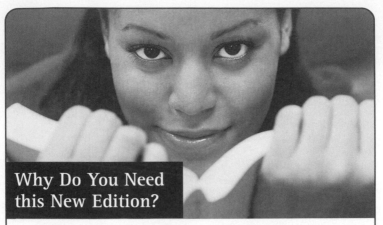

Why Do You Need this New Edition?

Why should you buy this new edition of *The Brief English Handbook*? Here are 4 good reasons!

1. **Part IX, on research,** has been completely rewritten to reflect the recently revised documentation guidelines from both the Modern Language Association (MLA) and the American Psychological Association (APA).

2. The revised Part IX now also includes **a rich array of examples from computer research, and a new sample student paper about plagiarism**—acknowledging the central role played by technology in your writing today.

3. **A new Researcher's Toolbox** complements the existing features, Writer's Toolbox and Editor's Toolbox, in offering specific, practical strategies for finding appropriate sources, evaluating them effectively, and documenting them correctly.

4. And a new section in Chapter 2, Basics of Critical Thinking, offers support for **developing and using skills in visual literacy**—a critical need in today's image-laden world.

THE

BRIEF ENGLISH

HANDBOOK

A Guide to Writing, Thinking, Grammar, and Research

Ninth Edition

EDWARD A. DORNAN
Late
Orange Coast College

ROBERT DEES
Orange Coast College

Longman

New York San Francisco Boston
London Toronto Sydney Tokyo Singapore Madrid
Mexico City Munich Paris Cape Town Hong Kong Montreal

Senior Sponsoring Editor: Virginia L. Blanford
Senior Supplements Editor: Donna Campion
Marketing Manager: Susan Stoudt
Production Manager: Jacqueline A. Martin
Project Coordination and Electronic Page Makeup: Nesbitt Graphics, Inc.
Cover Design Manager: Wendy Ann Fredericks
Cover Designer: Nancy Sacks
Visual Researcher: Rona Tuccillo
Senior Manufacturing Buyer: Alfred C. Dorsey
Printer and Binder: Edwards Brothers Inc.
Cover Printer: Phoenix Color Corporation/Hagerstown

For permission to use copyrighted material, grateful acknowledgment is made to the
following copyright holders: *page 14:* Photo by Mark Busse; *page 15: Top,* Digitalvision
Royalty-Free/Getty Images; *Bottom,* © Corbis Royalty-Free/Corbis; *page 353:* Used with
permission of the University of California at Berkeley Library.

Library of Congress Cataloging-in-Publication Data

Dornan, Edward A.
  The brief English handbook : a guide to writing, thinking, grammar, and
research / Edward A. Dornan, Robert Dees.—9th ed.
    p. cm.
  Includes index.
  ISBN 978-0-205-66141-1
  1. English language—Grammar—Handbooks, manuals, etc. 2. English
language—Rhetoric—Handbooks, manuals, etc. I. Dees, Robert. II. Title.
  PE1112.D67 2009
  808'.042—dc22
                                                        2008053517

www.pearsonhighered.com

Longman
is an imprint of

4 5 6 7 8 9 10—V069—12

ISBN-13: 978-0-205-66141-1
ISBN-10: 0-205-66141-6

Contents

PART VI   Punctuation   243

Contents   **xiii**

Preface

The Brief English Handbook has undergone dramatic changes over the last eight editions, yet this ninth edition is still full of down-to-earth advice that students can easily understand. Despite its compact size, the *BEH* serves as a complete writer's guide that thoroughly covers what students need to know about communicating in college and the workplace.

What's New in This Edition

The most important change in the ninth edition is the complete overhaul of the research section, Part IX. Both the Modern Language Association (MLA) and the American Psychological Association (APA) have made significant changes in their documentation format, and these changes are now incorporated in the documentation guidelines in this handbook. It is also time to acknowledge that virtually all writing is now done on computer, and that much (if not most) research is pursued online. As a result, Part IX—on researching and writing papers, and on documenting sources—is completely rewritten to provide a rich array of examples from computer research and a new sample student paper on plagiarism.

Another new part of this section is the feature Researcher's Toolbox, which complements the existing boxes, Writer's Toolbox and Editor's Toolbox, in offering specific, practical strategies for finding appropriate sources, evaluating them effectively, and documenting them correctly.

Also new to this edition is a section in Chapter 2, Basics of Critical Thinking, that offers support for developing and using skills in visual literacy—a critical need in today's image-laden world.

What You Will Find in This Handbook

As always, *The Brief English Handbook* differs from other handbooks in its emphasis on both critical and creative thinking and study skills—two areas in which today's students often need support. The *BEH* puts critical thinking to work: Students learn the levels of thinking identified by cognitive psychologists and then apply that knowledge by interpreting key words in writing assignments to determine the level of thinking an instructor expects an assignment to generate.

Part I: Integration of creative and critical thinking with writing
Part I, Effective Thinking, Writing, and Studying, illustrates the fundamental concepts of thinking and reasoning that play significant roles in learning to write effectively.

- Chapter 1 concentrates on how to use creative and critical thinking along with writing to clarify a problem and generate solutions.
- Chapter 2 shows how to distinguish fact from opinion, analyze inferences, and verify interpretations; how to identify common logical fallacies and propaganda techniques; and, in a new section, how to use visual literacy skills effectively.
- Chapter 3 explains the inductive and deductive reasoning processes that underlie traditional argumentation.
- Chapter 4 acknowledges that good study strategies help one become a more successful student and a better writer; it provides guidelines for planning and managing time, taking useful notes, and studying efficiently for tests.

Part II: Practical advice on the writing process   The *BEH* has always emphasized the writing process, perhaps more so than any other compact handbook. The seven chapters of Part II, The College Essay, methodically demonstrate how essays unfold from thought to written word. Students can follow the interplay of creative and critical thinking that goes into developing a traditional thesis-support essay.

To help students conceptualize the writing process, Chapter 5 presents a completed student essay with commentary early in the discussion, and the subsequent four chapters document the development of that same essay. The goal here is, first, to establish what a well-written student essay embodies and, second, to trace its evolution from idea to final draft to show the recursive nature of composition. This teaching strategy helps make concrete what students often see as abstract.

The entire process is illustrated with specific examples. Actual paragraphs from the writer's hand-edited first draft are reproduced with running commentary to show the editing process at work and to explain the reasons for making editing choices. The final chapter of the part provides guidance for peer review, a process that occurs in some eighty percent of freshman composition classrooms today.

Part III: Essentials of paragraph development   The six chapters of Part 3 concentrate on paragraphs, the essential building blocks of the essay. The emphasis is on paragraphs working together within fully developed compositions. Chapters 12–14 show how to write effective topic sentences, create unity, and maintain coherence. Chapters 15–17 consider development patterns by purpose: to describe or narrate, to explain, and to argue. These three chapters are each illustrated by fully annotated paragraph models.

Parts IV–VII: Thorough grounding in usage, structure, grammar, and mechanics These sections, the heart of the traditional handbook, offer comprehensive guidance in the use of language— sentence structure, grammar, punctuation, and mechanics—and include a wealth of exercises that allow students to apply what they are learning as they are learning it. The total reference tool, these four parts will remain valuable to students long after their college careers are completed.

Part VIII: Guidance for responding to the most common college writing assignments The three chapters of this part address the most common college writing challenges: argument essays, essays about literature, and essay exams.

- Avoiding jargon, Chapter 55 presents a direct approach to writing **an argument essay**. By building on critical thinking concepts presented in Part I, this chapter illustrates the importance of clear reasoning when trying to win others to one side of an issue. By following clear, precisely stated guidelines, students will find that writing an argument is no more difficult than writing an expository essay.
- Chapter 56 helps students conceive and develop **an essay about literature**. In guiding students from the writing of an effective thesis to the proofreading of the paper, this chapter addresses such knotty problems as using the historical present, attribution, summary, and paraphrase.
- Chapter 57 gives students clear guidelines to follow when writing **an in-class essay exam**—a situation that many students find extremely stressful. This chapter builds on strategies presented in Chapter 4 on study and test-taking skills and provides students with support for an often difficult task.

Part IX: Procedures and conventions for writing research papers The three chapters of Part IX, all newly written, cover computerized library resources and researching on the Internet, including the use of search engines and, of critical importance, the evaluation of Internet sources. Part IX also traces the development of a student research essay: choosing a topic with care; narrowing the thesis; introducing quotations, paraphrases, and summaries of source material; citing sources accurately; and avoiding plagiarism. This part concludes with current MLA documentation guidelines and citation models, followed by the basics of APA and CSE documentation styles, with citation models.

Part X: Communication beyond college   The *BEH* gives special attention to the everyday uses of writing and oral communication. The chapters of Part X offer solid advice on how to prepare résumés, business letters, and memos, as well as the more typical electronic communications of today's workplace. Additional chapters focus on designing Web sites and making oral presentations—both common tasks in contemporary business settings.

Part XI: A brush-up on basic skills   A focus on **common errors** gives students an easy-to-use review of grammar basics. Five chapters cover parts of speech and sentences, phrases, clauses, and sentence patterns in just enough detail to provide a ready resource to bring students up to speed in meeting the demands of freshman composition.

Part XII: Background for multilingual writers   The *BEH* also provides support for writers whose first language is not English by focusing on the nagging errors that many such students confront. Five chapters cover omitted words, noun markers, verb combinations, faulty repetitions, and errors in using present and past participles. Each chapter gives ample explanation and examples and provides one or more exercises.

Helping Students Become More Effective Writers

In addition to the comprehensive content outlined above, the *BEH* includes several unique features to help students become better writers. Three strategic Toolboxes offer specific guidance at each stage of the writing process:

 Writer's Toolbox   These boxes highlight resources available to writers and provide concise, specific advice on critical thinking and writing ranging from tips on decision-making and avoiding plagiarism to placing commas accurately and embedding key words in topic sentences.

 Editor's Toolbox   These boxes focus on strategies for developing and revising writing; they also highlight the problems with such editing tools as spellcheckers and grammar checkers.

Researcher's Toolbox New to this edition, these boxes provide hints and strategies for selecting a research topic, making a schedule, narrowing a database search, and creating a working bibliography.

In addition to the Toolboxes, *The Brief English Handbook* is rich with exercises—probably more than in any other compact handbook. A separate Answer Key is available to instructors.

Additional Supplements

Pearson's unique **MyCompLab**, available both as a course management system and online as a Web site, provides an extraordinary range of additional resources for freshman composition, including a grammar practice, ExerciseZone, with over 3,000 test research databases. Talk to your Pearson sales representative about packaging this remarkable resource with your handbook.

Acknowledgments

Although neither of the original authors of *The Brief English Handbook,* Chuck Dawe and Ed Dornan, is still alive, their voice and focus continue to animate this handbook. Their extraordinary early emphasis on critical thinking is the foundational principle for this book, and their insistence on including a wealth of exercises remains central. I am grateful to have had their wisdom to build on in creating this ninth edition.

I am grateful also to the reviewers who provided insightful comments in the preparation of this edition, including Kevin R. Clouther, Bridgewater College (VA); Jeannine McDevitt, Pennsylvania Highlands Community College; David Sharpe, Ohio University; Emmanuel Sigauke, Cosumnes River College (CA); Ann Volin, Rockhurst University (MO); and Eric Watkins, University of California, San Diego, as well as the many reviewers of previous editions whose comments have without exception made this a better book.

ROBERT DEES

PART I

Effective Thinking, Writing, and Studying

Writing is a concentrated form of thinking. I don't know what I think about certain subjects until I sit down and try to write about them. Let's not forget that writing is convenient. It requires the simplest tools. Young writers see that with words and sentences on a piece of paper that costs less than a penny they can place themselves more clearly in the world. Words on a page, that's all it takes to help them separate themselves from the forces around them, streets and people and pressures and feelings. They learn to think about these things, to ride their own sentences into perceptions.

—Don DeLillo, *novelist*

---

1 **Thinking and Writing** *think/write*

Thinking is as natural to all of us as flying is to eagles or swimming is to dolphins. Thinking effectively, however, is another matter. It is natural to think, but it is not natural to think effectively. That must be learned.

Thinking generally refers to any sort of mental activity ranging from daydreaming to complex mathematical analysis. In very simple terms, thinking can be divided into two distinctively different categories— creative thinking and critical thinking. To be an effective thinker and writer, you have to learn how to use both.

Creative Thinking

At the heart of **creative thinking** is association, a mental process that generates information, insights, and ideas from memory. Sometimes when you are thinking creatively the mind seems to float from one memory to another. You may recall loosely connected experiences, such as casual conversations, unexplainable hunches, startling ideas, fragments of conversation, details from lectures, even snippets from books, newspapers, songs, and films. In other words, the mind is associating one memory with another memory.

Random thinking and *reflective thinking* are two forms of creative thinking. Random thinking seems to have no purpose and takes place when the mind is adrift or in a twilight state, a mental world between conscious thought and sleep. When in a twilight state of mind, you are hovering on the edge of awareness, and your thoughts appear as a spontaneous flow of images, memories, or feelings with no apparent relationship to one another.

In contrast to random thinking, reflective thinking has a purpose. When you learn to think reflectively, you will be consciously using the power of association to gain access to the reservoir of experience and information stored just below the surface of consciousness.

Critical Thinking

At the heart of **critical thinking** is evaluation, a mental process that judges—or tests—the accuracy of information, insights, and ideas.

Creative thinking—that is, random and reflective thinking— provides the spontaneity that generates information and the intuition that ignites insight. In contrast, critical thinking evaluates the information, insights, and ideas that emerge from the creative process. When thinking critically, you test options, analyze assertions, reveal implicit assumptions, trace logical relationships, and apply standards of reasoning. It is critical thinking that helps you decide what to do or not to do, what is right or wrong, what works or does not work.

Creative and Critical Thinking Work Together

To think effectively you must be both a creator and a critic. For example, to publish a novel, a writer must first *create* the story and characters, but before sending the work to a publisher, he or she must *critically evaluate* it to be sure it is ready for publication.

In diagnosing an illness, a doctor must *create* possible diagnoses to explain a patient's symptoms; then to decide which diagnosis is accurate, he or she must *analyze* each of them through further examination or laboratory tests.

In solving a crime, a team of detectives must *create* possible solutions, and then they must *test* them against the evidence. At the heart of effective thinking, therefore, is knowing when to use creative thinking and when to use critical thinking.

Creative and Critical Thinking in Problem Solving

In everyday life, unfortunately, most people tend to be careless about the creative and critical aspects of thinking. When emotions are aroused, people often act first and think later, seizing on the first course of action that occurs to them.

When facing a problem and making a decision, all of us would be much wiser to recognize the significant role the interaction of creative and critical thinking can play. For instance, through creative thinking, especially through the effective use of association, you can generate information necessary to explore all the elements involved in any decision you have to make; through critical thinking, you can evaluate all the information creative thinking has generated to help you make the right decision.

The procedure for employing creative and critical thinking in problem solving involves a cycle of five phases. You do not have to follow the cycle rigidly. In fact, the phases will probably overlap as you work through them. You may even go back to an earlier phase or work on several phases simultaneously.

1a Use critical thinking to write a definition of a problem

Typically, the critical thinking process begins with the recognition of a problem followed by a careful definition of the problem. The problem may be quite simple or complex, such as deciding what to do with a free evening or choosing a career path. A class assignment always involves some problem, whether the assignment is a written research project on World War II or an analysis of which is more effective, Abraham Lincoln's Gettysburg Address or Martin Luther King's "I Have a Dream" speech.

You should carefully define a problem in writing. Class assignments, for example, are usually handed to you but are often stated in broad or vague language. It is your job to define the problem correctly before going on to the other decision-making phases. If you fail to define the problem, you risk completing the wrong task.

Some problems are personal and difficult to recognize. Suppose, for example, you learn that the soccer coach is going to cut you from the team. You get angry, deciding that the coach dislikes you. Without giving it much thought, you decide that the solution to your problem is to save face and to quit the team. This thoughtless definition of the problem and your consequent solution help you avoid embarrassment, but later you learn that the real problem was your negative attitude, which had been affecting the team's spirit. If you had defined the problem more accurately, in writing, you might have decided to discuss your attitude with the coach in order to figure out how to improve the situation.

Sometimes defining the problem is the most difficult phase of decision making. Once you have correctly defined the problem, however, the rest of the process is relatively easy.

Three Guidelines for Defining a Problem

A definition should not be too broad. Suppose you define a problem as the need to understand why you feel anxious in stressful situations when all you really want is to learn to relax during finals. The broader definition would set you aimlessly adrift in psychological analysis. If a problem is truly large, break it down into smaller problems and solve them one at a time.

A definition should not be too narrow. Suppose you define a problem as the need to overcome your fear of mathematics because you feel panic as an algebra final approaches. In reality, you experience test anxiety in all testing situations. The narrower definition might lead to your wasting additional hours reviewing algebra; the broader definition might lead to the pursuit of meditation or exercise.

A definition should not in itself be a conclusion. Suppose you notice that every time you approach finals you become seriously anxious. If you define your problem as the need to learn why finals create anxiety, your definition in itself embodies a conclusion—that is, that finals indeed cause anxiety. But the first problem should be to decide whether finals *do* cause anxiety. You might discover that something else that occurs near the end of each semester is causing your feelings.

1b Use creative thinking to generate information

Once you have defined a problem, you are ready to gather information about it. Many problems require hours of research as part of the information-gathering phase—and you will encounter research techniques in later chapters—but many more problems merely require the thorough exploration of what you already know from past experience. All you have to do is access the information.

At this point reflective thinking comes into play. By setting aside critical thinking and by allowing your mind to associate one idea to another, you can generate a great deal of information from past experience.

There are several techniques you can use, but they all require you to follow your own thought patterns. You must associate one idea with another without worrying whether the connections are logical. In this phase of problem solving, resist the urge to judge or to analyze what comes up. Instead, encourage the creative exploration of your imagination.

Brainstorming

Brainstorming, sometimes called *listing,* is a creative way to write out your thoughts. Begin by concentrating on the problem and then quickly write down your associations. Write your list in just enough detail to remind you of each item's significance when you review the material. Your goal in brainstorming is to write down thought fragments on the fly. Later you can add information that is appropriate to the problem.

Freewriting

Freewriting is valuable during any part of the information-gathering phase. Simply set aside a block of time, reflect on the problem, and write nonstop. Associate one bit of information with another. Do not judge your ideas or shut them out. Often the unexpected will present itself—ideas connecting to ideas in ways you could not have planned. Do not be concerned here with the technical aspects of writing; instead, immerse yourself in your own creative flow while holding in check the critical process.

Clustering

Listing or freewriting usually creates a hodgepodge of written material in random arrangement, but once you have enough information, you can begin to make connections among key ideas. In one sense, *clustering* brings order out of chaos.

Begin a cluster by writing what you have determined to be your problem in the center of the page. Draw a circle around it. As you carefully reread the listing or freewriting, arrange major ideas around the problem in orbits connected by lines. Also circle significant points. As you discover ideas related to the major ideas, draw another orbiting system.

Do all this using single words or brief phrases. Remember, you can always reread the original material to examine the full entry. Through this process, you are simply dividing and subdividing information, emphasizing facts, opinions, or insights that will help the decision-making process.

WRITER'S TOOLBOX

Generating Ideas for Essays

Brainstorming, freewriting, and asking questions play an important part in the process of composing a writing project. Just as you can use a computer to begin a personal dialogue to solve a problem, you can also use it to generate material for an essay assignment.

It's quite simple to do: Just bring up a blank screen and start writing. This personal dialogue might begin with a list of ideas, even ideas that seem unrelated to your central purpose. One idea might generate freewriting—that's great, go with it! If you get stuck, start asking yourself questions and then answer them.

The process will loosen your creative thinking much like stretching loosens tight muscles. When you finish, go back over your writing to determine what's useful and save it.

Asking Questions

Ask questions about a problem. These are sometimes referred to as reporter's questions: Who? What? When? Where? Why? and How? Not every question will be appropriate for every problem, but using the ones that are can ignite an association chain that will help you view a problem from different perspectives. Write down the questions, and write down your answers.

Consultation

You might become part of a problem-solving group that discusses class assignments. You might also consult a fellow class member, perhaps someone more experienced than you with the decision process. You might also engage your instructor in a discussion to test your ideas. Whenever you discuss a problem, take notes or use a tape recorder; don't risk letting good ideas slip away.

1c Use creative thinking to write a list of tentative options

When should you shift to this phase? Make the shift when you have enough information to suggest several possible options or courses of action. The goal is to create as many options for yourself as possible; the more options you have, the more likely you will discover a sound one.

As in the previous phase, your thinking here must be primarily creative. Continue to give your imagination complete freedom, and postpone critical thinking until the next phase of the decision-making cycle. If you try to find flaws in your options while still forming them, you risk dismissing sound ideas before they are fully developed. Instead of being too analytical, write down every option that comes to mind. Options you might reject as wild or irrelevant could turn out to be solutions.

1d Use critical thinking to test tentative options

When you have several options to choose from, it is time to subject them to critical scrutiny to test their reliability. All tentative options involve some kind of *inference,* that is, a process of reasoning that draws a conclusion from information.

For example, suppose that you read an article written by the CEO of a major software corporation. After an analysis of the economy, the CEO concludes that the most financially rewarding careers for today's college students will be in electronic technology. If you conclude from reading this article that you should major in computer science, your conclusion is the result of an inference you formed by combining two pieces of information: the assertion in the magazine article and the fact that you are searching for a major. If you rush to the registrar's office to declare a major in computer science, you might end up with a financially rewarding career, but you have ignored an important rule of effective decision making by forming one tentative option and deciding on it without testing its reliability. Although your decision might lead to a successful career, it is not reliable. An option is reliable only when it is known to be accurate. For an option to be accurate, the information it is based on must be known to be accurate. Your decision to major in computer science fails the test. Because the information in the article may be wrong, your inference is inaccurate.

1e Use critical thinking to evaluate reliable options and make a decision

When you begin testing your options by appropriate methods, you will probably discover that absolute reliability is rare. Usually there will be some weakness either in the information or in the interpretation of the information, or in both. The best you can hope for is a high degree of reliability. If you delayed decision making until you reached absolute reliability, you would seldom make a decision.

The minimum degree of reliability you should have before acting on an option varies with the circumstances. For example, a juror for a murder trial must have a high degree of reliability to find a defendant guilty. But most options you choose from will not be true beyond a reasonable doubt.

If a written evaluation of your tentative options shows that none of them are sufficiently reliable, then you should repeat the whole decision-making cycle. Each time you repeat the cycle you are likely to discover new information, which might suggest new and more promising options. The process should be repeated until you reach a decision with a degree of reliability sufficient for your purpose.

Exercise 1.1: Defining Problems

By referring to information in this chapter, complete the following exercises.

1. It is 9:30 p.m. of the second day of classes. Pre-med major Ron Tanaka has been studying a biology assignment since 7:30 p.m.

He pauses and looks at the rest of the assignment. At his current rate, he will need five more hours to finish. He has history and English assignments to prepare, too. What phase of the decision-making cycle has Ron reached?

Below are five definitions of Tanaka's immediate problem. Identify the guideline that each definition violates.

2. To call his parents to alert them that he is thinking about becoming a lawyer instead of a medical doctor.

3. To figure out how to finish his biology assignment in three hours.

4. To determine the average amount of study time per week all his homework assignments will require.

5. To learn how to make every minute count in all areas of his life.

6. To find out which of his friends understands biology.

Answer the following questions and problems.

7. Tanaka estimates that all his assignments will require 60 hours each week to complete. Moreover, class and lab time will take another 20 hours. What phase of the decision-making cycle is he working on?

8. If you were in Tanaka's situation, what would you do next?

9. Using one or more of the information-gathering techniques described in this chapter, develop several options Tanaka might choose from.

10. What option do you feel is the most reliable? Why?

Exercise 1.2: Making Decisions

Imagine you are a comedian on the edge of national success, but you are concerned with the state of your profession. It seems that the trend in comedy is gross-out humor. Moreover, it seems that the comedians most engaged in grossing out their audiences are the most successful. In the right hands, you feel gross-out humor can be very funny. But it's not always in the right hands. Moreover, you feel there are certain moral hazards in addressing the most basic aspects of human behavior, and this feeling disturbs you.

To prepare yourself for the next phase of your career in comedy, go through the decision-making cycle to figure out a course of action you will feel comfortable following.

2 Basics of Critical Thinking *crit*

In common usage, *critical* often refers to taking a negative view, finding fault, or even excessive nit-picking. We have all heard such comments as "They criticize my every move" when the speaker probably means *ridicule,* not *criticize.*

In academic usage, *critical* refers to complex intellectual activities required by interpretation, analysis, and evaluation. In the statement "The attorney has lost his critical perspective by becoming emotionally involved in the decision," *critical* is used with more academic accuracy.

To be a critical thinker does not mean that you judge every comment your friends make. It does mean that you approach life thoughtfully with an arsenal of skills that help you interpret, analyze, and evaluate experience and information.

2a Distinguish between facts and opinions

We live in an age of information overload. There are roughly 65 million copies of newspapers published worldwide each day. Approximately 10,000 magazines are published every month, and close to 50,000 new books are published each year. In the United States itself over 1,400 television stations broadcast programs to 93 million homes, and over 10,000 radio stations broadcast through nearly 500 million radios that play in homes, workplaces, cars, and anywhere else an iPod goes. And now we have the World Wide Web, with its infinite possibilities for dispensing information. How do you guard against being overwhelmed by the information onslaught, especially by misleading information?

Begin by distinguishing between two fundamental concepts: facts and opinions.

Fact

A *fact* in itself is not debatable. A factual statement reflects how something actually exists or happened and can be objectively verified. These are factual statements: Republican presidents held the White House for the twelve years from 1981 through 1992. The moon is earth's only satellite. Hawaii became a state in 1959.

Numerical facts are called *statistics.* For example, the average American uses three gallons of paint a week. This adds up to more than a billion gallons every year, enough to fill a lake 20 feet deep, 4 miles long, and 1 mile wide.

Statistics are often referred to as *alleged facts*. An alleged fact can be misleading. For example, the statement "The junk mail Americans receive in one day could produce enough energy to heat 250,000 homes" may be a fact, but it would not be accepted without further consideration. (How would people use energy from burning junk mail, anyway?) The alleged fact that the average American uses three gallons of paint a week misleads because of averaging: Many Americans never lift a paint brush, but the auto industry uses tens of thousands of gallons of paint every week.

Opinion

Statistical analysis, that is, alleged facts, often reflect an opinion. *Opinion* is what someone believes, and it is not necessarily true because someone believes it. Opinions take different forms.

A *preference* is an opinion that expresses personal taste—that is, what someone likes or dislikes. Such statements as "Suspense movies are my favorite" and "Racquetball is a great workout" express preferences, not facts. Generally, preferences do not cry out for critical examination. How can someone be wrong for liking a type of movie or a particular sport? Why would anyone want to challenge someone's taste?

A *judgment* is an opinion with a basis for support, and preferences can often be restated as judgments. For example, the statement "Suspense movies, more than romantic comedies or westerns, reflect society's ills" can be analyzed by considering the social criticism embedded in romance, western, and suspense movies. The statement "Racquetball offers a more sustained aerobic workout than tennis does" creates the opportunity to compare the physical demands of racquetball and tennis. Both statements clearly reflect opinions that can be evaluated.

2b Analyze inferences for reliability

An *inference* is an observation or conclusion based on a fact or set of facts. It is a statement about what is not known, made on the basis of what is known. A loan officer may infer a man's social status from how he dresses. An investigator may infer from the ruins how a fire ignited. A chess player may infer her opponent's next move from the position of the chess pieces on the board. A mechanic may infer the condition of a car's valves from the sound of the engine.

Inferences may be carefully or carelessly made. They may be made on the basis of years of experience or on a wild hunch. Inferences might be reliable or unreliable, that is, right or wrong. For example, suppose the following facts are true in your hometown:

1. The elementary school is overcrowded because of the school design.
2. No new teachers will be hired because of budget cuts.
3. A new apartment complex with 300 apartments is opening before school begins.
4. The city planners have just approved the construction of a thousand homes.

From these facts it may be reasonably inferred that next year the elementary school will be even more crowded than it is now, and therefore learning will be more difficult.

But, as with all significant inferences, this one should be subjected to critical examination, which might reveal the following:

1. The school overcrowding is caused by students in their last year of elementary school.
2. The budget cuts are tentative because the state budget has not been finalized.
3. The apartments are for senior citizens, not families with children.
4. Construction of the thousand new homes will not begin for at least two years.

These additional facts, revealed by close critical examination, show that the original inference is unreliable.

Inference is closely related to *implication*. When someone says, "Most of the people who have lawns in this neighborhood are white and speak educated English, but most of the people who mow the lawns are brown and speak no English," he is *implying* that there is an injustice in this situation. When we hear such a statement, we *infer* that indeed there is an injustice. A speaker *implies* and a listener *infers* (and the two words are frequently misused).

Exercise 2.1: Drawing Inferences

Draw tentative inferences from each set of facts given below. For each inference, explain which particular fact, or facts, served as its basis. By reviewing all your tentative inferences, write the options you believe are viable for the situation you find yourself in.

a. It's after midnight, you've had a couple of drinks at a party, and your car stops working on an underlit stretch of the freeway. You pull over to the side of the road to figure out what might have happened. Your mind goes back over the facts. You were driving about 65 miles an hour. You were listening to the radio. The car sort of sputtered. The steering became difficult. The engine stopped, and the brakes needed extra pressure to make them work as you struggled to pull off onto the shoulder.

b. You find that you are in an unfamiliar part of the freeway that parallels a housing development. You can see no neon signs or other indications of nightlife. Traffic is sparse.

c. A four-door sedan is slowing down, the driver looking back as the sedan passes. The sedan is dark, a couple of years old, and its license plate light is not working. The car pulls over ahead of you and begins to back up, stopping about 25 feet away.

d. A man, about 6'2" and wearing a dark suit, gets out of the sedan and looks around as if he were inspecting the area. A moment or two passes—he does not seem to be in a hurry—then he reaches back into the sedan for a small object, steps to the far edge of the freeway shoulder, and begins walking slowly toward your car while seeming to be carefully observing the nearby area.

2c Use visual literacy skills to interpret images

Visual literacy is the ability to understand, interpret, and respond critically to an image, just as linguistic literacy is required for listening or reading. How we view and comprehend an image determines to a great extent how we understand and react to our world. We learn at an early age to respond to a visual experience and to interpret it: A smiling or scowling face, a closed or open hand, an erect or slumped body—all are appearances that invite a response based on an interpretation or inference.

The thousands of images we see every day are both naturally occurring—the people, objects, and events we regularly encounter—as well as intentionally composed, meant to create an effect or to convey a particular message. Unlike a spontaneous visual occurrence, a composed image such as an advertisement, a graph, a painting, or a photograph (or even a series of images, such as a film) has its details purposely arranged for the viewer to see, interpret, and respond to. Yet as anyone who has ever been fooled by a magician, heard conflicting testimony from eyewitnesses, or damaged a fender while trying to park a car knows, accurately interpreting what we see is not always easy. Luckily, our ability to make correct inferences about what we see develops with experience and with practice in thinking critically about what we see and how we interpret it.

Look carefully at the photograph below of a woman perched on a doorstep and smoking a cigar. Consider your response to the photograph. Do you like it? What can you tell about the woman in the photograph? How would you describe the way she is dressed? Are the features of her clothing significant? What about the setting? Why the cigar? After studying all the elements that make up the photograph, what is your overall impression or feeling about the woman? What can you infer about her and her life? What is she like as a person? What do you think the photographer intended to say or to make you aware of in this photograph?

The last three questions require you to make inferences about the photograph's subject and the intentions of the photographer. (You may want to discuss the inferences you draw with others to see if they agree with your interpretations.) Although you may never know anything for certain about the woman in the photograph or the photographer's intentions, your critical study of the work will undoubtedly lead you to a different understanding of it than you had when you first saw it. In arriving at thoughtful inferences about an unfamiliar image in this way, you move from a collection of half-formed ideas about the work to a conscious, critical grasp of it and its message.

Exercise 2.2: Drawing Inferences from a Visual Image

Choose one of the images below to analyze and draw inferences about. Carefully study the image you select and then write two to three paragraphs analyzing its content and meaning. Begin by objectively describing or summarizing the content of the image, then explain the inferences you would make about its subject and its intended meaning or significance.

Image A

Image B

Image C

2d Verify the reliability of interpretations

An *interpretation* examines facts and opinions to make sense of them. An interpretation is always speculative. It is often an attempt to think beyond the obvious to find a deeper truth. Personal experience, literary works, and cultural, political, and historical events often supply the raw material for interpretation.

Like assertions, interpretations can reflect opposing views. For example, the Japanese military's surprise bombing of Pearl Harbor on December 7, 1941, took the United States into World War II. Later, some historians charged that President Roosevelt had had advance knowledge of the attack but did not warn our military. Their accusation is based mainly on the interpretation of one suspicious fact: By the summer of 1940, the United States had cracked Japan's top-secret diplomatic code, enabling intelligence agencies to monitor messages to and from Tokyo. Some historians interpret this to mean that President Roosevelt wanted to use the attack as a reason to involve the United States in World War II. To counter this interpretation, however, other historians have pointed out that the code-breaking intelligence could not have exposed the attack on Pearl Harbor because Japan sent no messages about the planned attack!

The reliability of an interpretation is usually difficult to verify. Often only a careful analysis will reveal whether a particular interpretation of an act or an event is accurate.

Exercise 2.3: Interpreting Facts

Read the following summary of an event that rocked Los Angeles several years ago and then respond to the task at the end.

In Los Angeles on the night of March 3, 1991, a bystander made a videotape that showed several police officers using police clubs to beat an African American named Rodney King into submission so they could arrest him. Subsequently the videotape was played on television, and it made viewers feel they were actually witnessing the beating. Did the videotape reveal all the facts? According to the police, it did not; they claim it failed to show the "trigger" elements that led to the violent arrest:

1. King racing at high speed in a seven-mile car chase prior to the event.

2. King, over six feet tall and muscular from hours spent in weight rooms, appearing violently psychotic from drugs.

3. King showing no effect from two jolts from a stun gun.

4. King throwing off several officers who tried to subdue him.

5. King charging one officer who had hit him with a baton.

But the video did foster two interpretations: First, to many viewers it showed police subduing a dangerous criminal who was resisting arrest; second, to other viewers it showed a gang of racist Anglo police officers using excessive violence by brutally clubbing an African American man into submission.

A year later, when a jury acquitted three officers of charges of using excessive force, the conflicting interpretations of the event triggered a riot. Fifty-four people died. Two thousand people were injured. Over eight hundred buildings burned.

Write a 100- to 150-word explanation that offers your interpretation of the two opposing interpretations made by most Los Angeles residents.

2e Identify the logical fallacies embedded in information

Logical fallacies are common mistakes in thinking. The word *fallacy* means deception or a fault in reasoning. Information tainted by logical fallacies is unreliable. As a critical thinker, you can avoid accepting unreliable information by recognizing common fallacies.

Ad Hominem Argument

The Latin phrase *ad hominem* means "to the man." Writers and speakers use the ad hominem argument when they attack the person who is connected with an issue rather than concentrate on the issue itself.

> The president has made an interesting case for drilling for oil in Alaska. No wonder! His family is heavily invested in oil companies.

In this statement the writer ignores the president's arguments for drilling in Alaska and focuses on his personal situation.

> Do not believe film critics. They are all frustrated actors or directors who could not succeed in the film industry.

The statement attacks the film critics rather than discussing inaccuracies or bias in their reviews.

Begging the Question

A frequent error that people make is reasoning in a circle, commonly referred to as *begging the question*. In its most fundamental form, a circular argument ends up where it began, having merely restructured the original assumption without introducing actual information.

> Welfare recipients are lazy because they don't like to work. Have you heard about someone on welfare who likes to work? That's because welfare recipients are lazy.

The argument travels in a circle, confirming only the assumption it makes in the opening assertion.

False Analogy

Someone using *false analogy* assumes that if two things are similar in one or more characteristics, then they are similar in other characteristics.

> Some people cannot be educated. You can't make a silk purse out of a sow's ear.

Applying the apparent wisdom of folk sayings to real-life situations usually results in false analogy. Education does not change valueless things into valuable things, as the folk saying suggests; it develops already existing intelligence further.

> The European experience in World War II is clear. The lessons should not be ignored. You cannot ignore the rise of a dictator, and you cannot successfully negotiate with one to avoid a war. The best solution is to attack an enemy before he attacks.

Conditions today are not the same as they were before World War II. To apply pre–World War II conditions to those in the world today is to fall into the trap of false analogy.

Faulty Either/Or Reasoning

Many writers and speakers commit *faulty either/or reasoning* by assuming there are only two alternatives when in fact there are many. The slogan "America, love it or leave it" implies that love of country must be unqualified, which has the effect of excluding constructive criticism.

> Drug use is destroying the social order of American cities. The drug problem is so monumental that no one can afford to be

neutral. Are we going to do nothing and let criminals rule our cities? Or are we going to give our police more power so that they can control drug traffickers, dealers, and users?

Of course, other actions may relieve the situation: initiating public education, funding rehabilitation for drug users, developing agreements with other countries to curtail drug traffic, and so on. The choices are not just between doing nothing and increasing police power.

Hasty Generalization

Writers and speakers commit *hasty generalization* when they draw conclusions from insufficient or unrepresentative evidence.

> In recent years, almost every major college athletic program has been investigated by the NCAA for recruitment violations. Every year, at least one team is placed on probation as a result of these investigations. Clearly those in charge of college athletics must be immoral.

The person who has drawn this conclusion has done so from insufficient evidence. Are all violations of complex regulations a matter of immorality? Perhaps some of the violations were inadvertent or technical. As for the investigations and penalties, they could indicate rigorous enforcement of the rules rather than widespread immorality.

> During the last year, three of five award-winning films concentrated on family violence. An examination of family violence was just broadcast on national television. No doubt these events indicate that family violence is on the rise.

Three films and a television program do not represent a trend. The conclusion that family violence is rising needs to be substantiated with statistics and reports from such authorities as psychologists, sociologists, and law enforcement officials.

Non Sequitur

The Latin phrase *non sequitur* means "it does not follow." People often commit this fallacy when their conclusions do not logically follow from their premises.

> Ryan Beach has the highest per capita income in the state, but it has the lowest-paid police force, city employees, and school-teachers. These facts are revealing. They show that those with money know how to keep government expenses under control.

Many factors contribute to per capita income. Perhaps in a small beach town a few wealthy landowners drive up the average income. Moreover, individuals do not directly pay for city government and schools, which are paid for by tax dollars that may come from state or local government. And, finally, elected city and school officials— none of whom, in this specific case, may be wealthy—determine employee salaries. Clearly, this writer's conclusion does not follow from the premises.

Oversimplification

People *oversimplify* when they ignore essential information in forming a conclusion, offering a simple explanation for a complicated problem.

> Getting a good grade in a composition class may involve a lot of your time, but there is nothing difficult about it. All you have to do is meet the required word length and avoid errors in grammar and punctuation.

As you probably know by now, getting a good grade in composition also requires clear thinking, organizational skills, and a good deal of effort and practice at writing.

Post Hoc Argument

When people assume that one event causes a second event simply because the second follows the first in time, they are committing the *post hoc, ergo propter hoc* ("after this, therefore because of this") fallacy.

> Some people think that microwave ovens are a health threat. I disagree. Our family purchased a microwave oven two years ago. Since then, none of us has seen a doctor.

The only relation between the purchase of a microwave oven and the good health of this family is that one followed the other in time. Time sequence alone cannot prove the existence of a cause-and-effect relationship.

Stereotyping

A *stereotype* is a person or idea presented as having certain characteristics just by virtue of belonging to a particular group. Stereotypes, which are usually negative, lead to prejudice—that is, the prejudging of individuals on their group identities rather than on individual merits: "Foreigners can't be trusted," "The English have no sense of humor," "People on welfare are lazy."

Stereotyping is similar to hasty generalization in that both are based on limited information. Stereotyping gains power when people accept a stereotype uncritically because it is perpetuated by the media.

> Politicians, whether currently in office or not, should not be allowed to sit on the boards of nonprofit organizations such as charities, foundations, and educational institutions. We all know that to win an election a person must always compromise common standards of ethics. Politicians are notorious for representing the individual interests of their supporters and then seeking their financial support in the next election. All of us should fight to keep nonprofit organizations free from this kind of corrupt behavior.

If you believe that all politicians are corrupt, that stereotype will be reinforced by the political scandals reported in newspapers and on television. Yet the reality is that only a few politicians of the thousands holding office are ever involved in corruption.

Exercise 2.4: Identifying Logical Fallacies

Identify the logical fallacies in these brief statements. Following the treatment of each example given above, write a brief explanation of how the item is fallacious.

1. We must reject gun-control laws or sacrifice a sacred right granted to us by the Constitution.

2. I think Mr. Delgado is the best math teacher at our school because he is really nice.

3. Glenview College always has a winning football team because its coach prays before every game.

4. The least promising students achieve the greatest success as adults. Winston Churchill's teacher predicted he would be a failure, and Albert Einstein dropped out of school.

5. Ancient religious leaders were responsible for the sun's rising because they went to high ground every morning and prayed for the sun god to return.

6. Sonia is intelligent and hardworking. There is no doubt she will rise to the top of her field.

7. A brain absorbs information just as a sponge absorbs water. But eventually a sponge becomes saturated; it cannot hold any more water. Students, too, reach a saturation point, and then it is foolish to expect them to soak up more information.

8. If I had not gone out of my way to pick up Mia this morning, the car would not have broken down.

9. I do not see how anyone can think he's a good football player; he has been arrested several times, and his wife left him because he was cruel.

10. Lola Allure, the star of stage, screen, and television, starts every day with Skinny Wafers. Don't you think you should, too?

2f Learn to recognize and evaluate propaganda techniques

Propaganda refers to information and images designed to motivate people by appealing to their desires rather than to their intellect. Seldom do advertisers try to sell products by presenting accurate statistics and reasoned arguments based on specific evidence. Instead, they use language and images to associate their products with the subconscious yearnings their research reveals consumers have. Not all propaganda is bad. Most people would argue that a police officer who tries to persuade a group of preteens not to join street gangs by appealing to their emotions is using "good" propaganda.

Here are five commonly used propaganda techniques.

Glittering Generalities

Glittering generalities are virtue words that appeal to such emotions as love, generosity, motherhood, brotherhood, the American way, the natural world, and so on. Propagandists offering glittering generalities frequently use such words as *truth, freedom, honor,* and *love* for the emotions they trigger.

Name Calling

Name calling is an obvious but surprisingly effective tactic. Often used in conjunction with ad hominem arguments, name calling is designed to belittle or arouse contempt for a person or an idea.

Testimonial

Testimonial involves loved or respected persons giving statements of support (testimonials) for a particular cause, idea, or product. The persons giving the testimonials may not be experts; in fact, they may know nothing at all about the subject.

Plain Folks

Plain folks is the opposite of testimonial. This appeal comes from the participation of ordinary people with ordinary backgrounds, as opposed to the rich and famous.

Bandwagon

Bandwagon appeals to the strong desire to be one of the crowd, or part of a peer group. It exploits the fear of being excluded.

2g Learn to evaluate Internet resources

Critical thinking is essential to the evaluation of information on the Internet. Because the Internet is unrestricted, you can find on it anything someone thinks is important, interesting, and—yes—even bizarre. The democratic nature of the Internet is one of its great values, of course, but this also means there's a lot of irrational junk out there. You must stay critically alert when sorting through it. Use the following questions to guide your assessment of any Internet source.

- *Fallacious Reasoning.* Does the author rely on faulty reasoning and propaganda techniques to advance a position?
- *Currency.* Is the information current? Has it been recently updated to keep it current?
- *Fairness.* Does the source offer multiple viewpoints, even opposing viewpoints? Does the author sound reasonable?
- *Evidence.* Does the information include verifiable evidence? Is there a clear separation of fact from opinion?
- *Credibility.* Is the information based on credible research? Are bibliographical sources listed? Is the information credible in the non-Internet world? Why and with whom?
- *Authorship.* Is the author identified? Are the author's qualifications listed? Does the author have academic degrees, awards, or other publications that can be substantiated?

No one guards the Internet door. You must be the judge of all Internet sources you rely on.

Exercise 2.5: Identifying Propaganda

Find two examples from newspapers or magazines, including editorials and advertisements, for each of the five propaganda techniques defined above. For each of your examples, write a brief explanation of how the technique works.

---

3 Critical Thinking and Reasoning *crit*

Critical thinking emphasizes *objectivity,* the ability to view experience without distortion, and deemphasizes *subjectivity,* the inability to think beyond a limited frame of reference.

Critical thinking is strongly affected by the fact that we each see and experience from a unique perspective. Being aware of this subjective perspective is especially important when working to reach group consensus. Subjectivity not only affects our ability to think effectively, it may even cripple it, especially when emotions become engaged.

Emotions are an indispensable part of our behavior. Where would the artist be without passion or the philanthropist without compassion? Yet even the mildest emotions can hamper our ability to reason logically and work productively with others. In any situation where objectivity is required, emotions tend to intensify self-defensive behavior, which always hinders reasoned discussion.

To reduce emotional intensity during group consensus building, you can try to see the world through the eyes of those with whom you are in conflict. When emotion derails the reasoning process, that is, the ability to think critically and logically, you must step back and reexamine each step of the process to be sure your conclusions are reliable and thoroughly understood by others.

3a Use reflective listening to achieve consensual agreement

The goal of reasoned discussion is to reduce conflict, not to enflame it. In reasoned discussion there should not be winners and losers; there should only be consensual resolution.

Some people feel so strongly about their opinions that they are deeply threatened by any challenge to them. Even when presented with irrefutable evidence that contradicts their position, they ignore it. At this point, emotion—not reason—controls their behavior.

A more effective strategy than engaging in emotional confrontation is to adopt a respectful, even conciliatory attitude by actively listening to anyone with an opposing viewpoint. After having heard out the other person, restate in your own words what you believe was said. Then ask if you paraphrased the points accurately. If so, then find common points of agreement, not just points of disagreement, before stating your position. Continue this process, emphasizing what you agree on, until everyone clearly understands the similarities and differences of the two positions. This technique, developed by the psychologist Carl Rogers, is called *reflective listening*. By pursuing reflective listening you can remove emotion from the discussion, and in doing this you make it easier to reach consensus, that is, a synthesis of every position that the group can agree on.

Applying the Rogerian Approach to Consensus Building

- Make an effort to understand opposing viewpoints. Try to "walk a mile in the other person's moccasins." Concentrate intently on what is being said, not on how you can counter it.
- In an unemotional fashion, paraphrase what you have heard. An objective description will show that you are open-minded.
- Acknowledge the value of some of the other person's points. An acknowledgment will show that you are fair and balanced, seeking an appropriate resolution, not one that has a winner and a loser. Identify areas of common ground—not just points expressed in the disagreement, but general areas such as values, beliefs, and goals.
- Present your position reasonably, with supporting evidence. By now the other person will realize that this is not a win/lose situation and will feel less defensive. Then it is time for the other person to paraphrase what you have said.

3b Maintain objectivity by retracing the inductive reasoning process

Whether in written arguments or group discussion, when objectivity seems to have given way to emotion, it's time to evaluate the steps in the reasoning process.

Inductive reasoning moves from specific evidence to a general conclusion. You have been using inductive reasoning throughout your life. Imagine, for example, that you were given a wrong date the first time you registered for college classes. Against all reason, you were not allowed to register even though you had waited in line for two hours. "Come back Friday," you were told. "That's the right day."

At registration for the second semester, you discovered that the class numbers had been printed incorrectly, and you had to return to revise your schedule.

The third semester, the procedure went well, but you discovered on the first day of classes that you were not on any class roster. "We just can't explain it," a clerk said. "I guess it was a computer glitch."

By induction—that is, by interpreting the meaning of these experiences—you conclude that your college's registration procedure is a shambles and you had better figure out how to use it effectively. Inductive reasoning thus builds to a conclusion piece by piece. As the evidence is presented and clarified, the conclusion becomes irresistible to reasonable people.

Another example: One student maintained that her college had an advanced gender awareness program. Others emphatically disagreed, claiming that nothing at all had been done to further gender awareness. To reach consensus, she retraced the evidence inductively by beginning with a question everyone agreed on.

QUESTION	Is Riverbank College responsible in the area of gender bias?

Then, one step at a time, she brought forward the supporting information, the evidence.

EVIDENCE	Riverbank College has gender awareness workshops for students, faculty, administrators, and support staff.
	The college has revised its course catalog, class schedule, and policy statements to embody gender-neutral language.
	The college has created a standing committee to review and arbitrate gender-related issues.
	The college has instituted new procedures to eliminate gender bias.
CONCLUSION	Evidence shows that Riverbank College has an advanced gender awareness program.

Through patient examination of the evidence and by listening reflectively to each group member's position, the group finally tended to agree with her, yet one group member still disagreed, adamantly maintaining that the conclusion was only partially true. In further reasoned discussion, she pointed out that there was pay inequity between the salaries of men and women doing the same job. After she presented her evidence during discussion, the group reached a final consensus.

GROUP CONSENSUS Although some inequity exists in salaries, Riverbank College is making a strong effort to eliminate gender bias.

Conclusions drawn from inductive reasoning are usually referred to as *probable conclusions*. They are, in fact, inferences subject to close examination. The acceptance of a conclusion that follows from inductive reasoning is often referred to as the *inductive leap*. When constructing or evaluating inductive reasoning, you must be sure that the probable conclusion is clearly connected to the evidence. If it is not clearly connected, then the reasoning is flawed and the argument must be revised to show the connection more clearly or must be abandoned for being illogical.

3c Maintain objectivity by reexamining the premises and conclusions of the deductive reasoning process

Deductive reasoning is the opposite of inductive reasoning. The process begins with general assumptions called *premises* and draws specific conclusions that follow logically from the premises.

In formal logic, this pattern is called a *syllogism*. Syllogisms always include a major premise, a minor premise, and a necessary conclusion that is the logical result of the two premises. The classic example of this deductive form comes to us from the philosopher Aristotle.

MAJOR PREMISE All humans are mortal.

MINOR PREMISE Socrates is human.

CONCLUSION Therefore, Socrates is mortal.

When you reexamine deductive reasoning, keep in mind that accuracy is the key to validity. If the major and minor premises are accurate, then the conclusion will be accurate and logically sound. Syllogisms, however, can be illogical. An inaccurate major premise may make the result of deductive reasoning illogical.

MAJOR PREMISE Computer programmers are shy and seldom socialize.

MINOR PREMISE Joan Adams is our first female computer programmer.

CONCLUSION Therefore, she will be shy and seldom socialize with fellow employees.

Clearly, the major premise, which reflects a stereotypical image of computer programmers, is inaccurate. Ask yourself: Are all computer programmers shy and antisocial? At one time or another, aren't most people shy and seeking to avoid social contact? Because the major premise is inaccurate, the reasoning is flawed and the conclusion is inaccurate.

Sometimes the slippery use of language makes deductive reasoning inaccurate. Consider the use of *good student* and *accept* in this flawed syllogism.

MAJOR PREMISE	All good students accept that teachers have the responsibility for grading their class performance.
MINOR PREMISE	Harold Ward is disputing his history grade from last semester.
CONCLUSION	Therefore, Harold is not a good student.

Good student is a concept too vague to identify a category of students accurately. And what does *accept* mean in this context? Teachers may make mistakes when grading; is it unreasonable to ask for a grade change because of a mistake? Colleges have provisions for challenging grades that students believe are unfair; does using this procedure mean a person is not a "good" student? Clearly, because language is used deceptively in the premises, the conclusion is illogical.

A conclusion resulting from deductive reasoning may also be illogical because the reasoning is improperly constructed. First, evaluate a properly constructed syllogism.

MAJOR PREMISE	All economists must master statistics.

In a properly constructed syllogism, the subject of the major premise—in this example, economists—must be repeated in the minor premise.

MINOR PREMISE	Leslie is an economist.

The conclusion then follows necessarily from the major and minor premises.

CONCLUSION	Therefore, Leslie has mastered statistics.

The syllogism is properly constructed and, therefore, logical. Now evaluate the following invalid syllogism.

MAJOR PREMISE	All economists must master statistics.
MINOR PREMISE	Social psychologists must master statistics.
CONCLUSION	Therefore, social psychologists are also economists.

This syllogism is improperly constructed because the minor premise does not repeat the subject of the major premise. The conclusion, therefore, is illogical.

Like inductive reasoning, deductive reasoning can help organize a discussion. Deductively reasoned conclusions, however, are seldom reached as simply as the skeletal form of syllogisms that illustrate them suggests.

Often the deductive reasoning process fails to state one of the premises the conclusion is drawn from. The missing premise must be inferred. Consider, for example, a deductively reached conclusion drawn from a major premise and a minor premise.

> Migrating Canada geese are disappearing from the marshes where they forage each winter. People frighten Canada geese. Therefore, we must restrict the use of the marshes during migration.

Now examine the same conclusion without the minor premise.

> Migrating Canada geese are disappearing from the marshes where they forage each winter, so we must restrict the use of the marshes during migration.

A deductively reasoned conclusion drawn from an unstated premise needs to be evaluated with care because the omitted premise may be inaccurate. In evaluating the preceding example, you might ask these questions: Do many people visit the marshes during winter months? Are fewer geese migrating south? Have the geese found better foraging sites? Of course, in most reasoned discussions, the group would anticipate these questions.

Exercise 3.1: Building Consensus

Join a group of no more than five people. Read the following statement of a problem an employee of a manufacturing company faces. By using consensus building, decide on a group-recommended course of action the person may follow.

First, establish a procedure for the group to follow, such as individually pursuing the decision-making cycle. Second, share the results of the individual activity. Third, develop a group-consensus position and state it in writing.

> I'm a supervisor for a small company in a community of 40,000 residents, many of whom work for the firm. Recently

I was told that the company was going to shift a substantial portion of its manufacturing activity to India, where labor is very inexpensive. I have been forbidden to tell the people I supervise about the plan. Several of my fellow supervisors are discussing the option of announcing the plan to the employees and then resigning en masse. What problems do you think I'm facing, and what is the morally correct thing to do?

Exercise 3.2: Reasoning Patterns

Study each item and determine the reasoning pattern embedded in it. If the reasoning is incomplete—that is, if it is missing a premise— state the missing element in your own words. Then state what logical conclusions you might draw from the information.

1. After hundreds of driving tests of American and imported automobiles, including subcompact, compact, midsize, and full-size vehicles, the consumer agency claims that full-size vehicles are the safest of all categories and that subcompact cars are the least safe.

2. An important skill in becoming a successful economist is the ability to interpret statistical information from a variety of sources. Sometimes that information comes from the far reaches of the world—that is, from undeveloped countries as well as highly developed countries. Wong Lian worked for the Economic Study Institute, a nonprofit institution, while she was a graduate student. Her job required that she analyze statistical information in key production areas.

3. Only a person who hated the victim could have committed such a brutal crime. Killers always leave a clue to their identity, though. Now I have examined all the evidence, that is, the details from the original crime scene, including photographs, the bloody but blurred shoe print, the unidentifiable smudged thumbprint, the pistol, and the angle the bullet entered the mouth and brain. It all points to murder, not suicide. That leaves us only one suspect, Bill Rimes, with whom the victim had a love-hate relationship. I have no doubt we will find that one of his shoes has blood on its sole.

4. You keep on jumping from lover to lover like that and you'll end up alone in life.

4 Effective Studying *eff*

The ability to think and reason critically and to make persuasive arguments may be the most important ingredient in college success. Certainly learning to think critically will make you a better writer. But sometimes college success is also rooted in more mundane strategies like knowing how to organize your time, find appropriate resources, and study efficiently. Just as you need a plan when you write a paper—which is what the next sections of this handbook will cover—you need a plan when you study. If you study haphazardly—a little or a lot depending on your mood, without a plan, sitting in front of a TV or in a noisy dorm lounge, always at the last minute, or with an iPod constantly plugged into your ear—you probably won't learn as efficiently as you might. To make the most of your study time, you need some strategies.

4a Make a plan

Developing a clear plan for organizing your schoolwork will make you a more effective student. First, create a weekly schedule. On a calendar, note when classes meet, when you work, when you have team practices or other regular responsibilities. Make sure to leave time for meals, sleeping, and relaxing, and for getting from one place to another. Now, look at what's left and identify blocks of time that you can use for studying.

Study Schedules

Successful students typically spend twice as much time studying or reading as they spend in class—that is, two hours of study time for every hour of class time. If you can manage, try to schedule your study time for each course before and after the class meets. You'll process information more efficiently if you review your class notes soon after, and read assignments shortly before, you participate in a class. Now write the study times you've identified on your calendar. But don't stop there; the key will be to follow your study schedule just as closely as you do your class schedule. It won't always be easy, but it will pay off in better grades.

You'll need to make adjustments, of course. Some weeks you'll have little to do for one class, but a major paper will be due in another. Shift your study times accordingly—but don't focus entirely on one course or another. Try to balance your work each week.

When you have a long-term assignment, don't leave it until the last minute. Identify steps—deciding on a topic, doing research, writing a draft, completing the paper—and space them out on your schedule.

4b Use your study time efficiently

You may not have as much time as you would like for studying, especially if you work or have family responsibilities in addition to school. So when you study, make the time that you do have work for you. Set realistic goals so you won't feel stressed or frustrated, and make every minute count.

Where you study can make all the difference in whether you study efficiently. You need a space that is quiet, comfortable, and offers room to spread out papers and books. Your dorm room or apartment may do, but if your roommate watches TV all the time or your desk is in your kids' play space, the library may be a better option.

Make sure that you have all the tools you need for work—not just the right textbook, but also pens, pencils, a calculator, paper, access to a computer—whatever you will need to work on an assignment.

Organize the time you have so that you get the most from it. Tackle your most difficult subjects first, while you're fresh. Break big assignments into manageable chunks. Set goals, and take regular short breaks as you achieve those goals. Review material right after a class meets, and study it again right before the class meets.

4c Use class time efficiently

Class is a time to listen, take notes, and ask questions. Don't let your mind wander to what you're planning to do this weekend or how you're going to pay your bills. And don't get so engrossed in note-taking that you stop hearing and understanding what is being said.

Taking Notes

Don't try to write down every word your professor says. (Research shows that students who record lectures, thinking that the recording will help them review material later, hardly ever listen to the tapes or CDs they create.) Instead, use a note-taking system that works for you. You may want to make up a "shorthand" of your own—symbols to mark important material, abbreviations for frequently used words and phrases. Listen for key words, and write down what the professor writes on the blackboard. Make sure that your notes provide a snapshot of what was covered in class.

Asking Questions

Your professors are the best resource you have. If you don't understand something, ask. If you're embarrassed to ask in class, see the professor during office hours or send an e-mail. Don't expect a professor to repeat the lesson for you or provide notes for a class you've missed (that's what classmates are for), but if you are genuinely confused by a point made in class, ask for an explanation—or ask how to find one. More often than not, your professor will provide more help than you ask for.

Reviewing Your Notes

Simply having notes doesn't do you much good unless you go back to them—and not just before the next quiz or test. Skim your notes as soon as you leave class. Is there anything you don't understand? Visit or e-mail your professor and ask for an explanation, or check the information in your textbook. And review again before the next class session starts; then you'll be ready to understand new material.

4d Read carefully and critically

Some people argue that what you read in college is what makes college worthwhile—that a college needs a good library more than it needs professors. The textbooks, articles, and other source materials that you are required to read in college demand more from you than the reading you may do in your daily life. We've talked already about critical thinking and analysis. These are skills you'll want to apply to your reading as well. But a number of fairly simple strategies will help you get the most out of your assignments.

Preview

Getting a sense of what you are about to read before you start reading will help you focus on the most important points and formulate goals for your reading. Look first at the elements that provide a general overview of the book or article you are about to read: for a textbook, the title, the back cover (which often provides a summary), the table of contents, the preface or introduction; for an article, the title and any heads that appear throughout. Look quickly at any illustrations. Sometimes important points are highlighted in charts, graphs, or images. Now think about what you've found. Can you begin to see the main ideas? The sequence of ideas?

Reading Strategically

Try to establish an overall purpose for your reading. If you are reading to obtain a general overview of a subject, you will read somewhat differently than if you want answers to specific questions. In either case, you can help yourself by using techniques to identify and remember main ideas.

- Turn titles into questions. Create a goal for each section you read by trying to answer the question raised by the title.
- Highlight important information. Don't fall into the trap of highlighting everything, however. Use your reading goals and the title-turned-question to locate main ideas, key terms, and other information you will want to be able to find quickly.
- Write notes in the margins. Jot down questions or a word or phrase that summarizes the important information.
- Make an outline. On a separate sheet of paper or on your computer, outline the ideas in the book or article. Your outline becomes a study guide for quizzes or tests.
- Reread.

Once you have read any material carefully, go over the notes you've made to see that your notes provide a logical summary of what you've read. If there are gaps, go back and read again to fill them in. Then skim the material one last time to make sure you have a clear overview in your head.

4e Prepare efficiently for tests

Do you start studying the night before a test? A better idea is to keep a calendar for quizzes and tests and schedule study time throughout the semester. When you take useful notes in class and on your reading, and review them regularly, you are already halfway there in preparing for a test or midterm.

Finding Out about the Test

Try to clarify what will be tested—but tread carefully. There is nothing that frustrates professors more than a student asking constantly, "Will this be on the test?" You'll also want to know what kind of test you'll be taking. Will it be a multiple choice test, or lots of short answers? Then you need to focus on reviewing and memorizing information—dates, names, relationships, and so on. Will it be several short essay questions? Or one long one? Then you need to focus on understanding the larger concepts you have learned and memorizing the details that support them.

Scheduling and Organizing

Whenever an instructor assigns a quiz or test, mark it on your weekly schedule. Find study blocks when you can focus on each test or quiz—and don't wait until the day before to begin studying. But do clear your schedule as much as possible the afternoon or evening before the test.

WRITER'S TOOLBOX

The Pop Quiz

Some instructors require unannounced, written responses to reading assignments. One kind of response might require you to apply information you've read. Another might want you to summarize key points. No matter what a quiz question calls for, you should try to use three key tactics:

1. Get organized. Quickly list the key points in any order and then make a scratch outline to rearrange them logically.
2. Begin quickly. State your purpose in the first sentence and create a blueprint of what will follow:

   President Lincoln had three criteria when he selected Grant and Sherman as his generals.
3. Use clear transitions. Begin each point with a brief sentence that starts with a clear transition.

   First, Lincoln expected his generals to have courage. Second, Lincoln expected his generals to be loyal. And third, Lincoln expected his generals to fight.

Remember that your reader wants you to answer two implicit questions: Have you read the assignment? Did you understand it?

Making a Study Plan

As you review notes from class and reading, create a study outline that focuses on the main ideas presented in both contexts. Fit your study guide into your study schedule—decide which chapters or what material you will study in what order—and then stick to the plan you make. And use strategies that will help you study effectively:

- Reread chapters or class notes out loud or rewrite the notes as you read to "lock" them in your memory. Skim material again after you have reread it carefully. Make sure that you remember, understand, and can discuss the main concepts in the course as well as the connections between them. Think about how topics relate to one another, and anticipate potential essay questions.

- "Chunk" information into related groups: In U.S. history, memorize dates for wars, then dates for land acquisitions, then dates for other major events, rather than try to memorize complete time lines. Research suggests that we have trouble holding a group of more than seven items in our memory at once.
- Use mnemonics, or tricks of memory, to help you memorize: for example, use HOMES to remember the names of the Great Lakes (Huron, Ontario, Michigan, Erie, Superior).
- Test yourself, or have a friend quiz you—or better, put together a small study group to share notes and ideas.

Taking tests—like writing papers—is a matter of planning ahead, structuring your time appropriately, and understanding the steps you need to take.

WRITER'S TOOLBOX

Secrets of Self-Motivation

Studying, like writing, is not only about reviewing notes or putting words on paper. It is also about keeping yourself going to the end. That takes motivation. Here are strategies for motivating yourself to continue when the going gets tough—when you're tired, when you just don't get it, when the words are just not coming.

- **Self-talk.** You must be in your own corner. Don't be afraid to talk to yourself about why you are bogging down. Maybe the obstacle is something you can change. Give yourself a pep talk.
- **Goal-setting.** Be specific. Set a time limit for reviewing the first chapter or writing the first draft. If you try to study everything in one sitting, or write a complete draft all at once, your goal may be unrealistic. Try to schedule breaks at specific hours. Stop when the break time comes.
- **Consultation.** If you are really stuck, talk to someone who has a positive attitude—your roommate, your spouse, a friend. State the problem in precise language. Ask for advice.
- **Control your space.** You may not be able to control the world, but you can control your own space. Nothing paralyzes the study process more than distractions. Study where there are none. Turn your cell phone off. Find a corner in the library. Face a blank wall. Don't tell anyone where you are.

Tell yourself that studying, like writing, is a positive experience, one that not only lets you learn but also teaches you something about how you think and work, and lets you demonstrate to yourself and others how much you really do know.

PART II
The College Essay

What's so hard about the first sentence is that you're stuck with it. Everything else is going to flow out of that sentence. And by the time you've laid down the first two sentences, your options are all gone.

Yes, and the last sentence in a piece is another adventure. It should open the piece up. It should make you go back and start reading from page one. That's how it should be, but it doesn't always work. I think of writing anything at all as a high-wire act.

—Joan Didion, *novelist*

5   **Write for a Reader**

6   **Begin the Composing Process**

7   **Write a Thesis Statement and Develop a Plan**

8   **Write a First Draft**

9   **Revise the First Draft**

10   **Standard Manuscript Form**

11   **Instructor and Peer Review**

5 Write for a Reader *essay*

Most papers you write in college are essays. College essays usually discuss a limited subject by relying on general knowledge, research, observations, experience, insight, or values. Effective college essays should be based on accurate information and embody a writer's deep understanding of a subject.

College essays differ from other kinds of writing. Works of imagination, such as poems or short stories, often dramatize a writer's personal experience and feelings; textbooks report facts and information; lab reports precisely detail the procedures of an experiment. In contrast, college essays tend to analyze or interpret a subject.

In college you will usually write for a highly informed reader, probably a professor who has made a career of processing information in a particular field. Less frequently, you will write for other students, especially those who are members of your writing or working group engaged in collaborative activities.

The Writer-Reader Relationship

When writing an essay, you are participating in a relationship. This relationship is between you and your reader. It is not enough to know a lot about a subject; you must also maintain the writer-reader relationship by effectively arranging what you know on the page, or you will risk confusing your reader.

Like every relationship, the writer-reader relationship has its obligations. One of your obligations as a writer is to meet your reader's expectation that you will use common essay principles to guide him or her through the reading process.

5a Readers expect an essay to have a dominant purpose

Readers adjust the way they read to fit an essay's *dominant purpose*. For instance, most readers approach descriptive writing much differently than they do persuasive writing. Description involves the senses, so readers reconstruct experience as they read. Persuasion involves the intellect, so readers trace the key points and counterpoints throughout a discussion.

Generally, the purposes of essays can be divided into four categories that represent the ways writers and readers approach a subject.

A **narrative essay** tells a story by relating a sequence of events. You might write a narrative essay on the criminal justice system by tracing the chronology of a typical day in the life of a district attorney.

A **descriptive essay** pictures a scene, a person, a setting, an object, or an event. You might write a descriptive essay that re-creates a courtroom scene for its emotional impact.

An **expository essay** explains, informs, analyzes, or interprets. You might explain the causes of a particular crime, inform your readers about several approaches to ending street crime, analyze the effects of crime on a community, or interpret what crime statistics suggest about a community.

An **argument essay** attempts to persuade readers to take some action or to accept your position on a debatable issue. You might try to persuade your readers to join a crime alert program or argue that the police harass teenagers.

These categories are not rigid. You might, for example, use expressive—that is, descriptive or narrative—techniques in an argument; you might supply useful and interesting information in a narrative. But keep in mind that readers will expect an essay to have a dominant purpose, one that allows them to adjust their reading style appropriately.

5b Readers expect an essay to have a clear structure

Structure comes from a Latin word that means to arrange in piles, to pile up, and therefore to build or construct. Many things look very different but have the same underlying structure. For example, humans are easily distinguished by their physical appearance, but beneath the skin their skeletal structure is very similar. Two automobiles may have the same inner system of frame, engine, and drive train, but the shape, color, and design of their bodies are entirely different.

The structure of expressive essays tends to be more fluid than that of expository and argument essays. Expressive essays are more exploratory, sometimes revealing the writer's personal experience and insight. As a result of their fluid nature, expressive essay structures are often very loose: They capture the flow of experience, not a reconstructed interpretation of experience.

In sharp contrast, expository and argument essays usually follow a structure that professors have come to expect college students to use: the thesis-support structure. Thesis-support essays are composed of several paragraphs, are typically 500 to 1,500 words in length, and have a clear structure that can be divided into three main parts: an introduction, a discussion, and a conclusion.

1. The introduction, usually no more than one or two paragraphs, presents the *thesis statement* and any background information that readers might need to understand the discussion. An effective introduction arouses reader interest and limits the discussion that follows.
2. The discussion usually contains several paragraphs, each organized by a *topic sentence* that relates to the thesis statement. Discussion paragraphs develop the ideas expressed in the thesis statement in a detailed, thorough manner.
3. The conclusion, usually no more than a single paragraph, gives a sense of completion to the essay. Often, though not always, the conclusion restates the thesis statement and touches on the essay's subpoints as expressed in the topic sentences.

Within the overall structure, an effective thesis-support essay should embody three other principles:

- An essay should be unified; that is, every part must clearly relate to the idea expressed in the thesis statement.
- An essay should be coherent; that is, the thoughts expressed in sentences should be connected by transitional techniques such as the repetition of key words and phrases, the rephrasing of key ideas, and the use of transitional words and phrases.
- An essay should have adequate development; that is, there should be thorough explanation and supporting detail.

5c Readers expect discussion paragraphs to follow clear development patterns

Just as readers expect essays to have a clear structure, they expect paragraphs, especially discussion paragraphs, to follow clear patterns. Since an essay is composed of several paragraphs, it might contain a variety of paragraph development patterns (see Chapters 12–17 on writing paragraphs).

1. *Examples* include typical and specific illustrations and concrete descriptions used to develop a point.
2. *Comparison and contrast* presents the similarities and differences between two subjects.
3. *Analogy* helps explain a complicated or abstract idea by comparing it to something familiar.
4. *Cause and effect* explains why something happened and the results of something that happened.

5. *Classification* organizes a subject into distinct categories.
6. *Definition* differentiates one concept from others.
7. *Process analysis* explains how to do something or how something works.

The sooner you master these development patterns, the sooner you will gain control of your writing.

A Student Essay for Study

Consider a college essay by student-writer Judith Park responding to a critical thinking assignment in freshman composition. Begin by reading what Park says about the essay.

> I'm afraid the final draft creates the impression that writing this essay was easy.
>
> It was not.
>
> I wrote it over a two-week period, writing and rewriting several drafts. Basically, I wanted to explain how merchandisers—people who sell us products—manipulate honest feelings.
>
> The essay's content came from class notes and my own experience. In the beginning, I had too much information. This made me work hard at organization. Establishing my dominant purpose early helped me sort all the parts out. Then carefully following the composing process helped me arrange the material in writing. I wrote a rough draft without being too critical. But when I wrote the final draft, the one you'll read here, I kept thinking how my reader would take in information. I revised the thesis statement with care and made sure all topic sentences and supporting information related to it.

Now examine Park's final draft. First, read the essay all the way through. Note how she effectively uses writing conventions to guide readers through her paper. Pay particular attention to the thesis statement and topic sentences, which appear here in italics to help you identify them. Then reread the essay along with the notes in the margin, which identify what readers expect in a college essay. This will help you understand the thesis-support structure.

Subtle Exploitation

Title suggests what the essay will cover (see 9c).

Whether aware of it or not, most of us have learned to respect a core of social values. Our parents, teachers, and the community at large have taught us that it is good to be socially accepted, repay favors, maintain consistent behavior, and respect authority. Without these values, community trust would break down. Friends and neighbors could not count on each other. The psychological power of social values has not been lost on sales representatives and advertisers. *Indeed, these merchandisers engage in the subtle exploitation of typical social values to influence what we buy.*

Introduction gives background information and showcases the thesis statement (see 8a).

Clearly written, limited thesis statement (see 7c).

Topic sentence 1 (see 12a).

The desire for social validation is one value merchandisers exploit. No one likes to be out of step with others. As children we turn to friends and grown-ups to see how to fit in. As adults we continue to seek social acceptance. For example, I recently attended my first formal dinner. The table was beautifully set with flowers, candles, crystal, and a mysterious array of silverware. When the salad was served, I was confused about which fork to use. Rather than face embarrassment by making a mistake, I took guidance from a guest seated across from me. My behavior reflected one form of social validation, that is, the natural tendency of one person turning to another as a model for public behavior. Advertisers often subtly exploit this desire to fit in. Think of advertisements for such retailers and products as Target, Coca-Cola, iPod, Lexus, or Calvin Klein. If consumers see themselves reflected in the advertisements, merchandisers hope they will also

Discussion section with topic sentences that develop one aspect of the thesis statement. Each discussion section paragraph developed according to a clear pattern (see 8b).

Clincher sentence closes the discussion (see 12a).

see themselves using the product as it has been modeled for them, thus successfully exploiting the desire for social validation.

*Topic sentence 2
(see 12a).*

The desire for reciprocity is another value merchandisers exploit. At the start of each school year, several merchandisers give away products and services to new students. For instance,

*Writer uses
development by
examples (see 16a).*

Gillette offers free toiletries; the *Times* offers free newspapers; 24 Hour Fitness Center offers free workout sessions. These are not merely kind

*Note how smoothly
the sentences blend
together: Writer
effectively uses
transitional
techniques
(see 14a, b).*

gestures; they are calculated efforts to influence what first-year students buy. Obviously, these companies are counting on students' liking the gifts and paying to use them in the future. But less obviously, these companies are also exploiting the social value of reciprocity. Most of us have been trained to repay a favor, even an unrequested favor. As a result, merchandisers know that some students will feel obligated to

*Clincher sentence
(see 12a).*

repay their kindness. After all, it does not take many razor-blade sales, newspaper subscriptions, and health club memberships to offset the cost of a few gifts, does it?

Most of us value consistent behavior. Such

*Opening sentences
give background.
Writer uses
"consistent" to
create unity (see 13).*

people as friends, coworkers, and instructors expect us to behave today as we did yesterday. We generally are consistent, for not to be consistent might lead to being rejected. Unfortunately, we are sometimes "mindlessly consistent"—that is, we are consistent when it

*Topic sentence 3
(see 12a).*

makes no sense to be. *High-pressure merchandisers are particularly adept at exploiting mindless consistency.* The tactic begins when someone follows a small commitment with a larger one and then an even larger one. This chain of commitments creates a consistent pattern that is hard to break. For example, recently my friend Lila and I stopped at an expensive boutique. A fashionably dressed saleswoman asked if we were interested in seeing the new spring line. "Yes," Lila said without hesitation. Merely walking into the store represents the first commitment, what salespeople call "putting a foot in the door." Responding with a "yes" to the initial question is a second commitment. Granted these are small commitments, but they lead to larger ones. The saleswoman then asked a series of questions designed to get a consistent "yes" response. "You're a size 8, aren't you?" She took a coat from a hanger and extended it for Lila to feel. "Feel that wool, soft isn't it?" Next she was holding it for Lila to try on. "Feels good to wear a fine coat, doesn't it?" Of course it does, and soon Lila was signing a credit card receipt while the saleswoman was smiling and assuring her she had just bought the finest coat in the store. Exploiting mindless consistency can be almost too subtle to detect, but the next time a telemarketing salesperson calls, listen carefully to the opening questions. They will be designed to get "yes" responses.

Writer develops paragraph through examples and cause-and-effect patterns. One response triggers another, in a causal chain (see 16c).

Topic sentence 4 (see 12a).

Writer uses definition pattern to explain key concept (see 16e).

Another value merchandisers exploit is an automatic respect for authority. Parents hold up doctors, teachers, police, politicians, athletes, and entertainers as authorities, people to be admired and trusted. Golf champion Tiger Woods is an example of an admired celebrity using his name

Writer uses example pattern (see 16a).

to advertise a wide range of products. Woods has won over sixty-five national and international championships, including the Masters Tournament, the PGA Championship, and the British Open Championship. He has used his fame to market not only DVDs on golf and his own line of clothing, he has also earned millions of dollars by endorsing Tag Heuer watches and products from American Express, Nike, and General Motors. Several well-known movie stars have also used their fame to promote personal causes and beliefs. Mel Gibson, for example, took advantage of his power as a Hollywood star and producer to film the movie *The Passion of the Christ,* which portrayed his own controversial version of Christ's life and death. Similarly, film star Tom Cruise exploited the media to advocate for his personal belief in Scientology. These actions generated huge amounts of public attention to and debate about the ideas held by both stars.

Conclusion rephrases the thesis statement and reidentifies key supporting points (see 8c).

No doubt merchandisers target our social values. They suggest their products will bring us social validation. They expect us to repay them for unrequested gifts. They twist our desire to be consistent and abuse our trust in authority. They exploit our fundamental values as if they were human weaknesses.

Park has met her responsibility to her readers. The essay has a clear purpose. It has a clear structure with an introduction that presents the thesis statement, a discussion that develops the subpoints of the thesis statement, and a conclusion that effectively closes the discussion. Finally, the discussion paragraphs reflect sound paragraph patterns.

WRITER'S TOOLBOX

Read with a Critical Eye

Try a new way of reading: Instead of reading strictly for information, practice reading as a writer does. Writers read to improve their writing craft—that is, they read with a critical eye. The critical eye examines another writer's purpose and writing strategies. The critical eye pierces a work's surface and reveals its bones and its heart. If you learn to read other writers' work with a critical eye, you will discover their writing techniques and be able to apply them in your own writing. As a start, analyze Elaine Kubo's "The Thirties: A Personal History" in the exercise below.

Exercise 5.1: Analyze a College Essay

Read the essay "The Thirties: A Personal History," by Elaine Kubo, from the perspective of the reader-writer relationship. The following tasks can serve as a guide. Review the appropriate sections in the *BEH* before completing each task.

1. Study 7a, then state the essay's dominant purpose.

2. Analyze the essay's overall structure.
   • Study 7b, then record the thesis statement.
   • Study 12a, then record the topic sentences.
   • Study Chapter 13, then identify key words that help create unity.
   • Study 14a–b, then identify words and phrases that help create coherence.

3. Study Chapter 16, then identify paragraph strategies you recognize.

The Thirties: A Personal History

   Members of my generation have grown up during a time when the majority of Americans have lived in relative comfort. Nevertheless, we have all seen photographs of the Great American Depression of the 1930s: images of anonymous men in dark suits and tweed caps selling apples on street corners; hollow-cheeked women cuddling infants in front of clapboard shacks; crowds milling before factory gates; hoboes gathered around campfires and eating from tin cans; Model T Fords loaded with chairs, tables, mattresses, and boxes of clothes crawling along desert highways toward the Pacific. These dreadful memories, preserved in history books, are grim. But besides the dreadful memories, there are positive aspects of the Depression that haven't been preserved in history books. These memories are carried by people who suffered yet lived through the thirties.

One positive aspect of the thirties my grandparents remember was the determination to overcome adversity it stirred in them. Like many Kansas farmers in the early thirties, they were suffering from the country's sudden economic collapse, but they still had land and raised some crops. Then nature turned against them. Unrelenting winds swept across the plains, destroying crops and swirling away the topsoil. A drought came with the wind and destroyed any chance they might have had to grow a crop. Finally, the bank demanded payment on the farm's mortgage. They couldn't scrape together the money, so they lost the farm. But if economic collapse and a senseless act of nature destroyed them financially, these events toughened their will to overcome adversity. They moved to a small Kansas town. Days, my grandfather worked as a clerk in his uncle's store; nights, he studied law. My grandmother, who had taught before marrying, worked at the local school. By 1938 my grandfather had passed the state examination allowing him to practice law. By the end of World War II, my grandmother was school superintendent.

I know there were many less fortunate than my grandparents, many who were fighting poverty all those years, but some people who lived through the thirties remember poverty as being different then. It seems that another positive aspect of the Depression was that people could be poor without losing personal dignity. My mother has a childhood memory of a gray-haired man who knocked at the kitchen door one day and asked to do some work in return for a meal. Her father refused to allow him to work, but invited him to join the family for a lunch of soup and biscuits. After the meal, he whittled little wooden birds for all the kids. My mother says that the whole family gave him the respect they would give any successful artist now. My retired neighbor knew out-of-luck businessmen and bankrupt investors who sold flowers on street corners and caddied at golf courses without losing a sense of personal dignity. Can you imagine such things today? Perhaps because there were so many people broke and hungry, it wasn't considered a failure not to have a regular job. People respected each other anyway.

Another positive aspect some people experienced during the thirties was the sense of community it created in them.

Many people tell stories about grocers who supplied out-of-luck neighbors with food on credit and charged no interest. Others talk about going to wedding showers without enough money to buy a nice gift and the guests all digging into their pockets and pooling their change to buy a community gift for the bride. My aunt remembers over a hundred people turning out to help repair a neighbor's house that had partly burned down. But perhaps the most startling example of the sense of community I've heard comes from my friend's family's experience. Her grandparents were forced to move from the countryside to Boston, where they rented a one-bedroom apartment. At the time, my friend's grandmother was eight months pregnant and started having labor pains. A doctor, selected at random from the phone book, came over immediately, completed a quick examination, then called for hot water. He delivered a healthy, six-pound girl. A week later the new parents got a bill for $7.32, the cost of home delivery. Since the move and rent had taken all their money, they couldn't pay. But when other people living in the building—all of whom had been complete strangers to them until the baby was born—heard of the couple's plight, they chipped in pennies, nickels, dimes, and quarters. They sent the fee to the doctor. Less than three days later, the doctor drove up with a back seat full of groceries. He said his nurse had sent the bill by mistake, so he used the payment to buy groceries for them. At one time I might have seen this aspect of the Depression as an act of charity; now I see it as an act of community.

Indeed, the historian's portrayal of the Depression as a grim time for Americans is accurate, but we must remember that a personal history that doesn't get into books parallels the social upheaval we've read about. It's the history carried in the minds of people who endured through that time. Often those memories have some positive aspects.

---

6 Begin the Composing Process *essay*

The composing process is not easy to define, teach, or learn. For writing purposes, think of it this way: It is an interactive process that uses creative and critical thinking to discover and develop a subject worth exploring in an essay.

Few writers can take up a pen or sit at a keyboard and write an effective essay from beginning to end. Instead, most writers develop their work in stages by using the composing process.

Creative thinking is characteristic of the early stages of the composing process. Using creative thinking, writers generate ideas, recall experience, develop examples, stimulate insights, and create figurative language—the raw materials of fresh, interesting writing (see 1b).

Critical thinking is characteristic of the later stages. Using critical thinking, writers evaluate content, shape structure, examine logic, and craft sentences—the analytical perspective that results in accurate, coherent writing (see 1d).

Simply stated, through creative thinking, writers invent material; through critical thinking, writers evaluate and organize material for their readers.

The composing process is not a linear, step-by-step process in which creative and critical thinking are neatly divided. Instead, it is a recursive process of exploration, inquiry, and evaluation that engages both modes of thinking at different times.

Using the composing process, you will construct an essay through several phases or drafts. Throughout the process you will constantly be selecting and rejecting information and making corrective decisions. In the end, after generating pages and pages of writing, you will have composed a final draft to submit for evaluation.

6a Analyze the writing situation

The writing situation has four key elements: the essay subject, the sources of information, the reader, and the essay's length and due date. Your critical analysis of the writing situation early in the composing process will save you time and trouble later.

Subject

The subjects of most college writing assignments are given to you. For example, in political science you might analyze an editorial cartoon or explain local campaign fund-raising restrictions. In business you might identify the reasons for the fluctuating value of the dollar. In literature you might interpret a short story or poem. In psychology you might describe the behavior of people in stressful situations.

The approaches in these assignments are clear: They are to analyze, explain, identify, interpret, and describe. When responding to an assignment, be sure to identify the approach your professor expects.

At other times, however, you can choose your own subject. In this situation, select a subject you know something about or one you can quickly research. In either case, build in a clear approach to your subject just as an instructor would.

Information Sources

Information sources for most academic papers are research materials, whether found in the library or on the Internet. But they are not the only legitimate sources. For example, in her essay "Subtle Exploitation," Judith Park relies on three information sources: personal experience, direct observation, and lecture notes.

Personal experience allows you to integrate information from your life—often the best source of information. You might, for instance, use your experience of having lived in a neighborhood that has changed over the years or of having experienced an event that changed your vision of the world.

Direct observation casts you in the role of observer. You might use your observations on the behavior of strangers gathered in confined places such as elevators, lunch counters, and crowded public transportation. You might include information drawn from watching a television program, a film, or a series of advertisements.

Reading and lectures form the basis of your college education. Many of the writing situations you face will be based on the careful reading of a text—that is, a book, essay, short story, or poem. In these situations, be sure not to let your paper become an extended summary; instead, concentrate on interpreting the work, and support your interpretation with details and examples from the text. You can also draw on your reading for brief examples to support a point or clarify an observation.

Questionnaires and interviews can serve as rich information sources for essays. A psychology instructor might ask you to use questionnaire information as the source for an essay on student attitudes toward such subjects as work, family values, child rearing, and marriage. A law professor might ask you to interview several legal authorities, such as a judge, a defense attorney, a prosecuting attorney, and a police officer, and then use the interview information in an essay.

Mixed sources orchestrate several kinds of information. Suppose, for instance, you plan to argue for security guards to be stationed on campus. To develop your argument, you might use the personal experience of having once attended another crime-plagued campus.

You might include the results of a student survey on crime. You might offer direct observations of illegal acts. And you might report crime statistics you found in the local newspaper. Combined, these sources could make a powerful argument.

Your Reader

Write each essay for a particular reader. In college writing, the reader is usually a professor. Your task is to convince him or her that you have fulfilled the assignment, your information is valid, and your conclusions are reasonable.

Other readers may include fellow students, professionals in a particular field, and community members. Often your readers will be very diverse. This is the universal reader. Here you must seek common elements that involve everyone in the audience. Common groups of readers might be consumers, males, females, students, teenagers, senior citizens. Once you have a sense of your universal readers, you can build cues into your essay that address them: "All consumers are targets . . . ," "No matter how many semesters you have completed at this campus . . . ," "For those of you would-be athletes over fifty-five. . . ."

Length and Time Limit

Writing professors usually specify an approximate length and a due date for essay assignments. The length of an essay and the time you have to write it have a direct bearing on the writing situation. You will need to restrict your subject more for a 500-word essay than you would for a 1,500-word essay. If you have two weeks to write an essay, you will not have much time to research the subject, and if you are writing an in-class essay, you will not have much time to plan the essay. In any case, first you must accurately assess the length of a paper and the time you have to write it. Then you can adjust your writing behavior appropriately.

Exercise 6.1: Analyze the Writing Situation

Identify information sources that could be used to develop the following subjects. Then identify who the audience might be.

1. Whether "franchise" food (McDonald's, Sbarro) at campus food courts provides appropriate nutritional choices

2. The influence of Carl Jung's psychiatric theory of the unconscious on the painter Jackson Pollock

3. The effects of consumer reports about energy efficiency on new car buyers

4. How photographs reveal family relationships

5. Unexpected sources of noise pollution

6b Find a subject in open-ended assignments

Some professors let you select an essay subject; that is, they make open-ended assignments. When that happens, always select a subject quickly. Do not wait for inspiration. Beware, though: not all subjects are suitable for college essays. For example, "My Summer Vacation" is an inappropriate subject under all circumstances.

Pick a subject that reflects the content and spirit of the course. Plunge into serious issues. Explore significant concepts. An effective subject should force you to use specific examples and concrete details. Remember, the quality of a subject is revealing; it can show that you are an engaged writer, not someone who is merely drifting through a course.

When a suitable subject does not come to mind immediately, find one through these strategies:

1. Make a list of possibilities. Give yourself thirty minutes of uninterrupted time. Jot down subjects that come to mind. Items on your list do not need to be extensive entries; a phrase or a sentence will do.

2. If you keep a journal, browse through it. Search for an engaging entry. If an entry engages you, it will engage readers.

3. Recall a classroom lecture. Perhaps a professor stimulated your curiosity or reminded you of a strong opinion you hold, either of which might inspire an essay.

4. Skim a news magazine or newspaper until a subject catches your attention. Jot down your thoughts; use them as a starting point.

6c Analyze the language of close-ended assignments

Usually professors carefully word their assignments to identify the subjects they want you to write about. That is, they make close-ended assignments.

Often a close-ended assignment is designed to test your level of thinking in a particular area of study. Cognitive psychologists have identified six levels of thinking that range from the simple to the complex.

Level 1	*Knowledge*—recognizing and recalling facts and specifics.
Level 2	*Comprehension*—interpreting, translating, summarizing, or paraphrasing given information.
Level 3	*Application*—applying information in a situation that is different from the one in which it was originally learned.
Level 4	*Analysis*—separating a complex whole into its parts until the relationship among the elements is clear.
Level 5	*Synthesis*—combining elements to form a new entity.
Level 6	*Evaluation*—making decisions or judgments based on a set of criteria.

A carefully phrased assignment will usually have a key word that reveals how a professor wants you to approach a subject and the thinking level it addresses. To meet your professor's expectations, it is important that you analyze the language of an assignment.

The following are examples of key words you should know, including what they mean in the context of a writing assignment, what levels of thinking they indicate (in parentheses), and how they might be used.

- *Analyze:* To distinguish the parts of something and discuss their relationship. (Analysis)

  Analyze three advertisements directed at working women in *Vogue, Vanity Fair,* or *Good Housekeeping.*

- *Apply:* To use material from one area of knowledge and relate it to another. (Application)

  Apply three techniques Stephen King uses to create terror in his novel *The Shining* to the techniques the director uses in *The Blair Witch Project.*

- *Assess:* To determine the success or failure of something. (Evaluation)

  Assess the social values expressed in five television commercials for comparable products.

- *Clarify:* To make a complex subject clear, which may involve defining words and concepts. (Comprehension)

  Clarify the phrase "liberty and justice for all."

- *Compose:* To create from diverse sources. (Synthesis)

  Compose an argument that justifies a ban on automatic weapon sales.

- *Criticize:* To analyze the strengths and weaknesses of a subject. (Analysis and Evaluation)

  Critically examine the photographic techniques in Orson Welles's *Citizen Kane.*

- *Discuss:* To consider as many elements as possible concerning a subject. (Comprehension)

  Discuss the effects of crime in the Hanson Projects.

- *Evaluate:* To give your opinion or judge the value of a subject. (Evaluation)

  Evaluate the argument that violent television shows stimulate violence in children.

- *Explain:* To clarify a subject that needs to be understood. (Comprehension)

  Explain the relationship between poverty and crime.

- *Interpret:* To offer what you believe a subject means. (Comprehension and Application)

  Interpret the symbolism of the "woods" in Frost's poem "Stopping by Woods."

- *Justify:* To argue that something is valid or correct. (Evaluation)

  Justify the assertion that illegal drugs should be legalized.

- *Relate:* To show the connections between subjects. (Knowledge and Application)

  Relate IQ scores to success in college.

- *Review:* To reexamine, summarize, or paraphrase a subject. (Knowledge)

  Review the reasons for practicing home schooling.

- *Summarize:* to relate the major points of a subject. (Knowledge)

  Summarize Thomas Hobbes's view of "self-interest."

- *Support:* To argue for or to justify something. (Synthesis)

  Support one of the following positions: using animals for laboratory research is humane or inhumane.

WRITER'S TOOLBOX

Write Now, Plan Later

The way effective writers work is different from what you might expect.

- Effective writers discover problems and solutions in the writing process. By contrast, less effective writers want to anticipate all problems before they write.
- Effective writers brainstorm first, then organize the results. Less effective writers organize first, then write.
- Effective writers bypass rigorous critical thinking until they edit their work. When the writing is difficult, tangled, and plodding, they write their way through. They go with their gut feelings.

What if they are wrong? They trust the writing process. To worry about being wrong puts obstacles in the way of clear thinking.

Judith Park's Writing Assignment

Before beginning the composing process, Judith Park, the author of the model essay in Chapter 5, carefully analyzed her assignment:

> In a 750- to 1,000-word essay, explain how common social influences are used to manipulate behavior. To develop your essay, feel free to use personal experience, observations, lectures, and reading assignments.

This assignment is relatively closed. Park knew that the key word "explain" meant she had to demonstrate her comprehension of the subject. To do so, she had to identify and clarify several common social influences.

An Idea List for Analyzing a Subject

Even though Park's assignment is closed, its subject is too general to write about in a 1,000-word essay. Therefore, Park shifted from analyzing her assignment to creating an idea list with the phrase "social influences" as the starting point.

Social Influences

1. Parents, relatives influence children—role models, authority, love, anger.

2. Teachers, police officers, other authority figures influence our behavior.
3. Political campaigns and politicians influence voters—image, favors, promises.
4. Religious figures influence their followers—guilt, love, kindness.
5. Television influences viewers—entertainment programs, news, commercials.
6. Charities try to influence donors.
7. Celebrities, such as music stars, film actors, television personalities, influence fans.
8. Influence tactics—guilt, trust, hope.
9. Trained behavior patterns are used to influence people.
10. Government lying—is this influence? No. It's deception.
11. Photography is a powerful influence in films such as *March of the Penguins* or *Walk the Line*.

Creating this idea list helped Park find a subject for further exploration. No particular entry gave her a clear subject, Park says, but the list externalized her thinking and began a more analytical process.

> When I first reviewed my idea list, I felt lost. Nothing would work as an essay. Then I began to examine the items differently.
>
> My thought went something like this: many items suggested authority figures who serve as role models. We emulate role models, and they give us advice. From them we also gain a sense of self-worth. These two ideas began to connect in my imagination.
>
> Then my attention fell on two brief entries, influence tactics and trained behavior. People are trained to listen to authorities and to trust authorities. Authorities give us self-worth, advice. How do authorities abuse their roles? They use trust, guilt, and hope. I felt I had found a direction.

Park's experience with this early stage in the composing process was not unusual. A subject or a direction presents itself only after a writer becomes deeply involved. Writers must reexamine their material, redevelop it, combine ideas, and seek patterns among existing ideas. This looping back into previously developed material reflects the recursive nature of the composing process.

6d Narrow the subject so that it can be covered in a single essay

Take charge of your subject by narrowing it to a manageable size. The first subjects you come up with will probably be too general. If you write on a general subject, your essay will consist of general assertions, not specific details and examples. Avoid this trap by working through a general subject to its specific aspects.

GENERAL	The anti–nuclear energy movement.
SPECIFIC	Three dangers residents living near the San Onofre nuclear plant face.
GENERAL	The history of television violence.
SPECIFIC	Violence on the 11 o'clock news.
GENERAL	Child development.
SPECIFIC	An eleven-year-old who killed an attacking dog.

Suppose you are asked to analyze gender roles on television. First you compose an idea list of possible subjects. Then you decide to explore one item from your list: the role of women in situation comedy. This subject, of course, is too general; you would have to examine all situation comedies with women—an enormous task.

You begin the narrowing process. You might concentrate on specific comedies: a current comedy, such as *Two and a Half Men* or *Family Guy* or a vintage comedy, such as *Get Smart* or *I Love Lucy*. Perhaps you have a special interest in *I Love Lucy*. You select that show for analysis. Your subject is now narrowed. Next, you might review several representative segments to identify the female roles the show portrays. In the end, you might concentrate on Lucy herself and examine her role in one show, thus narrowing the subject even more.

Judith Park Narrows Her Subject

Judith Park, the author of "Subtle Exploitation," narrowed her subject even further once she had formulated it from her idea list. She limited her subject to "methods used to influence our decisions." She decided to identify and explain some common tactics that affected her personally, the kind that most people probably experience.

Later, as she was brainstorming her subject, the idea of behavior came back. In this way, writers often change the scope or phrasing of a subject as they move through the composing process. Keep in mind that writing is a process of trial and revision; do not hesitate to change your subject if you see new possibilities as you proceed.

Exercise 6.2: Narrow a Subject

Narrow the following subjects by writing three progressively more limited topics. For example:

> Music
> Country and western music
> Male and female relations in country and western ballads
> Attitudes toward marriage in current country and western ballads

1. science
2. style
3. advertising
4. survival
5. the Internet
6. shopping malls
7. film
8. health
9. politics
10. conformity

6e Use association techniques to gather information

When you have decided on a specific subject, you are ready to gather information. During this information-gathering phase, you will rely more on creative thinking than on critical thinking.

Some assignments require hours of research. But for essays based on general knowledge and experience, you can gather information by exploring what you already know.

The information-gathering techniques presented here are the same as those you would use in decision making (see 1b).

Information-Gathering Techniques

Relax. Let your mind associate one thought with another. Resist analysis; encourage imagination.

> *Brainstorming* helps you capture thoughts on the fly by spontaneously creating an extended list of ideas.
>
> *Freewriting* immerses you in a creative flow by allowing you to automatically write everything that comes to mind while holding back critical thinking.
>
> *Clustering* makes visual connections between key ideas created from brainstorming and freewriting.
>
> *Asking questions* generates an association chain by considering who, what, where, when, why, and how.
>
> *Consultation* uses oral brainstorming and idea-sharing in working groups to create information.

Judith Park Mixes Information-Gathering Techniques

To generate the material that led to "Subtle Exploitation," Judith Park used several information-gathering techniques.

Once I narrowed the subject—ways common behavior is used to influence decisions—I took it to my writing group. We generated a long list of questions, several of which I found helpful.

What common behavior traits do most people share?

What behavior traits are used to influence people?

Who uses them?

Why do they use them?

How are they used?

Then we spent the rest of my group time brainstorming a response to the first question. For example, here are several of the items on the brainstorming list.

People are selfish.

People are self-sacrificing.

People feel guilt.

People trust authority.

People are insecure.

People need to be accepted.

> People need to be valued.
>
> People feel indebted to others.
>
> The next day I began to respond to the remaining questions.
> I used both brainstorming and freewriting to generate re-
> sponses. When I finished I had several pages to work through.

Using several techniques to gather information is not unusual. Once you begin to use associational thinking, you might find yourself, like Park, first making lists, then writing questions, then freewriting to explore the questions. No single technique is appropriate for all writing situations. Use one or a combination of several to explore your subject.

Exercise 6.3: Use Information-Gathering Techniques

To start a 750- to 1,000-word essay, select three of the following subjects, or choose three other subjects that interest you, and narrow their focus. For one subject, brainstorm until you have developed a list of at least fifteen items related to the subject, or freewrite about the topic for thirty minutes (see 1b).

For the second subject, create a list of appropriate questions based on who, what, where, when, why, and how. Follow each question with an answer, if possible (see 1b).

For the third subject, create a cluster of at least fifteen items. Include secondary clusters when appropriate (see 1b and 7b).

improving health	evolution
damaging health	fashion trends
gun control	angry students
making money	competitive sports
escaping the rat race	American memories
becoming involved	getting rich
messages in dreams	living in poverty
space travel	obtaining knowledge
effective teaching	being manipulated
lost causes	funny films

6f Evaluate prewritten information

Much of your information will be in fragments you jotted down to trigger your memory later. That's okay; this phase of the composing process is for your eyes only, not for your reader's eyes.

You will quickly find that much of the information is useless. Strike out pointless observations, odd digressions, clichéd thinking, stalled musings, and just plain dead-end ideas. Search for a fresh perspective, interesting ideas and observations you might develop as examples to connect with your reader's experience.

You will also learn what you do not know about a subject. You might have to get more information. If so, you can refer to published works, review your class notes, or engage in discussions with relatives, friends, or instructors. The more information you generate, the more you will have to work with later.

Judith Park Evaluates Freewriting

The fifth paragraph of Judith Park's "Subtle Exploitation" came from a critical evaluation of freewriting. Park began by rereading her notes. She crossed out useless information and made additional notes as ideas came to her.

Respect for authority is one idea Park used. In these freewriting fragments, she also uncovered typical examples from her own experience and reworked the examples for the final draft. Reread the following paragraph on "authority" from Park's final draft. Study how she reshaped details from her notes (shown in the margin) to fit into her discussion.

Authority. I had a strict religious childhood.

Church every Sunday . . .

I was trained to respect my elders . . .

Who has not been encouraged to respect authority? My parents held up doctors, teachers, police, politicians, athletes, and entertainers as models of success, people to be admired and trusted.

I remember taking up golf just because I had seen Tiger Woods on television. And I wore a Nike hat just like the one he did. I was not the only one. He looked so suave and self-assured. And those Buick commercials! They were awful, really, but Tiger

Another value merchandisers exploit is an automatic respect for authority. Parents hold up doctors, teachers, police, politicians, athletes, and entertainers as authorities, people to be admired and trusted. Golf champion Tiger Woods is an example of an admired celebrity using his name to advertise a wide range of products. Woods has won over sixty-five national and international championships, including the Masters Tournament, the PGA Championship, and the British Open Championship. He has used his fame to market not only DVDs on golf and his own line of clothing; he has also earned millions of dollars by endorsing Tag Heuer watches and products from American Express, Nike, and General Motors. Several well-known movie stars have also used their fame to promote personal causes and beliefs. Mel Gibson, for

Woods was famous. So I guess if you wanted to move in sophisticated circles like he did . . .

Open a magazine or turn on your TV and you will see fashion models, athletes, and entertainers selling cosmetics, athletic equipment, cars, and food. Or beliefs? Mel Gibson? Tom Cruise?

example, took advantage of his power as a Hollywood star and producer to film the movie *The Passion of the Christ,* which portrayed his own controversial version of Christ's life and death. Similarly, film star Tom Cruise exploited the media to advocate for his personal belief in Scientology. These actions generated huge amounts of public attention to and debate about the ideas held by both stars.

Exercise 6.4: Evaluate Prewritten Material

Select one of the three subjects you used to practice prewriting strategies in the previous exercise. Evaluate your prewritten material. (If you need more material to develop a 750- to 1,000-word essay, continue the prewriting process.) Strike out useless observations, odd digressions, and clichéd thinking. Identify the material you can use in an essay and note aspects of the subject that you might need more information about.

---

7 Write a Thesis Statement and Develop a Plan *essay*

College essays must have a clear thesis statement and should be arranged according to a plan. So far you have used a subject to guide the composing process. Now, before you write a thesis statement, you should clarify your subject and purpose.

7a Clarify your subject by stating a purpose

When stating your purpose you should identify your subject and how you propose to develop it. Later in the process, the purpose statement will become the basis for a working thesis statement.

An effective purpose statement can usually be made in a single sentence.

> I plan to analyze the role of Lucy as a gender stereotype in the classic situation comedy *I Love Lucy.*

The writer's subject here is quite clear: the character Lucy Ricardo seen as a gender stereotype. The writer will develop the subject by analysis, thereby writing an expository essay. Now consider another statement of purpose.

> I propose to argue that public rudeness damages campus life.

The writer's subject is clear—the effects of public rudeness on campus life—and it will be developed in an argument essay.

After analyzing her prewriting material, Judith Park wrote a purpose statement for her essay.

> I want to explain how people who sell products influence the public.

This purpose statement makes Park's subject clear: the methods used to influence consumers. She will develop her subject in an expository essay.

Keep in mind that a purpose statement can be revised during the composing process. Nevertheless, it is an effective tool for keeping a writer on track when developing an informal plan.

Exercise 7.1: Clarify a Dominant Purpose

Clarify a dominant purpose for the subject you evaluated in the previous exercise. State the purpose as directly and as clearly as you can. Write it in a complete sentence.

7b Sketch an informal plan

Use your purpose statement to sketch an informal plan for your essay. Think of this stage of the composing process as a matter of sorting and grouping your notes from prewriting.

More than likely, the sorting and grouping process began when you first critically evaluated your notes. Now, by sketching an informal plan, you will be organizing your material in a clear pattern designed to fulfill your purpose. By identifying major points and examples, an informal plan will help you structure your essay. It will also help you discover what other information you might need to gather.

Judith Park's Informal Plan

An informal plan should begin with a purpose statement, followed by a phrase list of major points.

> I want to explain how people who sell products use
> several ways to influence the public.

- Point 1. Social validation: monkey see, monkey do. Examples: formal dining; ads designed to teach product use.
- Point 2. Reciprocity: a compelling desire to repay a favor. Examples: what campus giveaways suggest.
- Point 3. Mindless consistency: avoid appearing "harebrained." Examples: high-pressure salespeople; telemarketing.
- Point 4. Authority: buy what I endorse. Examples: Tiger Woods' clothing; celebrities of all kinds, including politicians.

Clustering techniques you might have used to generate material during the invention process can also serve as an informal outline. Park's informal sketch in cluster form might resemble this one.

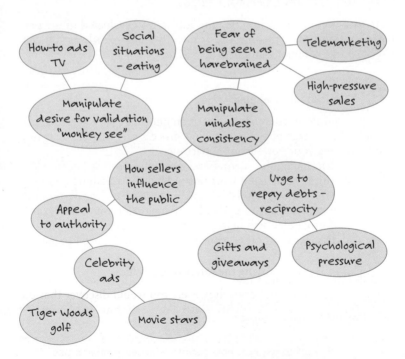

Cluster diagram for Park's informal plan.

Exercise 7.2: Sketch an Informal Plan

Examine the material you have developed for your 750- to 1,000-word essay, that is, the prewritten material and the purpose statement. Make an informal plan by selecting and organizing the ideas and information from your notes.

7c Write a working thesis statement that holds up to critical examination

If there is one moment in the composing process when an essay's final direction and shape become clear, it is when you write a thesis statement. A thesis statement serves as a college essay's intellectual center. It must withstand careful critical scrutiny.

The thesis statement plays a significant role in the writer-reader relationship, too. For writers, a thesis statement identifies and limits the subject, establishes the dominant purpose, and unifies the discussion. Once you have a clear thesis statement, you will find it easier to make decisions about what to include and what to exclude from the discussion paragraphs and how to conclude the essay. When you do not have enough material to develop your thesis statement adequately, then you know you must seek more information (either by returning to earlier drafts or by generating additional material).

For readers, a thesis statement tells what the essay will cover and helps put discussion paragraphs in perspective. Imagine how confused readers will be if you develop several paragraphs but fail to provide the necessary perspective to convey their purpose. A thesis statement provides that perspective.

An effective thesis statement, usually expressed in a single sentence, goes beyond a purpose statement by specifically identifying a subject and limiting the discussion. If you were writing about violence, for example, you might begin with the following thesis statement.

> Violence is destroying the safety of U.S. cities.

When writing your first draft, however, you would discover that the thesis statement is much too broad for a three- or four-page essay. At best you could develop only a few very general observations, all unsupported by specific details. As a consequence, you would have to limit the thesis statement.

Limit a Thesis Statement

Writers limit their thesis statements in two ways.

First, they limit the subject part of the statement. As it stands, the subject of the previous thesis statement is "violence." But violence covers a large territory—murder, muggings, police brutality, and so on. Concentrating on one aspect of violence would limit the subject.

> *Street violence* is destroying the safety of U.S. cities.
> *Gang violence* is destroying the safety of U.S. cities.
> *Random violence* is destroying the safety of U.S. cities.

"Street violence," "gang violence," and "random violence" are more limited than the general subject of "violence." However, these statements are still too broad for a brief essay.

Second, writers limit the predicate part of the statement—in the examples, the part that reads "is destroying the safety of U.S. cities." "U.S. cities" covers all cities from Bangor, Maine, to Honolulu, Hawaii. You could narrow the predicate part of these thesis statements to a particular city, town, or neighborhood.

> Street violence is destroying the safety of *Newport Heights.*
> Gang violence is destroying the safety of *my apartment complex.*
> Random violence is destroying the safety of *our campus.*

These thesis statements are now manageable—that is, they are limited enough to be effectively developed in a short essay. You could develop them from personal observation, interviews, surveys, police reports, and newspaper articles—all readily available information sources.

Phrase a Thesis Statement Precisely

An effective thesis statement does not have to be complex, but it should always be precise. Vague language and overly general assertions may misguide your reader. Use precise, not vague, language to phrase your thesis statement.

VAGUE THESIS

The examination of fairy tales is fascinating because it reveals stereotypical characteristics of women, even in today's world.

PRECISE THESIS

Cinderella reveals common stereotypes of women.

The second example, phrased precisely in specific language, leaves no room for confusion.

Make a Promise in a Thesis Statement

Finally, an effective thesis statement makes a promise: It announces to readers what the essay will cover. The writer must keep that promise or risk writing an unsuccessful essay. Consider, for example, three thesis statements.

> Films like *Curious George* and *The Pink Panther* represent different approaches to humor.

The writer promises to compare and contrast the ways by which two films achieve humor.

> Although murder is humankind's most repugnant crime, the death penalty should be abolished.

The writer promises to argue that capital punishment should be ended.

> Cigarette advertisements fall essentially into four broad categories.

The writer promises to classify cigarette advertisements.

Do Not Confuse Thesis Statements with Other Statements

When writing your thesis statement, do not confuse it with a title, a factual statement, or a purpose statement. *Titles* orient readers, but they are not detailed enough to reveal much about an essay's focus and direction. *Factual statements* do not lend themselves to development; they are dead ends. *Purpose statements* are often similar to thesis statements, but they are usually less refined and become stylistically intrusive when inserted into essays. Compare the following:

TITLE

Sesame Street: The Hidden Message

FACTUAL STATEMENT

Sesame Street is a successful children's education program.

PURPOSE STATEMENT

I am going to argue that *Sesame Street* emphasizes entertainment over education.

THESIS STATEMENT

Although it is identified as television's finest children's education program, *Sesame Street* communicates the message that entertainment is more important than education.

Only the thesis statement clearly announces the discussion that will follow.

Judith Park Composes a Thesis Statement

Judith Park's thesis evolved from the purpose statement she used to sketch her informal plan. After several attempts, Park phrased her thesis statement:

> Self-interested people use several ways to manipulate consumers based on typical conditioning.

By analyzing the elements of her thesis statement, Park could see that she was promising the reader that she would identify several typical behaviors and explain how self-interested people use them to manipulate others. Who are these self-interested people? By returning to her prewritten material, Park identified them mainly as advertisers and salespeople.

Remember, in a college essay a thesis statement must be able to stand up to critical examination. Be sure any thesis statement you write is limited, specific, and makes a clear promise.

Exercise 7.3: Write Precise Thesis Statements

The following statements are ineffective as thesis statements. Identify their problems and rewrite them so that they make effective thesis statements.

1. U.S. schools are not doing their job.

2. Film: A window to the world.

3. I want to explain how magazine advertisements use fear to sell products.

4. The state has set aside 3,800 acres of sand dunes for land preservation.

5. Help—the cry of the homeless.

Exercise 7.4: Write Your Thesis Statement

Write a working thesis statement that clearly sets up the discussion for the essay you have been developing. Do not confuse a thesis statement with a title, a factual statement, or a purpose statement. Remember, an effective thesis statement must be limited and precise, and it must make a promise.

WRITER'S TOOLBOX

Forecast an Essay's Subpoints

Sometimes you may want to use a thesis statement to forecast an essay's subpoints. First, write out the subpoints in brief parallel words or phrases. Next, integrate them into your thesis statement.

> Rude behavior is increasing within our college community, noticeably *in local movie theaters, on campus,* and *at social functions.*

or

> Rude behavior *in local movie theaters, on campus,* and *at social functions* is increasing within our college community.

Forecasting an essay's subpoints generally works well for in-class writing assignments. A forecast not only alerts your reader to an essay's key points; it also serves as a brief outline to help you concentrate while writing under pressure.

7d   Consider audience when you draft a formal outline

If you have not done so already, now is the time to determine who your reader is.

Your reader will influence your choices about an essay's content. If you were writing an in-class essay for an instructor, you would want to show the full range of your understanding. Writing for fellow students, you would select examples that relate to their experience. Writing for a universal audience, you would select examples that reflect broad experience.

Judith Park, responding to a freshman composition assignment, decided to direct her paper to members of her writers' group. She knew she would have to select common examples and explain her ideas in ways that students would understand. This decision and the formulation of her working thesis meant that she was ready to develop a more formal plan for her essay.

For a short essay, an informal outline may be effective, but for longer essays a formal outline will provide a more detailed view of an essay's final arrangement.

Characteristics of a Formal Outline

A formal outline identifies the thesis statement, the subpoints, and various levels of detail depending on the subject's complexity. You can compose a formal outline in topic or sentence form.

Identify the main points by roman numerals, the first sublevel of items by capital letters, the second sublevel by arabic numerals, the third sublevel by lowercase letters, the fourth sublevel by arabic numerals enclosed in parentheses, and the fifth sublevel by lowercase letters enclosed in parentheses. All letters and numbers at the same level are indented to fall directly under one another. (You will rarely need all six levels for a college essay.)

Formal Outline Structure

I.
   A.
   B.
      1.
      2.
         a.
         b.
            (1)
            (2)
               (a)
               (b)
II.
   A.
   B.
      1.
      2.
         a.
         b.
            (1)
            (2)
               (a)
               (b)

Notice that each level is a division of the level above it. There must be at least two items at every level because, logically, a topic cannot be divided into one item—there cannot be an A without a B or a 1 without a 2. Of course, there may be more than two items at any level.

All items at the same level must have parallel grammatical structure, and the first word of each item must be capitalized.

Judith Park's Formal Outline

The following is a formal sentence outline for "Subtle Exploitation."

> Thesis: Self-interested people use several ways to manipulate consumers based on typical conditioning.

I. Social validation relies on conformity.

    A. Etiquette is important.

    B. Advertisements teach consumers.

II. Reciprocity suggests some people are compelled to repay favors.

    A. Companies give away free samples on campus.

        1. Gillette offers toiletries.

        2. The *Times* offers free newspapers.

        3. 24 Hour Fitness Center offers free workouts.

    B. A calculated effort is made to create indebtedness.

III. Mindless consistency exploits the desire to appear consistent.

    A. High-pressure salespeople use the "foot-in-the-door" tactic.

    B. Telemarketers use the same tactic.

IV. Celebrity authorities influence decisions.

    A. Golf champion Tiger Woods uses celebrity to sell his own golf CDs and other products.

    B. Movie stars use celebrity to sell beliefs.

        1. Mel Gibson supports conservative Catholicism through making *The Passion of the Christ*.

        2. Tom Cruise advocates Scientology while advertising movies.

V. These manipulative strategies are based on common values.

Developing a formal outline forced Park to arrange the subpoints and the particulars of her material for a reader. Throughout the process of constructing her outline, Park relied on the informal outline she had constructed earlier, her prewriting material, and other material she had collected. About her outlining process, Park says:

> To start, I laid out my informal plan, prewriting, and class notes. I kept moving through the material and

experimenting with the outline. Since I was writing for
members of my writing group, I knew I needed to include
more examples of experience similar to their experience,
such as being offered free samples on campus.

I also realized I needed to collect more information on
Tiger Woods, Mel Gibson, and Tom Cruise. Everything else
came directly from my experience.

Too often, beginning writers want to skip formal planning, yet a
formal plan can be an important part of the composing process, one
that will help you determine your essay's final arrangement.

Exercise 7.5: Draft a Formal Outline

If appropriate, develop a formal outline for your essay. Identify the
main points by roman numerals (I, II, III, IV), the first sublevel by
capital letters (A, B, C), the second sublevel by arabic numerals (1, 2, 3),
and the third sublevel, if you have one, by lowercase letters (a, b, c).

8 Write a First Draft *essay*

A first draft will never be a final draft. Trying to write a perfect first
draft will force you to start and stop: *Do I put a comma here? Is* strategy *spelled with two t's? This sentence doesn't make sense, or does it?*
Starting and stopping will dry up your creative juices, fresh ideas and
insights will whither, and spontaneity will die.

Instead of perfection, seek writer's flow. Try to keep your writing
moving by concentrating on the big picture: content and structure.
Later you can polish your essay.

To begin a first draft, keep everything in front of you—brainstorming
lists, freewriting, clusters, purpose statement, outlines. Having everything before you, including mojo charms if you like, will prime the
flow of ideas.

There is no hard and fast rule about where to start a first draft.
Some writers like to start at the beginning and move step by step
to the end. That's okay. Other writers start with the discussion
and then write the introduction and conclusion. That's okay, too.

An effective tactic is to begin with information that engages your imagination. In this way you can draw yourself more deeply into the writing flow.

Remember your goal: Keep writing toward a completed first draft. You can circle back and fill in later.

8a Write an introduction with a thesis statement that captures a reader's interest

In a thesis-support essay, the introduction is your chance to grab your reader. Do not throw that chance away. Here is how an effective introduction works.

First, showcase the thesis. The thesis embodies your promise to the reader, and the promise will bring him or her into the discussion.

Second, give your reader background information. Place your thesis in context. Not to provide the right context for your thesis is like letting someone stumble through a dark room without knowing the light switch location.

Third, make your writing interesting. Never whine on the page about the rigors of the assignment. Use specific language and images to engage the reader's imagination.

For a thesis-support essay, the introduction will seldom be longer than a paragraph, certainly no longer than one-fifth of your paper. The most effective strategy is to open with sentences that engage the reader and conclude with the thesis statement. In the following examples of opening paragraphs, the thesis statements are italicized.

> From a page in a high-fashion magazine, a stunningly attractive woman in boots, jeans, and bomber jacket stares directly at the reader. From the back cover of a news magazine, a rugged cowboy in Stetson and sheepskin coat leans casually on a fence post and gazes at the distant mountains. On another page, a handsome young couple sit in a tavern and look longingly into each other's eyes, and on yet another page a camel in tuxedo struts its stuff in a nightclub. These are all central images in cigarette advertisements, and each figure is smoking. *Generally, to sell their products cigarette advertisers appeal to deep consumer desires.*
>
> —Student-writer Joan Akers, "Burning Desire"

> "Attitude" is in. I don't mean good attitude; I mean bad, real bad, attitude. You're probably attracted to it, and your parents, like mine, probably hate it. It's a combination of

arrogance, anger, and dark humor. Raw comedians have attitude. Cool actors have attitude. Sullen rock stars have it, too. Dennis Leary, Chris Rock, and Axl Rose—all are soaked in attitude. Is it strictly a male trait? Hardly—Whoopi Goldberg, Madonna, and the Spice Girls all have serious attitude. *Attitude doesn't come easily, but you can acquire it if you follow five simple steps.*

—Student-writer Phyllis Booker, "Attitude"

Here are strategies professional writers use to grab the reader's attention.

1. Create vivid details that engage a reader's senses.
2. Dramatize statistics that relate to the thesis.
3. Use eye-catching quotations that arouse a reader's curiosity.
4. Ask a question that alerts the reader.
5. Relate an anecdote with which the reader can identify.
6. Define a key word or concept in an unusual way.

In short papers, especially those that give straightforward information, you might choose to open with the thesis statement instead of showcasing it last.

A page titled "Conditions of Contract" on airline tickets could serve as a syllabus for a course in travel education. In fine print, it answers several questions.

—Student-writer Tim Potts, "Read the Fine Print"

WRITER'S TOOLBOX

Writing a First Draft on a Computer

If you can type "cold" onto the computer—that is, type a first draft without a rough handwritten draft—you will save a lot of time. But not everyone can or wants to do this; most writers are more comfortable writing by hand first. They start by roughing out sentences and paragraphs, then they enter them into the computer.

Remember: Write the first draft quickly. Even when your typing is weak, a computer can increase your speed. Mistakes can be corrected later. Keep in mind, too, that your first draft will be filed and easily accessed for revision. If you find yourself stuck on an important concept, write a reminder note in parentheses or in all capitals and boldface so you will remember to return to it later.

Exercise 8.1: Write an Introduction

Write an introduction to your essay. In some respects, the introduction can be your essay's most important section. Indeed, writing an effective introduction might take more creative effort than writing any other part of the essay.

Many writers compose an introduction after they have composed the discussion. These writers need to know exactly where they are taking their readers.

Whether or not you start your first draft by writing the introduction makes no difference. Either way, you should use the introduction to showcase the thesis, provide necessary background information, and make your writing interesting by using one of several tactics.

1. Create vivid details.
2. Dramatize statistics.
3. Use eye-catching quotations.
4. Ask a question.
5. Relate an anecdote.
6. Define a key word or concept.

8b Write a discussion several paragraphs long, organized by topic sentences

In a thesis-support essay, each discussion paragraph develops one aspect of the thesis statement. Furthermore, a topic sentence serves as the main idea of a discussion paragraph just as a thesis statement serves as the main idea of an entire essay. Topic sentences and supporting information—that is, the discussion—keep the promise that is implied in a thesis.

For a full review of paragraph structure, see Chapters 12–17 on writing paragraphs, especially Chapter 12, Topic Sentences, and Chapter 16, Expository Paragraphs.

To be effective, discussion paragraphs should be unified, coherent, and well developed.

Unity.   Discussion paragraphs are unified when the information they present clearly relates to the idea expressed in the topic sentence. Remember: A topic sentence advances a thesis statement's promise by identifying and developing one key aspect of the thesis.

Coherence. Discussion paragraphs are coherent when readers move smoothly and logically from one sentence to another—that is, when the main idea advances from sentence to sentence along a well-constructed verbal path. When a paragraph lacks coherence, readers become distracted and lose interest.

Development. How long should a discussion paragraph be? Paragraph length depends on several considerations, such as the complexity of the information, the development method, and the lengths of the paragraphs before and after it. Use this as a guiding principle: A discussion paragraph should be developed just enough to do justice to its main idea as presented in the topic sentence.

While composing an essay, you might discover that you need more information to develop an effective paragraph. There are several actions you can take. First, you can return to your prewriting for another idea. Second, you can provide greater detail to the idea at hand. Third, you can consult outside sources for more information. The process of gathering information may continue until the final draft is complete.

Well-developed paragraphs might contain examples, definitions, comparisons, causes, effects, facts, and statistics—all presented in enough detail to make a paragraph over a hundred words long.

When a discussion paragraph becomes exceptionally long, writers often divide it into two or more paragraphs to ease the reading process, even though all the information amplifies the main idea of a single topic sentence.

Transition Paragraphs

In an extended thesis-support essay, a brief paragraph often serves as a transition when a significant shift occurs in the discussion. Usually no longer than two or three sentences, the transition paragraphs purpose is to remind a reader of the thesis statement and indicate that the discussion is shifting emphasis.

> Clearly, body alteration through scarring and tattooing in primitive cultures communicated a variety of social messages. In contrast, body alteration today is merely decorative. Tattooing and piercing are fads, much like styles of clothes.

This transition announces that the discussion is turning from the purpose of body alteration in primitive cultures to the purpose of body alteration today.

Exercise 8.2: Write a Discussion

Use your thesis statement and outline to sketch out the discussion section of your essay, organizing each paragraph around a topic sentence. Begin by roughing out each topic sentence. Then flesh out each paragraph, keeping in mind the principles of effective paragraphs. Remember, this is a first draft. Do not seek perfection; your goal is to complete a solid first draft.

Even so, you want to write paragraphs that approximate effective discussion paragraphs.

1. Concentrate on a single aspect of the thesis statement.
2. Open with a topic sentence.
3. Maintain unity.
4. Retain coherence.
5. Develop the idea adequately.

8c Write a conclusion that effectively closes the discussion

Too often, beginning writers treat conclusions in a perfunctory manner: a couple of general statements about the subject and a rapid "That's all, folks" to close.

Experienced writers use a different approach, one based on the simple principle that readers remember best what they read last. Experienced writers, therefore, treat writing a conclusion as a challenge that demands skill and concentration, and they have several strategies for concluding their essays.

Give a brief summary. In college writing, the most common practice is to restate the thesis statement and then summarize the subpoints to reinforce what has come before. This summary method often seems mechanical, but it can be effective when it is handled in an interesting way. A summary conclusion does have one strong advantage: It is clearly linked to the rest of the essay.

Draw an inference. You can use the conclusion to deepen a dimension of an essay. One student ended a paper on being threatened at pistol point and robbed by shifting from the external detail of the experience to an implicit psychological fact. Notice how she uses questions to put the reader in a reflective mood:

> What does it mean when somebody holds you up? Just the loss of a few dollars? Or just the loss of a wallet and some mementos— a few peeling photographs, worn identification cards, tattered

ticket stubs? Yes, it means that. And it means more. It means you have become part of that chosen group that no longer feels it is safe to walk the neighborhood streets after dark.

Use an anecdote. You can conclude an essay with an anecdote, a brief story that puts the thesis statement in clear perspective.

Link the subject to the reader. You can conclude by drawing a lesson from the discussion that links the subject to the reader's experience.

Close with a quotation. You can conclude with an apt quotation, one that echoes the main idea of the essay and will resonate in the reader's memory.

Remember that a conclusion must flow logically from the essay. If it does not, it will seem to be merely tacked on.

Exercise 8.3: Write a Conclusion

Write a conclusion for your first draft. Remember, a conclusion should echo the entire essay. Use one of these common strategies:

1. Give a brief summary.
2. Draw a significant inference.
3. Present a meaningful anecdote.
4. Link the subject to the reader.
5. Close with a quotation.

9 Revise the First Draft *essay*

Although you cannot actually talk to a reader during the revision process, you can do the next best thing: Imagine that you are seeing your first draft through a reader's eyes.

Seeing through a reader's eyes will give you the critical perspective you need to evaluate your own work. Through this act of imagination, you will recognize passages where the reader might get bogged down. You will spot where you need to delete or add information. You will rewrite for clarity and logic.

Remember, revision engages the critical thinking process. You will critically evaluate your work and consciously revise it to fulfill an informed reader's expectations. Keep in mind, too, that revision does not take place in one swoop. It unfolds in phases.

9a For phase 1 revision, improve the major elements

Examine your first draft with an eye toward improving the major elements first. You might have to add or delete information, sharpen the thesis and topic sentences, improve the unity, and make the point of view more consistent. Throughout the process, you will always be improving the clarity of your essay.

Some writers revise on the computer. Others print out copies of the first draft and revise by hand. If you choose to revise on screen, make a copy of the original first draft before you begin to make changes. This way you will not risk losing information you might decide to reinstate later. If you choose to revise on hard copy, do not be timid. Scratch out passages, rewrite in the margin, and make notes that reflect what you plan to add. When all that is done, write a second draft to accommodate the changes.

Add Content.   Reread your first draft to see if you need more information. Some writers skimp on content in their first drafts. They choose to move quickly through the draft, hitting the high points and planning to add detail during revision. To develop more content, they sometimes return to the beginning of the composing process, which means they return to thinking creatively. If you need to add information, you will develop a new list of details, create another cluster, or seek more information.

Delete Content.   Reread your first draft to eliminate unnecessary information. Some writers purposely overwrite their first drafts, knowing that they are generating excessive information. Other writers may overemphasize a minor point or include too much detail to support it. In all these cases the content must be trimmed, and to delete content effectively requires a sharp critical eye. You must read and reread passages to figure out what can be cut and how to combine information in other sentences.

Examine the Structure.   Reread your first draft with an eye toward improving its organization. At the most general level, this draft should already have a distinct introduction, discussion, and conclusion. But more than likely the unity will be flawed, that is, the thesis will not clearly relate to the topic sentences. Reread the thesis. Be sure it is specific and limits the discussion. Check to see that each of the topic sentences relates directly to one aspect of the thesis. If necessary, rewrite the thesis and the topic sentences so that each embodies a key word. The relationship between thesis and topic sentences must be clear because each serves as a signpost for the reader. Sometimes repeating a key word makes the link clear.

Once you know your thesis and topic sentences work together, check each discussion paragraph separately to be sure its information relates directly to the topic sentence. This evaluation is as important as checking to be sure that the thesis and topic sentences are clearly linked.

Finally, examine the conclusion to see that it follows logically from the discussion. It is important to make sure your conclusion directly restates, or at least echoes, the thesis statement.

Examine the Point of View.   In the broadest sense, writers present their material from a personal or impersonal point of view. The personal point of view is characteristic of essays based on personal experience and observation; the impersonal point of view is characteristic of objective reports and research. A personal point of view places the writer in the experience, which is signaled by personal pronouns (I, me, my, we, us, our). Sometimes writers address their readers directly, using second-person pronouns (you, your). An impersonal point of view seldom directly addresses the reader or uses first-person pronouns.

Your material will usually dictate the appropriate point of view to use. You would not write about your childhood experiences in an impersonal way, nor would you write about historical, social, or scientific research in a personal way.

When revising for point of view, ask yourself where the material came from: from research? from reports by others? from personal experience? The proper point of view will follow from your answer.

In "Subtle Exploitation," Judith Park had no choice but to write from a personal point of view. Much of her information comes from her own experiences and observations. Although many writing professors caution against using the personal point of view, it is sometimes the only appropriate point of view to use. The key to making your decision is reflected in your essay's content. Like Park, if you use examples from your own experience, then the personal point of view is appropriate.

One caution: When you use the personal pronoun *I* to signal a personal point of view, do so judiciously. Do not pepper your essay with *I*'s. To do so might create the impression that you, not your subject, are the center of the essay.

Judith Park's Phase 1 Revisions

Judith Park extensively revised her first draft of "Subtle Exploitation." For this phase, she kept her eye on the larger elements, knowing she would concentrate on the smaller elements in another phase. Examine the changes she made along with her comments about the reasons she made them.

I added details to show how many forces influence social values. I also wanted to subtly introduce my supporting points.

Unfortunately, most people have learned to [Parents, teachers, and the community at large teach] respect a core of social values. ~~Most of us want~~ [that it is good to be socially accepted, repay favors,] ~~to be socially acceptable, repay favors, maintain~~ [maintain consistency, and respect authorities.] ~~consistency, and show respect for authorty.~~

I revised the thesis to be specific. "Exploitation" works better here. Later, I could make "exploit" a unifying word.

Without these values community trust would not work. No one could count on anyone. The power of social values has not been lost on merchandisers, ~~that is, those who want to sell us their products.~~ [merchandisers engage in] These ~~self-interested people use~~ [the subtle exploitation of typical social values.] ~~several ways to manipulate consumers based on typical conditioning.~~

I added detail to enliven this example.

I used "mysterious" to emphasize my confusion.

[beautifully set with flowers, candles, and a mysterious array of silverware.]

The desire to be socially validated is a common desire advertisers use to manipulate consumers. No one likes to be out of step with others. [As children we turn to friends and grown-ups to see] ~~When confused in a social situation, most~~ [how to fit in. As adults we continue to seek social] ~~people will turn to someone else for direction.~~ [acceptance.] I recently attended my first formal dinner. The table was ^ ~~beautiful but confusing.~~ When the salad was served, I was confused about which fork to use. Since I was afraid to face embarrassment by making a mistake, I watched a guest seated across from me. This behavior reflected one form of social validation, which is the natural tendency of one person looking at another as a [for public behavior.] model. ^ [Advertisers subtly exploit this desire to fit in.]

Trying to see my essay through a reader's eyes, I decided that this paragraph was unnecessary and overwritten so I combined it with the previous one.

~~The manipulation of the desire for social validation is a powerful strategy when used to influence people.~~ Think of advertisements for such retailers and products as Target, Coca Cola,

iPod, Lexus, or Calvin Klein. ~~They usually~~

~~feature models using the products in social~~

see themselves reflected in

situations. ~~If consumers~~ ~~identify with the models~~

the advertisements, merchandisers hope they will also

~~and situations, then the advertiser is successfully~~

see themselves using the product as it has been

~~using social validation to influence them.~~ How

modeled for them. They are successfully exploiting

~~does this tactic work? By showing~~ consumers

the desire for social validation.

~~that it would be appropriate to use the product in~~

~~similar situations in their lives. Manipulating the~~

~~desire for social validation is only one of several~~

~~strategies used to influence our decisions.~~

The desire for reciprocity is another value

~~Merchandisers frequently use the desire to~~

merchandisers exploit. For instance, Gillette offers

~~repay a favor, which is called "reciprocity," to~~

free toiletries; the Times offers free newspapers; 24

~~influence our decisions. Reciprocity is at work~~

Hour Fitness Center offers free workout sessions.

~~when a company gives out free samples of a~~

~~product. I know of one maker of razor blades,~~

~~shaving creams, and after-shave lotions who~~

~~offers free samples at the beginning of each~~

~~school year. One local newspaper offers a two-~~

~~month free subscription to all registering~~

~~students. A local athletic club offers one free~~

~~month of workout sessions to first-year students.~~

These are not merely kindnesses, they are

calculated efforts to influence what

~~attempts to get~~ first-year students to buy, certain

products. Obviously, these companies are

ing and paying to use

counting on students to like the gifts. ~~First, it~~

~~makes sense for these companies to get students~~

~~used to using their products and services so that~~

they will pay to use them in the future. ~~Second,~~

But less obviously,

~~at a more complex level,~~ these companies are

I revised this topic sentence to parallel the one in the preceding paragraph and added "exploit" to help create unity. I identified the companies by name to be more specific. I also cut down the wordiness.

also ~~using reciprocity as a subtle way to~~ exploit^ing^
the social value of reciprocity. Most
~~students. They know that~~ most of us have been

I felt the "psychologically painful" reference might distract a reader. I added the closing detail to remind the reader that these gifts are insignificant next to potential sales.

trained to repay a debt, even an unrequested

As a result, merchandisers know that some
debt. ~~In fact, for many people not to repay a debt~~
students will feel obligated to repay their kindness.
~~can become psychologically painful.~~

It does not take many razor blade sales, newspaper subscriptions, or health club memberships to offset the cost of a few gifts, does it?

Exercise 9.1: Phase 1 Revisions

Always start with a clean draft. Reread your essay for content and eliminate unnecessary information. Note points that might need more development or support. Generate more content and work it into your paper. Then reread for organization, making sure that the discussion paragraphs reflect the thesis statement. Next, reread for point of view, making the necessary revisions to keep the point of view consistent. Revise once again, integrating your changes into this draft.

EDITOR'S TOOLBOX

Making Phase 1 Revisions

Most writers like to make phase 1 revisions on hard copy, that is, a printed version of the essay, with plenty of space between the lines to accommodate changes. But some writers have learned to revise on the computer.

A computer can make phase 1 revisions easy. To move long passages, use the computer's Cut and Paste function. To check paragraph unity, you can use the Find feature to trace how frequently you use key words to keep your central purpose before the reader. To keep track of the changes you make, turn on the Track Changes function of your word-processing program.

Judith Park Integrates Phase 1 Revisions

The following are three revised paragraphs from Judith Park's draft. What she deleted is lined out, and what she added appears in italics.

Unfortunately, most people have learned to respect a core of social values. ~~Most of us want to be socially acceptable,~~ *Parents, teachers, and the community at large teach that it is good to be socially accepted,* repay favors, maintain consistency, and show respect for authority. Without these values community trust would not work. No one could count on anyone. The power of social values has not been lost on merchandisers. ~~that is, those who want to sell us their products. These self-interested people use several ways to manipulate consumers based on typical conditioning~~ *merchandisers engage in the subtle exploitation of typical social values.*

The desire to be socially validated is a common *value* advertisers use to manipulate consumers. No one likes to be out of step with others. ~~When confused in a social situation, most people will turn to someone else for direction.~~ *As children we turn to friends and grown-ups to see how to fit in. As adults we continue to seek* acceptance. I recently attended my first formal dinner. The table was beautiful*ly set with flowers, candles, crystal, and a mysterious array of silverware,* ~~but confusing.~~ When the salad was served, I was confused about which fork to use. Since I was afraid to face embarrassment by making a mistake, I watched a guest seated across from me. This behavior reflected one form of social validation, which is the natural tendency of one person looking at another as a model *for public behavior. Advertisers subtly exploit the desire to fit in.* ~~The manipulation of the desire for social validation is a powerful strategy when used to influence people.~~ Think of advertisements for such retailers and products as Target, Coca Cola, iPod, Lexus, or Calvin Klein. ~~They usually feature models using the products in social situations.~~ If consumers identify ~~with the models and situations, then the advertiser is successfully using social validation to influence them. How does this tactic work? By showing consumers that it would be appropriate to use the product in similar situations in their lives. Manipulating the desire for social validation is only one of several strategies used to influence our decisions~~

see themselves reflected in the advertisements, merchandisers hope they will also see themselves using the product as it has been modeled for them. They are successfully exploiting the desire for social validation.

Merchandisers frequently ~~use the desire to repay a favor, which is called "reciprocity," to influence our decisions. Reciprocity is at work when a company gives out free samples of a product.~~ *The desire for reciprocity is another value merchandisers exploit.* ~~I know of one maker of razor blades, shaving creams, and after-shave lotions who offers free samples at the beginning of each school year. One local newspaper offers a two-month free subscription to all registering students. A local athletic club offers one free month of workout sessions to first-year students.~~ *For instance, Gillette offers free toiletries; the* Times *offers free newspapers; 24 Hour Fitness Center offers free workout sessions.* These are not merely kindnesses, they are ~~attempts to get~~ *calculated efforts to influence* what first-year students ~~to buy~~ certain ~~products.~~ Obviously, these companies are counting on students to ~~like~~*ing* the gifts *and paying to use them.* ~~First, it makes sense for these companies to get students used to using~~ their ~~products and services so that they will pay to use them~~ in the future. *But less obviously,* ~~Second, at a more complex level,~~ *these* ~~These~~ companies are also ~~using~~ reciprocity ~~as a subtle way to~~ exploit*ing* ~~students~~ the social value of reciprocity. ~~They know that~~ *Most* of us have been trained to repay a debt, even an unrequested debt. ~~In fact, for many people not to~~ ~~repay a favor can become psychologically painful.~~ *As a result, merchandisers know that some students will feel obligated to repay their kindness. It does not take many razor blade sales, newspaper subscriptions, and health club memberships to offset the cost of a few gifts, does it?*

9b For phase 2 revision, improve the smaller elements

When you have integrated your revisions into your first draft, you are ready to focus on smaller elements. Revise your sentences with an eye for effectiveness, for clarity, for coherence—that is, clear transitions in thought—for conciseness, diction, and style.

Consider Your Essay's Tone. Now is the time to consciously think about *tone*. Tone embodies your attitude—it is embedded in the words you use and how you use them. In college writing, try to achieve a reasonable tone, one that shows you understand your subject and have respect for it and for your readers. Most college writing requires standard American English, which can be formal or informal writing.

Although readers appreciate lively language, they can be repelled by sarcasm or slang inserted into serious discussion. They can also be repelled by pompous language. College writing often becomes pompous when inexperienced writers use the thesaurus to find words that sound more "intelligent" to replace words they have already used. Generally, the words will be unnecessarily abstract and inaccurate. Extensive reading with a dictionary in hand is the effective way to acquire a working vocabulary.

For phase 2 revision, start again with a clean draft. To sharpen your critical examination, try reading it slowly, preferably out loud. (The ear is often more critical than the eye.) As you read, make your improvements.

When you see that individual sentences are precise, edit them for correctness: Check their grammar, spelling, mechanics, and punctuation. Make these changes directly on the page or screen, integrate the revisions, then print out a clean, new draft.

Judith Park's Phase 2 Revisions

For her second-phase revisions, Judith Park found herself concentrating on improving coherence, that is, providing clear transitions to guide readers through her essay. She changed several words and passages to reflect her thought more accurately. She also improved the wording of her thesis and topic sentences so they signaled a clear movement in the discussion. Finally, she made sure that the identity of her readers was embedded in the introduction. Read the following passage with Park's phase 2 revisions, then read her comments on the revision, which appear in the margin.

"Unfortunately" is inaccurate.
"Our" is the start of my attempt to define a reader. It suggests that I'm writing for readers my own age.

Whether aware of it or not, most of us
~~Unfortunately, most people~~ have learned to respect a core of social values. Our p Parents, teachers, and the community at large ~~teach~~ have taught that it is good to be socially accepted, repay favors, maintain consistency, and show respect for authority.

I think "friends and neighbors" personalizes what I'm saying.

Without these values community trust would ~~not break down. friends and neighbors work. No one~~ could count on anyone. The power of social values has not been lost on sales representatives and advertisers. ~~merchandisers. that is, those who want to sell us their products~~. These merchandisers engage in the subtle exploitation of typical social values to influence what we buy.

I tried to show a purpose, so I added "to influence what we buy."

Some small changes: "advertisers" to "merchandisers" because I use merchandisers as a key term.

The desire ~~to be~~ for socially ~~validated~~ validation is ~~a~~ one. common value ~~advertisers use to manipulate consumers.~~ merchandisers exploit. No ono likes to be out of step with others. As children we turn to friends and grown-ups to see how to fit in. As adults we continue to seek acceptance. For example, I recently attended my first formal dinner. The table was beautifully set with flowers, candles, crystal, and a mysterious array of silverware. When the salad was served, I was confused about which fork to use. Rather than ~~Since I was afraid to~~ face embarrassment by making a mistake, I ~~watched~~ took guidance from a guest seated across from me. ~~This~~ My behavior reflected one form of social validation, ~~which~~ that is, the natural tendency of one

Added transitional phrase.

I wasn't "afraid"; I didn't want to be embarrassed.

I was "guided" by the guest. "Watched" is inaccurate.

"Turning to" works better than "looking at." Added "often" to qualify the assertion.

~~turning to~~ person ~~looking~~ at another as a model for public behavior. Advertisers *often* subtly exploit the desire to fit in. Think of advertisements for such retailers and products as Target, Coca Cola, iPod, Lexus, or Calvin Klein. If consumers see themselves reflected in the advertisements, merchandisers hope they will also see themselves using the product as it has been modeled for them, *thus* ~~They are~~ successfully exploiting the desire for social validation.

I combined these sentences to show the result more effectively.

The desire for reciprocity is another value merchandisers exploit. *At the start of each school year,* ~~For instance,~~ Gillette offers free toiletries; the *Times* offers free newspapers; 24 Hour Fitness Center offers free workout sessions. These are not merely kindnesses, they are calculated efforts to influence what first-year students buy. Obviously, these companies are counting on students liking the gifts and paying to use them in the future. But less obviously, these companies are also exploiting the social value of reciprocity. Most of us have been trained to repay a debt, even an unrequested debt. As a result, merchandisers know that some students will feel *After all, it* obligated to repay their kindness. ~~It~~ does not take many razor blade sales, newspaper subscriptions, and health club memberships to offset the cost of a few gifts, does it?

I left all this untouched. It worked for me.

Added a transitional phrase, "after all."

EDITOR'S TOOLBOX

Making Phase 2 Revisions

For phase 2 revisions, you can probably revise on the screen without much difficulty. Chances are you've already revised some sentences during phase 1 revisions. Now is the time to evaluate the sentences as each relates to the other.

Experiment with phrasing. Change words to create a different effect. Try different sentence structures to increase reading speed.

If you decide to make your essay more impersonal, use the Find feature to spot each use of "I." Then see if you can revise the sentence to eliminate it. If you want to avoid sexist pronoun references, use Find to trace all the uses of masculine pronouns to be sure they have masculine referents. If they don't, rewrite the sentences to remove the gender bias.

Meet Reader Expectations

Academic readers expect that a college essay will be organized by a thesis statement and developed through a series of topic sentences, one for each discussion paragraph. During proofreading, scan your thesis statement and topic sentences one more time to be sure they clearly relate to each other. Judith Park scanned her thesis statement and topic sentences as follows:

THESIS STATEMENT IN THE INTRODUCTION

Merchandisers engage in the subtle exploitation of typical social values to influence what we buy.

TOPIC SENTENCE IN THE FIRST DISCUSSION PARAGRAPH

The desire for social validation is one value merchandisers exploit.

TOPIC SENTENCE IN THE SECOND DISCUSSION PARAGRAPH

The desire for reciprocity is another value merchandisers exploit.

TOPIC SENTENCE IN THE THIRD DISCUSSION PARAGRAPH

High-pressure merchandisers are particularly adept at exploiting mindless consistency.

TOPIC SENTENCE IN THE FOURTH DISCUSSION PARAGRAPH

Another value merchandisers exploit is an automatic respect for authority.

Exercise 9.2: Phase 2 Revisions

Begin with a clean draft of your essay. Read it to improve the smaller elements. Try to read as critically as you can through the eyes of your imagined reader. Do not fall into the trap of making negative judgments by telling yourself "this isn't any good," or "this part sounds stupid," or "it was dumb to pick this subject." Instead, decide what is effective and what is not. Leave the effective writing alone and figure out how to fix what is ineffective.

Revise the entire essay, reading and rereading to see that the sentences fit together, then integrate your improvements by completing another draft and reviewing it. If necessary, improve that draft, too.

9c For phase 3 revision, proofread the final draft and write a title

When you have thoroughly revised and edited your essay, you are ready to prepare the final manuscript (see Chapter 10) and write a title.

Proofread with Care. Proofreading requires a special kind of attention. You are looking for such errors as misspellings, missing words, dropped endings of words, and typographical mistakes. Some writers proofread their manuscripts by reading them backward, one sentence at a time. Reading backward in this fashion will distract your mind from each sentence's meaning so that you can concentrate on the technical features. Keep in mind that you are now preparing the draft your reader will see. A carefully proofread essay will reflect the effort you have given the entire project.

Create an Appropriate Title. Often the last step in the composing process is writing the title. Yet a title should not be an afterthought, a phrase hastily typed at the top of the page before you rush to class. Because a title actually begins the essay, it should suggest the general subject while serving as an invitation to read. A title should be brief but interesting and may be taken directly from the essay itself. Frequently a title will echo a thought that runs through the essay.

Exercise 9.3: Phase 3 Revisions

Proofread your essay and create a title. Accurate proofreading is demanding. Many writers are not good proofreaders of their own work because they are too close to it to see it objectively. They concentrate on what they thought, not whether they said it correctly. Their eyes, as a result, ignore the errors that will be obvious to other readers.

EDITOR'S TOOLBOX

Making Phase 3 Revisions

Phase 3 revisions, careful proofreading, can be done on the screen. During this phase you should concentrate on catching errors in grammar, punctuation, and spelling.

Pay particular attention to homonyms, words that sound alike but are spelled differently, such as *your* and *you're; to, two,* and *too; there, their,* and *they're; it's* and *its.* Your computer's Spellcheck feature will not pick up misuses of these words.

By setting an essay aside for a day or two, you will be able to examine it more objectively. In reality, the due date may be near, and you will not have time to postpone proofreading. If so, at least reread your essay with one eye on your personal list of frequent errors. At the very least, errors in homonyms and typos will leap out at you.

EDITOR'S TOOLBOX

Making a Frequent Error List

Throughout the semester, compile your own frequent error list to refer to during proofreading. The list should be composed of errors you make repeatedly. Examples of troublesome words include:

it's = it is
its = possessive pronoun
you're = you are
there = a place
their = possessive pronoun
they're = they are
strategy, *not* stradegy
judgment, *not* judgement (British spelling)
effect *means* result or to cause
affect *means* to influence

Write such errors on a Post-it note and paste it to your computer when proofreading your essay.

---

10 **Standard Manuscript Form** *essay*

Academic readers expect college essays to be properly formatted. Following standard manuscript form is a courtesy to the reader. The formatting guidelines outlined below, which follow those of the Modern Language Association, help make essays easy to read.

Most instructors today require that papers be written on computer and printed out in hard copy, although more and more are accepting—or requiring—papers submitted electronically. Most instructors strongly discourage handwritten papers, and many will no longer accept them. If you do not have access to a computer, talk with your instructor; your college probably offers computer and printer access at a computer lab accessible to all students.

Materials

- **Use standard size 8½″ × 11″), good quality white paper**, and print on only one side of the paper.
- **Use a standard, easily readable typeface**. Make sure that the regular type contrasts clearly with the italic version of the same typeface, so that titles and other italicized information can be readily identified.

Spacing and Margins

- **Double-space the entire paper**, including the list of works cited.
- **Leave 1″ margins all around**—top, bottom, left, and right. Don't justify the right margin—on most computers, justifying the right margin creates awkwardly spaced lines.
- **Indent the first line of every paragraph uniformly**. (If you use the Tab key on your keyboard to create indents rather than the space bar, your indents will be consistent.)

Course Information and Title

- **Put at the top of your paper the information required by your instructor** (usually your name, your instructor's name, the course title and number, and the date).
- **Center the title of your paper** two lines below the course information and date. Start your first paragraph two lines below the title.

Don't underline your title or put quotation marks around it. (If the title of another work or a quotation is part of your title, then use italics and quotation marks appropriately.)

- **Capitalize every word in your title** except articles, conjunctions, and prepositions.

Paging

- **Put your last name and the page number on every page**, so if the paper falls apart, your instructor can easily reassemble it. (You can use your computer's Insert function to create a page number and header for every page.)
- **Use a paper clip to hold your paper together**, unless your instructor specifically requests that you staple it. Most instructors do not want stapled papers, which are more difficult to read and grade.

Judith Park's Formatted Paper

Judith Park's paper, "Subtle Exploitation," illustrates the proper format for a typed college essay.

Park 1

Judith Park

Dr. Craft

English 1

22 October 2008

Subtle Exploitation

Whether aware of it or not, most of us have learned to respect a core of social values. Our parents, teachers, and the community at large have taught us that it is good to be socially accepted, repay favors, maintain consistent behavior, and respect authority. Without these values, community trust would break down. Friends and neighbors could not count on each other. The psychological power of social values has not been lost on sales representatives and advertisers. Indeed, these merchandisers engage in the subtle exploitation of typical social values to influence what we buy.

The desire for social validation is one value merchandisers exploit. No one likes to be out of step with others. As children we turn to friends and grown-ups to see how to fit in. As adults we continue to seek social acceptance. For example, I recently attended my first formal dinner. The table was beautifully set with flowers, candles, crystal, and a mysterious array of silverware. . . .

11 Instructor and Peer Review *essay*

Many instructors give developing writers plenty of commentary on essays written early in the semester. This commentary will generally concentrate on the larger elements rather than on refinements. A student can expect to hear whether the thesis is limited, whether the structure is effective, whether the discussion is unified, whether the conclusion works.

Generally, commentary will come from two sources: the instructor and a student's classmates.

Instructor Commentary

Writing professors approach essays differently. Some will simply collect an essay, make notes in the margin, and return it. Others will write or type extensive notes that they attach to the essay before returning it. Others will meet with students for individual conferences to discuss the essay. Some professors—a growing number—will evaluate essays through e-mail or fax: Students submit their drafts electronically, and the professor responds electronically.

No matter what method your professor uses, read any commentary with care. If the professor uses correction symbols, refer to the correction chart to be sure you understand what each symbol means. If you meet with your professor in conference, be sure to make notes of his or her oral comments.

Keep in mind that a writing professor is not only trying to improve a particular essay but is also laying the foundation for your writing success in future classes.

Peer Commentary

Some writing instructors organize formal peer-review sessions; that is, they require their writers to submit early drafts of their essays to other class members for comments. Peer review is often done in established peer-review groups whose members work together throughout the semester. At other times, professors form new groups every few weeks to give everyone in class a chance to work together.

In either case, writing professors usually set aside class time for the groups to complete their reviews. In addition, professors generally provide peer-review guidelines based on the particular requirements of the assignment.

If your professor does not require formal peer-review sessions, you and other classmates may want to set up an informal review group. Or you may choose to work with another class member to review each other's work. Either way, your goal will be the same: to see your work through another reader's eyes. You will be surprised how often a passage—even an entire essay—that may be perfectly clear to you will be confusing to a reader who has intellectual and emotional distance from the material.

Peer-Review Responsibilities

You have two main responsibilities during the peer-review process: to receive informed advice and to give informed advice in a collegial manner.

Receiving Advice. Writing isn't easy, and sometimes it is the flawed piece of writing that receives a writer's most focused emotional energy. When a writer's work is criticized, the natural tendency is to defend each paragraph, each sentence, each word against what may be perceived as an attack. But when writers can look at responses to their work unemotionally, it is easy to see that reviewer comments are offered as suggestions for improvement, not challenges. So your job is to relax when receiving advice and to judge the observations by what you are trying to accomplish.

Once your work has been reviewed, read all the written responses with care. Although they may be brief, they may still be valuable. Moreover, you can follow up written responses by asking the reviewer questions that will help to clarify or amplify any written advice.

Be sure to consider all oral responses, too. Jot down the advice you feel will help improve your draft. When a reviewer asks you a question, answer it, but do not feel you have to justify any decision you made during the composing process. Most important, *don't become defensive.* Always remember that your reviewers are evaluating the effectiveness of writing, not you or your character.

Should you incorporate reviewer suggestions in revising? That is your decision. Reviewers' responses sometimes conflict, often reflecting reviewers' inexperience or misunderstanding. At other times, reviewers' responses may agree, giving you a clear direction for revision. Only you can decide which responses are appropriate or inappropriate for your paper. The responsibility for a final draft lies solely with you.

Giving Advice.   When reviewing another writer's work, keep in mind that your task is not to rewrite the draft but to respond to it as an informed reader and offer advice for improvement. It is up to the writer to write the next draft.

What must you do to give good advice?

Know the assignment. Each draft you read will have been written in response to a writing assignment. To respond intelligently, you must be familiar with the assignment. Chances are you will be writing an essay for the same assignment, but if not, it is your job to know what the assignment calls for. Keep those requirements in mind when reviewing an essay.

Apply your knowledge. You will likely have studied the same information as the writer whose essay you are reading. Use that knowledge. Applying the information will help you make accurate observations and give you the specialized vocabulary to describe your observations in a way the writer will understand.

Offer specific advice. Identify a draft's strengths and weaknesses as specifically as you can. Vague and general observations do not help. The following two responses represent the extremes; consider first the ineffective response.

> Good work. I like the way it reads, even though it isn't always clear. Also good use of words. Keep it up.

Clearly, this response is of no help. Perhaps the reviewer fears hurting the writer's feelings, or perhaps he is just plain lazy. Who knows? The fact remains: The student offers only vague, feel-good responses.

Consider now a much more specific and thus effective response.

> One strong point is your active verbs: "shrieked," "maul," "cavort," and so on. They add specific detail and color to the whole essay.

One problem is unity. You seldom refer to your thesis in topic sentences. To fix it wouldn't take much. I suggest you add a key word to the thesis, such as "dysfunctional," and use it, or use its synonyms, in the topic sentences. For example, "The theme of dysfunctional personal lives runs throughout nearly ever episode of *Will and Grace*." Whatever you do, you'll need to improve the unity somehow.

This reviewer's response is helpful. She identifies strengths and weaknesses in specific language. Where she can, she gives advice to help the writer revise. She does all this specifically and clearly.

Do not be distracted by surface errors. It is not your job to correct grammar, punctuation, and mechanics. Tell the writer that the errors exist, but remember that it is the writer's job to proofread carefully and correct surface errors. Your job is to concentrate on the larger elements.

Staying on Track in Peer Review

Peer-review sessions can get bogged down. Keep on track by specifying the session's purpose clearly.

- Be sure every writer is prepared. Everyone should know what's expected well before the session begins.
- Communicate whether the session is for brainstorming, reading rough drafts, or proofreading.
- Remind each other of the purpose whenever the discussion drifts.

To avoid getting bogged down, everyone should agree on group guidelines that clarify what's expected of each member.

In order to stay on track, use the following five questions to guide the review process.

1. Does the draft meet assignment requirements?
2. What is the dominant purpose, and does the organization logically reflect that purpose?
3. At what points is the draft confusing?
4. Is the draft adequately developed, or does it need more information and examples?
5. What are the draft's main strengths and weaknesses?

The first step in the review process is usually done in writing. After the writer reads the review, the reviewer and the writer will usually get together to discuss the comments.

Above all else, always respond sensitively when you discuss with its author your review of an essay. Most developing writers have no experience of submitting their work for peer review. They may misconstrue genuine advice for negative criticism. To avoid sounding negative, make objectively descriptive comments instead of subjectively evaluative comments. Your responsibility is to help other writers improve their work, not to criticize them for making mistakes.

 EDITOR'S TOOLBOX

Effective Peer Review

When discussing with a writer your responses to a draft, keep in mind the following guidelines.

1. Use the review session to hold a dialogue, not a debate.
2. Ask questions that might help you develop a clear understanding of the writer's goals.
3. Take notes while reading a draft and use them to discuss the draft's strengths and weaknesses. Emphasize the strengths, but remember that the writer needs to know about the weaknesses.
4. Make suggestions for improvement in relation to the writer's intent.
5. Close your response by summarizing ways the writer can improve the draft.

Peer Review by E-Mail

In many classrooms, gone is the day when instructors passed around photocopies of every paper to every student and asked students to write comments on them. That process (like many other processes) has become electronic—often through one of the peer-review programs offered by textbook publishers (like Longman's *Exchange*) or simply through the exchange of papers by e-mail. Peer review programs typically encourage thoughtful responses, but e-mail does not always do the same. If you are asked to provide responses to classmates' papers by e-mail, you need to remember that you are evaluating someone's hard work, and you should keep these guidelines in mind:

- Whenever possible, compose your comments off-line first. Once you've finished writing, reread your comments to make sure they are reasonable, professional, and say exactly what you want them to say. Then copy and paste them into an e-mail, or send them as an attachment.

- Many people are casual about e-mail, perhaps seeing it as an extension of oral conversation rather than as written communication. (Indeed, whole alphabets of symbols and signs have grown up in cyberspace.) Make sure that your e-mail is easy to read. Check for spelling errors, and follow standard punctuation and grammar conventions. Remember that you are engaged in a classroom interaction, not a street conversation.

The emphasis is always on improvement, both for the writer as a writer and for the reviewer as a reader.

EDITOR'S TOOLBOX

Watch Your Tone

When responding online to someone's writing, be careful of your tone. While you may think you are offering constructive criticism, the writer may feel that he or she is under attack. For example, using all capital letters or boldface when pointing out an error can make a helpful comment seem like a personal attack.

Exercise 11.1: Peer-Review Groups

If your instructor does not establish a process for peer-review sessions, you and other classmates can hold your own peer-review sessions.

1. Identify students interested in peer commentary.

2. Have everyone review this chapter before beginning.

3. Meet as a group; read the papers; write comments and discuss them. Remember, concentrate on the large elements: thesis, structure, discussion, conclusion.

PART III
Paragraphs

I thought of myself as like the jazz musician: someone who practices and practices and practices in order to be able to invent and to make his art look effortless and graceful. I was always conscious of the constructed aspect of the writing process, and that art appears neutral and elegant only as a result of constant practice and awareness of its formal structures.

—Toni Morrison, *novelist*

---

12 Topic Sentences ⌥

Paragraphs are sometimes brief. Paragraphs in newspaper articles, for example, are brief. Transitional paragraphs, the kind that guide a reader from one part of an essay to another, are brief, too.

In college writing, however, paragraphs are seldom brief. They are usually fully developed, each one a significant part of an essay. Excluding introductory and concluding paragraphs, fully developed paragraphs advance a reader's understanding of an essay's thesis statement. An effective, fully developed paragraph has four characteristics:

- A topic sentence that advances the controlling idea in an essay's thesis statement.
- Full development with enough information to convey the idea in a reasonably thorough manner.
- A unified structure that shows the relationship of supporting information to the topic sentence.
- Coherence techniques that move the reader smoothly from one sentence to the next.

In a sense, essay paragraphs may be looked at individually as brief compositions in themselves, but they may also be looked at as related building blocks in an essay's overall structure.

12a State a paragraph's subject and controlling idea in a brief topic sentence

In the following paragraph, student-writer Maria Dallas opens with a brief topic sentence to focus her reader's attention. Then she fully develops the topic sentence with supporting information.

> Earning a college degree is a sound investment. College tuition can cost anywhere from $2,000 a year at a state-supported university to as high as $40,000 a year at an expensive private university such as Harvard, Stanford, or Chicago. When you add another $10,000 a year for books and living expenses, the final spread is $12,000 to $50,000 a year or $48,000 to $200,000 for an entire four years. No matter where you fall within the range, this price tag is hefty, especially if you could be earning money on a job instead of attending college. But the payoff from earning a degree is substantial also. The difference between having a college degree and a high

school diploma these days is $600,000 in income over a working lifetime. Calculating forty years on the job, that amounts to a $15,000-a-year differential for college graduates. Clearly, college is a sound investment, but as my grandmother used to say, "It takes money to make money."

Topic sentences are usually placed first in paragraphs. Sometimes a topic sentence will be placed in another part of the paragraph, often following a transitional sentence that links a paragraph to the preceding one, or it will be placed last for dramatic impact. In any case, a college writer should have a strong reason for not placing a topic sentence first.

Effective Topic Sentences

Like a thesis statement, a topic sentence makes a promise. The subject of a topic sentence promises what the paragraph will be about. The controlling idea promises what aspect of the subject the writer will discuss.

> Hong Kong has a fascinating mixture of European and Asian traditions.

This topic sentence promises the reader that the paragraph subject will be Hong Kong. The controlling idea promises the reader that a discussion of Hong Kong's European and Asian traditions will follow. The paragraph will not cover Hong Kong's crime rate, economy, population, or style of government. Other paragraphs might do that, but not this one.

Limit the Subject and the Controlling Idea. Do not promise a reader more than you can deliver. Topic sentences should not be overly general, or you will not be able to contain the development within a single paragraph, even a fully developed one. You must limit the scope of discussion by making the topic sentence less general and more specific. You can control the scope of a topic sentence in two ways—by limiting the subject and by limiting the controlling idea.

GENERAL TOPIC SENTENCE

The works of James Agee often include information from several academic disciplines.

LIMITED SUBJECT

James Agee's *Let Us Now Praise Famous Men* includes information from several academic disciplines.

LIMITED CONTROLLING IDEA

James Agee's *Let Us Now Praise Famous Men* includes information from history.

GENERAL TOPIC SENTENCE

Authorities can reduce the danger associated with concerts.

LIMITED SUBJECT

Concert promoters can reduce the danger associated with concerts.

LIMITED CONTROLLING IDEA

Concert promoters can reduce *the number and severity of spectator injuries by following a few simple rules of crowd control.*

GENERAL TOPIC SENTENCE

Bolivia is unstable.

LIMITED SUBJECT

Bolivia's military government is unstable.

LIMITED CONTROLLING IDEA

Bolivia's military government is *being threatened by peasant revolutionaries in the countryside.*

Write a Topic Sentence That Can Be Developed.   The controlling idea of a topic sentence must lend itself to development; that is, it has to be one that can be amplified or illustrated. For example, a fact does not make an effective topic sentence—unless you are merely reporting information.

FACT

In 1957, the Soviet Union launched Sputnik, the first satellite to orbit the earth.

An effective topic sentence may embody a fact, but it must also lead to discussion.

TOPIC SENTENCE

American educators panicked when the Soviet Union launched Sputnik, the first satellite to orbit the earth, in 1957.

This topic sentence leads to a discussion of how the first Sputnik threatened American educators.

Like a fact, the expression of an attitude does not make an effective topic sentence.

ATTITUDE

Analyzing nonverbal behavior is interesting.

Phrasing an attitude as a topic does not signal that an informed discussion will follow. In fact, it invites immediate reader resistance: Oh yeah? I think it's a hoax!

TOPIC SENTENCE

Analyzing nonverbal behavior accurately is the secret to winning at poker.

Now this topic sentence could lead to an interesting discussion, at least for would-be poker players.

WRITER'S TOOLBOX

Insert Key Words in Topic Sentences

Here is an effective way to show readers that you are advancing a topic sentence. In a topic sentence, insert key words that you will then repeat at strategic moments. One key word might refer back to an essay's thesis, another to the controlling point of the particular paragraph.

> Advertisers often *exploit* a *desire* for *economic* and *social independence.* Women are frequently the target of such *exploitation.* For example, no company has *exploited* this *desire* more effectively than Philip Morris in a campaign to sell Virginia Slim cigarettes. Each advertisement in the campaign features images of strong, *independent* women; one riding a motorcycle, another standing behind a man who is cooking, and yet another of an *independent* woman in a leather jacket, leaning on a sports car door. Each advertisement is accompanied by a sentence declaring the woman's *economic and social independence:* "I don't necessarily want to run the world, but I wouldn't mind taking it for a ride"; "Equality comes with no apron strings attached"; and "I always take the driver's seat." Moreover, each advertisement features the slogan, "You've come a long way, baby," now a buzz phrase to announce that a woman has fulfilled a *desire* for *independence.*

12b Develop a paragraph fully

How long should a paragraph be? Paragraph length depends on several things: the complexity of the idea; the method of development; the length of adjacent paragraphs; and the age, knowledge, interest, and education of the reader. In college writing, thoughtful paragraphs usually range from 125 to 150 words because of their complexity.

Excessively long paragraphs may seem more intellectual and weighty, but too many of them can discourage a reader and make a subject appear more difficult and complex than it is. Short paragraphs are easy to read, but a paper consisting of a series of brief paragraphs indicates that an essay's thesis statement is inadequately developed.

The best approach is to take the middle ground. Include enough supporting information to make your point, and avoid skimpy, undeveloped paragraphs.

The following paragraph lacks the specific detail needed to adequately develop the topic sentence.

> A number of curious experiences occur at the onset of sleep. A person just about to go to sleep may experience an odd physical sensation. A nearly universal occurrence at the beginning of sleep (although not everyone recalls it) is a sudden jerk of the body. The onset of sleep is not gradual at all. It happens in an instant.

The paragraph needs more specific information and concrete details to support the topic sentence adequately. Now study the original paragraph as Peter Farb wrote it. Notice how the addition of information and specific details turns an underdeveloped paragraph into a fully developed one.

> A number of curious experiences occur at the onset of sleep. A person just about to go to sleep may experience an *electric shock, a flash of light, or a crash of thunder. The most common sensation is that of floating or falling, which is why "falling asleep" is a scientifically valid description.* A nearly universal occurrence at the beginning of sleep (although not everyone recalls it) is a sudden, *uncoordinated* jerk of the *head, the limbs, or even the entire* body. *Most people tend to think of going to sleep as a slow slippage into oblivion, but* the onset of sleep is not gradual at all. It happens in an instant. *One moment the individual is awake, the next moment not.*

12c Close a paragraph with a clincher sentence

Writers will often end a paragraph with a *clincher,* a sentence that restates the controlling idea in different words, summarizes the discussion, or gives the writer's response to the material, which may be ironic or humorous. The next example closes with a clincher.

Topic sentence opens the paragraph.

> As sources of ideas, professors simply cannot compete with books. Books can be found to fit almost every need, temper, or interest. Books can be read when you are in the mood; they do not have to be taken in periodic doses. Books are both more personal and more impersonal than professors. Books have an inner confidence which individuals seldom show; they rarely have to be on the defensive. Books can

Supporting information advances the topic sentence's controlling idea.

> afford to be bold and courageous and exploratory; they do not have to be so careful of boards of trustees, colleagues, and community opinion. Books are infinitely diverse; they run the gamut of human activity. Books can be found to express every point of view; if you want a different point of view, you can read a different book. (Incidentally, this is the closest approximation to objectivity you are likely ever to get in humanistic and social studies.)

Clincher sentence closes the paragraph.

> Even your professor is at his best when he writes books and articles; the teaching performance rarely equals the written effort.
> —William G. Carleton, "Take Your College in Stride"

Closing with a clincher is especially effective in long paragraphs. A clincher will remind readers of the paragraph's main point and can be used to transition into the next paragraph.

Exercise 12.1: Revising Topic Sentences

The following topic sentences are either too general or too factual. Revise each to make it more effective.

1. Some states require motorists to use hands-free cell phones.

2. Petty crime is a problem in some urban areas.

3. Many Americans try different diets from time to time.

4. Going to college is expensive.

5. Grading policies are different for different professors.

6. Everyone believes that travel is educational.

7. Large stores usually have consumer complaint departments.

8. In spite of all the evidence, my sister believes that eating carbs will make you healthier.

9. I like people who assume responsibility for their actions.

10. Hollywood films have both good and bad features.

Exercise 12.2: Writing Paragraphs

Using one of the topic sentences you revised for Exercise 12.1, write an effective paragraph. Remember, an effective paragraph has the following characteristics.

• It advances the main point in an essay's thesis statement.

• It has enough information to convey the idea in a reasonably thorough manner.

• It shows the relationship of supporting information to the topic sentence.

• It moves the reader smoothly from one sentence to the next.

13 Unified Paragraphs ¶

Just as academic readers expect a thesis sentence to be the organizational center of an essay, they expect a topic sentence to be the organizational center of most paragraphs. Information that does not advance a topic sentence disrupts the train of thought of the reader moving from the topic sentence to the clincher. When the reader's train of thought is disrupted, paragraph unity is flawed.

A paragraph is unified when all the information it contains clearly relates to the controlling idea expressed in the topic sentence. Study the following paragraph. Analyze the relationship of supporting information to the controlling idea, which asserts that many

people oppose hunting even where animal populations are danger-
ously large.

> (1) *Many Americans mindlessly oppose hunting, even in
> cases where animal populations are dangerously high.*(2) In
> some areas of Alaska, wolves have become so prolific they are
> running out of hunting ground and prey heavily on moose,
> deer, and occasionally dogs. (3) Wolves run in packs and
> hunt with more cunning than any other predator in North
> America. (4) In the past, game managers curbed wolf
> populations by trapping and aerial hunting without wiping
> out the species. (5) Still, whenever they propose to do this
> nowadays, they receive tens of thousands of letters in protest.
> (6) Growing deer populations in parts of California threaten
> to starve themselves out. (7) No doubt images of Bambi rise
> up in the minds of hunting opponents. (8) Sea-otter colonies,
> burgeoning along the Pacific coast, are fast running out of
> fodder, too, as well as putting commercial fishermen out
> of business. (9) Because otters are so cute, ecologists have
> rushed to their aid.

Sentences 3, 7, and 9 disrupt the train of thought. They do not relate
directly to the controlling idea expressed in the topic sentence. They
should either be integrated into other sentences or deleted.

Now read the paragraph as Lael Morgan actually wrote it in "Let
the Eskimos Hunt." Examine how all the supporting information and
details relate to the topic sentence's controlling idea.

> *Many Americans mindlessly oppose hunting, even in cases
> where animal populations are dangerously high.* In some areas
> of Alaska, wolves have become so prolific they are running
> out of hunting ground and prey heavily on moose, deer,
> and occasionally dogs. In the past, game managers curbed
> wolf populations by trapping and aerial hunting without
> wiping out the species. Still, whenever they propose to do
> this nowadays, they receive tens of thousands of letters in
> protest. Growing deer populations in parts of California
> threaten to starve themselves out. Sea-otter colonies,
> burgeoning along the Pacific coast, are fast running out
> of fodder, too, as well as putting commercial fishermen out
> of business.

With the unrelated sentences deleted, the paragraph is unified and
reader attention remains focused on the key point, that is, "many

Americans mindlessly oppose hunting." The writer's train of thought has been freed of disruption.

Exercise 13.1: Achieving Unity

The following sentences are taken from Robert I. Tilling's "A Volcanologist's Perspective." Several sentences are from one paragraph. Others are from different parts of the article. Determine which sentences should be included in a unified paragraph with the topic sentence, "Volcanic eruptions have had a profound influence on mankind."

1. Civilizations have flourished in regions blessed with fertile soils derived from the breakdown of nutrient-rich volcanic materials.

2. The volcanoes in the Ring of Fire zone are what scientists call composite volcanoes.

3. The violent, destructive unleashing of volcanic fury that accompanied the catastrophic blast of Mount St. Helens have imprinted their marks on mind and landscape.

4. Some of the world's most majestic and inspirational mountain and seashore scenery, including the entire state of Hawaii, has been created by volcanic action and subsequent erosion.

5. Most of the world's approximately five hundred active volcanoes are located along or near such boundaries between shifting plates.

6. The Pacific Basin provides excellent examples of these two types of volcanoes.

7. The earth's surface is broken into lithospheric slabs, or plates.

8. As one volcano dies, however, a new volcano begins to form behind it over the hot spot.

9. More fundamentally, life on earth as we know it would not have evolved at all were it not for volcanic exhalations that occurred over hundreds of millions of years and formed the primitive but life-giving atmosphere and oceans.

10. Composite volcanoes predominantly erupt highly viscous (sticky) magma.

---

14 Coherent Paragraphs ¶

When a paragraph is coherent, the writer's thought flows from the first sentence to the last. When coherence breaks down, the sentences do not work together. They seem disconnected, and the writer's thoughts do not unfold smoothly from sentence to sentence.

14a Achieve coherence with transitional words and phrases

One method for achieving coherence is to use transitional words and phrases. These words show the relationship among ideas or signal readers that there will be a transition in thought.

TO SHOW SIMILARITY

likewise, similarly, moreover

TO SHOW DIFFERENCE OR CONTRAST

but, however, still, yet, nevertheless, on the one hand/on the other hand, on the contrary, in contrast

TO SHOW ADDITION

moreover, and, in addition, equally important, next, first, second, third, again, also, too, besides, furthermore

TO SHOW TIME AND PROCESS

soon, in the meantime, afterward, later, meanwhile, while, earlier, finally, simultaneously, next, the next step

TO SHOW DIRECTION

here, there, over there, beyond, nearby, opposite, under, above, to the left, to the right, in the distance

TO ANNOUNCE AN END

in conclusion, to summarize, finally, on the whole

TO ANNOUNCE A RESTATEMENT

in short, in other words, in brief, to put it differently

TO INDICATE A RESULT

therefore, then, as a result, consequently, accordingly, thus, thereupon

The following narrative paragraph achieves coherence through the use of transitional words and phrases (shown in italics) that trace the time order of the events.

> At first glance Todd seems to be a typical four-year-old: scruffy, sun-bleached hair, a few freckles, worn cords, short-sleeved shirt, and tattered tennis shoes. But behind his boyish appearance he seems to be a loner. *During the first class,* he was the only child who did not raise his hand to answer a question or share an experience. He was attentive *at first* but soon lost interest. *Once* he reached out a finger to poke a boy in front of him, and then he stopped, perhaps thinking better of it. *Finally,* his thumb went into his mouth. *As soon as* the class broke up, he headed for the monkey bars, where he climbed to the highest rung and sat, his eyes staring toward a distant hill. No one tried to approach him, however. The other children, most of whom chased around the play yard, seemed to respect his wish for privacy. *Later,* when the class regrouped for story time, Todd didn't show as much interest as he had during the sharing session. He seemed more interested in using a fingernail to trace the cracks in the wall than in listening to *Winnie-the-Pooh.*

14b Achieve coherence through the repetition of key words

A writer can maintain coherence by repeating key words and phrases to emphasize the major points and to smooth the flow of the sentences. Pronouns referring to clearly established antecedents function in the same way. In the following paragraph the repeated words appear in italics.

> Public speaking differs from acting in that the *speaker* rarely, if ever, reveals any character or personality traits other than his own. A central problem of the *actor* is to create a character for his audience. There are other differences. The *public speaker* usually works alone. The *actor,* unless he is performing a monodrama, usually works with a group. A *public speaker* does not ordinarily use scenery, costume, or make-up to help him express and communicate as the *actor* does. He may on some occasions employ special lighting effects and platform decorations to reinforce his message. Further, the *public speaker* deals only with his own composition while the *actor,* like the oral reader, has all the problems of interpreting the words of another. He serves as a sort of middleman for the playwright and reveals the intentions of a director. Thus, the purposes of

the *actor* are at once like and unlike those of the *public speaker.*
The *actor* may seek to elicit primarily utilitarian responses or to
gain aesthetic responses depending upon the nature of the
material with which he works.

—John F. Wilson and Carroll E. Arnold,
Public Speaking as a Liberal Art

EDITOR'S TOOLBOX

Analyzing Paragraphs for Coherence

The mind can be tricky. When rereading your own work, you, like
most writers, make the transition from one sentence to another in
your mind when there are no actual transitions on the page. The
reason for this is simple: You have already made the connections
mentally, so you automatically fill them in.

One way to be sure you have put transitions in place is to underline
them in your paper. In this way you will know they are there.

> The researchers found that the participation of women in
> sports activities was a significant indicator of the health and
> living standards of a country. Today, gradually, women have
> begun to enter the sports world with more social acceptance
> and individual pride. In 1952, researchers from the Finnish
> Institute of Occupational Health who conducted an intensive
> study of the athletes participating in the Olympics in Helsinki
> predicted that "women are able to shake off civil disabilities
> which millennia of prejudice and ignorance have imposed
> upon them." No doubt myths die hard, but they do die.

14c Achieve coherence by using parallel structure

By repeating a particular grammatical structure in successive sentences, a writer can create a parallel form that will guide a reader
smoothly from the first sentence to the last. The repeated structure
emphasizes the relation of the sentences to the paragraph's controlling idea. Parallel structures are italicized in the following paragraph
from Mark Reuter's impressionistic essay on California.

> Historically, California has been a place as much in the
> imagination as a place on any map. *In the minds of the '49ers,*
> *California offered* gold nuggets, shallow streams, and meadows.
> *In the minds of farmers wiped out in the Depression, California*
> *offered* rich soil and abundant potential. *In the minds of impres-*
> *sionable teenagers, California offered* champagne, silver slippers,
> and fame at the corner of Sunset and Vine. But too often

adventurous Easterners sold everything to pursue the dream of gold and ended up losing it all to swindlers. *Depression victims were* sometimes greeted by hostile ranchers who carried rifles and drove them away from the fertile valleys. And many *young actors ended up* living on the streets, the stars in their eyes faded.

In this example, Reuter creates parallel form by repeating the prepositional phrase, "In the minds of . . ." and the adjective-noun combinations, "adventurous Easterners," " "Depression victims," and "young actors."

Exercise 14.1: Identifying Transitions

Select an article from a popular news site on the Web. Print out the article and read it with care. Underline the transitions you find and identify them as transitions, key-word repetition, or parallel structure.

Exercise 14.2: Creating Parallel Structure

Revise the following paragraph from William G. Moulton's "Linguistics." Make the three supporting points parallel by revising key sentences and by using "with" and "shares" as key words.

> Linguistics has been described as being, at one and the same time, the most scientific of humanities and the most humanistic of the sciences. In both theory and practice it shares elements of many other disciplines, even though it cannot be neatly classified with one of them. It uses the same method of observation, classification, and generalization, and the search for countable units and describable structures as the natural sciences. It is interested like the social sciences in group behavior as revealed through the actions of individuals. And with the humanities it shares an interest in the uniquely human, in language as a phenomenon which distinguishes humans as "the talking animal" most sharply from all other living beings.

15 Descriptive and Narrative Paragraphs ❡

To describe is to picture experience in words. Effective description makes the general more specific by engaging the senses. The sound of thundering surf, the smell of ripe apples, the sight of darkening clouds, the taste of chocolate cake, the feel of soapy water—each appeals to one of the senses. Because sensory experience is so powerful, descriptive writing will often snap readers to attention and pull their imaginations into a discussion.

To narrate is to tell a story. Simple narratives play an important role in everyday thinking. In discussion with friends or acquaintances, a speaker may spontaneously shape raw experience into a narrative: "Let me tell you what happened in psychology today." "I learned an important lesson when my car wouldn't start." "I'll never ride a bicycle again." Each of these snippets of conversation would probably lead to a narrative illustrating a personal insight.

15a Write active description that appeals to the senses

Take a page from the creative writer's notebook: Use description to engage readers' senses. When writing a descriptive passage, make your readers see, hear, smell, taste, touch, and sense movement in your writing.

Developing writers often believe that adjectives and adverbs make for good descriptive writing, so they pile them up against their nouns and verbs. This makes for slack, not active, prose.

> Some of my city friends think horses are *cute, loving* animals. That is not *necessarily* true. Yesterday I watched a young wrangler try to ride a *skittish* stallion. He *quickly* swung himself into the saddle and held the saddle horn *tightly*. The *big chestnut* stallion bucked *angrily* and *easily* tossed the *wide-eyed* wrangler to the *dusty* ground. The stallion then *viciously* attacked him. The *panicked* wrangler rolled toward the fence. The stallion tried to trample him before he *desperately* pulled himself under the fence post before the *sharp* hooves pummeled him.

This anecdote has elements of effective description, such as the use of specific nouns and verbs, but the writer could make it even more effective. Rather than use the adverbs *quickly, tightly, angrily*, and rather than use the adjectives *skittish, dusty, panicked*, the writer could have created active description by filling in more sensory detail in phrases. The overuse of adverbs and adjectives short-circuits the descriptive process by providing ready-made words for general experience. Better to look at experience in more detail in order to write more engaging description. Revised, the passage might read:

> Some of my city friends think horses are cute, loving animals. That is not necessarily true. Yesterday I watched a

~~young~~ wrangler try to ride a ~~skittish~~ stallion *that snorted and twitched as he put his foot in the stirrup. Pushing up with one leg,* he ~~quickly~~ swung himself into the saddle and *gripped* the saddle horn ~~tightly~~ *as if he had hopped on a roller coaster.* The ~~big chestnut~~ stallion bucked ~~angrily~~, *arching its back, its hooves lifting from the ground,* and ~~easily~~ tossed the wrangler, *his eyes popping in panic,* to the ~~dusty ground~~ dust. The stallion ~~then viciously attacked him~~ *reared back on its hind legs, its hooves pawing the air, its mane whipping around its neck.* The ~~panicked~~ wrangler rolled toward the fence, *gasping for breath, dust filling his nostrils and coating his lips and teeth.* The stallion's *hooves* ~~tried to trample him before he desperately pulled himself under the fence post before the sharp hooves~~ *clubbed the ground, and again it reared up, a whinny erupting from deep in its throat, echoing over the ranch, as the wrangler grabbed the bottom fence post, his hand raked with slivers, and scrambled from the corral before the hooves, flashing sunlight,* pummeled him.

EDITOR'S TOOLBOX

Thinking Critically about Description

When writing description, our first impulse is to use "descriptive" words, that is, to use adjectives and adverbs.

> The *shiny red* Porsche drove *quickly* through the *wet* streets.

But adjectives and adverbs pile up against the nouns and verbs they describe, slowing down the reader. It is more effective to turn adjectives and adverbs into phrases that describe more accurately and more actively. Begin your revision by crossing out adjectives and adverbs.

> The ~~shiny red~~ Porsche drove ~~quickly~~ through the ~~wet~~ streets.

Then rewrite the sentence by turning adjectives and adverbs into active descriptive phrases and by selecting more specific verbs, such as changing *drove* to *raced* in the example.

> The Porsche, *sunlight glinting from its red paint, raced* through the *rain-slickened* streets.

Not only does this sentence read more easily, it gives more specific information.

Now this descriptive paragraph is vivid, alive with action and detail. The writer kept two adjectives and one adverb, all three in the opening two sentences that set up the description. Then he relied on descriptive phrases to do most of the work.

15b Balance subjective responses with objective description

Descriptive writing is usually a mixture of subjective and objective detail. In subjective description, writers select language and a point of view that show they are participants in an experience. In objective description, writers concentrate on examining a subject rather than their personal experience of it.

The purpose of subjective description is to show the impact of an experience on the writer, that is, to create an impressionistic description of the experience. The purpose of objective description is to show how the experience might impact anyone, that is, to create an entirely factual description of the experience. But seldom is a passage purely subjective or objective.

Peter Schjeldahl, in the opening paragraph of "Cyclone," writes at the extreme of subjective description while including some objective detail to support his personal responses. His aim is to describe how he feels riding the Coney Island roller coaster, not to give an objective picture of the ride. The two brief passages of objective description are shown here in italics.

> The Cyclone is art, sex, God, the greatest. It is the most fun you can have without risking bad ethics. I rode the Cyclone seven times one afternoon last summer, and I am here to tell everybody that it is fun for fun's sake, the pure abstract heart of the human capacity for getting a kick out of anything. Yes, it may be anguishing initially. (I promise to tell the truth.) Terrifying, even, the first time or two the train is hauled upward with groans and creaks and with you in it. *At the top then—where there is sudden* strange *quiet but for the fluttering of two tattered flags, and you have a* poignantly *brief view of Brooklyn, and of ships far out on the Atlantic*—you may feel very lonely and that you have made a serious mistake, cursing yourself in the last gleam of the reflective consciousness you are about, abruptly, to leave up there between the flags like an abandoned thought-balloon. To keep yourself company by screaming may help, and no one is noticing: try it. After a couple of rides, panic abates, and after four or five, you aren't even frightened, exactly, but stimulated, blissed, sent.

The squirt of adrenaline you will never cease to have at *the top as the train lumbers, wobbling slightly, into the plunge,* finally fuels just happy wonderment because you can't, and never will, believe what is going to happen.

Schjeldahl's subjectively charged description would not be effective without some objective description to show literally what the ride is like.

A passage from student-writer Clarita Tan's "Imaginatively Chaotic Art" mixes objective and subjective description effectively. Tan expresses her subjective view by using a simile, comparing the artist to an orchestra conductor, and an allusion, a reference to the "Sorcerer's Apprentice." Tan's brief subjective response is shown here in italics.

> The final phase of his method is captured in the fifth photograph. The canvas is now raised upright on the plywood base, a practice that deviates from Pollock's and that of other abstract expressionists. Here McNeil stands with his back to the camera and faces the massive canvas. He is hunched forward with an upraised brush held *like a symphony conductor's baton, and I think of composer Paul Dukas's "Sorcerer's Apprentice." Indeed, McNeil is performing artistic sorcery,* for he is creating images that suggest themselves from the splattered configurations on the canvas.

It is the objective description that sets up Tan's subjective response near the end of the passage. She then develops the artist-as-magician image throughout her entire essay.

15c Select an effective arrangement for descriptive paragraphs

Descriptive paragraphs lend themselves quite readily to a **spatial arrangement**—that is, to proceeding like a camera panning from left to right, from right to left, from near to far, from the center outward, and so on. In the following paragraph from a gallery report, Alice Lee describes a painting from the top down. Notice how Lee effectively guides the reader by using clear transitions (shown here in italics). She skillfully centers the reader's concentration on the painting's key focal point.

> *At the top* of Doree Dunlap's "Picnic," clouds are gathering as if ready to erupt with rain. *Between* the sky and shore, *in the*

upper middle, the sea is edged with whitecaps and a line of sailboats lean into the wind, heading for safe harbor. *On shore, in the lower foreground,* two children stand facing the sea and a third stares back at a man and woman sitting on the sand, a fearful expression on the child's face. The couple she stares at *are the focus of the canvas, taking up a third of the space.* Dunlap represents only the back of the man's head and just a slice of his profile. He seems to be staring beyond the children at the impending squall. The woman is staring at him, a neutral expression on her face, but she appears to have the faint trace of a bruise on her cheek. *Behind her, in the lower left corner,* is a watermelon with a butcher knife leaning against it, the knife tip in the sand.

Another arrangement common to descriptive paragraphs is **movement from the specific to the general.** In the following paragraph from *The Way to Rainy Mountain,* N. Scott Momaday moves from specific detail to a general observation—that is, from physical details of Rainy Mountain and the surrounding plain to the generalization (shown here in italics) that one can imagine creation having begun in such a spot.

> A single knoll rises out of the plain in Oklahoma, north and west of the Wichita Range. For my people, the Kiowas, it is an old landmark, and they gave it the name Rainy Mountain. The hardest weather in the world is there. Winter brings blizzards, hot tornadic winds arise in the spring, and in summer the prairie is an anvil's edge. The grass turns brittle and brown, and it cracks beneath your feet. There are green belts along the rivers and creeks, linear groves of hickory and pecan, willow and witch hazel. At a distance in July or August the steaming foliage seems almost to writhe in fire. Great green and yellow grasshoppers are everywhere in the tall grass, popping up like corn to sting the flesh, and tortoises crawl about on the red earth, going nowhere in the plenty of time. *Loneliness is an aspect of the land. All things in the plain are isolate; there is no confusion of objects in the eye, but one hill or one tree or one man. To look upon that landscape in the early morning, with the sun at your back, is to lose the sense of proportion. Your imagination comes to life, and this, you think, is where Creation was begun.*

Notice how, after the opening sentences, Momaday uses objective description to set up his subjective response.

15d Arrange narrative paragraphs in a clear time sequence

Description frequently plays a significant role in narrative writing. Vivid descriptive details help readers visualize the unfolding events. In narration, however, the emphasis is on the events, not on the descriptive passages.

Narrative paragraphs—those that tell a story or tell of a series of incidents—take place in time and are usually arranged in **chronological time,** that is, as the events unfold step by step.

Student-writer Mark DeLap arranges the following narrative paragraph chronologically and relies heavily on description to create a vivid picture of events. DeLap also uses clear transitional techniques (shown here in italics) to guide readers through the time sequence.

> Bill Meek, a marine biologist and entrepreneur, manages an unusual enterprise. Using a hoe, a suction hose, and lots of elbow grease, Meek rakes and vacuums up mussels that cling to the long legs of oil platforms located off the coast. He sells the mussels to restaurants that pay top prices for them. *His day begins at sunrise* on a dock where he checks his equipment and meets his small crew for the three-mile trip to the oil platform. *Once at the platform* the sun is well up and he peers into the aquamarine depths to take an informal inventory. The mussels grow rapidly on the platform legs to a depth of forty feet, but below forty feet there isn't enough light to nourish the plankton on which mussels feed. *By 8 o'clock* the harvesting work begins. Two divers in wet suits jump into the sea. They are equipped with air hoses and mouthpieces for breathing, a hoe, and a corrugated plastic tube to suck up the mussels. One man will loosen the mussels while the other vacuums. *Once the work is under way,* a compressor generates the pressure that sucks the mussels through the tube to the surface, where they are collected into a tumbling wire-mesh container. The container turns throughout the collecting process, allowing barnacles, seaweed, and salt water to cascade back into the ocean while retaining the larger mussels. *By early afternoon* the harvest is done and the crew heads for shore. *Within hours,* the mussels will be steaming on the stoves of local restaurants.

Narrative paragraphs are not always arranged in chronological time. Sometimes they are arranged in **psychological time,** that is, as events might be connected in memory. Here the writer shifts back and forth in time, emulating the way the mind recalls experience while keeping the events moving forward.

Student-writer Richard McKnight uses psychological time in a flashback to previous experience and then returns to the present.

> *Just two weeks earlier, a hot-shot from Hawaii paddled out in the heavy surf that a Mexican storm had kicked up.* He sat on his board beyond the breakers and waited for the big swells to roll in. Suddenly, he swung his board's nose toward shore to catch the day's biggest wave. He seemed to do everything right: He quickly leaped to his feet, cut sharply left, moved to the board's nose to gain speed as he shot ahead of the curl—but not in time. The massive wave broke over his shoulder and tossed him into the roiling foam. The breaking wave's force snapped his board in half and swept him over the reef. He survived, but barely. Lifeguards raced him to an emergency ward where doctors hovered above his body for two hours with needles and thread. *Now the old man was in that kind of danger but with one difference—he was well past his prime, much too old to be riding in dangerous waters.*

McKnight uses the first and last sentences (italicized here) to set up the time frame. Although the sentences that take place in the past move chronologically toward the present, the paragraph is still arranged according to psychological time.

Exercise 15.1: Identifying Subjective and Objective Description

Analyze the following paragraphs. Underline the words and phrases that represent objective description. Explain whether or not each paragraph is written to create an impressionistic or a literal picture of the experience. What details from the paragraphs support your contention?

> The reef was generally exposed as the tide went down, and on its flat top the tide pools were beautiful. We collected as widely and rapidly as possible, trying to take a cross section of the animals we saw. There were purple pendent gorgonians like lacy fans; a number of small spine-covered puffer fish which bloat themselves when they are attacked, erecting the spines; and many starfish, including some purple and gold cushion stars. The club-spined sea urchins were numerous in their rock niches. They seemed to move about very little, for their niches always just fit them and have the marks of constant occupation. We took a number of slim green and brown starfish and the large slim five-rayed starfish with plates bordering the ambulacral grooves.
>
> —John Steinbeck, *The Log from the Sea of Cortez*

I've been out in the back today checking beehives. When I leaned over one of them to direct a puff of smoke from my bee smoker into the entrance to quiet the bees, a copperhead came wriggling out from under the hive. He had been frightened from his protected spot by the smoke and the commotion I was making, and when he found himself in the open, he panicked and slithered for the nearest hole he could find which was the entrance to the next beehive. I don't know what went on inside, but he came out immediately, wearing a surprised look on his face. I hadn't known that a snake could look surprised, but this one did. Then, after pausing to study the matter more carefully, he glided off to the safety of the woods.

—Sue Hubbell, *A Country Year*

Exercise 15.2: Arranging a Descriptive Paragraph

The following sentences were originally a coherent paragraph, but their order has been changed. By following an appropriate order of development, rearrange the sentences so that the descriptive paragraph is coherent once again.

1. On this oval embankment a fair-size audience could gather to take part in a ceremony or watch the priests.

2. The most unusual is the great Serpent Mound, a masterpiece in earth sculpture.

3. What went on there we shall never know, since no traditions have come down to us.

4. More than a thousand feet of sinuous serpent body extends along the backbone of a ridge, ending on the brow of a cliff overhanging a small river.

5. The modeling is so good that the visitor can all but see the movement suggested.

6. The serpent's head rests on this cliff, its tail back upon the ridge, partly coiled; its long body is posed as if gliding along the crest of the ridge.

7. The tourist driving through the state of Ohio may see some of the world's finest prehistoric earthworks.

8. But we can feel sure that the beliefs clustering around this earth sculpture were in keeping with its magnificence.

9. The enlarged head is an oval embankment, in the center of which is a heap of stones, possibly a fireplace and altar.

Exercise 15.3: Arranging a Narrative Paragraph

The following sentences were originally a coherent paragraph, but here their order has been changed. By following an appropriate order of development, rearrange the sentences so that the narrative paragraph is coherent once again.

1. Before I started grammar school, I knew all the neighborhood's marvelous places: the avocado tree where my friends and I used to climb to an ancient tree house that had been built by children before us, the park where old-timers would sit on the benches and laugh at our wild games, the abandoned garage where we used to spy at the neighborhood through knotholes.

2. My earliest memories center on playing in that house: pushing trucks over the hardwood floors, my pajama knees mopping up the morning dust; rummaging through my mother's pan drawers and banging pans on the linoleum; and hiding behind the over-stuffed couch whenever I was called for lunch.

3. Driven out by a severe drought, my parents came from the corn-fields of Nebraska to the house where they lived for thirty-five years.

4. I was born in the back bedroom because, as my mother said, "There just wasn't enough time to get to a hospital."

5. When I first began to walk, the backyard seemed to stretch the length of a football field, and there I would chase my older brothers and sisters until I would fall down, breathless and sweating.

Exercise 15.4: Responding to Photographs

Clip a photograph from a newspaper or magazine or select one from a photo album of your own. First, write an objective description that's a factual rendering of what is in the photograph. Second, write a subjective description that's a personal impression based on the photograph.

---

16 Expository Paragraphs ¶

Expository writing concentrates, or sets forth, information, ideas, and analysis. For this reason expository writing is often referred to as **informative writing** because its main purpose is to *inform* a reader.

When you write a college essay to inform, your readers will expect you to write with a minimum of bias. Think of informative writing this way: Your purpose is to educate readers, not to persuade them to take action.

Writers have historically used six traditional methods to develop information. They are development by examples, comparison and contrast, cause and effect, process analysis, definition, and classification.

These development methods are not arbitrary. They reflect the way people organize information in their minds—how they think. For instance, people think of examples to illustrate an idea, they compare and contrast experiences to clarify them, they grope for the causes and effects of events in order to explain why things happen. These patterns of thinking, along with the other three, provide the internal structure that molds our rational thoughts into usable forms. How well they are used depends on each person's ability to think critically.

16a Use examples to illustrate a point

An *example* is a single experience that embodies the characteristics of many experiences. The word *example* is derived from *exemplum,* a Latin word that refers to "one thing selected from the many." Writers use examples with the same intentions as speakers: to illustrate a point, to make a general assertion specific, or to electrify an audience.

The following paragraph illustrates with details the effects of DDT spraying.

> Soon after the spraying had ended there were unmistakable signs that all was not well. Within two days dead and dying fish, including many young salmon, were found along the banks of the stream. Brook trout also appeared among the dead fish, and along the roads and in the woods birds were dying. All the life of the stream was stilled. Before the spraying there had been a rich assortment of the water life that forms the food of salmon and trout—caddis fly larvae, living in loosely fitting protective cases of leaves, stems or gravel

cemented together with saliva, stonefly nymphs clinging to rocks in the swirling currents, and the wormlike larvae of blackflies edging the stones under riffles or where the stream spills over steeply slanting rocks. But now the stream insects were dead, killed by the DDT, and there was nothing for a young salmon to eat.

—Rachel Carson, *Silent Spring*

Examples are of three types: specific, typical, and hypothetical. *Specific examples* include single events, behaviors, or facts. They are specific because they represent one particular experience, not generalized experience. The examples in the following paragraph are separated to emphasize how they support the topic sentence.

Opening sentence leads to the topic sentence. *Topic sentence.* *Third sentence sets up series of examples.*	The popular image of the frontier as a place of violence is only partly due to the fact the place often was violent. *Most of it is due to hype, particularly Hollywood hype.* The truth is many more people have died in Hollywood westerns than ever died on the real frontier (Indian wars considered apart).
Example 1: Dodge City.	In the real Dodge City, for example, there were just five killings in 1878, the most homicidal year in the little town's frontier history—scarcely enough to sustain a typical two-hour movie.
Example 2: Deadwood City.	In the most violent year in Deadwood, South Dakota, only four people were killed.
Example 3: Tombstone and the OK Corral. The writer adds additional information to make the last example in the sequence the most dramatic.	In the worst year in Tombstone, home of the shoot-out at the OK Corral, only five people were killed. The only reason the OK Corral shoot-out even became famous was that town boosters deliberately overplayed the drama to attract new settlers. "They eventually cashed in on the tourist boom," historian W. Eugene Hollon says, "by inventing a myth about a town too tough to die."

—Richard Shenkman,
Legends, Lies, and Cherished Myths

Typical examples, in contrast to specific examples, are generalized from many specific experiences. Student-writer Daniela Taylor makes use of typical examples in her essay on discourteous behavior in public places, "We Are Not Alone."

Taylor opens with a topic sentence that indicates she will be writing about "typical" behavior.

Last week I began to notice typical discourteous behavior that seems to have recently developed.

Example 1: Roller bladers. Notice that Taylor's example is based on a composite of experiences, not on a single specific one.

First, roller bladers apparently find a challenge in weaving in and out of pedestrians strolling on public walkways. They seem to lack common courtesy, failing to keep in mind that a pedestrian walking at a much slower pace than their skating pace cannot always predict their movements. Their discourteous behavior can turn a relaxing afternoon stroll into a nerve-racking game of dodge the speed blader.

Example 2: Cellular phone use. She continues to offer composite experiences rolled into one typical example.

Typical examples work because most readers will probably have had similar experiences.

Second, the increase of cellular phones has given rise to a new kind of public discourtesy. People must no longer retreat to enclosed public phone booths to make private phone calls. They can now phone friends, loved ones, and business associates while standing in a crowd. Often their voices rise well above normal speaking range, thus disrupting the casual conversations of people who share the public space.

Hypothetical examples, like typical examples, are a composite of many events, yet they are not necessarily based on actual experience. Unlike typical examples, hypothetical examples are fictional; that is, the writer makes them up to clarify an abstraction or a generalization. The writer, of course, should make it clear that the example has been imagined, not actually observed.

In the following paragraph from *Mediaspeak,* media critic Donna Woolfolk Cross creates a hypothetical example to illustrate the general role children have played in soap operas.

Cross opens with a topic sentence and background information to provide the reader a context for the discussion.

Children on soap operas are secondary. Because they serve largely as foils for the adult characters, their development does not follow the slow, steady pattern of the rest of the action. Their growth is marked by a series of sudden and unsettling metamorphoses as new and older juvenile actors assume the role. On Tuesday, little Terence is cooing in his cradle. On Monday next, he is the terror of the Little League. By Thursday, his voice begins to change. Friday night is his first date. He wakes up on Monday a drug-crazed teenager, ready to be put to use creating heartbreak and grief for his devoted mother and her new husband. He stays fifteen years old for about two to five years (more if he managed to get into lots of scrapes), and then one day he again emerges from the off-camera cocoon transformed into a full-fledged adult, with all the rights, privileges, pain, and perfidy of that elite corps. And so the cycle continues.

She uses one extended example to illustrate her point. The example is clearly hypothetical, but it serves her purpose by clarifying her topic sentence.

Little Terence springs from Cross's imagination, not from the television screen. Clearly, though, she illustrates her point: Children are secondary to adult soap-opera characters.

Exercise 16.1: Explaining with Examples: The Paragraph

Write a paragraph developed by examples on one of the prompts listed below. First develop a topic sentence, then organize the examples you will use. Your paragraph may include a mixture of specific and typical examples.

a. Watching television teaches lessons about life.

b. People's houses reveal their character.

c. Games teach children important lessons about independence and cooperation.

d. Exercise can be detrimental to health.

e. A half hour of the evening news reveals a deeply divided United States.

f. Public places are disrupted by piped-in music.

g. Some people argue that hip-hop lyrics promote violence.

h. Some media celebrities symbolize more than success.

i. Americans are wasteful people.

j. Intelligent people often lack common sense.

k. Parents are too involved in their children's education.

l. Anything worth doing is worth doing badly.

m. There are several alternatives to public schools.

Exercise 16.2: Explaining with Examples: The Essay

Write a full essay, using examples, based on one of the following situations.

a. Everyone worries about drivers on cell phones making highways dangerous, but similarly, sidewalks in many large cities have become hazardous for pedestrians dodging nonstop talkers. Take a walk through campus or on a busy downtown street. Determine the percentage of people who are walking while talking. Identify the possible dangers and use examples to write an essay illustrating them.

b. Over the last few years, college courses of study have changed to reflect the concerns of women and minorities. Examine your college's programs and courses of study. Determine how they successfully or unsuccessfully address concerns of women and ethnic minorities. Write an essay using examples that illustrate what you discovered.

c. People today seem to yearn for the simple life. Perhaps this desire is fueled by the perception that there is never enough time to get everything done. To survive this caffeinated jungle, people wear digital watches that beep on the quarter hour or clutch their day organizers like life preservers. Examine your life for examples of the impact of time on you and the people you know; then write an examples essay as a warning to others to give up the "rat race" and seek a simplified existence.

d. Magazine advertisers seldom only praise their products. They also associate them with pleasing images to attract consumers, images such as physically attractive men and women, people in prestigious professions, an outdoor life, or the life of leisure. Write an essay using advertisements as examples to illustrate that advertisers entice consumers to buy products for the wrong reasons—that is, not because of product quality but because of pleasing associations.

16b Use comparison to explain similarities and differences

To identify similarities is to *compare;* to identify differences is to *contrast.* Showing similarities and differences, that is, *comparison,* is common not only in daily decision making but in all forms of writing. Sometimes the content of a comparison paragraph is presented side by side—that is, all the details of one side of the comparison are presented first, followed by all the details of the other side. Student-writer Tom Henry uses side-by-side comparison in the following paragraph.

Topic sentence clearly indicates that a comparison will follow.

When I first saw the reproduction of the prehistoric mastodon, I thought of elephants I had seen in circuses and zoos.

Similarities between the elephant and the mastodon.

Like the modern elephant, the mastodon was large, with legs that remind me of sturdy tree trunks. The ancient beast had large, floppy ears and a long trunk that he could use as a tool for gathering food.

Transitional sentence indicates a shift from similarities to differences.

But after a closer look, I saw some major differences between the modern elephant and the prehistoric mastodon.

Differences between the elephant and the mastodon.

The mastodon's tusks grew longer and curved upward at a sharper angle. Unlike the elephant with its thick, almost hairless hide, the mastodon was matted with long thick hair. And although the mastodon was large, it was not as tremendous in size as its modern descendant.

Comparisons can also be organized by the point-by-point method. This method is most useful when many points must be covered. In the following paragraph, student-writer Jim Cartozian begins a comparison of the American writers Ernest Hemingway and William Faulkner.

The topic sentence introduces the subjects to be compared and clearly indicates this will be a comparison.

Point 1: Both won the Nobel Prize. Hemingway had a temper.

No modern American writers have gained as much worldwide critical recognition as Ernest Hemingway and William Faulkner, and no two could be more different.

Both did win the coveted Nobel Prize for literature, but when the mild-mannered Faulkner won first, Hemingway is said to have lost his temper and then sulked.

Explaining Similarities and Differences **129**

Point 2: Both published early, but Hemingway had more success early.	Both were publishing at a young age, but Hemingway attracted popular attention early in his career, whereas Faulkner worked in near obscurity.
Point 3: A longer passage contrasts their public images; Hemingway as media star, Faulkner as recluse.	Hemingway became America's first modern literary media star. Magazines featured spreads of his war exploits, his African safaris, and his bullfighting adventures. Faulkner, in contrast, was never a media celebrity. Instead, he seemed to embody the lifestyle of small-town southern gentry, spending most of his quiet life in Oxford, Mississippi.
Continues Point 3.	Hemingway's novels and stories were often set in exotic locales like France, Spain, and Cuba; Faulkner set his works in the South, primarily in the mythical Yoknapatawpha County.
Transition sentence shifts discussion to personal visions.	Each dealt with very different visions.
Point 4: Two contrasting sentences compare their separate visions.	Hemingway's work displays psychologically wounded characters struggling to establish a personal code of values in an absurd world. Faulkner's work displays characters who are victims of history, suffering because of the sins of their ancestors, the men who wrenched the land from Native Americans and enslaved Native Africans.
Point 5: Hemingway's and Faulkner's deaths were dramatically different.	In 1961 Hemingway died violently by his own hand; in 1962 Faulkner died peacefully.

An *analogy* is a figurative comparison that helps explain a complicated or abstract idea by comparing it to a simpler idea or more concrete image. In an analogy, the items compared are from different classes. For example, a writer might compare the life of a human being to a river. In most ways the two are not alike, but in *suggestive* ways they are alike: Both flow smoothly at times, turbulently at other times; both change as they follow their paths; both find destinations that change their very nature. Analogies can help you show things to your reader in different ways, but you must take care not to press an analogy too far or it can become foolish.

The following paragraph from Lester del Rey's *The Mysterious Sky* compares the earth's atmosphere to a window. The writer succeeds because he uses our familiarity with windows to enlighten us about the functions of the atmosphere.

The topic sentence clearly indicates an analogy will follow.	The atmosphere of Earth acts like any window in serving two very important functions.
Similarity 1.	It lets light in and it permits us to look out.
Similarity 2.	It also serves as a shield to keep out dangerous or uncomfortable things.
Similarity 3.	A normal glazed window lets us keep our houses warm by keeping out cold air, and it prevents rain, dirt, and unwelcome insects and animals from coming in.
Similarity 4.	As we have already seen, Earth's atmospheric window also helps to keep our planet at a comfortable temperature by holding back radiated heat and protecting us from dangerous levels of ultraviolet light.

Exercise 16.3: Explaining Through Comparison

Write a fully developed comparison on one of the following topics. Keep in mind that you can alter the suggestion you choose to fit your own interests and knowledge.

a. Two groups that have contrasting values, such as smokers and nonsmokers, vegetarians and meat eaters, exercisers and couch potatoes.

b. Two campus groups who hold opposing values.

c. Two contrasting characters on a TV series. If appropriate, compare their physical appearance, their psychological makeup, and their actions. Conclude with an observation about what each represents.

d. Two ways of losing weight.

e. Coverage of an event by a newspaper and on television.

f. Two classic films from the same category, such as westerns, science fiction, thrillers, romances, or supernatural tales.

g. Watching an actual sports event and watching one on television.

h. Children's games yesterday and children's games today.

i. A film and the novel from which it was made.

j. Two talk-radio commentators (Al Franken and Bill O'Reilly, for example).

k. The pros and cons of two controversial points of view.

l. Two approaches to raising children.

m. How two people from different economic conditions, cultures, or age groups would view the same experience.

Exercise 16.4: Explaining Through Analogy

Write an analogy that relates an abstract idea, a process, an experience, or the odd behavior of someone you know to one of the subjects on the following list.

a poker hand	a flood
a merry-go-round	a game of solitaire
crashing waves	a flowering tree
gardening	dancing
a spiderweb	a leaking faucet
walking through a forest	a soaring bird

16c Use cause and effect to reveal reasons and results

Paragraphs of *cause and effect* reveal why something happened or explain what happened as a result of something else.

Sometimes such a paragraph deals only with causes because the effects are already clear. For example, a paragraph might explore the reasons for a late movie star's popularity without needing to demonstrate that the person really was a star.

At other times a cause-and-effect paragraph might concentrate on effects because a given cause clearly exists and the only question remaining is, What happened as a result? For example, a paragraph might explain the effects of unemployment or an increase in taxes.

Sometimes it is appropriate to discuss both causes and effects in one paragraph. The following paragraph from Victor B. Cline's "How TV Violence Damages Your Children" reveals both the causes and the effects of television violence on behavior.

The topic sentence suggests, but does not explicitly state, that the paragraph will reveal causes and effects of TV violence.	Much of the research that has led to the conclusion that TV and movie violence could cause aggressive behavior in some children has stemmed from the work in the area of imitative learning or modeling which, reduced to its simplest expression, might be termed "monkey see, monkey do."
Cause and effect 1: Brief exposure to aggressive acts on TV influences behavior.	Research by Stanford psychologist Albert Bandura has shown that even brief exposure to novel aggressive behavior *on a one-time basis* can be repeated in free play by as high as 88 percent of the young children seeing it on TV.
Develops cause and effect 1 further.	Dr. Bandura also demonstrated that even a single viewing of a novel aggressive act could be recalled and produced by children six months later, without any intervening exposure.
Cause and effect 2: Because children watch excessive TV, violence becomes commonplace in their minds.	Earlier studies have estimated that the average child between the ages of 5 and 15 will witness, during this 10-year period, the violent destruction of more than 13,400 fellow humans. This means that through several hours of TV watching, a child may see more violence than the average adult experiences in a lifetime. Killing is as common as taking a walk, a gun more natural than an umbrella.
The overall effect.	Children are thus taught to take pride in force and violence and to feel ashamed of ordinary sympathy.

Revealing cause-and-effect relationships can be difficult because they are usually complex. To write a meaningful cause-and-effect analysis, you must go deeper than the obvious. Sometimes you will find that a cause will have many effects that a quick look would fail to reveal. At other times you will find that cause-and-effect relationships occur in a sequence often called a causal chain.

Causal chain refers to cause-and-effect relationships appearing in a sequence, each event contributing to the following event, which then creates another event. You can use a causal chain to arrange a cause-and-effect paragraph, or an entire essay for that matter. In the following paragraph, student-writer Laura Topolte reveals the causal chain behind the violent teenage encounters in her hometown.

Topic sentence and background information announce that the writer is going to trace a pattern of violence.

A manhood ritual in my hometown of about 75,000 people centers on Friday-night violence among teenage boys. Parents usually explain the underlying cause of the violence by saying "boys will be boys," suggesting that their children are motivated by mysterious hormonal explosions beyond anyone's understanding. Though the actual details of these violent encounters may vary from one Friday night to another Friday night, the general pattern is always predictable.

The causal chain sequence is set in motion by a sports event.

Typically, an encounter is set in motion during a sports event in which a team from Northwood High School opposes a team from South Hills High School.

Event 1: Winners taunt losers.

Since the competition between the two schools is strong both on and off the playing field, the sports event usually ends with the winners taunting the losers and the losers vowing revenge.

Event 2: Rowdy students withdraw to beer parties.

The rowdier students often withdraw to beer parties where they continue to brag about the victory or threaten their arch rivals.

Event 3: Police break up parties.

As the parties become rowdy, the neighbors complain, and at about midnight the police disperse the teenagers, ordering them to go home.

Event 4: Rowdy students gather at local hangouts.

Many do, but others gather at their favorite hangouts, Northwood's Taco Bell and South Hills's Denny's.

Event 5: Cruising students taunt other students.

Eventually, a boisterous group, usually the winners, will cruise the opposition's hangout and shout obscenities from their cars.

Event 6: Students give chase.	The losers will typically respond with obscene gestures, climb into their cars, and give chase.
Event 7: Both groups meet and continue to taunt each other.	Eventually the two sides will meet up in a parking lot or community park where they call each other's manhood into question.
Event 8: A fight breaks out.	The final result is several broken noses, skinned knuckles, and expensive dental bills—after all, "boys will be boys."

When analyzing a causal chain, be aware of the immediate causes or effects (those occurring near an event) and the remote causes or effects (those occurring further away in time). In Topolte's paragraph, for example, the rivalry between Northwood and South Hills is the remote cause of Friday-night violence and the verbal and physical confrontations are immediate effects. Topolte is also aware that an even more remote cause for the rivalry might be at work: the unknown developmental or psychological forces that parents dismiss by saying "boys will be boys."

Exercise 16.5: Determining Causes and Effects

Respond in writing to one of the following questions, concentrating on cause (reasons), effect (results), or both together. If necessary, narrow the focus of the question so that it can be discussed within a reasonable length. With your professor's agreement, you may also rewrite any of these questions or create a subject to reflect your own particular interests.

a. Is using your intuition an effective way to solve problems?

b. What have been the indirect effects of a historical figure in your life, someone such as a political leader, an artist, or a philosopher?

c. What have been the effects of a significant public event in your life?

d. Why do some artistic works affect you?

e. Why does a particular television show, song, or film succeed?

f. What are the causes of homelessness, child abuse, gang violence, or another social phenomenon?

g. What are the causes of a family, institutional, or social custom?

h. Should children be treated like adults?

i. Why does the burning of the American flag enrage many Americans?

j. What effects does a particular advertisement attempt to create in the minds of consumers?

k. What are possible influences of action-oriented cartoons on children?

l. How does conformity impact individuals?

Exercise 16.6: Explaining Immediate and Remote Causes and Effects

John Holt, a critic of education, finds fault with schools for the ways they have of humiliating children:

> From the very beginning of school we make books and reading a constant source of possible failure and public humiliation. When children are little, we make them read aloud, before the teacher and other children, so that we can be sure they "know" all the words they are reading. This means that when they don't know a word, they are going to make a mistake, right in front of everyone. Instantly they are made to realize that they have done something wrong. Perhaps some of the other children will begin to wave their hands and say, "Ooooh! O-o-o-o!" Perhaps they will just giggle or nudge each other, or make a face. Perhaps the teacher will say, "Are you sure?" or ask someone else what he thinks. Or perhaps, if the teacher is kindly, she will just smile a sweet, sad smile—often one of the most painful punishments a child can suffer in school. In any case, the child who has made the mistake knows he has made it, and feels foolish, stupid, and ashamed, just as any of us would in his shoes.

Write your own paragraph using cause-and-effect analysis to explain the results of being publicly humiliated in school. What were the causes of the humiliation and its effects, both immediate and remote?

16d Use classification to arrange information in categories

Classification is a method of organizing information into general categories. The purpose of such grouping is to clarify the nature of each category. In this sense, classification is a kind of indirect or implied comparison because the qualities that place an item in one class also distinguish it from items belonging to other classes.

In the following example, Elena Peralta offers an informal classification of comic book collectors. She introduces her categories in the opening of the paragraph, then sketches broad characteristics that each group possesses and cites specific comic book titles appropriate for each category. Peralta also identifies her categories by assigning each group a name, which helps readers keep the categories separate.

Opening description creates a sense of who collects comic books.

One fascinating offbeat hobbyist is the comic book collector. Usually pale, wearing glasses, bushy-haired and disheveled, collectors can be found rummaging through pile after pile of unsorted secondhand comics in magazine marts across the country. *Comic book collectors, the serious ones, seem to fall into four major groups: Antiquarians, Mercenaries, Idolators, and Compulsive Completers.*

Topic sentence identifies four categories of comic book collectors.

Category 1: The Antiquarian.

The Antiquarian cares only for age value; subject matter is of no concern. He is looking for a 1933 *Funnies on Parade* from the days when men were men and comics were comics.

Category 2: The Mercenary.

To the Mercenary, value is all-important. Certain numbers and titles ring a bell in his cash-register brain and start him furtively checking through a half dozen price sheets. A pristine first edition of *Action Comics* (value: $4,000) would suit him just fine.

Category 3: The Idolator.

The Idolator couldn't care less about age or value. He's looking for favorites: a *Sheena,* a *Flash Gordon,* or another *Incredible Hulk.* Hiding in a corner, reading those he can't afford to buy, the Idolator will be the last one out of the mart at night and the first one back in the morning.

Category 4: The Compulsive Completer.

The most frustrated collector is the Compulsive Completer. He'll examine and reject thousands of comics in his search for a badly needed *Felix the Cat* to complete a

year's set or the one *Howdy Doody* missing
from his collection.

Closes with a
clincher statement.

But no matter what the reason for collecting,
these hobbyists share a common trait: They
love the thrill of the hunt.

Exercise 16.7: Explaining Through Classification

Categorize elements in one of the following subject groups.

a. Books, CDs, or DVDs you own

b. Unusual sports that are seldom televised or reported in newspapers

c. Talk show hosts

d. "War" toys, family-oriented toys, or intellectual toys

e. People who like to hunt

f. Lies

g. Ways to read a novel or poem

h. Ways to watch a horror movie

i. Kinds of photography

j. Attitudes revealed by bumper stickers

k. Alternative marriages and family groups

l. Tattoos

m. New ways to learn

n. Kinds of good or bad luck

16e Use definition to clarify unusual words

One kind of *definition* is the dictionary definition, which provides a
synonym (*slice* = to cut) or shows how a word fits into a general class
(*astronomy* = the science that studies the universe).

Writing a paragraph-long definition for an unusual term goes beyond the scope of a dictionary definition by allowing for a thorough
discussion. Such a paragraph might begin, as does a dictionary definition, by identifying a term as belonging to a general class. It will then

differentiate it from other members of the class. It might also include synonyms, illustrate the word with examples, discuss the word's origins, compare it to similar words, or tell what it is not.

Consider Jan Harold Brunvand's definition of "urban legend," from *Alligators in Sewers*.

The opening places urban legends in a general class.	Urban legends are realistic stories that are said to have happened recently. Like old legends of lost mines, buried treasure, and ghosts, they usually have an ironic or supernatural twist.
Differentiates urban legends from classic legends.	They belong to a subclass of folk narratives that (unlike fairy tales) are set in the recent past, involving ordinary people rather than extraordinary gods and demigods.
Differentiates urban legends from rumors.	Unlike rumors, which are generally fragmentary or vague reports, legends have a specific narrative quality and tend to attach themselves to different local settings. Although they may explain or incorporate current rumors, legends tend to have a longer life and wider acceptance; rumors flourish and then die out rather quickly.
Identifies the chief characteristics of urban legends.	Urban legends circulate, by word of mouth, among the "folk" of modern society, but the mass media frequently help to disseminate and validate them. While they vary in particular details from one telling to another, they preserve a central core of traditional themes.
Completes the definition with two examples.	In some instances these seemingly fresh stories are merely updatings of classic folklore plots, while other urban legends spring directly from recent conditions and then develop their own traditional patterns in repeated retellings.
Example 1: "The Vanishing Hitchhiker."	For example, "The Vanishing Hitchhiker" describes the disappearance of a rider picked up on a highway. It evolved from a 19th-century horse-and-buggy legend into modern variants incorporating freeway travel.

Example 2:
"Alligators in
the Sewers."

A story called "Alligators in the Sewers," on the other hand, goes back no further than the 1930s and seems to be a New York City invention. Often, it begins with people who bring pet baby alligators back from Florida and eventually flush them down the drain.

Exercise 16.8: Explaining Through Definition

Define one of the following terms. Explore the word beyond its dictionary meaning, using a variety of methods to develop your definition. As part of this or any extended definition, differentiate your word from others in the same class.

humanity	male liberation	maverick
education	corruption	imagination
Armageddon	intuition	tragedy
terror	liberation theology	confidence
honesty	social responsibility	luck
science	obsession	genocide
evil	team player	blindsided
female liberation	sociopath	fashion

Exercise 16.9: Explaining Through Definition and Example

From the following list of seldom-used slang terms, choose and define one. After you explain the term, create a situation in which it might apply, using the term in several sentences as a speaker might. Also include examples of current slang that have a similar meaning.

hoodwink	peacenik	macho
greenhorn	bamboozled	bonehead
whoopee	boodle	jive

16f Use process analysis to show how to do something or how something works

Process analysis explains how to do something or how something works. Process paragraphs are usually developed step by step in a chronological or logical sequence. For example, Caroline Sutton in

How Do They Do That? explains how manufacturers get the stripes in a toothpaste tube.

Sutton's opening prepares the reader for process analysis.

Although it's intriguing to imagine the peppermint stripes neatly wound inside the tube, actually stripes don't go into the paste until it's on its way out.

This sentence prepares readers for the process explanation that follows.

A small hollow tube, with slots running lengthwise, extends from the neck of the toothpaste tube back into the interior a short distance.

First step: filling the tube with red paste.

When the toothpaste tube is filled, red paste—the striping material—is inserted first, thus filling the conical area around the hollow tube at the front. (It must not, however, reach beyond the point to which the hollow tube extends into the toothpaste tube.)

Second step: filling the remainder of the tube with white paste.

The remainder of the dispenser is filled with the familiar white stuff.

Third step: squeezing the tube.

When you squeeze the toothpaste tube, pressure is applied to the white paste, which in turn presses on the red paste at the head of the tube.

Fourth step: the merging of white and red paste.

The red then passes through the slots and onto the white, which is moving through the inserted tube—and which emerges with five red stripes.

Exercise 16.10: Explaining a Process

Use process analysis to explain one of the following subjects. Explain the process one step at a time and be sure to provide your reader with enough detail to make each step clear.

a. How you set a table

b. How you live without a car

c. How you would tame a wild creature such as a falcon or a rabbit

d. How you would get rid of pests without using poisons

e. How you show appreciation for others

f. How you buy a used motorcycle or car

g. How you toss a Frisbee, a football, a baseball

h. How you bluff at cards

i. How you overcome shyness

j. How you cope with crowds

k. How you win others to your point of view

17 Argument Paragraphs ∫

Argumentative or **persuasive** writing attempts to change or reinforce someone's opinion or to convince someone to take action. When writers emphasize rational thinking, they are writing *logical argument.* When they emphasize emotion, they are writing *persuasive argument.* Since most argumentative writing mixes rational thinking with emotion, the term *argument* includes both argumentation and persuasion.

Refutation Paragraphs

Like all essays, an argument essay is composed of paragraphs, and it usually employs a variety of paragraph modes, such as paragraphs developed by examples, comparison and contrast, cause and effect, and definition. One paragraph structure, however, is unique to argument. This is the *refutation* paragraph, which presents a brief summary of an opposing argument and then offers the author's argument. For example, in a paragraph from "Politics and the English Language," George Orwell refutes an argument point that opposes his position.

> I said earlier that the decadence of our language is probably curable. Those who deny this would argue, if they produced an argument at all, that language merely reflects existing social conditions, and that we cannot influence its development by any direct tinkering with words and constructions. So far as the general tone or spirit of a language goes, this may be true, but it is not true in detail. Silly words and expressions have often disappeared, though not through any evolutionary process but owing to the conscious actions of a minority.

Orwell's refutation paragraph follows a common structure, or sequence of sentences. He begins by stating his position. He then states a counterargument. Next he writes a sentence that swings the direction from the counterpoint to his response. He closes with an interpretation that supports his opinion.

Student-writer Rhonda Burris follows this pattern in "Here's Looking at Reality, Kid." Her essay argues that the government should require film producers to announce the dangers of smoking when characters in a film smoke.

The writer states her position, then uses a transition sentence to lead to the opposition's argument point.	I'm urging that warnings about smoking be required on films that glamorize smoking, nothing more and nothing less. I can hear opponents now.
She summarizes what she believes her opponents will claim.	One more law designed to control personal freedom, they will charge. Following this logic, if government wants to protect people, it should put warnings about cars on films with car chases or warnings about guns on films with shoot-outs. But they would be wrong. Cars and guns don't kill people, drivers and gun owners kill people.
She uses a brief transition, "In contrast," to show the shift back to her position. She states her response to the opposing argument.	In contrast, cigarettes *do* kill people, even people who don't smoke but inhale cigarette smoke for years, and that's a well-documented fact. Moreover, the government has already taken action to warn consumers about the dangers of smoking.

Refutation Paragraphs and Development Patterns

Often writers employ a particular development pattern in refutation paragraphs. In the following paragraph from "Scientist: I Am the Enemy," the pediatrician Ron Karpati responds to accusations made by animal-rights activists with stunning brief examples. Notice how Karpati first summarizes the activists' point before countering it.

Karpati gives a very brief summary of one point in the opposing position.	Much is made of the pain inflicted on animals in the name of medical science. The animal-rights activists contend that this is evidence of our malevolent and sadistic nature. A more reasonable argument,

He writes a brief transitional sentence and develops his persuasive counterpoint, which leans on emotion.

however, can be advanced in our defense. Life is often cruel, both to animals and human beings. Teenagers get thrown from the back of a pickup truck and suffer severe head injuries. Toddlers, barely able to walk, find themselves at the bottom of a swimming pool while a parent checks the mail. Physicians hoping to alleviate the pain and suffering these tragedies cause have but three choices: create an animal model of the injury or disease and use that model to understand the process and test new therapies; experiment on human beings— some experiments will succeed, most will fail—or, finally, leave medical knowledge static, hoping that accidental discoveries will lead us to the advances.

He further enhances his position by presenting alternatives to using animals for scientific research.

In "The Futility of the Death Penalty," Clarence Darrow used comparison and contrast to refute a counterpoint.

Darrow opens with a general belief.

It seems to be a general impression that there are fewer homicides in Great Britain than in America because in England punishment is more certain, more prompt, and more severe. As a matter of fact, the reverse is true. In England the average term for burglary is eighteen months; with us it is probably four or five years. In England, imprisonment for life means twenty years. Prison sentences in the United States are harder than in any country in the world that could be classed as civilized.

He then writes a transitional sentence to shift the discussion to his position.

Consider now two examples of refutation paragraphs that make use of analogy and process analysis. Civil rights leader Martin Luther King, Jr., used analogy in "Letter from Birmingham Jail" to refute a public statement made by Alabama clergymen who opposed civil rights demonstrations because they broke the then existing law.

In your statement you assert that our actions, even though peaceful, must be condemned because they precipitate violence. But is this a logical assertion? Isn't this like condemning a robbed man because his possession of money precipitated the evil act of robbery? Isn't this like condemning Socrates because his unswerving commitment to truth and his philosophical inquiries precipitated the act by the misguided populace in which they made him drink hemlock? Isn't this like condemning Jesus because his unique God-consciousness and never-ceasing devotion to God's will precipitated the evil act of crucifixion? We must come to see that, as federal courts have consistently affirmed, it is wrong to urge an individual to cease his efforts to gain his basic constitutional rights because the quest may precipitate violence. Society must protect the robbed and punish the robber.

In "Concerning Abortion: An Attempt at a Rational View," Charles Harshrone uses process analysis to refute the view that a fertilized egg in its early stage is a human being.

> Anti-abortion advocates argue that human life begins at the moment of conception. But this is not accurate. The fertilized egg is an individual egg, but not an individual human being. For such a being is, in its body, a multicellular organism, a *metazoan*—to use the scientific Greek—and the egg is a single cell. The first thing the egg cell does is to begin dividing into many cells. For some weeks the fetus is not a single individual at all, but a colony of cells. During its first weeks there seems to be no ground for regarding the fetus as comparable to an individual animal. Only in possible or probable destiny is it an individual. Otherwise it is an organized society of single-celled individuals.

Although stating an opposing argument point in order to refute it is not used by all argument writers, doing so does show your reader that you have thoroughly considered the issue, thus making your argument all the more convincing.

Exercise 17.1: Convincing a Reader

Select one of the subjects below as the prompt to write a refutation paragraph that follows this common pattern:

• State your position.

• Write a transitional sentence that leads to the opposing argument.

• Summarize the opposing argument.

- Write a transitional sentence to shift to your response to the opposing argument.

- Develop your response by using a traditional development pattern.

a. Movie ratings

b. Reinstating the military draft

c. Propaganda in commercial advertising

d. Home schooling

e. Sex education provided in junior high and high schools

f. Internet pornography

g. Moving the driving age to twenty-one

h. Vegetarianism

i. Violence on television

WRITER'S TOOLBOX

Developing a Refutation Paragraph

Time yourself. Take five minutes to draw up two lists, side by side. Begin by stating your position at the top. In one list write points opposing your position; in the other, give points supporting your position. This is a quick way to generate ideas; Rhonda Burris used this tactic to develop an example paragraph that appeared earlier in this chapter.

> I believe films that glamorize smoking ought to have warning announcements about the dangers of smoking.

Oppose	Support
New laws limit personal freedom.	Laws requiring warnings on cigarette ads already exist.
Should be warnings on cars.	People driving cars kill people in accidents.
Should be warnings on guns.	People using guns kill people on purpose or in accidents.
	Smoking does kill people directly and indirectly through sidestream smoke.

Use your list as a guide when writing the refutation paragraph. Because the list will be a rough one, do not hesitate to delete some points and rearrange others.

j. Burning the American flag

k. The sex life of Congress (House and Senate) members and of the president and vice president of the United States

l. Solving problems by intuition

m. The death penalty

n. Gay marriage

o. Lowering the drinking age to eighteen nationwide

PART IV
Sentence Clarity, Variety, and Word Choice

It's my dream that teaching become a glamorous profession. There should be a teacher Hall of Fame. It should be the biggest event, even bigger than the Oscars—"Ms. Smith of P.S. 13 has just made a big breakthrough in teaching the dangling participle. She gets Teacher of the Year!"—with everybody jostling to get near Ms. Smith to shake her hand.

—Frank McCourt, *memoir writer*

18 Emphasize Equal Ideas; Deemphasize Unequal Ideas *emph/deemph*

When a single sentence has more than one idea, the ideas may be given equal or unequal emphasis. To show equal emphasis use **coordination,** and to show unequal emphasis use **subordination.**

Coordination

To emphasize main clauses (that is, word groups that can stand alone as a sentence) in a single sentence equally, select the appropriate coordinating word, that is, a coordinating conjunction, correlative conjunction, or conjunctive adverb, or use a semicolon to coordinate them.

COORDINATING CONJUNCTIONS

and   but   for   nor   or   so   yet

◆ Many teenage athletes who overeat are obsessed with losing
weight, ~~Others~~ *, and others* who overtrain are obsessed with lifting weights.

When coordinating main clauses, be sure to place a comma after the first main clause and before the coordinating conjunction.

CORRELATIVE CONJUNCTIONS

either . . . or   both . . . and   not only . . . but also
neither . . . nor   whether . . . or

◆ *Either*
Venice will sink into the sea, ~~The~~ *, or the* Italian government will
spend $1 billion to stabilize its foundation.

CONJUNCTIVE ADVERBS

consequently   furthermore   however   meanwhile
moreover   nevertheless   therefore   thus

◆ Steward Enterprises, Inc., services funeral homes, ~~It~~ *; furthermore, it* now wants
to extend its services to hospitals.

Be sure to place a semicolon after the first main clause and a comma after the conjunctive adverb. You can also substitute a semicolon for a period to show a coordinate relationship between main clauses:

◆ Gamblers trust luck, ~~Investors~~ trust figures.
               ; *investors*

Subordination

When ideas in a sentence are unequal in significance, subordinate the minor idea to the major idea. You can subordinate ideas in two ways.

Rewrite Minor Ideas as Subordinate Clauses.   To show an unequal relationship among clauses, use a subordinating conjunction or a relative pronoun to link the minor idea to the main idea.

COMMON SUBORDINATING CONJUNCTIONS

after	because	since	until
although	before	so that	when
as	if	that	whenever
as if	in order that	though	where
as though	inasmuch as	unless	while

RELATIVE PRONOUNS

that	which	whoever	whomever
whatever	whichever	whom	whose

◆ ~~Chess~~ players are known for concentration, ~~Great~~ chess players are also known for intuition.
   Although chess   , *great*

◆ Thigh anxiety is taking over local gyms. ~~Both men and women are afflicted with it.~~
             , *which afflicts both men and women,*

Rewrite Minor Ideas as Subordinate Phrases.   A phrase, unlike a clause, does not have a subject and a predicate. Unlike a main clause, a phrase cannot stand alone as a sentence. Using phrases is an effective strategy for showing the relationship among major and minor ideas.

◆ ~~Geneticist~~ Wes Jackson thinks replanting grass may lead to a green revolution. ~~He has spent his life on the Kansas prairie.~~
   After spending his life on the Kansas prairie, geneticist

◆ High-tech employees spend almost all their time at work, ~~They~~ kill themselves to make deadlines.
     ing

18a Combine choppy sentences

Stringing together short sentences is a tipoff that you are not distinguishing major from minor ideas. One short sentence in a series of longer sentences may add emphasis, but too many short sentences in sequence probably means you are giving equal weight to each idea.

CHOPPY   China invaded Tibet in the 1950s. Tibetans by the thousands escaped to different countries. Most of them fled to India. Some of them immigrated to the United States. Others settled in Switzerland.

REVISED   When China invaded Tibet in the 1950s, Tibetans by the thousands escaped to different countries. Most of them fled to India, and some of them immigrated to the United States and Switzerland.

◆ Bell Rice_^ *who* has published four novels_/ ~~She~~ lives in Phoenix_/ *and* ~~She~~ just sold her first novel_^ *Alcatraz in the Mind,* to a film producer. ~~It was *Alcatraz in the Mind.*~~

18b Avoid faulty or excessive coordination and subordination

In a sentence, faulty coordination mistakenly emphasizes unequal or unrelated clauses. Revise faulty coordination by putting part of the sentence in a subordinate clause or phrase.

◆ Members of Doctors Without Borders travel on an hour's notice to third-world hot spots_/ *while* ~~and~~ their at-home practices languish.

◆ *While members* ~~Members~~ of Doctors Without Borders travel on an hour's notice to third-world hot spots, ~~and~~ their at-home practices languish.

◆ Rosa Parks_^ ~~was~~ the African American woman who would not go to the back of the bus_^ ~~and she~~ set the civil rights movement in motion.

Excessive coordination—stringing main clauses together with coordinating conjunctions for no apparent purpose—can become monotonous for the reader. Excessive coordination also fails to show the relation between clauses.

◆ Dan Jenkins~~,~~ who is a recognized sculptor ~~and he~~ works~~,~~ing in San

Francisco, ~~and he~~ has received grants from the Guggenheim

Foundation and the National Endowment for the Arts.

Faulty subordination occurs when the major clause is placed in a subordinate position in a sentence or when the expected relation between clauses is reversed.

◆ Although ~~F~~oreign-made goods are popular with American consumers,

~~although~~ they pose a serious threat to the incomes of American

workers.

◆ ~~Although~~ She easily won the Olympic trial, although she had been

training for only six months.

Excessive subordination should be avoided. It occurs when a sentence contains a series of clauses, each subordinate to an earlier one, as in this sentence:

The lonesome trapper, who was a retired railroad worker who lived in a small cabin, enjoyed the rare occasions when a group of hikers wandered by his place, which was inaccessible for most of the year.

Exercise 18.1: Revise to Improve Coordination

Revise the following sentences to correct faulty or excessive coordination.

1. Georgia O'Keeffe was an American artist, and she lived to be almost 100, and she painted and sculpted almost until her death despite dimming eyesight.

2. O'Keeffe was the ignored child of a large midwestern family, and she lacked confidence in art school, so she became an art teacher in Texas.

3. O'Keeffe blossomed after her art was discovered by the much older photographer Alfred Stieglitz, and their romance was legendary but unusual.

4. O'Keeffe fell in love with the Southwest after a visit to New Mexico in 1929, and she spent long months there every year despite the objections of her husband, and her best art was done there.

5. After Stieglitz's death, O'Keeffe moved permanently to New Mexico, where she painted desert scenes and sensuous flowers and her most famous painting, the 24' × 8' depiction of clouds that hangs in Chicago's Art Institute, and where she lived a very private life.

Exercise 18.2: Revise to Improve Subordination

Combine each pair of sentences below into one sentence, subordinating one idea to another.

1. My sister Carla loves to shop at airport duty-free stores. Her first overseas trip was to Paris.

2. Carla gets to take several overseas trips every year. She works for an importing firm in Atlanta.

3. Duty-free shops are not really duty-free to the consumer. She still saves money on perfumes, watches, scarves, and ties.

4. Carla arrives at the airport early and checks in. She heads for the duty-free shops.

5. She prefers the large selection of the airport duty-free shops. On-plane duty-free shopping is cheaper.

Exercise 18.3: Revise to Improve Subordination

Rewrite the following sentences, revising the faulty or excessive subordination in each. You may need to write more than one sentence for each item.

1. Eimi Yamada, who had been a teacher for more than twenty years, retired from Stanton University, which was founded in 1829 and which has an international reputation in the biological sciences, last year.

2. Professor Yamada, who is noted for her work on the chemistry of cells, has most of her research materials housed in her garage,

which she has used as a library for a decade, ever since someone stole her Buick.

3. Her ancient Buick, which was a 1940 Century convertible that had been purchased for her by her mother when Professor Yamada graduated from high school, had been admired by every student who had ever seen her drive it through the streets of Stanton.

4. The man who stole Professor Yamada's Buick, which was beige and maroon, once failed the biology course that Professor Yamada taught.

5. Stanton University's student body, which numbers over two thousand, took up a collection and bought Professor Yamada a retirement present, which was another automobile to replace the one that was stolen many years ago.

---

19 Use Parallel Structure for Emphasis //

Use parallel structure to emphasize two or more words or ideas of equal importance by expressing them in the same grammatical form. Such elements as coordinate word groups, compared and contrasted word groups, and correlative word groups should be expressed in parallel form—that is, a noun must be matched with a noun, a verb with a verb, a phrase with a phrase, and a clause with a clause. Parallel structure can add clarity, interest, and impact to your writing.

19a Use parallel structure for coordinate elements

To earn a living, he worked *as a busboy at the faculty club* and *as a bellhop at the Bayshore Inn.* [Parallel prepositional phrases]

Clearing tables and *lugging suitcases* often left him *tired, disgusted,* and *discouraged* by Sunday night. [Parallel phrases and parallel predicate adjectives]

When coordinate elements are not expressed in parallel grammatical form, sentences can be awkward and hard to understand.

◆ Desmond's favorite pleasures are ~~the dances~~ *dancing* at Hotspur's and sleeping until noon.

Words such as the prepositions *by* and *in,* the *to* of an infinitive, the articles *a* or *an* and *the,* and the subordinate conjunction *that* should usually be repeated when they apply to both elements in a parallel construction.

◆ By reading extensively and ^{by}voting wisely, Americans

   contribute to the democratic process.

Clauses beginning with *and, who, or,* and *which* can be coordinated only with *who* or *which* clauses that precede them.

◆ May Lin, a student and ~~who has been~~ a salesclerk, won election

   to the school board.

19b Use parallel structure to compare and contrast ideas

You can underscore comparisons by arranging them in parallel structure.

◆ Most New Yorkers would rather put up with the hectic pace of

   the big city than ~~moving~~ ^{move} to a little backwater town and ~~wasting~~ ^{waste}

   time.

◆ The author of *ReMax* wants to live fully and ~~then hopes he will~~ ^{to}

   have a quick death.

19c Use parallel structure for correlative constructions

Either . . . or, not only . . . but also, both . . . and, and similar correlative constructions should link parallel sentence elements.

◆ De Campo sent copies of his speech not only to his senators

   and representatives but also ^{to}his friends and relatives.

◆ Even at night she can usually be found in her office either

   listening to student problems or ~~she works~~ ^{working} on her research.

Exercise 19.1: Create Parallel Structure

Correct faulty parallel structure in the following sentences.

1. Endurance training helps not only the lungs but also is good for the heart.

2. The human body contains both slow-twitch muscle fibers and it contains fast-twitch.

3. Slow-twitch fibers are difficult to train but they are employed easily.

4. Usually, strenuous exercise will not only deplete the normal supply of stored glycogen, the body's ready-to-use sugar, and cause a sense of fatigue known to athletes as "the wall."

5. Some of the best exercises are running, swimming, and walks.

6. Gymnasts may work out using parallel bars, rowing machines, and lifting weights.

7. All spectators enjoy watching athletes performing well and those who win gracefully.

8. The outcome of many football games next season will depend on whether the kicker is successful, whether the quarterback will make the right calls, and if the team is healthy.

9. Coaches aid athletes both physically and with their emotions.

10. Champions are made and not the product of birth.

---

20 Create Sentence Variety *var*

A good writer avoids writing monotonous paragraphs and essays by varying the length and structure of sentences. The following paragraph has interesting content but too little variety in sentence length and structure.

> Cockroaches are about half the size of a thumb. They have hard shells and are dark in color. They are nocturnal insects who hate the light. Roaches can eat almost anything. They can survive on virtually nothing. They like sweet foods. They like foods that contain protein and oils. They will eat anything from oats to library paste. They will eat the glue on a postage stamp. Twelve of them can live more than a week on this glue. If there is no food, that's OK. The large brown American roach can live a month on water. It can even live for weeks on nothing. The German cockroach can fast for two months.

Every sentence in the paragraph begins with the subject and follows a similar pattern. Many of the sentences are between five and eight words long, a pattern that gives the paragraph a repetitive dreariness. Most important, each sentence stands as an isolated fact; therefore, the relations among ideas are not clear. Revised to create sentence variety, the paragraph might read as follows.

> About half the size of a thumb and with hard, dark shells, cockroaches live in the night. Although they are small, roaches can live on almost anything or virtually nothing. When they eat, they like sweet foods that contain protein and oils. But if their favorite food isn't available, they are not choosy. A hungry cockroach will eat anything from oats to library paste, even the glue on a postage stamp, which cockroach lore says will sustain twelve of them for more than a week. If there is no food, that's OK. A large brown American roach can live a month on water or even for weeks on nothing. Some cockroach observers claim that the German variety can fast for two months.

Of course the first paragraph was written poorly to illustrate by contrast the value of creating variety in sentence length and word order. The second paragraph differs from the first paragraph in other ways, too, but the point should be clear: Vary sentence beginnings, vary sentence structure and length, and change the word order to create writing that is lively, interesting, emphatic, and rhythmic.

20a Vary sentence beginnings

BEGIN WITH A SUBJECT	*Americans* chew millions of pounds of chewing gum each year.
BEGIN WITH AN ADVERB	*Surprisingly,* well over half of this gum is used in armed forces combat rations.
BEGIN WITH A PHRASE	*Before the importation of chicle from Mexico in the mid-1880s,* Americans chewed paraffin wax.
	Seeking greater chewing pleasure, Americans soon switched to chicle.
	To advertise his gum, William Wrigley, Jr., mailed free sticks of gum to every telephone subscriber in the United States in 1915.

BEGIN WITH A CONJUNCTION	I don't like candy. I don't like cookies. I don't like cakes or pies. *But* I can't live without my chewing gum!
BEGIN WITH A TRANSITION	Doctors used to believe that chewing gum was a health hazard. *However,* most doctors now agree that chewing gum contributes to a sense of well-being.

Exercise 20.1: Vary Sentence Beginnings

For each of the following model sentences, write another sentence that imitates its structure. Identify how each sentence begins.

1. Near the state border, the two escaped convicts surrendered.

2. At his first Olympics, Shaun White won gold in the snowboard halfpipe.

3. Reluctantly, the salesclerk told Clyde that his credit card had expired.

4. The New Orleans levees breached during Hurricane Katrina.

5. To encourage the team, the coach gave a pep talk.

20b Vary sentence structures

You can achieve variety by alternating sentence structures. A **simple sentence** has only one main clause.

> Nobody owns a cat.

A **compound sentence** has two or more main clauses but no subordinate clause.

> Nobody owns cats, but many people feed them.

A **complex sentence** has one main clause and at least one subordinate clause.

> If a cat likes you, it will live with you.

A **compound-complex sentence** has at least two main clauses and at least one subordinate clause.

> If a cat dislikes you, it may disappear, and no matter how hard you search, you will not find it.

Exercise 20.2: Vary Sentence Structure

Identify the sentence structure of each sentence.

1. Tiny bones in a fish's ear tell the life story of the fish.

2. The bones are called otoliths, and they grow in rings.

3. Because otoliths are affected by known weather conditions, scientists can tell the age of the fish, and they can tell when the fish migrated.

4. In addition, if the fish has had a behavior change, the ear bones have recorded it.

5. Because the otoliths absorb heavy metal, scientists can examine them for signs of water pollution.

20c Vary sentence forms

A **loose sentence** has its subject and predicate first, followed by modifiers and other amplification.

> Arteries carry blood, which is rich in oxygen, to the extremities of all warm-blooded animals, including birds.

A **periodic sentence** has most of its modification and amplification before the subject and predicate.

> Even with a temperature below ten degrees Fahrenheit, pheasants have warm bodies.

A **balanced sentence** is a compound or compound-complex sentence in which the clauses are parallel.

> Arteries transmit warm blood, and veins return the cooler blood. [Compound sentence]

> While they were studying zoology together, Bebe kept humming, and Ching kept mumbling. [Compound-complex sentence]

Exercise 20.3: Vary Sentence Forms

Identify the form of each of the following sentences.

1. The Senate confirmed the new Supreme Court nominee after a long debate.

2. The Democrats threatened a filibuster, and the Republicans threatened to change the Senate rules in return.

3. In the closing hours of the session, the Senate voted along party lines to confirm the nominee.

4. The president wanted to fill the empty Supreme Court seat, and the American people wanted that to happen, too.

5. While the senators were debating, reporters were interviewing party leaders and the candidate herself in the lobby of the Capitol.

Exercise 20.4: Vary Sentence Forms

Write sentences that conform to the following descriptions, using the model sentence as a prompt.

1. Write a simple, loose sentence.

   Ether burns brightly.

2. Write a simple, periodic sentence.

   An organic compound, ether has industrial uses.

3. Write a complex, periodic sentence.

   While Donna Lee was experimenting in her laboratory, some ether caught fire.

4. Begin a simple sentence with a prepositional phrase.

   Before noon, her laboratory was destroyed.

5. Begin a complex sentence with a dependent clause.

   When the firefighters arrived, they saw only embers.

6. Write a loose, complex sentence.

   The firefighters returned to their station while Donna Lee remained at the scene.

7. Begin a simple sentence with a participial phrase.

   Reading her insurance policy, the young scientist looked sad.

8. Write a periodic sentence containing two clauses.

   After talking to her insurance agent, she called her father, and then she sat down to eat dinner.

9. End a complex sentence with a prepositional phrase.

> While she was eating, her brother walked into the kitchen.

10. Begin a compound-complex sentence with a dependent clause.

> After Donna Lee told her brother about her accident, he helped her with the dishes, and later he helped her rebuild her laboratory.

21 Rewrite Misplaced Modifiers *mm/dm*

To avoid confusing readers, be sure to place modifiers, whether single words, phrases, or clauses, so that a reader will be certain what word or words they modify.

21a Place modifying phrases and clauses near the words they modify

A misplaced phrase or clause may mislead readers or force them to reread to figure out what a sentence means.

CONFUSING	Our neighbor borrowed our lawn mower with a smile.
CLEAR	With a smile, our neighbor borrowed our lawn mower.
CONFUSING	The car has bad tires that I sold today.
CLEAR	The car that I sold today has bad tires.

Exercise 21.1: Revising Sentences with Misplaced Phrases and Clauses

Revise the following sentences by relocating the misplaced modifying phrases and clauses.

1. The woman cashed her check with a French accent.

2. His trial was postponed for three months for tax evasion.

3. The explorer described an earthquake during his lecture.

4. After the party the hostess gave balloons to all the children in the shape of fantastic animals.

5. The senator examined the rocks in his office taken from the moon.

21b Avoid writing squinting modifiers

A squinting modifier can seem to modify a word either preceding or following it. The ambiguous result can confuse a reader.

SQUINTING	Mia told Antonio immediately to call the police. [Does *immediately* refer to *told* or to *to call*?]
REVISED	Mia immediately told Antonio to call the police.
REVISED	Mia told Antonio to call the police immediately.

Exercise 21.2: Revising to Correct Squinting Modifiers

Revise the following sentences to clarify the confusion that squinting modifiers create.

1. Walking to work occasionally is an interesting experience.

2. News that the water had been shut off completely mystified me.

3. Reading his novel thoroughly delighted me.

4. Taking coffee breaks frequently disrupts production.

5. Young children given allowances often waste the money.

21c Place limiting modifiers with care

Limiting modifiers, such as *only, hardly, just, nearly, almost,* and *ever,* can function in many positions in a sentence, but they modify only the expression that immediately follows them. Therefore, as these limiting modifiers change position in a sentence, the meaning of the sentence also changes.

I will go only if he asks me. [Otherwise I will stay.]
Only I will go if he asks me. [The others will not go.]
I will go if only he asks me. [Please, ask me!]
I will go if he asks only me. [If he asks others, I will stay.]

Exercise 21.3: Revise Sentences to Correct Misplaced Limiting Modifiers

Write another version of each sentence by moving the italicized modifier to a different position. Briefly describe the difference in meaning of the two sentences.

1. Henrietta lost *almost* one thousand dollars.

2. *Only* Clyde is ten years old.

3. Rachel *nearly* memorized a hundred Chinese verbs.

4. Andy *even* has a job.

5. Mr. Kobe *just* stared at Mike.

21d Move awkwardly placed modifiers

Avoid placing a lengthy modifying phrase or clause between key sentence elements.

AWKWARD	The cost of attending college, *because of inflation and reduced federal support*, has risen sharply in recent years.
REVISED	The cost of attending college has risen sharply in recent years *because of inflation and reduced federal support*.
AWKWARD	Anton seemed, *to those who had visited him during the several weeks following his operation*, discouraged.
REVISED	*To those who had visited him during the several weeks following his operation*, Anton seemed discouraged.
AWKWARD	Margo could have, *if she had not joined the army*, been a police officer.
REVISED	*If she had not joined the army*, Margo could have been a police officer.

You may place short modifiers between a subject and a predicate.

The cost of attending college, *unfortunately*, has risen sharply in recent years.

Anton seemed *mildly* discouraged.

He discovered he had been *cruelly* deserted.

21e Avoid splitting infinitives

An infinitive consists of *to* plus the plain form of a verb: *to run, to complain, to speak.*

SPLIT INFINITIVE	When the locusts descended, the prairie residents prepared to hurriedly depart.
REVISED	When the locusts descended, the prairie residents hurriedly prepared to depart.

Occasionally a split infinitive will seem natural and appropriate. In fact, not splitting an infinitive can sometimes create an awkward or misleading sentence.

His inability to *clearly* explain the issues cost him the election.

In this sentence, the alternatives are more awkward than the split infinitive. *Clearly to explain* and *to explain clearly* sound excessively formal, and *to explain the issues clearly cost him the election* produces a squinting modifier.

Exercise 21.4: Revise to Correct Awkward Modification

Change the position of the italicized modifier in each sentence to correct the awkward construction.

1. Tenochtitlan, *until it was destroyed by Cortés's army in 1521,* served as the capital city of the Aztec empire.

2. Following the destruction of the capital, Cortés's men built, *with the forced labor of the Aztec survivors,* a magnificent new city.

3. Mexico City is *by many visitors today* considered one of the most beautiful cities in the world.

4. Some demographers expect the population of Mexico City to, *by the year 2011,* number over 30 million people.

5. A visitor today will, *if romantically inclined,* enjoy the numerous sidewalk cafés and strolling musicians.

21f Avoid writing dangling modifiers

A dangling modifier is a phrase or clause that is not clearly attached to any word in the sentence. To correct a dangling modifier, change the subject of the main clause or rewrite the modifier as a complete clause.

DANGLING PHRASE	*Walking through the supermarket,* the oranges looked tempting. [The oranges were walking?]
REVISED	*Walking through the supermarket,* I noticed that the oranges looked tempting.
REVISED	*As I was walking through the supermarket,* the oranges looked tempting.
DANGLING PHRASE	*To understand world affairs,* a daily newspaper should be read.
REVISED	*To understand world affairs,* a person should read a daily newspaper.
DANGLING PHRASE	*After recovering from the treatments,* my doctor told me to be more careful in the future.
REVISED	*After I had recovered from the treatments,* my doctor told me to be more careful in the future.
DANGLING PHRASE	*While a student at Rutgers,* Shakespeare was my favorite author.
REVISED	*While I was a student at Rutgers,* Shakespeare was my favorite author.

Exercise 21.5: Revise to Correct Dangling Modifiers

Revise the following sentences to eliminate dangling modifiers.

1. To learn about zombies, Haitian voodoo tradition was studied by E. Wade Davis.

2. After receiving a sample of "zombie powder," it was found by Davis to contain one critical ingredient: tetrodotoxin.

3. Being a powerful poison, Davis said tetrodotoxin is 160,000 times more potent than cocaine.

4. Produced by a species of puffer fish, a soldier passed out for twenty-four hours after he handled roasted fish entrails containing tetrodotoxin.

5. Under constant tetrodotoxin intoxication, researchers noted that people acted like the zombies described in literature.

Exercise 21.6: Revising to Correct Misplaced Modifiers

On the basis of what you have learned throughout this chapter, recast the following sentences so that they illustrate clear writing. Some sentences have more than one error.

1. Denton Cooley, once an assistant in many heart operations and now a world-famous heart surgeon in his own right, estimates that he has at least performed 65,000 heart operations.

2. He has one of the lowest mortality rates anywhere of any heart surgeon.

3. He has nearly performed ninety-one heart transplants.

4. Dr. Cooley also developed and implanted the first temporary heart.

5. His career includes, among a number of adventures and awards so richly deserved, the world's first heart operation.

6. He in the mid-1950s invented one of the early heart-lung machines.

7. In excess of $20 million, he has amassed a personal fortune.

8. In early December 1967, Dr. Christiaan Barnard, Cooley heard on the radio, had done the first human heart transplant.

9. Cooley was, like most surgeons, dumbfounded.

10. Cooley predicted the newly transplanted heart would fail immediately within forty-eight hours.

---

22 Revise for Consistency *shift*

The use of person, number, mood, subject, and voice should remain consistent within sentences. Faulty shifts in any of these elements indicate that the writer's thinking is not clear, and the meaning of the sentence will be obscured. Always review your sentences for consistency.

22a Write sentences consistent in person and number

Most faulty shifts in person take place between second person and third person.

FAULTY SHIFT	If a beginning driver studies the vehicle code thoroughly, you should be able to pass the written test for a driver's license. [Faulty shift from third to second person]
REVISED	If a beginning driver studies the vehicle code thoroughly, he or she should be able to pass the written test for a driver's license. [Consistent third person]
REVISED	If you study the vehicle code thoroughly, you should be able to pass the written test for a driver's license. [Consistent second person]

Number refers to the singular or plural form of nouns and pronouns. Most faulty shifts in number result from the use of a plural pronoun to refer to a singular noun. (See agreement of pronoun and antecedent, Chapter 30; indefinite pronouns, 30b.)

FAULTY SHIFT	When a mud flat dries up, they do so in regular patterns of cracks. [Shift from singular to plural]
REVISED	When a mud flat dries up, it does so in regular patterns of cracks. [Consistently singular]
FAULTY SHIFT	When a chemist experiments with toxins, they exercise great caution. [Shift from singular to plural]
REVISED	When a chemist experiments with toxins, he or she exercises great caution. [Consistently singular]
REVISED	When chemists experiment with toxins, they exercise great caution. [Consistently plural]

22b Write sentences consistent in tense

Tense refers to the time of an action as indicated by the verbs in a sentence. Shifts in verb tense are often required to report time sequences accurately, but faulty shifts can confuse a reader. (See verb tense, 33g.)

FAULTY SHIFT	The suspected bicycle thief ran around the corner and falls into the arms of the police officer.
REVISED	The suspected bicycle thief ran around the corner and fell into the arms of the police officer.
FAULTY SHIFT	The escaping driver speeds around the corner and veered directly into the path of a motorcyclist.
REVISED	The escaping driver sped around the corner and veered directly into the path of a motorcyclist.

22c Write sentences consistent in mood

The mood of a verb can be indicative, imperative, or subjunctive. Statements and questions are in the indicative mood; commands, in the imperative mood; and wishes and statements contrary to fact, in the subjunctive mood.

Most faulty shifts in mood occur when a writer fails to follow through with the initial use of the imperative mood.

FAULTY SHIFT	Save coffee grounds, and you should sprinkle them around your rosebushes.
REVISED	Save coffee grounds and sprinkle them around your rosebushes.

22d Write sentences consistent in subject and voice

A shift in subject or a shift from active to passive voice is awkward and possibly confusing.

FAULTY SHIFT	In the game of curling, a player slides a heavy stone over the ice toward a target, and the ice in front of the stone is swept to influence its path.

Because the subject shifts from *player* in the first clause to *ice* in the second clause, and the voice shifts from active *(slides)* to passive *(is swept),* a reader may wonder who is doing the sweeping.

REVISED   In the game of curling, a player slides a heavy stone over the ice toward a target, and the player's teammates sweep the ice in front of the stone to influence its path.

A shift in subject and voice sometimes results in a dangling modifier.

FAULTY SHIFT   Shaking with fear, the sound of an intruder could be heard in the kitchen. [The sound is shaking?]

The subject of the main clause is *sound*. The introductory phrase *shaking with fear* is a dangling modifier because it does not sensibly relate to sound.

REVISED   Shaking with fear, we heard the sound of an intruder in the kitchen.

Now the subject is *we,* which clearly connects to *shaking with fear.*

22e   Avoid shifts between direct and indirect discourse

Direct discourse reports the exact words of a speaker. Indirect discourse reports the gist of what a speaker said but not the speaker's exact words.

DIRECT DISCOURSE   Father said, "I will be home at noon."

INDIRECT DISCOURSE   Father said that he would be home at noon.

FAULTY SHIFT   "I'll be home at noon," Father said, and I should not eat the cookies.

REVISED   "I'll be home at noon," Father said. "Don't eat the cookies." [Direct discourse]

REVISED   Father told me that he would be home at noon and that I should not eat the cookies. [Indirect discourse]

Exercise 22.1: Correct Faulty Shifts

In these sentences, label each faulty shift in person, number, tense, mood, subject, voice, or discourse and revise each sentence to be consistent. If any sentences are already correct, mark them with a C.

1. The river itself, cleaner than it had been when Sharon was a child, glimmered softly in the moonlight and winds like a snake through the valley.

170   *Revise for Consistency*

2. Across the river, climbing the opposite hill, was Otawnee, its narrow frame houses jammed together shoulder to shoulder as if they gather strength from one another.

3. Sharon felt a twinge of sadness as she gazes at the shadowy outlines.

4. Maybe if she hadn't concentrated so much on getting out, she thought, you might have had more time to find out what was good about it.

5. She let her gaze fall to the foot of the hill, to the river and the mill yards that hover on either side of it.

6. The same sounds are in the air that had been there the night before: the heavy, muffled breathing of the blast furnace, the occasional echoing clash of metal on metal.

7. "You know, I like the sounds best of all," Sharon said, hardly aware that she was speaking.

8. They were quiet for a moment, and sounds they knew from childhood were heard.

9. A puff of orange smoke rose far below them as a glowing ingot is loaded into the blooming mill.

22f   Avoid shifts in grammatical plans

> In Faulkner's often anthologized story "Barn Burning" poignantly reveals the conflicting loyalties in a young boy's life.

"Barn Burning" is used in this sentence as the object of the preposition *in,* but it is also used as the subject of the verb *reveals.* A word or group of words cannot function as both the object of a preposition and the subject of a main clause.

If the sentence begins with a prepositional phrase, the main clause has to have a subject of its own.

> In the often anthologized story "Barn Burning," Faulkner poignantly reveals the conflicting loyalties in a young boy's life.

If "Barn Burning" is to serve as the subject of *reveals,* the prepositional phrase must be eliminated.

> Faulkner's often anthologized story "Barn Burning" poignantly reveals the conflicting loyalties in a young boy's life.

22g Avoid faulty predication

Faulty predication occurs when the subject and the predicate of a sentence do not fit together in meaning.

FAULTY PREDICATION	The issue of gun control is an easy solution to a complicated problem. [The issue is not the solution]
REVISED	The issue of gun control is complicated.
REVISED	Gun control is an easy solution to a complicated problem.
FAULTY PREDICATION	Nepotism is when [or where] officials appoint their relatives to desirable positions. [Nepotism is neither a time nor a place]
REVISION	Nepotism is the appointing of relatives to desirable positions.
FAULTY PREDICATION	The reason he failed the examination is because he had a toothache.
REVISED	The reason he failed the examination is that he had a toothache.
REVISED	He failed the examination because he had a toothache.

Exercise 22.2: Correct Sentences for Consistency

Revise the following sentences to avoid shifts in grammatical plan and faulty predication.

1. Banking is an idea that has always interested me.

2. While I was eating at the Turkish restaurant, is where the music excited me so much that I felt like dancing.

3. All over the campus seemed to be alive with flowers.

4. Pearls are when gems are formed inside oysters.

5. In *Light in August* by William Faulkner is difficult to understand.

Exercise 22.3: Correct Sentences for Inconsistencies

1. In 60 percent of a new engine is made of plastic.

2. By using plastic makes the engine lightweight.

3. The engine can sit in a child's wagon, and the wagon can be easily pulled by them.

4. When a child does pull the wagon loaded with the powerful engine, they feel proud.

5. The new engine is called the Polimotor, and they were designed by Matthew Holtzberg.

6. When Holtzberg spoke to a recent engineers' meeting, he spoke calmly, saying most to the engine's moving parts are made of Torlon, and he also said that Torlon is a heat-resistant plastic resin.

7. In the engine block itself is made of a graphite-fabric of epoxy composite.

8. In the future is when drivers will have fewer mechanical problems because of their Polimotors.

9. In the design of the engine will probably be standard in cars in ten to twenty years.

10. According to Holtzberg, the first question everyone asks when they see a plastic engine is why the thing doesn't melt.

---

23 Add Omitted Words *inc*

Add missing words to complete sentences. Most incomplete sentences are sentence fragments, but some sentences that are not fragments may still be incomplete because words that complete the thought are missing.

23a Complete all comparisons

It is easy to leave your thought incomplete, unclear, or illogical when comparing one thing with another because the comparison is obvious in your own mind. But remember, you are writing for a reader who does not know what you know.

INCOMPLETE   Ace Construction Company treats its employees better.

COMPLETE	Ace Construction Company treats its employees better than other contracting firms treat their employees.
UNCLEAR	Susan is closer to me than Serena.
CLEAR	Susan is closer to me than Serena is.
CLEAR	Susan is closer to me than she is to Serena.
ILLOGICAL	The silence of the desert at night was more terrifying than a coyote.
LOGICAL	The silence of the desert at night was more terrifying than the howl of a coyote.

23b Add missing words in compound word groups

You may leave out words in compound word groups as long as the words you leave out are common to both groups.

◆ CEOs must provide strong visible leadership for all employees

and ~~provide~~ clear verbal direction for senior management.

The second *provide* is unnecessary because it is grammatically parallel with the first provide.

◆ There are only two lasting bequests we can give our children:

one is roots; the other‚ is wings.

The verb *is* can be left out before *wings* with no confusion in meaning. In fact, the omission serves to emphasize wings. The added comma indicates the omission.

◆ At eighteen I knew everything; at forty,‚ ~~I knew~~ nothing.

I knew can be omitted before *nothing*. The added comma indicates the omission.

Done properly, sentences can be strengthened by omissions. If, however, omitted words are not consistent in grammar or idiom, then the sentence is flawed.

◆ At eighteen I knew everything; now,‚ ^{I know} nothing.

◆ Humans have a strong belief‚ⁱⁿ and a desire for love.

23c Add the word *that* to prevent misreadings

If doing so does not cause a misreading, *that* may be left out of a sentence when it begins a subordinate clause.

◆ In 1968, Criswell predicted ~~that~~ the world would end on

August 18, 1999.

If there is a risk of creating confusion or a misreading by leaving out *that,* then include it.

◆ Studying his crystal ball, Criswell predicted in 1968ₐthe world

would end on August 18, 1999.

23d Add the articles *a, an,* and *the* for grammatical clarity

Check your sentences very carefully to see whether you have mistakenly left out articles.

◆ Negotiators cannot decide on a meeting date let alone reach
   ₐagreement.

Exercise 23.1: Add Missing Words

Rewrite the following sentences to make all comparisons complete, clear, and logical and to correct faulty omissions.

1. Many people believe that pit bulls are more dangerous.
2. Jake's wife Melinda always had confidence and admiration for Jake's pit bull, Simon.
3. Unlike some, Simon has never attacked anyone or anything.
4. Personally, I believe that Melinda loves Simon more than Jake.
5. To me, the soft fur of a cat is better than any kind of dog.
6. My cat does scratch the furniture, however, not Simon.
7. When my cat was a kitten, she slept on my bed all the time; now, never.

8. I would like to get a new kitten, except for hurting my cat's feelings.

9. I just know I would never get a pit bull, or any kind of dog, because of my cat's friendliness.

---

24 Use Appropriate Language *appr*

English can be divided into two very general categories: standard and nonstandard English. Standard English is used in most mainstream publications, business, politics, television broadcasts, and education. Nonstandard English consists of variations of standard English (especially in certain pronoun cases and verb forms) not found in the writing of formally educated people.

STANDARD	The guest *brought* homemade pie for dessert.
NONSTANDARD	The guest *brung* homemade pie for dessert.
STANDARD	Nina is the woman *who* broke the record.
NONSTANDARD	Nina is the woman *what* broke the record.
STANDARD	He sings to *himself.*
NONSTANDARD	He sings to *hisself.*

Standard American English can be divided into formal or informal (sometimes called *colloquial*) writing. Informal writing is characterized by common expressions taken from spoken English.

INFORMAL	If the mayor would *get together with* the city manager, *they'd* solve the problem.
FORMAL	If the mayor would *meet with* the city manager, *they would* solve the problem.
INFORMAL	I *don't get* why the refund took *all these* weeks to *get here.*
FORMAL	I *do not understand* why the refund took *several* weeks to *arrive.*

Informal writing is easily identified by contractions such as *they'd, don't, you're,* and *it's.* In formal writing contractions are usually written out: *they would, do not, you are, it is.* Most of the writing you do in college and in a profession—serious essays, theses, reports, and memos—will be formal.

24a Avoid slang, regional expressions, neologisms, and obsolete words

Slang comes from a specialized, often colorful vocabulary that is related to the experience of groups with common interests, such as actors, astronauts, athletes, computer scientists, copywriters, musicians, street gangs, teenagers, truckers, and so on.

Eventually, some slang passes into standard usage. *Jazz* and *A-bomb* were once slang words but are now standard English words. More often, slang makes its appearance, increases in use, and then shifts its meaning or becomes dated.

Generally, you should avoid using slang in college writing; it is imprecise and may be confusing or misleading to a reader.

◆ *Jean de Florette* is a ~~downer~~ to watch. The ~~flick~~ portrays a ~~smack~~ from Paris who lacks the ~~smarts~~ to survive on a farm.

[handwritten corrections: depressing (above "downer"); film (above "flick"); an intellectual (above "smack"); intelligence (above "smarts")]

◆ The journalist was ~~bummed~~ after the judge ~~laid a heavy trip on him~~ for contempt of court.

[handwritten corrections: stunned (above "bummed"); fined him (above "laid a heavy trip on him")]

Neologisms are words or terms that have come into use so recently that they may still be unacceptable in general writing. Some former neologisms, such as *astronaut, bookmobile, fallout, supersonic,* and *smog,* have become acceptable. But most neologisms pass quickly from use, and you should avoid using them unless they become widely accepted.

Regional expressions are common to speech in a geographical area. Do you *carry* or *drive* your friends to the mall? Do you *draw water* or *run water* from a *faucet,* a *spigot,* or a *tap?* Such regional words as these will not confuse your reader, but in writing you should avoid expressions that are not generally used outside a particular region.

◆ The committee had a ~~right nice~~ meeting. We wish ~~you all~~ could have come.

[handwritten corrections: productive (above "right nice"); all of you (above "you all")]

Obsolete or *archaic* words have fallen from general use. Obsolete indicates that a word or a specific meaning is no longer used at all. *Coy* meaning "to caress" and *cote* meaning "to pass" are labeled obsolete. Archaic indicates that a word or meaning appears only in special contexts. *Anon* meaning "at once" and *methinks* meaning "it seems" are labeled archaic.

24b Use technical terms, or jargon, with care

When writing for a group of literature specialists, you may use the terms *persona, verisimilitude,* and *motif* with confidence that your readers will understand them. These are technical terms that literature specialists freely use. Most fields and activities have technical vocabularies, and a person who studies a field or pursues an activity soon learns the specialized vocabulary that characterizes it. A person who has studied finance will use the terms *put, call,* and *margin* with ease. A skier will feel equally at ease talking about *moguls, whiteouts,* and *schussing.* But without explanation, such terms are inappropriate for a general audience. When you are writing for a general audience, therefore, avoid using technical terms. If you must use them, be sure to define them.

Exercise 24.1: Revise Using Formal English

Revise the following paragraphs by changing words or phrases that may be informal, slang, regional, obsolete, or archaic expressions, neologisms, or technical terms. Feel free to consult a dependable dictionary that includes usage labels to determine the appropriateness of expressions and to find suitable substitutes.

In 1945 Vice President Harry S. Truman unexpectedly became president when Franklin Roosevelt died in office. When Truman took the oath of office, he was so jittery that the words would not come to him and his voice petered out, so he took out a slip of paper with the oath written on it and held it on top of the Bible. Then his voice began to function, and he read the words in a real nice manner. The next day he laid his feelings on a group of reporters: "Boys, if you ever pray, pray for me now!" During his first months in office, Truman could not duck the decision to use the atomic bomb against Japan, a decision that not only brought World War II to an end but also demonstrated that human beings had created the power to waste the entire world.

After the war, Truman lost the heavy-duty political support Roosevelt had previously gathered; consequently, in the 1946 midterm elections Republicans gained control of both houses of Congress for the first time since 1930. Betwixt the attacks of the opposition party and the sniping of rebellious members of his own party, Truman appeared to be on the ropes politically, yet he continued his plans to run for reelection in 1948.

24c Avoid pretentious language

Write in simple English. Beginning writers often make their writing excessively showy, perhaps from a misconceived desire to sound impressive or even poetic. Unfortunately, the result is often pretentious.

◆ At ~~day's end the evening solitude descended on the sea-swept~~ *sunset the beach grew quiet.*

~~coast.~~

◆ This college ~~is predicated on the belief that diligent and~~ *rewards hard work.*

~~sustained effort will be rewarded.~~

To write in simple English, always choose the common word over the fancy one. If you want to say "Drinking will destroy the liver," do not write "Imbibing alcoholic beverages in vast quantities will lead to the degeneration of one of the body's most important organs."

Exercise 24.2: Eliminate Pretentious Language

While keeping the basic meaning, revise the following sentences by using simple English.

1. The ability to orate before the multitude is accrued through repetitive effort.

2. *Vinification* is an ancient art that has been revitalized by modern technological innovations.

3. Dr. Chen's verbal meanderings amaze and mystify her students.

WRITER'S TOOLBOX

Avoiding IM Jargon

With the exploding popularity of instant messaging (IM), we are all becoming more accustomed to using abbreviations and symbols as substitutes for standard language. So "See you later" becomes "C U ltr" and "I'll wait for you" becomes "I'll wait 4 U." Always remember that this kind of substitute language is unacceptable in any communication except between peers and good friends. Don't allow yourself to slip into this in e-mail messages—let alone in formal papers.

4. Among his peers he was the sole champion for those who wished to privatize the U.S. Postal Service.

5. We must face the dangers of an inexorable rise in population today or find an agreed-upon solution for thousands of starving infants and children in the near future.

24d Avoid sexist language

In your writing, avoid usage that may disregard or insult your readers or that relies on stereotypes. English traditionally contains an implicit sexual bias, such as in the use of the masculine pronouns *he, him,* and *his* to refer to individual members of a given occupation or of a group composed of both men and women.

BIASED	A mystery *novelist* concentrates on *his* plot, whereas a suspense *novelist* concentrates on *his* action.
BIASED	A *doctor* must pass the state medical examination before *he* can be licensed to practice.
BIASED	*Man* must assume responsibility for the preservation of the natural world.
BIASED	*Freshmen congressmen* must serve several years before they gain enough seniority to become committee *chairmen.*

These sentences ignore the fact that women also occupy these positions or participate in these groups; thus these sentences implicitly diminish their achievements.

You can avoid sexual bias in your writing by applying several techniques.

1. Replace masculine pronouns with an article (*a, an, the*).
2. Change nouns and pronouns from singular to plural.
3. Revise a sentence to eliminate the need for a pronoun.
4. Use compounds such as *he or she* and *him or her.*
5. Avoid the traditional masculine and feminine stereotypes by using gender-neutral language to refer to both men and women.

◆ A mystery *novelist* concentrates on *his* plot, whereas a suspense *novelist* concentrates on *his* action.

◆ A *doctor* must pass the state medical examination before he can be licensed to practice.

◆ Man must assume responsibility for the preservation of the natural world.

◆ Freshmen *congressmen* must serve several years before they gain enough seniority to become committee *chairmen.*

SEXIST	NONSEXIST
actor, actress	actor
chairman	chairperson, chair
coed	student
councilman	councilwoman, council member
fireman	firefighter
gal Friday	assistant
man, mankind	humankind, people
policeman	police officer
poetess	poet
stewardess, steward	flight attendant
waiter, waitress	server
weatherman	meteorologist, weather forecaster
workman	worker

Exercise 24.3: Revise Sexually Biased Language

Revise the following passage to eliminate gender bias. Use any of the methods explained in this chapter.

A writer's primary task is to fulfill the purpose of his book. He must first develop a sense of his reader and a strategy for addressing him: Whom is the essay directed to? How much does his reader know about the subject? How much time is he likely to spend reading the book? Will he want a straightforward treatment of the subject? Will he want extensive background information? These are questions every writer must ask himself. If he doesn't, he will not develop a feel for his reader, that is, for the person who sits behind his desk or in his easy chair, book in hand, under his reading lamp.

Exercise 24.4: Replace Sexually Biased Words

Find nonsexist words to replace sexist words.

1. chairman
2. stewardess
3. actress
4. Father Christmas
5. Mother Nature

6. sportsmanship
7. ladylike
8. mailman
9. anchorwoman
10. airman

---

25 Revise Wordy Sentences *wordy*

Make your writing concise by deleting words and phrases that add nothing to your meaning. Scrutinize your sentences: Look for empty phrases, needless repetition, and euphemism. Cross them out and search your vocabulary for more direct and forceful ways to say what you are thinking. Being concise does not necessarily mean that your writing will be skimpy; it means your writing will be free of useless words.

25a Avoid empty phrases

Empty phrases do little more than add useless words to your writing. Whenever they appear in your work, cut them out or revise them.

◆ ~~In the world of today,~~ eighteen-year-olds can find only

minimum wage jobs.

Today

Many empty phrases develop from such all-purpose words as *angle, area, aspect, case, character, fact, factor, field, kind, nature, process, situation,* and *type*. Watch for them and cut wherever you can.

Often one word will do the work of an entire empty phrase; if so, substitute the single word for the phrase.

FOR	SUBSTITUTE
at all times	always
at this point in time	now
at that point in time	then

at any point in time	whenever
by means of	by
come into conflict	conflicted
due to the fact that	because
for the purpose of	for
for the reason that	because
give consideration to	consider
give encouragement to	encourage
in order to	to
in the event that	if
in the final analysis	finally
make contact with	call, contact
of the opinion that	think, believe
regardless of the fact that	although
in fact that	that
until such time as	until

Exercise 25.1: Revise Empty Phrases

Revise the following sentences by deleting empty words or phrases or by substituting single words for empty phrases.

1. At the present time, sales indicate that biographies of film stars are the type of book more readers want.

2. It is usually the case that these tales give encouragement to the public's fantasies.

3. The 1966 story of film star Hedy Lamarr's life was so steamy that in order to keep an aspect of her public dignity, she claimed that the book revealed too much and denounced it as obscene.

4. But at this point in time stars seem pleased to reveal shocking details of their lives due to the fact that confession sells books by the millions.

5. Given the large amounts of money at stake, it's not hard to come to the realization that biographies of film stars are not to be relied upon for their accuracy.

25b Avoid careless repetition

At times you will repeat words for parallel structure or for emphasis. But careless repetition leads to awkward, wordy sentences.

◆ The grizzly ~~bear~~ is probably North America's most ferocious bear.

◆ Economists say that the recession will continue, and I ~~continue to~~ believe them.

25c Avoid redundant phrases

A redundant phrase says the same thing twice: *visible to the eye, large in size, cooperate together, close proximity, basic essentials, true fact.* Always revise sentences to eliminate redundancies.

◆ The central character in this novel is a mysterious figure○ ~~beyond understanding.~~

The following list cites common redundancies. Be aware of them and watch for them and others in your own writing. Whenever you find a redundancy, strike it. The italicized words in the list are redundant.

advance *forward*	*important* essential
disappear *from view*	revert *back*
autobiography *of her life*	combine *together*
end result	repeat *again*
basic fundamentals	consensus *of opinion*
factual truth	round *in shape*
circle *around*	continue *to go on*

Exercise 25.2: Revise for Repetition and Redundancy

Improve these sentences by revising them for ineffective repetition and redundancy.

1. From my point of view, I believe parents do not allow their children enough time to discover their creative interests.

2. Twice a day millions of people listen to public radio while continuing on their daily schedules.

3. In the United States, American citizens often make heroes out of the country's severest critics.

4. The book puts forth an extraordinary and exceptional deception aimed at convincing readers that philosophy is superior to and better than any other intellectual pursuit.

5. Nearly square in shape and reddish brown with yellow stripes in color, the puffer fish is covered with spines that make it look more like a spiny medieval weapon than a fish.

25d Avoid excessive euphemism

A *euphemism* is a word or phrase substituted for other words that are considered harsh or blunt. The funeral industry, for instance, substitutes *loved one* for *corpse, vault* for *coffin,* and *final resting place* for *grave.*

Common euphemisms generally refer to experiences in our daily lives: birth, bodily functions, sex, aging, death. They are often necessary for tactfulness. No doubt most of us prefer to ask a waiter for directions to the *rest room* rather than to the *toilet.*

Although common euphemisms such as *rest room* are harmless, other euphemisms, especially those created by private and public institutions, are often designed to distract us from the realities of poverty, unemployment, and war. We've become accustomed to the euphemisms *low income, inner city,* and *correctional facility* as substitutes for *poor, slum,* and *prison.* Plumbers may be referred to as *sanitation engineers,* teachers as *learning directors,* and salespeople as *account executives,* yet they still fix pipes, correct papers, and sell products. In wartime the act of burning villages and herding people into detention camps has been called *pacification,* and the lies of public officials have been termed *inoperative statements.*

Because euphemism is pervasive in our society, you must guard against its slipping into your finished work. When you identify euphemisms in your writing, replace them with more accurate, concrete language.

◆ The whole area was ~~underdeveloped and~~ crowded with ~~the~~ *a slum*
starving people
~~disadvantaged,~~ who seemed to ~~be living on a marginal diet.~~ *have no more to eat than rice water.*
Several families ~~often lived together in a small dwelling,~~ *crammed themselves into two-room hovels made of cardboard and sticks. The only water they had came from*
~~sometimes with no more than~~ a single ~~water source to serve~~ *tap shared by fifteen or twenty such shacks.*
~~them and several other homes together.~~

Use euphemism when tact calls for you to do so, but avoid using it when your work requires a direct rendering of the material. Do not use it to deceive.

Exercise 25.3: Make Sentences Concise

Make these sentences concise by eliminating jargon and euphemism and recasting them into plain, straightforward English.

1. The history of new regulatory provisions over the years is generally an immediate resistance to them.

2. A romantic relationship is ongoing between Marge and Craig.

3. When I was a young girl living in a deteriorating residential section of town, I vowed to develop the capital necessary to purchase a ranch when I grew up.

4. On the basis of information from visual surveillance, the air force chief of staff ordered the squadron to carry out a surgical bombing action over the enemy's capital.

5. My Uncle Ramsey passed away while staying overnight at a nearby motor lodge in the company of a female companion whom the family had never met and who was unfamiliar to them.

26 Choose Exact Words *exact*

Find words that best fit the meaning you wish to convey. To do this, you will need to develop a keen sensitivity to the differences in tone of some words. To be inexact is to risk misleading or confusing your reader.

26a Distinguish between a word's denotation and its connotation

Denotation refers to a word's concrete meaning as found in the dictionary. **Connotation** refers to what a word implies or suggests. According to one dictionary, the word *snake* denotes "any of a wide variety of limbless reptiles with an elongated, scaly body, lidless eyes, and a tapering tail."

For some people the word *snake* may connote treachery or evil; for others, wisdom or healing. Pay close attention to both the denotation and the connotation of words. Otherwise your words might clash, as in the following sentence.

> The speaker manipulated the audience by presenting the evidence to refute their arguments.

Manipulated has the connotation of deviousness on the part of the speaker, but *refute* denotes reasonably proving something false. The two words do not fit well together. To correct the clash of meanings, the writer should use words with more compatible denotations and connotations.

◆ The speaker ~~manipulated~~ convinced the audience by presenting the

  evidence to refute their arguments.

◆ The speaker manipulated the audience by presenting only the

  evidence ~~to refute~~ that would disprove their arguments.

Take special care when selecting a word from among synonyms, words that have nearly the same meaning. *Depart, retreat,* and *flee; emulate, copy,* and *mimic* are two groups of synonyms. Like most synonyms, they are close in their denotations, but they differ in their connotations. Similarly, "Harold's speech was funny" conveys a different meaning than does "Harold's speech was laughable."

When the connotations of words arouse exceptionally strong feelings, we consider the words *loaded.* Loaded words appeal to emotion and bias rather than to reason. A public relations expert might claim his company is carrying on the tradition of *free enterprise* while insisting that a competitor is *price gouging.* A politician might call himself or herself a *progressive* while labeling an opponent a *do-gooder.* Loaded words are the tools of propagandists; if you use loaded words, your writing will seem not only inexact but also biased.

Exercise 26.1: Select Exact Words

Replace each italicized word with a word that has a similar denotation but a connotation better fitted to the sentence.

1. To be a successful high-fashion model, a woman or a man must be *emaciated* and graceful.

2. Success also depends on an ability to improve from hearing a photographer's constant *ridicule* and to survive arduous hours in a studio.

3. Unlike actors, models are not hired because of their *quirky profiles.*

4. Instead, their facial features must be *bland,* and their bodies must seem to come from the same mold.

5. Successful high-fashion modeling has its *payoffs* but also its draw-backs—constant routine and *relentless* dieting.

Exercise 26.2: Eliminate Loaded Words

Revise the following paragraph to replace any loaded words and phrases with language that is less emotionally charged.

> Secretly, the president's agents in Congress are threatening to smother hardworking Americans with new taxes. These greedy politicians are plotting to impose a value-added tax to support social boondoggles that conservative legislators have always resisted. Patriotic taxpayers throughout the heart of the country are beginning to resist, too.

26b Do not rely exclusively on abstract and general words

Be as concrete and specific as you can.

Abstract words refer to qualities, ideas, and actions that we cannot experience through our senses: *culture, friendship, loyalty, democracy.* **Concrete words** refer to things we can experience through our senses: *orange, blood, scream, laugh, hug, tick, swamp.*

General words refer to large groups of people or things. The word *athlete* includes everyone who seriously pursues a sport. **Specific words** refer to a particular part of a general group. *Professional athlete* limits the group of athletes to those who are paid for their athletic performances. Other specific terms for *athlete* include *professional tennis player; professional female tennis player; top ten female tennis players;* and *Venus Williams, one of the top ten female tennis players.* Notice that *general* and *specific* are relative terms and that language becomes more specific as it moves from the general group to a unique example of the group—from *athlete* to *Venus Williams* in this case.

Experienced writers know the value of concrete and specific words. Inexperienced writers tend to overuse abstract and general words; consequently, their work is often inexact and lifeless.

◆ In English 170 we studied the ~~world's leading contemporary~~ *works of Alice Walker, Ursula K. Le Guin, Gabriel García Márquez, and Raymond Carver.* ~~writers.~~

◆ After major trials, jurors are often interviewed ~~for their~~ *by newspaper and television reporters who seek to find out the jurors' versions* ~~opinions.~~ *of the deliberations.*

◆ The ~~amount~~ *$13,000* set by the government as the poverty level for a *will not buy many $15 T-shirts or $35 jeans, let alone bread, milk,* family of four ~~is not much to live on.~~ *vegetables, and meat.*

WRITER'S TOOLBOX

Using a Software Thesaurus

A thesaurus identifies words that have similar meanings. Word-processing software will often include a thesaurus that a writer can call up to find a replacement for an inexact word. A thesaurus can be very helpful when composing an essay. If you use a word that does not quite express your thought, you can highlight the word, go to Tools on the menu bar, and click on Thesaurus. A window will open that offers several replacement suggestions. You can then select the one that more accurately expresses what you want to say.

Sometimes inexperienced writers will misuse a thesaurus. Instead of using it to find the right words they need, they use it to find more abstract words, that is, words that sound more "intelligent" to their untrained ear. This practice is a mistake; writers should select words for their accuracy, not their complexity.

Exercise 26.3: Use Specific Language

Make these sentences more precise by replacing the general words and phrases with concrete and specific language.

1. The film was *thrilling*.

2. The city was *quickly destroyed*.

3. The sea was *dangerous*.

4. The senator *lost her temper*.

5. My brother *irritates me*.

26c Use idioms correctly

An idiom is a fixed phrase with a single meaning that cannot be determined from the definitions of the individual words in the phrase. Hearing that "the waiter *flew into a rage*," most native speakers of English would understand that the waiter became angry. If, however, a non-native speaker were to translate the phrase *flew into a rage* word by word, the meaning would seem absurd.

People learn the idiomatic expressions of their language naturally and have little difficulty understanding and using most of them. Occasionally, however, even experienced writers make errors in using an idiom that combines an adjective or a verb and a preposition. "Independent *of* outside influence" is a correct idiom, whereas "independent *from* outside influence" is not.

Whenever you are in doubt about which preposition to use with a word, look up the word in a dictionary. Here are common idioms and examples of their use.

abide *by*	We must abide by the rules.
according *to*	According to the evidence, he must be innocent.
agree *with* (a person)	I agree with John.
agree *to* (a proposal)	I cannot, however, agree to his proposal.
agree *on* (a course of action)	We cannot agree on a common plan.
angry *with*	The children are angry with the babysitter.
charge *for* (a purchase)	The charge for cocoa butter is excessive.
charge *with* (a crime)	The manager has been charged with fraud.
comply *with*	Everyone must comply with the regulations.
compare *to* (something in a different class)	Do not compare psychiatry to witchcraft.
compare *with* (a person)	You can compare a Freudian with a Jungian.
concur *with* (a person)	Jones concurs with Fussel.
concur *in* (an opinion)	I concur in your wish to transfer.
confide *in* or *to*	Ching had no time to confide her secret to me. She confides in her roommate.

die *of* or *from*	He may die from grief.
differ *with* (disagree)	Ruth differs with Trent over who should be a presidential candidate.
differ *from* (be unlike)	Gibson's style differs from Redford's.
differ *about* or *over* (a question)	We differ about how food should be cooked.
different *from*	Living in a dormitory is different from living in an apartment.
identical *to* or *with*	One cannot be identical to the other.
ignorant *of*	Sally is ignorant of table manners.
inferior *to*	Is a life of toil inferior to a life of ease?
occupied *by* (a person)	We found our cabin occupied by a hiker.
occupied *in* (thought)	He was occupied in thought when the pain struck.
occupied *with* (a thing)	She is occupied with a novel.
prior *to*	Prior to being married he played drums.
superior *to*	Rhonda feels superior to Linda.

26d Use figurative language carefully

Writers use figurative language to draw a comparison between two things that are essentially different but alike in some underlying and surprising way.

By making comparisons, writers not only help their readers understand what is being said but also add vigor to their prose. The most common figures of speech are simile and metaphor.

In a **simile** a writer may express a comparison directly by using *like* or *as*.

> Her forward expression was steady and driving like the advance of a heavy truck.
>
> —Flannery O'Connor

> The bowie knife is as American as the half-ton pickup truck.
>
> —Geoffrey Norman

In a **metaphor** a writer may express a comparison indirectly, without using *like* or *as.*

> A sleeping child gives me the impression of a traveler in a very far country.
>
> —Ralph Waldo Emerson

> I refuse to accept the notion that nation after nation must spiral down a militaristic stairway into the hell of nuclear war.
>
> —Martin Luther King, Jr.

Personification and **hyperbole** are less common figures of speech. Writers use personification to give ideas, animals, and objects human qualities.

> When the wind swept through the forest, the trees moaned, and among their branches birds complained.

Through hyperbole a writer creates an exaggeration.

> Mike Finnegan's tennis game has hit bottom, unless he returns to the court another time.

To be exact, a figure of speech must always clarify a writer's thought by making it understandable in other terms. Sometimes, however, a figure of speech will miss the mark or fall flat because it is trite or overblown.

> Her smile is as warm as a crackling fire on a snowy evening.

Another figure of speech gone wrong is the *mixed metaphor,* which combines two or more incompatible comparisons.

MIXED METAPHOR	Ideas that *blaze* in his mind often *crash* in his writing.
REVISED	Ideas that *blaze* in his mind often *smolder* in his writing.
REVISED	Ideas that *race* in his mind often *crash* in his writing.

Exercise 26.4: Make Comparisons Consistent

Revise the following mixed metaphors to make the comparisons consistent.

1. The scalpel cuts through the flesh, leaving a road of blood.

2. The speaker bathed her audience in a blanket of nonsense.

3. She stirs figurative language into her writing the way a cook adds vegetables to a stew—a dash of simile, a pinch of metaphor.

4. His arms flapping, the student flew to the lectern and barked for silence.

5. Reformers once imagined that prisons could be lapidary shops where the soul would be polished after the flaws had been surgically cut away.

26e Avoid trite expressions

A **trite expression,** sometimes called a *cliché* or a *stock phrase,* is an expression that was fresh and striking at one time but by overuse has become stale.

Trite phrases include exhausted figures of speech (*hit the nail on the head*), wedded adjectives and nouns (*a well-rounded personality*), and overused phrases (*the finer things in life*).

Trite expressions may come easily to mind when you feel rushed. But when you revise your writing and come across one, strike it out and reword your thought in a fresh way. These are common trite phrases to avoid:

a must	as a matter of fact
a thinking person	at this point in time
all in all	cold as ice
all walks of life	depths of despair
aroused our curiosity	face the music
flat as a pancake	none the worse for wear
in a very real sense	pure as newly fallen snow
in the final analysis	quick as a flash
in the world of today	sadder but wiser
last but not least	silent as the grave
method in his madness	smart as a whip
never a dull moment	strong as an ox

Exercise 26.5: Eliminate Trite Expressions

Revise the following sentences, substituting fresh thoughts for trite expressions.

1. It is safe to say that Tom Pham looks like a timid tax attorney who would feel butterflies in his stomach if he ever heard a raised voice.

2. But looks are deceptive. Pham is a fierce negotiator who takes the bull by the horns and never gives an inch in collective bargaining sessions.

3. His endurance is such that he can go nose to nose with an opponent for twelve hours straight and leave the table none the worse for wear.

4. Although some see collective bargaining as child's play, Tom realizes that the incomes of two thousand union members hang in the balance.

5. He takes seriously his responsibility to get the best deal he can and never drops the ball—or a dime.

PART V
Sentence Errors

If you want to write, the sentence is your point of departure. Part of the art of creating a sentence is knowing the substance and elements of which it is composed. We all know, or let us assume, that sentences are made of words. But words come in various guises, whatever they are intended to hide or reveal, and so we must begin with them—seeing just what they think they are and bringing them together into the realm of sense.
—Karen Elizabeth Gordon, *novelist*

27 Rewrite Sentence Fragments

28 Revise Run-on Sentences

29 Examine Subject-Verb Agreement

30 Examine Pronoun-Antecedent Agreement

31 Check Pronoun Reference

32 Use Appropriate Pronoun Case

33 Select Accurate Verb Forms and Tense

34 Use the Appropriate Mood

35 Write in Active Rather Than Passive Voice

36 Select Adjectives and Adverbs with Care

| **27** | **Rewrite Sentence Fragments** *frag* |

A sentence fragment is a word group that is punctuated as if it were a complete sentence. Sentence fragments are usually serious errors, suggesting that the writer does not understand the basic principles of sentence structure.

27a Revise fragmented subordinate clauses

A group of words introduced by a subordinating conjunction (such as *when, while, although, because, if, until*) or by a relative pronoun (such as *who, which, that*) functions as a subordinate clause. Although subordinate clauses have subjects and verbs, they are not main clauses. When they are punctuated like main clauses, they are actually sentence fragments, that is, *fragmented subordinate clauses.*

You can correct such fragments by attaching the subordinate clause to a main clause, by rewriting the subordinate clause as a complete sentence, or by rewording the clause to eliminate the subordinating conjunction or relative pronoun. (See subordinating conjunctions and relative pronouns, Chapter 18.)

◆ Dragon stories abound in the myths and legends of people

everywhere, ~~As~~ a study of early civilization will reveal.

◆ One type of dragon popular in art is a huge beast with an

armorlike skin and several heads capable of breathing fire.
These features make the dragon
~~Which makes it~~ difficult to subdue.

◆ Drawings from widely separated cultures show dragons that

are grotesque combinations of several animals, ~~That are~~

familiar to the people living in that area.

27b Revise fragmented phrases

A phrase is a word group used as a noun, verb, adjective, or adverb. Since such word groups lack a subject, a predicate verb, or both, they cannot stand alone as if they were sentences. (See phrases, Chapter 69.)

Fragmented phrases can be corrected by joining them to main clauses or by rewriting them as complete sentences.

◆ Some scholars have spent years studying ancient texts from civilizations around the globe, ~~S~~earching for a common origin of all later dragon lore.

◆ One candidate for the honor is Zu, a water monster of Sumerian myth, ~~who~~ Zu was slain by Ninurta, ~~A~~ warrior god who took for himself the names and characteristics of all the creatures he killed.

◆ In Babylonian stories about battles between dragons and gods, ~~T~~he defeated dragons were forced to live under the sea.

◆ These dragons struggled constantly, ~~T~~o free themselves and destroy the world.

27c Revise compound predicates and word groups punctuated like sentences

Two or more predicates joined by a coordinating conjunction form a compound predicate and share the same subject. Compound predicates should not be separated and punctuated like separate sentences.

◆ According to one Greek tradition, dragons sleep with their eyes open, ~~A~~nd see with them shut.

Word groups introduced by expressions announcing that examples or a list will follow should not be punctuated like a sentence.

◆ Network television ignores many sports, ~~S~~uch as rock climbing, skateboarding, surfing, archery, and snowboarding.

EXPRESSIONS THAT INTRODUCE EXAMPLES OR A LIST

also	for example	like	or
and	for instance	mainly	such as
but	in addition	namely	that is

27d *frag*

27d Use fragments in special situations

Use fragments in special situations sparingly and only when your purpose is clear.

QUESTIONS AND ANSWERS	What next? Another term paper.
EXCLAMATIONS	Awesome!
IN DIALOGUE	"Of course." "Wonderful."
FOR EMPHASIS	I've been patient, understanding, attentive, and gentle. Now it's over. *No more Mr. Nice Guy!*
AS TRANSITIONS	My final point.

Exercise 27.1: Revise Sentence Fragments

Correct the following sentence fragments by (1) attaching them to main clauses, (2) rewriting them as main clauses, or (3) rewording them to eliminate subordinating conjunctions or relative pronouns.

1. Woodblock prints are illustrations made from carved blocks of wood and printed on paper. First used in Japan in the 1600s to illustrate books.

2. When readers became more and more interested in the illustrations for their artistic value. Publishers hired skilled artists to create prints.

3. By the end of the 17th century, techniques to produce many copies of a print from one woodblock had been developed. Making this fine art available to the general public.

4. The most famous Japanese woodblocks were made during the 1700s and 1800s. Scenes from everyday life or the theater, beautiful women, and landscapes.

5. Later, European artists admired the Japanese woodprints. Their bold colors and unusual designs.

6. Dinosaurs became extinct some 65 million years ago. According to the best estimates of scientists.

7. Dinosaurs had roamed the earth for more than 100 million years before their sudden demise. The cause of which remains a mystery.

8. Although there are many theories about why the dinosaurs became extinct. Some theories, such as the conjecture that alien space creatures kidnapped the dinosaurs, are rather implausible.

9. Until a few years ago, most scientists agreed on the most likely cause of dinosaurs' extinction. Their inability to adapt to a changing climate.

10. Many scientists now believe that a giant meteor struck the earth. Causing a huge explosion followed by a series of earthquakes.

Exercise 27.2: Revise Fragmented Phrases

Correct the following phrase fragments by joining them to the accompanying main clauses or by rewriting them as complete sentences.

1. Dragons appear in a variety of roles. Symbolizing evil cultures, wisdom to others, and power to still others.

2. Sumerians thought of dragons as embodiments of evil. A concept later attached to the devil.

3. The Gnostics, early religious cults of Europe and Asia, used a figure of a dragon biting its own tail. To symbolize the cyclic nature of time and the continuity of life.

4. To convince the people that their leaders had the dragonlike qualities of strength and goodness. Early Chinese emperors adopted the dragon as a symbol of imperial power.

5. Although you may not believe they ever existed, the image of dragons survives in art, fiction, religious stories, and dreams. In every corner of the world.

Exercise 27.3: Correcting Fragments

Correct each of the following fragments either by attaching it to a main clause or by rewriting the fragment as a complete sentence. Mark correct items with a C.

1. What explains the popularity of belief in dragons? In the absence of any scientific evidence that they ever existed.

2. Some scholars suggest that dragon stories originated from dim memories of prehistoric animals. And were passed on to later generations. Who embellished them to explain the history of their people.

3. The problem with this theory is that dinosaurs, pterodactyls, and similar animals that could have been the ancestors of dragon stories ceased to exist millions of years ago. Before human beings appeared on earth.

4. Others theorize that dragon stories represent a human psychological need. To imagine ourselves triumphant over enemies and evil forces.

5. The hero battles the many-headed monster threatening the beautiful young woman. Restores order to the world, and allows us to feel that we can control our lives, too.

6. Whatever the reason, dragons show a remarkable ability to survive. No matter how many have been killed, they are still with us.

7. Those of us who have not had the good fortune to see a live dragon can read about them. Or see them in our neighborhood theaters.

8. If books and films do not satisfy your urge to go dragon hunting. Find a damp, grassy, but rocky hillside remote from human habitation.

9. There, you may spot a particularly beautiful stone. That is really a dragon egg.

10. If you are patient, you may be witness to a dragon's hatching. Take a lunch. Sometimes it takes a thousand years.

---

28 Revise Run-on Sentences *run-on*

Like unintentional sentence fragments, run-on sentences are serious errors because they show that the writer is either careless or unaware of sentence structure.

In speaking, you quite naturally run clauses together, linking or separating them with breaths and pauses. In writing, you must use coordinating conjunctions or punctuation marks to link or separate clauses.

There are two types of run-on sentences: fused sentences and comma splices. When main clauses are not separated by a punctuation mark or joined by a coordinating conjunction, the result is a **fused sentence.**

FUSED SENTENCE

Main Clause
Spiritual insight produces one kind of
Main Clause
knowledge reading critically produces another.

When main clauses are joined by a comma without a coordinating conjunction, the result is a **comma splice.**

COMMA SPLICE

Main Clause
Meditation requires inactive sitting, reading
Main Clause
critically requires active page turning.

Comma splices and fused sentences can be corrected in four ways.

1. Use a period to make two separate sentences.

◆ Some composers put notes down as rapidly as their hands can move across the paper, others write and rewrite slowly.

◆ In earlier centuries most composers were employed by churches or noblemen now they are usually employed by universities.

2. Use a semicolon to show a close relation between the main clauses.

◆ Some athletes work out four hours a day, others work out four days a week.

◆ For centuries, artists didn't just reimagine history sometimes they wrote its first draft.

NOTE: When two main clauses are joined by a conjunctive adverb—such as *nevertheless, consequently, however,* or *therefore*—a semicolon must come before the clause containing the conjunctive adverb. (See note on conjunctive adverbs, 67g.)

◆ In earlier centuries most composers were employed by churches or noblemen, however, now they are usually employed by universities.

3. Use a comma and a coordinating conjunction to show the appropriate relation between main clauses. (See coordinating conjunctions, 67g.)

◆ Painting history was drudgery, *and* all too often it showed.

◆ She manages a career, a family, and the household assets, *but* she is still the average woman.

4. Use a subordinating conjunction to introduce the less important clause. (See subordinating conjunctions, 67g.)

◆ *Although* Hart has an extensive collection of toy soldiers, he still spends more time searching for classic comic books.

◆ *Even though* Mary Barkenwagen used to fear the unknown, now she faces challenges joyfully.

Exercise 28.1: Identify and Correct Run-on Sentences

Label each sentence as correct (C), fused (FS), or containing a comma splice (CS). Correct the fused sentences and comma splices in any of the four ways listed in the text.

1. Although she has studied for only two years, Laurie has already earned a black belt in aikido.

2. The meeting place for aikido practice is called a dojo the teacher is called the sensei.

3. The students at Laurie's dojo work hard, many practice two or three hours every day.

4. Some of the movements are difficult to master however, everyone improves with practice.

5. Each movement is demonstrated by the sensei, he repeats the demonstration in slow motion.

6. Aikido is a fairly new martial art, it was developed in this century by Ueshiba Morihei of Japan.

7. The aikido form of self-defense involves neutralizing an attacker's power and causing him to become the victim of his own momentum.

8. Aikido students learn they do not need strength to repel an attack they use the attacker's strength against him.

9. Each training session begins with warm-up and stretching exercises then the students practice a movement until they can perform it in a smooth, seemingly effortless, motion.

10. By applying the physical and philosophical aspects of aikido to their daily lives, students learn self-defense and self-control.

Exercise 28.2: Correcting Run-on Sentences

Correct the ten comma splices or fused sentences in the following paragraph.

Jazz is an American form of music that is difficult to define there are many kinds of jazz. Almost any popular music can be played as a jazz piece such an interpretation gives it a special swing or jump. Jazz musicians take the basic idea of a piece they are playing and change it to fit a personal style personal touch is known as improvisation, consequently jazz musicians can speak directly to their audience. Jazz rhythms are syncopated they have a bounce to them stressing weak beats is at the heart of this rhythm. When jazz first started, it was always improvised. With the popularity of large dance bands that developed later, jazz arrangements were written down, at least for portions of the selection, nevertheless, individual performers improvised solos between the arranged sections. Arranging jazz is difficult it is almost impossible to write everything down on paper, individual performers must rely on their feelings at the moment to supply the rest. Each band has its own style, therefore a new performer must fit his or her personal style to the group.

29 Examine Subject-Verb Agreement *agr*

When a word refers to one person or thing it is *singular* in number. When a word refers to more than one person or thing, it is *plural* in number.

SINGULAR	PLURAL
person	people
woman	women
ox	oxen

this	these
either	both
he, she, it	they

A verb must always agree with its subject in number. Singular subjects take singular verbs.

> A jet lands every four minutes.

> The winner was carried from the field.

Plural subjects take plural verbs.

> Jets land every four minutes.

> The winners were carried from the field.

When a verb immediately follows a subject, you will probably have little trouble making them agree. But sometimes you'll write a sentence in which a subject or its number may be hard to identify.

29a Make verbs agree with their subjects even when other words intervene

Words coming between a verb and its subject often obscure an agreement error. Usually these words will modify a subject and include a noun that seems to be the subject but is not. By reading the sentence without the modifying words, you will usually be able to spot the agreement error.

◆ Archery [as practiced by Zen masters] require^s concentration.

◆ The detectives [working with the witness] ~~was~~ *were* expected to solve

  the theft immediately.

Expressions such as *together with, as well as, in addition to, accompanied by,* and *along with* do not make a singular noun plural.

◆ The major [accompanied by four scouts] ~~are~~ *was* traveling west.

29b Examine compound subjects to determine if they take a plural or a singular verb

When two or more subjects are joined by a coordinating conjunction such as *and* and *or,* they form a compound subject. Compound subjects joined by *and* usually take a plural verb.

◆ Spiritual growth and psychological insight among artists ~~is~~ *are* not

  uncommon.

An exception to this guideline comes when the parts of a compound subject function as a single idea or refer to a single person or thing. In these cases the subject should take a singular verb.

◆ Meat and potatoes, once a staple of American cuisine, ~~are~~ *is* banished from low-fat diets.

◆ The Stars and Stripes wave*s* over the battlefield.

When a compound subject is preceded by *each* or *every*, the verb should be singular. Although these words refer to more than one, they imply consideration of one at a time.

◆ Every hotel, bed and breakfast, and campground ~~are~~ *is* filled.

When a compound subject is followed by *each*, the verb should be plural.

◆ Diplomacy and threat each require skilled execution.

When a compound subject is joined by *or* or *nor*, make the verb agree with the part of the subject nearer to the verb.

◆ The James Boys or Billy the Kid ~~are~~ *is* the Wild West's most written about outlaws.

Even though the preceding sentence is now correct, it does not sound right. Better to correct such a sentence by rearranging the order of the compound subject so it rings truer in a reader's mind. *Billy the Kid or the James Boys are the Wild West's most written about outlaws.*

◆ Neither the atomic bomb nor space flights ~~has~~ *have* influenced human events as powerfully as the Bill of Rights.

29c Generally, use singular verbs with indefinite pronouns as subjects

Indefinite pronouns refer to unspecified subjects. Most indefinite pronouns—such as *everyone, someone, no one, everything, anybody, neither,* and *something*—are singular and take singular verbs.

◆ Most everyone in Utah support*s* keeping 22 million acres of wilderness.

◆ Neither partner, GM nor IBM, ~~are~~ *is* discussing the agreement.

A few indefinite pronouns—such as *all, any, none,* and *some*—may be singular or plural. Whether you use a singular or a plural verb depends on the number of the noun that the indefinite pronoun refers to.

◆ The judge announced that all of the jury ~~was~~ were present.

◆ The judge said that all of the report ~~were~~ was helpful.

29d Use singular or plural verbs with collective nouns depending on how the nouns are used and with nouns ending in -*s*

Collective nouns—such as *army, audience, class, committee, faculty, group, herd, public,* and *team*—are singular even though they name groups of individuals. When referring to a group as a single unit, a collective noun takes a singular verb.

◆ The American public eventually sees the truth.

When you wish to draw attention to individual members of the group, a collective noun will take a plural verb.

◆ The faculty argue among themselves in department meetings.

Treat units of measurement like singular collective nouns when they refer to a single unit. *By mid-game one-third of the crowd was gone. Five dollars is the cost of a ticket.*

Most nouns that are plural in form but singular in meaning take singular verbs. Nouns such as *athletics, civics, economics, mathematics, measles, mumps, news, physics,* and *species* are singular and take singular verbs.

◆ Mumps in adults ~~are~~ is dangerous.

Words like *trousers* and *scissors* are regarded as plural and take plural verbs, except when used after *pair.*

◆ This pair of socks ~~have~~ has holes in the toes.

29e Examine miscellaneous subject-verb agreement problems

A verb must agree with its subject even when the subject follows the verb. Verbs generally follow subjects; when the subject-verb word order is reversed, examine the sentence to see that the subject and the verb agree.

◆ In the back of his mind <s>is</s> *are* the pain of abuse and the joy of

recovery.

Do not mistake the expletives *there* and *here* for subjects. They merely signal that the subject follows the verb.

There are several strong points in his argument.

Be sure the verb following *who, which,* and *that* agrees with its subject. *Who, which,* and *that* are relative pronouns; the words they refer to are called *antecedents.* When a relative pronoun serves as a subject, the verb must agree with the pronoun's antecedent.

◆ Wind that blow*s* over the peaks create*s* massive snow plumes.

In a sentence that uses *one of the,* examine its meaning to determine if the verb should be singular or plural.

◆ He is one of the critics who <s>is</s> *are* joining the argument.

The antecedent of *who* is *critics,* not *one.*

◆ He is the only one of the critics who care*s.*

The antecedent of *who* is *one.*

Use a singular verb when its subject is a title or words named as words.

◆ *Six Days and Seven Nights* seem*s* to last at least that long.

◆ *Chitlins* refer*s* to pig intestines used as food.

Exercise 29.1: Correct Subject-Verb Agreement Errors

In the following sentences, correct any errors in subject and verb agreement. If you find a correct sentence, mark it with a C.

1. A total of over $400 million were spent to turn the Meadowlands marsh in New Jersey into a sports and entertainment complex.

2. Every wireless phone package are not the same.

3. The committee are expected to announce the decision today.

4. There is at least three different breeds of dog at the dog run.

5. If you look at the map, you will see there is three different routes the mail carrier have to cover each day.

6. Our children is the only hope we have for the future.

7. Either the students or the teacher order the theater tickets every month.

8. All of the seventeen-page information booklet are required reading.

9. The senator commented that politics are the art of the possible.

10. Where is the pants I bought last weekend?

11. The only chance we have to win rest with the point guards.

12. Managers respect the advice of employees who work hard.

13. Every one of the journalism students want to attend the conference.

14. Ham and eggs are a popular American breakfast.

15. Here are a list of all the printing shops in our area.

16. Both Pedro Martinez and Johnny Damon has moved from the Boston Red Sox to a New York team.

17. The police officer as well as the onlookers were applauding the little girl's performance.

18. All the performers are from Brazil, and all the musical selections have a Latin beat.

19. The group argue about the fund-raising activities hour after hour.

20. Jerry Hopkins and his neighbors enjoys the peaceful summer evenings at the lake.

Exercise 29.2: Correct Subject-Verb Agreement Errors

In the following paragraph, correct the errors in subject and verb agreement.

Computerized psychological testing services around the country is gaining widespread use. A report published in recent months indicate that almost everybody taking the tests are pleased by the method. The automated testing proceeds in the following fashion: Sitting before a TV-like screen, a patient answers a group of questions that demands true/false responses or offers multiple-choice answers. Either a psychiatrist or a clinician who has been trained in psychiatry sit in another room and score the data and analyze the results. Immediately following the test, doctor and patient meets to discuss the outcome and plans an initial treatment. Some critics of computerized testing claim the testing dehumanizes the doctor-patient relationship, but neither doctors using the method nor patients undergoing the process seem to agree with the critics.

---

30 Examine Pronoun-Antecedent Agreement *pron agr*

The antecedent of a pronoun is the word or words a pronoun refers to. An antecedent and its pronoun must agree whether they are singular or plural.

SINGULAR   The *director* took *her* cinematographer to Peru.

PLURAL   The *writers* kept working at *their* computers.

30a Examine compound antecedents with care to determine whether to use a plural or singular pronoun

For antecedents joined by *and,* use a plural pronoun.

Hayes and King rearranged *their* priorities.

For compound plural or singular antecedents joined by *or* or *nor,* use a pronoun that agrees with the nearest antecedent.

◆ Once a year, the players or the coach host͡s a banquet at their

favorite restaurant.

When sentences that follow this convention sound awkward or puzzling, writers usually recast them.

◆ Once a year, ~~the players or~~ the coach ^{or the players} host a banquet at their

favorite restaurant.

30b Generally, use a singular pronoun to refer to an indefinite pronoun that functions as an antecedent

Indefinite pronouns refer to nonspecific persons or things.

anybody	either	everything	no one
anyone	everybody	neither	someone
each	everyone	none	something

Although they may seem to be plural, indefinite pronouns are treated as singular antecedents in writing.

◆ Every one of the women donated time to ~~their~~ ^{her} favorite

charities.

◆ Everybody passing through the office offered ~~their~~ ^{his} advice.

Traditional grammar used the masculine pronoun *his (he)* to refer to persons of either sex when the gender of the antecedent was unknown. This practice, however, reflects a sexual bias in English. To offset the bias, use *his or her (he or she)* in place of a masculine pronoun. Or you may rewrite the sentence to reflect the same meaning.

◆ Everybody passing through the office offered his ^{or her} advice.

◆ Everybody passing through the office offered ~~his~~ advice.

30c Generally, use a singular pronoun to refer to collective nouns

Collective nouns include words such as *army, audience, class, committee, group, herd, jury, public,* and *team.* Even though they identify a class or a group having many members, collective nouns are usually singular because the members are seen to be acting as a single unit.

◆ The jury of five women and seven men spoke with one voice. ~~They~~ ^{It} declared the defendant guilty as charged.

When a passage makes clear that the members of a group are acting individually, use a plural pronoun.

◆ The jury ~~members~~ could not agree. ~~It~~ ^{They} deliberated for three

days before the judge declared a mistrial.

30d Use a singular pronoun to refer to a generic noun

Generic nouns refer to typical members of a group. They are always singular.

◆ A law student must study hours every night if ~~they are~~ ^{he or she is} to

graduate.

Such a sentence can also be recast to reflect the same meaning.

◆ A law student must study hours every night if they are to

graduate.

◆ A law student must study hours every night ~~if they are~~ to

graduate.

30e Use accurate pronouns with *who, whom, which,* and *that*

Who refers to persons and sometimes to animals that have been named in the passage.

> *Armando, who* lives in New Mexico, once worked as a guide to the Carlsbad Caverns.

> *Lassie* was the first Hollywood dog *who* had a fan club.

Which refers to things or places and unnamed animals.

> *Darby, which* has become a yuppie retreat, is located on the Bitter Root River in Montana.

> Tony's *cat, which* is highly curious, disappeared for two weeks.

Whose, the possessive form of *who,* can be used to refer to animals and things to avoid awkward constructions using *of which.*

◆ This is a riddle ~~the~~ *whose* answer ~~of which~~ no longer interests me.

◆ *Okay* is a word ~~the~~ *whose* origin ~~of which~~ puzzles linguists.

That also refers to things or places, unnamed animals, and sometimes to persons when they are collective or anonymous.

> The dry *hills that* border Los Angeles ignite easily when the Santa Ana winds sweep Southern California.

> The *earthquake faults that* run under Los Angeles are dangerously active.

EDITOR'S TOOLBOX

Grammar Checkers and Sentence Errors

Grammar-checking features may or may not raise red flags—and that's the problem you face when using one. Too often they fail to identify errors, and too often the errors they identify are correct.

- Grammar checkers do not flag errors in parallel structure because computers cannot assess whether ideas are parallel in meaning.
- Grammar checkers cannot identify most missing words, although they can sometimes flag some missing verbs and articles.
- Grammar checkers cannot flag errors in modifiers (such as dangling modifiers).
- Grammar checkers cannot flag shifts in verb tense, mood, or voice.
- Grammar checkers tend to flag most sentence fragments and run-on sentences but not all of them. Sometimes they flag correct sentences as incorrect.

The best practice is to develop your own understanding of common sentence errors. Then you can serve as your own grammar checker.

Exercise 30.1: Make Antecedents and Pronouns Agree

Correct the antecedent-pronoun errors in each of the following sentences. If a sentence is correct, mark it with a C.

1. Sophie got a new kitten, and she feels very much at home already.

2. Brooke and Daria both have new bikes, and hers has six gears.

3. Both groups bought its own supplies.

4. Skiers must select his or her equipment carefully.

5. Everyone passed their exam.

6. Anyone who cares about their grade will study every day.

7. Every family in our neighborhood takes good care of their lawn.

8. Neither the sales force nor the manager received their instructions on time.

Exercise 30.2: Make Antecedents and Pronouns Agree

Rewrite the following sentences according to the directions in brackets. Be sure to make all the changes necessary to keep the agreement of pronouns and antecedents correct.

1. The catalog and the schedule of classes contain the registration information you are seeking. [Change *and* to *or.*]

2. The counselors agree that English composition should be taken in the first year of college. [Change *The counselors* to *Each counselor.*]

3. Each year the dean or the president has her portrait painted by an outstanding art student. [Change *or* to *and.*]

4. The board of trustees submitted its proposals yesterday. [Change *The board of trustees* to *Some members of the board of trustees.*]

5. Someone attending the mother-and-daughter banquet forgot her coat. [Change *mother-and-daughter* to *father-and-son.*]

6. Either the crew or the rugby team uses the weight room on Monday afternoons. [Change *Either . . . or* to *and.*]

7. The class, which usually meets on Wednesday, forgot that it had agreed to meet on Saturday. [Change *The class* to *Some class members.*]

8. By using attractive visual displays, the business manager or the budget committee chairman can communicate his plans for spending tax money wisely. [Change *budget committee chairman* to *members of the budget committee.*]

9. The bear mascot, which is paraded at all home games, was donated to the university by the game wardens' association. [Change *The bear mascot* to *Bruno, the bear mascot*.]

10. Students who study every evening will perform well on examinations. [Change *Students* to *Anyone*.]

---

31   Check Pronoun Reference   *ref*

Pronoun reference refers to the relation between a pronoun and its antecedent. (See antecedent, 67b; agreement of pronoun and antecedent, Chapter 30.) If the pronoun reference is unclear, the sentence will confuse or misinform a reader.

31a   Avoid using a pronoun to make a broad reference to an entire sentence or clause

Sometimes inexperienced writers use *this, that,* or *it* to refer to an entire sentence or clause, which can create confusion. Rewrite such references or use a summary noun for clarification.

◆ *I needed the sense of mystery*
   ~~Mystery is what~~ I felt during my nightly walks through the
   streets of Paris. ~~That is what I needed.~~

◆ Mystery is what I felt during my nightly walks through the
   This feeling was
   streets of Paris. ~~That is~~ what I needed.
               ^

◆ Good managers know when to delegate responsibility. This ‸ *knowledge*
   allows them to concentrate on the broader aspects of a project.

◆ Good managers know when to delegate responsibility‸ *which* ~~This~~
                                                        ^
   allows them to concentrate on the broader aspects of a project.

31b   Avoid the indefinite use of *it, they,* and *you*

In conversation *it* and *they* are often used to make vague reference to people or situations. In writing, use more precise identification.

VAGUE	*It* is said that gold prices are rising.
CLEAR	Today's newspaper predicted that gold prices will rise further this year.
VAGUE	*They* said it would rain tomorrow.
CLEAR	The KTTV weather forecaster predicts rain.

You is commonly used in conversation to refer vaguely to people in general. In writing, however, use the more formal *one* or the less formal *a person* or *people*. *You* should be used as a personal pronoun.

VAGUE	When traveling in a foreign country, *you* should respect local customs.
CLEAR	When traveling in a foreign country, a person should respect local customs.

The use of *you* to refer to "you, the reader" is perfectly appropriate in all but the most formal writing.

> If you plan to become a history teacher, *you* should begin *your* education by reading Herodotus.

31c Make a pronoun refer clearly to one antecedent

CONFUSING	After Yoshi studied with Kim for a week, she discovered that she still did not understand calculus.
CLEAR	After studying with Kim for a week, Yoshi discovered that Kim still did not understand calculus.
CONFUSING	After Carlos bought the shingles and the boards, he discovered they were full of termites.
CLEAR	After Carlos bought the shingles and the boards, he discovered the shingles were full of termites.
CLEAR	After Carlos bought the shingles and the boards, he discovered the boards were full of termites.
CLEAR	After Carlos bought the shingles and the boards, he discovered that both were full of termites.

31d Use a pronoun ending in *-self* or *-selves* only to refer
to another word in the sentence

Stacy returned the book to the library *herself.*

People who expect riches without effort are fooling *themselves.*

Avoid using pronouns ending in *-self* or *-selves* in place of a grammatically correct pronoun.

◆ Between you and ~~myself~~ *me*, I think our team will win.

Exercise 31.1: Correct Faulty Pronoun References

Correct the faulty pronoun references in the following sentences.
You may need to change words or rewrite entire sentences. For
example:

Mary decided to live with Liz because ~~her~~ *Liz's* roommate had

moved out.

1. Jason gave the notes to Raul that he had taken during the lecture.

2. After hours of lessons, he learned to water-ski, but this didn't impress his girlfriend.

3. I heard they're planning to widen the expressway to eight lanes.

4. Among Jose, you, and myself, the secret will be safe, but if we tell Alberto, we will hurt ourselves.

5. Joe Louis and Rocky Marciano were two great heavyweight boxing champions; however, after Marciano beat him in 1950, he never fought as well again.

6. I sometimes buy clothes at discount stores because they are good values.

7. As the tiny robot approached the cat it started hissing loudly.

8. The enchiladas are for ourselves and the fajitas are for them.

9. Tonya survived the three-car accident, which is evidence of her luck.

10. John changed his major and then had to drop all his classes. That's typical.

Exercise 31.2: Correcting Faulty Pronoun Reference

Rewrite the following sentences to correct faulty pronoun reference.

1. Lena saw a television movie and ate a TV dinner. She enjoyed that.

2. After she saw the movie, she turned it off.

3. Sharlene combed her hair and brushed her teeth. She did it every night.

4. It was going to be cold tomorrow, they said.

5. Rita took her coat and hat from the closet and put it on the couch.

6. Although Al had neither read the novel nor seen the TV movie, he said that he might do it.

7. When you drive on a dark night in the rain, it can be dangerous.

8. They said that they will disconnect our telephone if we do not pay our bill.

9. After Carole and Joanne shared an apartment for a year, she moved.

10. I blame me for not turning it off before the generator's engine ran out.

---

32 Use Appropriate Pronoun Case *case*

The **case** of nouns and pronouns indicates how the words function in a sentence. Nouns and most pronouns have only two case forms (that is, the spelling of the word when it is used in a particular case): the plain form (*day, someone*) and the possessive form (*day's, someone's*).

The pronouns *I, we, he, she, they,* and *who* have three different case forms: the subjective form, the objective form, and the possessive form.

The pronouns *you* and *it* have one form for both the subjective and the objective case and a different form for the possessive case. (See possessive pronouns, 67b.)

	SUBJECTIVE	OBJECTIVE	POSSESSIVE
PERSONAL PRONOUNS			
SINGULAR			
First person	I	me	my, mine
Second person	you	you	your, yours
Third person	he, she, it	him, her, it	his, her, hers, its
PLURAL			
First person	we	us	our, ours
Second person	you	you	your, yours
Third person	they	them	their, theirs
RELATIVE OR INTERROGATIVE PRONOUNS			
SINGULAR	who	whom	whose
PLURAL	who	whom	whose

32a Use the subjective case of pronouns for subjects and for predicate nominatives

Alicia and *I* went shopping. [Subject]

Since Marcus and *he* returned to Detroit, *she* has been lonely. [Subjects]

The scouts who had the most badges were Salvador and *he*. [Predicate nominative]

NOTE: When the subject is a compound, as in *Alicia and I* and *Marcus and he,* beginning writers sometimes become confused about the selection of a pronoun. They would not write *Me went shopping,* but they might write *Alicia and me went shopping.* To avoid this error with compound subjects that include pronouns, try reading each subject separately with the verb.

In speech it is common practice to use the objective forms of personal pronouns as predicate nominatives in expressions beginning with *it is* or *it's: It's me, It is him, It's us, It's them.* Such use of the objective form is unacceptable in writing. Instead use the appropriate subjective pronoun: *It is I, It is he, It is we,* and *It is they.* By carefully examining pronoun use, you will avoid making this common pronoun error. (See linking verb, 67c.)

32b Use the objective case when pronouns are direct objects, indirect objects, and objects of a preposition

Bernie met Naomi and *me* at the museum. [Direct object]

The doorman gave *us* a map of the exhibits. [Indirect object]

A man dressed in a caveman costume sat by *me* on the bench. [Object of a preposition]

Exercise 32.1: Using Subjective and Objective Pronouns

For each of the following sentences, select the correct pronoun from the pair in parentheses. Identify each selected pronoun as a subject (S), a predicate nominative (PN), a direct object (DO), an indirect object (IO), or an object of a preposition (OP).

1. The lecture on Etruscan pottery interested Nguyen and (*I, me*).

2. The ones who laughed the most were Monica and (*she, her*).

3. I know I blushed when Sonia and (*she, her*) sat near (*we, us*).

4. That group's achievement is impressive, but the faculty expected (*they, them*) to excel.

5. Jorge wanted to use the car, so I gave (*he, him*) the keys.

32c Use the appropriate case when the pronoun *we* or *us* comes before a noun

If the pronoun functions as a subject, use *we*.

We linguists meet once a year at a major university. [We meet.]

If the pronoun functions as an object, use *us*.

A number of us mycologists regularly collect mushrooms in the foothills. [A number of us collect.]

32d When a pronoun is used as an appositive, its case depends on the function of the word it refers to

Two chemistry majors, Margarita and *he*, won science foundation awards. [The pronoun refers to *majors*, the subject of the sentence, so it is in the subjective case.]

Science foundation awards received by two chemistry majors, Margarita and him, highlighted the program. [*Majors* is now the object of the preposition *by,* so the pronoun is in the objective case.]

Exercise 32.2: Using Proper Pronoun Case

Select the correct pronoun in each of the following sentences.

1. The artists, (*she, her*) and Shawn, will be at the festival booth all day.

2. (*We, Us*) customers are waiting for the festival to begin.

3. Many of (*we, us*) have been here since seven this morning.

4. The stormy weather ruined the day for the artists, Shawn and (*she, her*).

5. Nevertheless, (*we, us*) early birds enjoyed the chance to see the exhibits.

32e In elliptical, or incomplete, comparisons following *than* or *as,* the case of the pronoun depends on the meaning of the sentence

In comparisons, *than* and *as* often introduce incomplete comparisons. The case of the pronoun in such constructions depends on how the incomplete clause would be completed.

Use the subjective case when the pronoun functions as the subject of the omitted clause.

> I have been studying Spanish longer than *they* [have been studying Spanish].
>
> She works as hard on projects as *he* [works on projects].

Use the objective case when the pronoun functions as the object in the omitted clause.

> For information, I rely on him more than [I rely on] *her.*
>
> I see Ngoc as much as [I see] *him.*

32f Use the objective case for pronouns that are subjects or objects of infinitives

> The attorney considered *him* to be a prime suspect. [Subject of infinitive]

He tried to trap *him* with tough questions. [Object of infinitive]

32g Usually, use the possessive case of a pronoun or noun preceding a gerund

A gerund is the present participle of a verb used as a noun. (See gerund and gerund phrases, 69e.)

What was the reason for his appearing tonight? [*His* modifies the gerund *appearing.*]

Dr. Rodriguez's running for office pleased us all.
[*Dr. Rodriguez's* modifies the gerund *running.*]

The possessive is not used when the present participle serves as an adjective. (See present participles, 69d.)

The crowd watched him tottering on the tightrope.
[*Tottering* is a present participle used as an adjective modifying *him.*]

I often hear Tom talking in his sleep. [*Talking* is a present participle used as an adjective modifying *Tom.*]

Avoid using the possessive with a gerund when doing so creates an awkward construction.

AWKWARD	I am pleased about Nadeem's cooking dinner.
REVISED	I am pleased about Nadeem cooking dinner.
BETTER	I am pleased that Nadeem is cooking dinner.

Exercise 32.3: Using Proper Pronoun Case

Select the correct pronoun for each of the following sentences.

1. The president ordered (*he, him, his*) to be ready at dawn.

2. Do you know the reason for (*he, him, his*) erratic driving?

3. Bok Hee has been more generous than (*they, them, their*).

4. The whole group watched (*he, him, his*) cooking the quesadillas.

5. We wanted to prove (*he, him, his*) wrong.

32h The case of the pronoun *who* is determined by its function in its own clause

You can usually determine which case to use in interrogative sentences by answering the question the sentence poses.

Who led England to victory? [The prime minister led England to victory: subject.]

Whom shall we hold responsible? [We shall hold her responsible: direct object.]

Whom is the letter addressed to? [The letter is addressed to her: object of the preposition *to*.]

In dependent clauses use *who* or *whoever* for all subjects; use *whom* or *whomever* for all objects. The case of the pronoun depends only on its function within the clause, not on the function of the clause in the sentence.

The Sisters of Mercy give help to *whoever* requests it. [*Whoever* is the subject of the clause *whoever requests it*. The entire clause is the object of the preposition *to*.]

I do not remember *whom* I met at the party. [*Whom* is the direct object of *met*. The entire clause *whom I met at the party* is the direct object of the verb *do remember*.]

To determine whether to use *who, whom, whoever,* or *whomever*, substitute a personal pronoun for the relative pronoun. The case of the personal pronoun is the correct case for the relative pronoun. If necessary, change the word order of the clause.

I do not recall (who, whom) I lent the book to.

I lent the book to him (or her). [Objective case]

Therefore, *whom* is the correct relative pronoun:

I do not recall *whom* I lent the book to.

Sometimes a dependent clause includes an expression such as *I think* or *he said*.

She is the woman (who, whom) he said called last night.

To decide between *who* and *whom* in such a construction, repeat the sentence without the intervening expression.

She is the woman *who* called last night.

Exercise 32.4: Using *Who* and *Whom*

Select the correct pronoun in each of the following sentences.

1. The National Book Award will be given to (*whoever, whomever*) the committee chooses.
2. With (*who, whom*) shall I file my report?
3. (*Who, Whom*) will download the files?
4. The honor goes to (*whoever, whomever*) I select.
5. The master is loved most by those (*who, whom*) share his beliefs.

33 Select Accurate Verb Forms and Tense *verb*

Every verb has three principal forms: the infinitive (the plain form of the verb), the past, and the past participle.

Verb Forms

INFINITIVE	PAST	PAST PARTICIPLE
dance	danced	danced

The **infinitive** form of the verb usually appears in combination with *to*, forming a verbal that functions as a noun, an adjective, or an adverb (see 69c). A **participle** is a verbal that functions as an adjective, an adverb, or a part of a verb phrase (see 69d).

All verbs form the **present participle** by adding *-ing* to the infinitive form. Neither a present participle nor a past participle can function as the verb in a sentence unless it is combined with one or more helping verbs.

Any verb may be combined with helping (or auxiliary) verbs to express time relations and other meanings. *Shall* and *will; have, has,* and *had; do, does,* and *did;* and forms of the verb *be* (*am, are, is, was, were, been, being*) are helping verbs used to indicate time and voice. (See tense, 33a; voice, Chapter 35.) *Can, could, may, might, must, ought, shall, should, will,* and *would* are helping verbs used to indicate necessity, obligation, permission, or possibility.

You *could* learn to ski.

You *must* attend.

She *should* know better.

Verbs have either regular or irregular forms. A regular verb forms its past and past participle by adding *-d* or *-ed* to the infinitive.

INFINITIVE	PAST	PAST PARTICIPLE
live	lived	lived
jump	jumped	jumped

An **irregular verb** forms its past and past participle in a different way from regular verbs. This difference may involve a change in spelling or no change at all from the infinitive form. Spelling changes usually involve a change in vowels or the addition of an *-n* or *-en* ending.

INFINITIVE	PAST	PAST PARTICIPLE
swim	swam	swum
throw	threw	thrown
hit	hit	hit

The major difficulty you will confront in the use of irregular verbs is in selecting the correct past or past participle form. When in doubt, consult a dictionary. If a verb is regular, the dictionary does not include the past and past participle. If the verb is irregular, the dictionary includes the irregular forms.

IRREGULAR VERBS

INFINITIVE	PAST	PAST PARTICIPLE
begin	began	begun
bite	bit	bitten
blow	blew	blown
break	broke	broken
bring	brought	brought
catch	caught	caught
choose	chose	chosen
come	came	come
creep	crept	crept
dig	dug	dug
dive	dived or dove	dived
do	did	done
draw	drew	drawn
dream	dreamed or dreamt	dreamed or dreamt

drink	drank	drunk
drive	drove	driven
eat	ate	eaten
fall	fell	fallen
feel	felt	felt
find	found	found
fit	fit or fitted	fit or fitted
fling	flung	flung
fly	flew	flown
fly (baseball)	flied	flied
forbid	forbade or forbad	forbidden
forget	forgot	forgotten or forgot
get	got	got or gotten
go	went	gone
hurt	hurt	hurt
know	knew	known
lay (place or put)	laid	laid
lead	led	led
lend	lent	lent
lie (recline)	lay	lain
light	lighted or lit	lighted or lit
lose	lost	lost
pay	paid	paid
ride	rode	ridden
rise	rose	risen
run	ran	run
say	said	said
see	saw	seen
set (place or put)	set	set
shine	shone or shined	shone or shined
shoot	shot	shot
sing	sang or sung	sung
sink	sank or sunk	sunk
sit (take a seat)	sat	sat
sleep	slept	slept
steal	stole	stolen
sting	stung	stung
swim	swam	swum
tear	tore	torn
throw	threw	thrown
wear	wore	worn
win	won	won
write	wrote	written

Exercise 33.1: Practice Using Irregular Verbs

Working with another student, test yourself on the principal forms of the irregular verbs in the list above.

Exercise 33.2: Look Up Irregular Verbs

Use a dictionary to determine the correct forms of the irregular verbs necessary to complete each sentence.

1. We knew the strawberries _____ a great deal, but we had _____ to love them. (*cost, grow*)

2. By the time we _____ for the airport, he had _____ less nervous. (*leave, become*)

3. The parents had _____ a slide and _____ it to the children. (*build, give*)

4. We had _____ our views, but they had not _____ them. (*speak, hear*)

5. I had just _____ the window when the sky _____ up. (*shut, light*)

Verb Tense

Verb forms change to show the time of the action they express. The change in time (past, present, or future) is called *tense*.

33a The present tense expresses action about something occurring now, at the present time

I *believe* you.

The light from below *creates* huge shadows on the wall.

The present tense also serves special functions in writing:
Use the present tense to state a general truth or fact.

Automobiles *require* fuel.

A yard *equals* thirty-six inches.

Use the present tense to state what a writer does in his or her written work or to describe a character's activities in a written work.

Tonya *argues* for mandatory installation of air bags.

The hero *discovers* the truth about the Lost Canyon Mine.

Use the present tense to describe elements in artistic works.

In *Mishima,* Eiko Ishioka's designs *intrigue* the audience.

The nonsensical conversation in Philip's stories *makes* readers uncomfortable.

Use the present tense to state habitual action.

She *studies* in the library every day.

Jeff always *keeps* his car sparkling clean.

Use the infinitive form with *do* to create emphasis.

I *do get up* early!

NOTE: In all tenses you can show continuing action by using the **progressive tense,** which is the present participle of the verb together with a form of the helping verb *be.*

Li-Ching *is attending* Kettler College.

33b The past tense expresses action that occurred in the past and does not continue into the present

I *slipped* on the icy street several times.

I *was slipping* on the ice when he grabbed my arm.

Use the infinitive form with *did* to create an emphatic form.

I *did slip* on the ice.

NOTE: Past action may be shown in other ways.

I *used to slip* on the icy streets.

33c The future tense expresses action about something that will happen in the future

The visitors from Oxford *will debate* four of our prelaw students next week.

The visitors from Oxford *will be debating* four of our prelaw students next week.

NOTE: Future action may be shown in other ways.

The visitors from Oxford *are going* to debate four of our prelaw students next week.

The visitors from Oxford and four of our prelaw students *are* about to debate.

33d The present perfect tense expresses action occurring at no definite time in the past or action occurring in the past and continuing into the present

Environmentalists *have enlisted* the help of sensitive businesspeople. [The action has not occurred at a specific time in the past.]

Environmentalists *have been enlisting* the help of sensitive businesspeople. [The progressive form indicates that the past action continues into the present.]

33e The past perfect tense expresses action completed in the past before another past action occurred

I *had flown* in a glider before I flew in a single-engine Cessna. [Flying in the glider preceded flying in the Cessna.]

After I *had been flying* for three months, I gave it up. [Flying for three months preceded giving it up.]

33f The future perfect tense expresses action that will be completed in the future before another action occurs

By the end of the year 2011, the Galaxy Probe *will have traveled* through space for fifteen years.

By the end of the year 2011, the Galaxy Probe *will have been traveling* through space for fifteen years.

33g Use an appropriate sequence of verb tenses

Sequence of verb tenses refers to the time relation expressed by verbs in main clauses and verbs in dependent clauses, infinitives, or participles. In the sentence *The crowd cheered when he served an ace,* the past tense of the verb *cheer* (*cheered*) is in sequence with the past tense of the verb *serve* (*served*). (See subordinate clauses, 70b; verbals and verbal phrases, 69c and 69d.)

Dependent Clauses

When the verb in the main clause of a complex sentence is in any tense other than the past or past perfect, make the verb tense in the dependent clause consistent with the meaning of the sentence.

> Our political leaders hope that we will decrease our dependence on foreign oil significantly by the year 2015. [The sequence moves from the present tense, *hope,* in the main clause to the future tense, *will decrease,* in the dependent clause.]

> The president of the company will visit our department after she has met with the board. [The sequence moves from the future tense, *will visit,* in the main clause to the present perfect tense, *has met,* in the dependent clause.]

> Kayla will change her major because she thinks that the computer field will soon be too crowded. [The sequence moves from the future tense, *will change,* in the main clause to the present tense, *thinks,* and the future tense, *will be,* in the dependent clauses.]

When the verb in the main clause is in the past or past perfect tense, use the past or past perfect tense in the dependent clause, except when the dependent clause is a general truth.

> The pianist blushed as the audience cheered. [Past tense in both the main clause and the dependent clause]

> The scout troop had sold a hundred coupons before the Christmas trees even arrived. [Past perfect tense in the main clause and past tense in the dependent clause]

> The visitors from Taiwan soon learned that Americans love Chinese food. [Although the verb in the main clause is in the past tense, the verb in the dependent clause is in the present tense because *Americans love Chinese food* is a general truth not related to a specific time.]

Infinitives

Use the **present infinitive,** which is composed of the plain form of the verb preceded by *to* (as in *to dance, to sing, to grow*), to express action that takes place at the same time as or later than that of the verb in the main clause. Use the **present perfect infinitive,** which is composed of *to have* followed by a past participle (as in *to have danced, to have sung, to have grown*), to express action that takes place before that of the verb in the main clause. (See infinitives, 69c.)

> Last July I wanted to attend summer school. [Present infinitive: Action takes place at the same time as that of the main verb, *wanted.*]

> They hoped to go. They hope to go. [Present infinitive: Action takes place at a time later than the main verbs, *hoped* and *hope.*]

> Maurice would like to have entered last week's race. [Present perfect infinitive: Action takes place before that of the main verb, *would like.* Note that *to enter,* the present infinitive, is not the correct form.]

> Maurice would have liked to enter last week's race. [Present infinitive: Action takes place at the same time as that of the main verb, *would have liked.*]

Participles

Use the **present participle** to express action that takes place at the same time as that of the main verb. Use the **past participle** or the **present perfect participle** to express action that takes place earlier than that of the main verb. (See present participle, 69d.)

> Running in the woods, he felt free of worries. [Present participle: The running occurs at the same time as the feeling.]

> Encouraged by friends, Pat decided to attend college. [Past participle: The encouragement took place before the decision.]

> Having danced all night, Maria slept past noon. [Present perfect participle: The dancing took place before the sleeping.]

Exercise 33.3: Use Correct Verb Forms

Select the verb form that is in sequence with the other verb or verbs in each of the following sentences.

1. The sudden ringing of the alarm clock reminded me that I (*have, had*) an appointment with the dentist in a few hours.

2. I am confident that I (*can, could*) pass the next history test.

3. I know that she will call me if she (*is, will be*) visiting the campus on her next trip.

4. Turning the corner to Rose Street, the mail carrier remembered that she (*had been, was*) bitten by a dog on this street.

5. (*Finishing, Having finished*) his shopping, Larry went to the Red Lion Inn for lunch.

6. The chief engineer will conduct further tests himself because he (*doubts, doubted*) that the first report (*is, was*) accurate.

7. Harold wrote his library report on Alice Walker because he (*knows, knew*) she (*wrote, writes*) with compassion and insight.

8. Rosa told Felipe that she (*will be, would be*) studying in the library last Friday.

9. His experiments proved that water (*boiled, boils*) at 212° F.

10. When I saw the movie, I thought that I (*will be, would be*) more frightened than I (*had been, was*).

Exercise 33.4: Practicing Past Tense

Rewrite the following paragraph as if you were living in the twenty-second century and the events had happened in the past. Change verb tenses wherever necessary. Your opening sentence will read:

> Years ago throughout Orange County, visitors seemed unable to tell where fantasy ended and real life began.

> Throughout Orange County, visitors seem unable to tell where fantasy ends and real life begins. One reason is theme architecture, which accounts for perhaps as much as 60 percent of the county's buildings. Within the county you can find triplex homes that look like English Tudor mansions, restaurants that look like a French chateau or a Mississippi riverboat, and a motel that resembles a Persian mosque. Theme architecture adds a dash of Disneyland to most neighborhoods. Visitors can travel from one exotic land to another within a few blocks. The variety bewilders visitors, but local residents take it in stride. The themes divide into several categories. Some homeowners prefer a Spanish mission style. Others choose the Mediterranean look. Still others want Tudor, Cape Cod, or plantation designs. One aspect of all this diversity is tragically real: As developers hack down the orange groves, they replace the trees with glittering fantasy structures.

Exercise 33.5: Practicing Future Tense

Rewrite the following passage as if the events described were going to take place at some time in the future. Change verb tenses wherever necessary. Your opening sentence will begin: Tomorrow's female writer will face . . .

> Today's female writer faces a peculiar confusion because she is susceptible to the images of women in literature. She goes to poetry or fiction looking for her role in the world, but she is disappointed. She is looking for guides, models, possibilities. But what she finds are many images of women in works by men. She discovers a terror and a dream. She encounters literary heroines such as a Belle Dame sans Merci and a Daisy Buchanan. She does not find an image of herself, the struggling female writer.

---

34 Use the Appropriate Mood *mood*

The three **moods** of a verb indicate a writer's intent. The **indicative mood,** the one most frequently used, states a fact or an opinion or asks a question. The **imperative mood** gives a command or direction (usually with the subject *you* implied: *Be here at ten sharp*). The **subjunctive mood** expresses doubt or uncertainty, a condition contrary to fact, or a wish.

You will rarely have a problem with mood. In fact, the subjunctive mood, which can be problematic, is rarely used in current English. Nevertheless, you should master the remaining forms and the three uses of the subjunctive mood.

Forms of the Subjunctive

In the present tense the subjunctive mood consists of only the infinitive form of the verb no matter what the subject is. (See infinitives, 69c.)

> The choreographer urged that Boris *consider* a ballet career. [Present subjunctive]

> The guidelines demand that procedures *be* in effect tomorrow. [Present subjunctive]

In the past tense the only commonly used subjunctive verb form is *were*.

If I *were* retired, I would live a carefree life. [Past subjunctive]

Uses of the Subjunctive

34a Use the subjunctive form *were* to express a wish and in contrary-to-fact clauses beginning with *if*

I wish she *were* my teacher. [But she is not my teacher: expresses a wish.]

I would be able to finish all my work if the day *were* thirty hours long. [But the day is twenty-four hours long: contrary-to-fact clause.]

34b Use the subjunctive form in *that* clauses following verbs that demand, request, or recommend

Jano's aunt urged *that Brian save the money.*

The attorney asked *that the witness be ready to testify.*

NOTE: Often writers find substitute constructions for the subjunctive in sentences such as those above.

Jano's aunt urged Brian to save the money.

34c Use the subjunctive form in some standard phrases and idioms

Peace *be* with you.

Heaven *forbid!*

Come rain or *come* shine.

So *be* it!

Exercise 34.1: Use the Appropriate Subjunctive Form

Revise the following sentences by using appropriate subjunctive forms.

1. If I was in charge, I would change the way we process health claims.

2. Since the costs of health care have risen steeply, I wish the process was faster and more generous.

3. The present system requires that each department head signs off on the claim before it can be paid.

4. I think the process would be easier and faster if each claim was processed by a single department.

5. People laugh when I suggest these changes, as if I was a standup comic.

6. Meanwhile, people with major health problems wait for months to get reimbursed, when they must be wishing that they got paid right away.

7. If we had a national health care policy, everyone's health costs are covered.

8. That is the most efficient way to do it, if everyone agreed to vote for it.

---

35 Write in Active Rather Than Passive Voice *pass*

Voice is the quality in verbs that shows whether a subject is the actor or is acted upon.

> The Tanaka Construction Company built the Statler Bridge. [The subject *Tanaka Construction Company* is the actor.]

> The Statler Bridge was built by the Tanaka Construction Company. [The subject *Statler Bridge* is being acted upon.]

Effective writing is vigorous and direct. In nearly all circumstances, the active voice achieves vigor and directness better than the passive voice. Consequently, use the active voice except when you do not know the doer of an action or when you want to emphasize the receiver of an action or the action itself.

> Demonstrators from the New Earth Alliance closed the nuclear plant. [Active voice]

> The nuclear plant was closed by demonstrators from the New Earth Alliance. [Passive voice]

These sentences contain the same information, but each emphasizes a different point. The active construction emphasizes the demonstrators because *demonstrators* is the subject. The passive construction emphasizes the nuclear plant because *nuclear plant* is the subject.

Transitive verbs have both active and passive voice. When a verb is in the **active voice,** the subject performs the action and the object receives the action. When a verb is in the **passive voice,** the subject receives the action. (See transitive verb, 67c.)

To form a passive construction, move the direct object of the sentence ahead of the verb; it thus becomes the subject. Use a form of *be* as a helping verb; the actual subject may be contained in a prepositional phrase. (See direct object, 68e.)

> William Faulkner won a Pulitzer Prize in 1963. [Active voice]
>
> A Pulitzer Prize was won by William Faulkner in 1963. [Passive voice: The direct object from the previous sentence, *Pulitzer Prize,* becomes the subject; *was* is added to the verb *won;* and the subject of the previous sentence, *William Faulkner,* becomes the object of the preposition *by.*]

Active sentences that have direct objects often have indirect objects also. When rewritten in a passive construction, either the direct object or the indirect object can become the subject, and the actual subject can be dropped. (See indirect object, 68e.)

> The committee awarded Thuy a scholarship. [Active voice]
>
> Thuy was awarded a scholarship. [Passive voice: Indirect object, *Thuy,* becomes the subject; the original subject, *committee,* is dropped.]
>
> A scholarship was awarded to Thuy. [Passive voice: Direct object, *scholarship,* becomes the subject; the original subject, *committee,* is dropped.]

Although the meaning of each of the above sentences is the same, as the subject changes so does the emphasis: from the committee to Thuy to a scholarship. The choice depends on the writer's intention.

In most situations, use the active voice for several reasons:
The active voice is more concise.

> An ancient soothsayer predicts the end of the world. [Active voice: nine words]
>
> The end of the world is predicted by an ancient soothsayer. [Passive voice: eleven words]

The active voice emphasizes the actual subject and is therefore more direct.

The detectives who investigated the case earned the admiration of their fellow officers. [Active voice]

The admiration of their fellow officers was earned by the detectives who investigated the case. [Passive voice]

The active voice is more forceful.

Starks rifled a pass to Ewing under the basket. [Active voice]

A pass was rifled to Ewing under the basket by Starks. [Passive voice]

The passive voice is appropriate in several situations:
When you do not know the doer of the action.

The clubhouse was left a shambles, and the parking lot was littered with cans and garbage.

When you want to emphasize the receiver of the action.

Tomaso was wounded by falling bricks.

When you want to emphasize the action itself.

A curved incision was made behind the hairline so the scar would be concealed when the hair grew back.

Exercise 35.1: Revise to Make Passive Sentences Active

Revise the following sentences by changing passive voice to active voice.

1. The warehouse was destroyed by fire.

2. Fortunately, or suspiciously, the paintings had been removed by the owner the day before.

3. One woman was seriously burned by falling cinders.

4. She was rushed to the emergency room by the paramedics.

5. It was reported by the fire chief that the fire was set deliberately.

6. Copies of the proposed fire guidelines were provided by the safety committee.

7. The repairs on the warehouse were done by an inexperienced contractor.

8. A detailed rendering for a new building was submitted by an architect.

9. An award is to be given to the architect by the Fine Arts Association.

10. The awards banquet will be sponsored by Arnald Forde, a well-known art collector.

Exercise 35.2: Change Passive Voice to Active Voice

Rewrite the following passage, changing the passive constructions into active constructions.

> A poison ivy rash is considered by some to be humorous. But it is not funny at all. A rash that has the intensity of a fresh mosquito bite and lasts for several days is caused by contact with the plant. The poison ivy reaction has been studied by scientists for centuries, but no preventive pill or inoculation has been found. The poisonous substance in the plant is called urushiol. After the skin has been touched by urushiol, the exposed area will soon be covered by blisters and weeping sores.
>
> What can you do after coming into contact with poison ivy? First, the urushiol should be washed off as soon as possible. Any available hand soap and plenty of scrubbing should be used. Then take a cold shower and soap yourself all over. The course of the reaction seems to be shortened by cold water. Finally, see a doctor.

36 Select Adjectives and Adverbs with Care *adj/adv*

Adjectives and adverbs are frequently misused in writing. Errors involving adjectives and adverbs are easy to correct once you understand how the words function in a sentence.

Adjectives modify nouns and pronouns. Adverbs can modify verbs, adjectives, and other adverbs. You can form adverbs by adding *-ly* to adjectives (*rapid, rapidly; complete, completely; happy, happily; desperate, desperately*). But not all words ending in *-ly* are adverbs; some are adjectives (*womanly, lonely, saintly*). Some adverbs and adjectives have the same form (*well, late, early*), and some adverbs have two forms (*slow, slowly; quick, quickly; cheap, cheaply*).

36a Use adjectives to modify nouns and pronouns; use adverbs to modify verbs, adjectives, and other adverbs

An adjective modifies a noun or a pronoun.

> José is a *swift* runner.
>
> I prefer the *checkered* one.

An adverb, not an adjective, modifies a verb.

> José ran *swiftly*.

An adverb, not an adjective, modifies an adjective.

> José is *terribly* swift.

An adverb, not an adjective, modifies an adverb.

> José ran *very* swiftly.

36b Use an adjective after a linking verb to refer to the subject; use an adverb to refer to the verb

The most common linking verb is *be* and its forms—*am, are, is, was, were,* and *been*. Other common linking verbs include *seem, appear, become, grow, remain, prove,* and *turn,* along with verbs of the senses—*feel, look, smell, hear, taste*. When these verbs link the subject with a modifier, use an adjective as the modifier. When the modifier describes the verb, use an adverb.

> The climber felt *uneasy* about the darkening sky. [Adjective: *Uneasy* describes the climber.]
>
> The climber felt *uneasily* for a firm handhold. [Adverb: *Uneasily* describes how the climber used a hand to find a firm place to grip.]

36c After a direct object, use an adjective to modify the object; use an adverb to modify the verb

> The judges ranked the wine *excellent*. [Adjective: *Excellent* describes wine.]
>
> She revised her papers *thoroughly*. [Adverb: *Thoroughly* describes revised.]

36d Use the words *bad* and *badly* and *good* and *well* correctly

Bad is an adjective; *badly* is an adverb. Since verbs of the senses—*feel, look, smell, hear, taste*—require adjectives to modify the subjects, use *bad*, not *badly*, after them.

> The diners felt *bad* after the third course.
>
> The rendering plant smells *bad* this evening.

Good is always an adjective, never an adverb.

INCORRECT	The team played *good* last night.
CORRECT	The team played *well* last night.
CORRECT	The team played a *good* game last night.

Well may be used as either an adjective or an adverb. As an adjective, *well* has three meanings.
To be in good health:

> He seems *well* considering his ordeal.

To be advisable or prudent:

> You would do *well* to study before the test.

To be satisfactory:

> All is *well*.

Exercise 36.1: Selecting Adjectives or Adverbs

Choose the correct word to complete each sentence. Explain the function of each adjective or adverb you select.

1. The band marched (*brisk, briskly*) down the field.
2. Mario felt (*bad, badly*) about the argument.
3. Choosing what car to buy is becoming (*increasing, increasingly*) difficult.
4. The driver considered the route (*safe, safely*).
5. Mai takes a (*brisk, briskly*) walk every morning.
6. The pedestrian looked (*careless, carelessly*) at the traffic.
7. Carlos shook his head (*sympathetic, sympathetically*).

8. It was an (*extreme, extremely*) clever plan.

9. The quarterback executed the play (*well, good*).

10. The pedestrian looked (*careless, carelessly*) standing there.

36e Use the correct forms of adjectives and adverbs when making comparisons

Adjectives and adverbs have three forms or degrees: the **positive,** or plain form, which only describes; the **comparative,** which compares two things; and the **superlative,** which compares three or more things.

The comparative and superlative of most adjectives and adverbs are formed either by adding *-er* and *-est,* respectively, to the positive form or by placing *more* and *most* (or *less* and *least*), respectively, before the positive form.

Using *more* and *most* (or *less* and *least*) is the only way to form the comparative and superlative for most adverbs of two or more syllables and for adjectives of three or more syllables. Some adjectives of two syllables can add either *-er* and *-est* or *more* and *most.*

	POSITIVE	COMPARATIVE	SUPERLATIVE
ADJECTIVES	thick	thicker	thickest
	happy	happier	happiest
	beautiful	more beautiful	most beautiful
		less beautiful	least beautiful
ADVERBS	fast	faster	fastest
	often	more often	most often
	sadly	more sadly	most sadly

A few adjectives and adverbs change their spelling to form the comparative and superlative.

POSITIVE	COMPARATIVE	SUPERLATIVE
bad, badly	worse	worst
good, well	better	best
many, much	more	most
little	littler, less	littlest, least

Use the comparative form to compare two things.

In August the sea seems *bluer* than the sky.

Although the two tours cost the same, the one to Paris will be the *more* exciting.

Her client was *less* anxious today than yesterday.

Use the superlative form to compare three or more things.

Of the three agents, Bozarth has the *deadliest* charm.

Apparently the *most* skilled of all the drivers, Randolph wins nearly every race.

This novel is the *least* interesting in the series.

36f Do not use double comparatives or double superlatives

◆ They are the ~~most~~ happiest couple I know.

36g Do not use comparative or superlative forms with words that cannot logically be compared

Words such as *unique, perfect, dead, empty, infinite,* and *impossible* are absolute. That is, their positive form describes their only state. They cannot, therefore, be compared.

◆ Dr. Nastasi is ~~the most~~ *a* unique surgeon.

Exercise 36.2: Correct Errors in Adjective and Adverb Forms

Identify and correct any errors in the use of adjectives and adverbs in the following sentences.

1. When the four skaters came around the last lap, Apolo Ohno seemed to have the greater stamina.

2. Although he was the same size as the Korean skater, his strides seemed the longest, and he was able to cross over the easiest.

3. Ohno won the 500-meter race in record time, proving to be the fastest short-track skater to win the Olympic gold.

4. After the race, Ohno said, "That was the most perfect race I've ever skated."

5. Whether Ohno was right or wrong, today he was definitely the better skater.

PART VI

Punctuation

My attitude toward punctuation is that it ought to be as conventional as possible. The game of golf would lose a good deal if croquet mallets and billiard cues were allowed on the putting green. You ought to be able to show that you can do it a good deal better than anyone else with the regular tools before you have a license to bring your own improvements.

—Ernest Hemingway, *novelist*

37 Comma ,

The comma is a critical mark of punctuation. It helps the writer show the logical relationships within a sentence by indicating groups of words that belong together and by separating words that do not. If writers fail to group and separate information logically, they risk misguiding the reader.

The comma also has several conventional uses, such as in dates and addresses. Since the comma is the most frequently used, and misused, punctuation mark, you will be well on your way to controlling punctuation errors by mastering its use.

37a Use a comma before a coordinating conjunction joining two main clauses

When a coordinating conjunction—that is, *and, but, or, nor, yet, so,* and *for*—joins two main clauses, place a comma before the coordinating conjunction.

◆ The aging process is relentless, but most of us fight growing
  ^
  old.

◆ Professional athletes begin their careers out of a love for sports,
  and a few keep that love.
                              ^

◆ The road was littered with household goods, for the refugees
  could not carry the extra weight.
                         ^

NOTE: Not every coordinating conjunction in a sentence joins main clauses. Often coordinating conjunctions create compound subjects or compound predicates.

> Every Saturday the lawyer walked seven miles to the widow's cabin *and* chopped a week's supply of firewood for her.

The coordinating conjunction *and* joins two verbs, *walked* and *chopped.* It is incorrect to separate two parts of a compound predicate with a comma.

> We enjoy bagels *and* cream cheese for breakfast.

WRITER'S TOOLBOX

Placing Commas

To test whether you need a comma before *and, but,* or *or,* the most frequently used coordinating conjunctions, place a period before it. Then reread each part, before and after the period, without the conjunction. If each part works as a complete sentence, write your sentence using a comma before *and, but,* or *or.* If not, leave out the comma.

EXAMPLE

The printing press was invented in 1450. [but] only a small percentage of the Western world's population could read.

Because each part works as a sentence, the full sentence needs a comma before *but.*

REVISED

The printing press was invented in 1450, but only a small percentage of the Western world's population could read.

EXAMPLE

Teenagers in the 1950s had no music of their own. [and] no influence in the fashion market.

Because the second part does not work as a sentence, the full sentence does not need a comma before *and.*

REVISED

Teenagers in the 1950s had no music of their own and no influence in the fashion market.

The coordinating conjunction *and* joins two nouns, *bagels* and *cream cheese;* do not use a comma.

Exercise 37.1: Using Commas with Coordinate Main Clauses

Insert a comma before each coordinating conjunction joining main clauses. If a sentence is correct, mark it with a C.

1. The British used the name *America* to refer to the British colonies and the colonists used the term *American* to refer to natives.

2. The emerging country needed to establish a name or it would always be seen as an extension of Europe.

3. In 1697 Cotton Mather popularized the word *American* to mean an English colonist in America and by 1780 our language was called *American*.

4. By 1782 a citizen of the United States was called *American* but the term *Americanism* was not used until 1797.

5. Citizens of the United States call themselves *American* but seldom remember that citizens from other Western Hemisphere countries are also American.

6. Many common names for things have interesting histories but only etymologists, word historians, study them.

7. *Hamburger,* for example, is an interesting word yet few people who eat at McDonald's know its background.

8. Russian Tartars introduced eating shredded raw meat and the practice found its way to Hamburg, Germany. Hamburg residents began cooking the meat so people began calling the result *Hamburg steak.*

9. Hamburg steak appeared in the United States around 1884 and was soon called *hamburger steak.*

10. Soon Americans were putting their hamburger steaks on a bun and *hamburger* came to mean the sandwich.

Exercise 37.2: Commas with Coordinate Main Clauses

Insert a comma before each coordinating conjunction joining main clauses. If a sentence is correct, mark it with a C.

1. Some words are unacceptable and should never be used yet the history of these words shows that they have legitimate beginnings.

2. *Ain't* is such a word and some linguists claim it is a very good and useful word.

3. The use of *ain't* began in England in 1706 and the word was soon used in America.

4. *Ain't* developed as a contraction of *am not* so it was first spelled *an't.*

5. In 1778–1779 *an't* had become *ain't* on both sides of the Atlantic but some New Englanders still pronounced it with a broad *a* like *an't*.

6. By the 1830s *ain't* was still used, but many people had begun to misuse it.

7. *Ain't* was an obvious contraction of *am not* yet people began to use it as a contraction for *is not* and *are not* also.

8. Educated people began to criticize its common use for they believed it was unacceptable in all its forms.

9. Teachers say we are not supposed to use *ain't* anymore yet people still use it.

10. The educated use it with a self-conscious smirk and the uneducated use it naturally.

37b Use a comma to set off introductory phrases and clauses from main clauses

A comma following an introductory clause or phrase shows its subordinate relationship to the information in the main clause.

INTRODUCTORY PREPOSITIONAL PHRASE

◆ By the end of next month, life in this house will change.

◆ On the north shore of Kauki, two sharks attacked surfers.

INTRODUCTORY VERBAL PHRASE

◆ To sail solo around the world, you must have courage.

◆ Beaten by relentless winds, the caravan returned to the oasis.

◆ Diving into the field, the hawk pursued its prey.

INTRODUCTORY CLAUSE

◆ If the Alaska king crab population plummets, crab fishers will be bankrupted.

◆ Whenever heavy rains hit Southern California, hillside homes begin to slide.

Be careful to distinguish verbal modifiers from verbals that function as subjects. Verbal modifiers are usually separated from the main clause by a comma; verbals functioning as subjects never take a comma. (See gerunds and gerund phrases, 69e.)

VERBAL AS MODIFIER

◆ Parachuting from an airplane‸Darryl realized the joy of

floating on the wind.

VERBAL AS SUBJECT

◆ Parachuting from an airplane⸝ is Darryl's favorite pastime.

You may omit a comma after a very short introductory clause or phrase if the omission does not cause a misreading.

CONFUSING	On each weekday morning exercise class begins at six.
CLEAR	On each weekday, morning exercise class begins at six.
CLEAR	In science we need to know when to persevere and when to quit.

Usually no comma is needed to separate adverb clauses placed at the end of a sentence. (See unnecessary commas, Chapter 38.)

◆ Presidential news conferences offer more entertainment than

information⸝ because reporters do not ask pointed questions.

Exercise 37.3: Use Commas with Introductory Clauses and Phrases

Insert commas where needed after introductory phrases and clauses in the following sentences. If a sentence is correct, mark it with a C.

1. In spite of an apparently inexhaustible supply the numbers of wild creatures are being depleted because of greed.

2. If you are tempted to spend $25,000 for a leopard-skin coat remember that each coat requires the pelts of seven animals.

3. Specializing in killing and stuffing a taxidermist in California illegally offered bighorn sheep to wealthy customers.

4. After exposure he confessed and paid a fine.

5. Handicapped by low budgets authorities seem to be losing the battle against poachers.

6. With the help of naturalists, a Senate committee concluded that hunting is viewed as a traditional right in America.

7. To hunt illegally is also part of the tradition.

8. Resorting to historical records hunting enthusiasts point out that poaching on private lands was one way the poor fed themselves during tough times.

9. Hunting endangered species, stuffing them, and selling them as trophies is not the same as hunting for survival.

10. When hunting is done illegally isn't it the responsibility of authorities to arrest those involved?

37c Use a comma or commas to set off nonrestrictive elements; do not set off restrictive elements

A **restrictive element** defines or identifies—that is, it restricts—the meaning of the noun it modifies and is essential to the meaning of the sentence. A **nonrestrictive element** may add important information to a sentence but is not essential to the meaning of the sentence.

> RESTRICTIVE A student who sets academic goals will graduate in four years.

The clause beginning with *who* is essential to the meaning of the sentence. Without the clause, the sentence will say something else: A student will graduate in four years.

> NON-RESTRICTIVE Robin Crisp, who studies five hours daily, will graduate in three years.

The clause beginning with *who* adds factual information but is not essential. The basic meaning of the sentence is clear without it: Robin Crisp will graduate in three years.

Restrictive clauses and phrases are not set off by commas.

◆ Citizens, who are interested in politics, should run for public office.

◆ Anyone, caught cheating, will be expelled.

NOTE: Clauses beginning with the relative pronoun *that* are almost always restrictive.

◆ The belief, that human beings, are driven by subconscious

drives is common among psychoanalysts.

◆ Medical treatments, that are not approved by the American

Medical Association, may be dangerous.

In a restrictive adjective clause, the relative pronoun introducing the clause may be dropped when it does not function as the subject of the relative clause.

◆ A tax increase is the only way ~~that~~ our government can

continue to function.

◆ Dr. Diaz could not find a politician ~~whom~~ she respected.

NOTE: Clauses and phrases modifying indefinite pronouns are almost always restrictive.

◆ Walt Disney is a genius to those, who make animated

cartoons.

◆ Anyone, sleeping in the park, was awakened.

Nonrestrictive clauses and phrases should be set off by commas.

◆ Venice, which is noted for its Piazza San Marco, was a favorite

haunt for American writers.

◆ The right to free speech, like breathing itself, is essential to

life.

NOTE: Clauses and phrases that modify proper nouns are always nonrestrictive. (See proper nouns, 67a.)

◆ Ernest Hemingway, who had an interest in art, claimed to have

learned to write fine descriptions by studying impressionist

paintings.

Sometimes a clause or phrase may be either restrictive or nonrestrictive. The writer must indicate how it is to be interpreted by using or omitting commas.

RESTRICTIVE   The engineers who were trained as pilots provided the technical advice.

The *who* clause restricts or defines *engineers.* The sentence means that not all engineers provided technical advice; only the ones trained as pilots did.

NON-
RESTRICTIVE   The engineers, who were trained as pilots, provided the technical advice.

This sentence means that all the engineers were trained as pilots, and they gave the technical advice. The *who* clause is not essential to the meaning of the sentence.

Nonrestrictive appositives should be set off by commas; restrictive appositives should not.

A restrictive appositive defines the noun it refers to in such a way that its absence from the sentence would leave the meaning unclear.

NON-
RESTRICTIVE   Cal Worthington, a frequent personality on late-night television, made millions selling used cars.

NON-
RESTRICTIVE   Baby gray whales, huge creatures at birth, consume up to fifty gallons of milk daily.

NON-
RESTRICTIVE   "Mending Wall," one of Robert Frost's narrative poems, deals with two differing worldviews.

RESTRICTIVE   The actor Whoopi Goldberg is known for both her comedic and her dramatic roles.

RESTRICTIVE   The Greek hero Perseus slew the dragon and freed Andromeda.

RESTRICTIVE   James Dickey's poem "Looking for the Buckhead Boys" portrays a middle-aged man's attempt to reconnect with his youth.

WRITER'S TOOLBOX

Setting Off Nonrestrictive Elements

You will usually use commas to set off information that is not essential (nonrestrictive elements), but you may use dashes or parentheses instead, depending on the importance of the information to the meaning of a sentence.

Use commas for important information.

> No painter or sculptor, not even Michelangelo, had been as famous as Pablo Picasso was in his own lifetime.

Use dashes to emphasize nonessential information.

> Pablo Picasso—the twentieth century's dominant painter and sculptor—lived to be ninety-two.

Use parentheses for interesting but less important information.

> Picasso's *Guernica* (perhaps equaled in drama only by Goya's etchings *Disasters of War*) captures the madness of modern warfare.

Exercise 37.4: Set Off Nonrestrictive Elements

In the following sentences, insert commas to set off nonrestrictive clauses, phrases, and appositives. If a sentence is correct as written, underline the restrictive or nonrestrictive element and mark the sentence with a C.

1. Edgar Allan Poe a nineteenth-century American writer wrote the first murder mystery.

2. "The Murders in the Rue Morgue" published in 1841 presents C. Auguste Dupin the world's first modern detective.

3. In Dupin, Poe created a detective who solved murders through observation and reason often drawing a solution that appears miraculous.

4. Poe also created the "locked room" story a mystery in which a murdered victim is found in a room locked from the inside.

5. James Fenimore Cooper another American writer created the first espionage novel.

6. Cooper's *The Spy* which was based on historical notes from the American Revolution appeared even before Poe's work.

7. Cooper who is known for his romantic American Indian tales created a formula that future espionage writers would use.

8. Mark Twain who is not considered to be a mystery writer contributed to detective fiction by being the first author to use fingerprints to help solve a crime.

9. Mystery writers today must use new methods of detection since crime technology has become so sophisticated.

10. Anyone who reads or writes mysteries must wonder if science will put an end to the fine art of fictional murder.

Exercise 37.5: Combine Sentences Using Restrictive or Nonrestrictive Elements

Combine the following sentences according to the directions given in brackets. After you have combined the sentences, be sure to punctuate them correctly. For example:

> The tradition of detective stories with murder in the family is an old one. Human beings have always had murder in their hearts. [Use *since* to form an adverbial clause.]
>
> **Combined:** Since human beings have always had murder in their hearts, the tradition of detective stories with murder in the family is an old one.

1. Cain killed his brother Abel in an Old Testament story of the first murder. Cain was jealous of Abel. [Use *who* to form an adjective clause.]

2. Some serious mystery readers claim that *Oedipus Rex* is the first detective story. *Oedipus Rex* is an early Greek play. [Use an appositive phrase.]

3. Oedipus seeks his true identity. He has inadvertently killed his father and married his mother. [Use *who* to form an adjective clause.]

4. Clearly, *Oedipus Rex* is a murder mystery. The play ends ironically when the detective discovers he is the killer. [Use *that* to form an adjective clause.]

5. Shakespeare's *Hamlet* can also be viewed as a mystery. *Hamlet* is an Elizabethan tragedy. It deals with a brother's murdering his

brother and ascending to the throne of Denmark. [Use an appositive phrase and an adjective phrase beginning with *that*.]

6. Hamlet must first prove that his uncle murdered his father. Hamlet was the son of the slain king. [Use an appositive phrase.]

7. Both *Oedipus Rex* and *Hamlet* concentrate on solving a family murder. They thrill many audiences today. [Use a present participial phrase.]

8. Modern detective writer Ross Macdonald also wove his mysteries around family crimes. They often use murder or a disappearance to motivate the investigation. [Use *which* to form an adjective clause.]

9. *The Galton Case* begins with a mother who wishes to be reconciled with her son. *The Galton Case* is an early Macdonald mystery. The son has disappeared without a trace. [Use an appositive phrase and an adjective clause beginning with *who*.]

10. By the novel's end, Macdonald's detective has revealed a murder and unraveled the family's snarled history. The detective's name is Lew Archer. [Use an appositive.]

37d Use commas between words, phrases, and clauses in a series consisting of three or more items of equal importance

When three or more items—words, clauses, or phrases—are arranged in a series, they should be separated from one another with commas.

- Three well-known Japanese novelists were Junichiro Tanizaki, Yasunari Kawabata, and Yukio Mishima.

- To plan successfully you must clarify the goal, define the objectives, establish a deadline, and charge ahead.

- Driving luxury sedans, eating gourmet food, and drinking fine wine are Camelita's fantasies.

- Aaron did not know who he was, where he had been, or what would happen next.

Although the final comma in a series is optional, including it can prevent misreading.

> I took the following courses: digital computers, software manufacturing, word processing, and data retrieval. [The final comma makes it clear that word processing and data retrieval are separate courses.]

NOTE: No commas are necessary between items in a series all joined by *and* or *or.*

> Whole grains and nuts and yogurt are the staples in Quintan's diet.

37e **Use a comma between coordinate adjectives not joined by *and;* do not use a comma between cumulative adjectives**

Coordinate adjectives are two or more adjectives that modify the same noun or pronoun and could appear in any order.

> Informative, imaginative, appealing advertising should be more common.

> Advertising is often no more than a deceptive, dull appeal to consumer insecurity.

NOTE: A comma is never used between the last adjective in a series and the noun it modifies.

Cumulative adjectives modify the adjectives that follow them as well as a noun or pronoun, and their order cannot be changed.

◆ His life was dedicated to achieving a single, personal goal.

◆ The exhibition of ancient, Tunisian mosaics will close next week.

Exercise 37.6: Using Commas in a Series

Insert commas as necessary within a series or between coordinate adjectives in the following sentences. Include the last comma in a series. If a sentence is correct, mark it with a C.

1. Early colonists brought such words as *bandit robber highwayman* and *outlaw* with them from England.

2. Freezing weather personal dignity or increasing population demanded that the first privy be built.

Knowing the Difference Between Coordinate and Cumulative Adjectives

Two simple tests can help you tell the difference between coordinate and cumulative adjectives. If you can change the order of the adjectives or place the word *and* between them, the series is coordinate and requires commas.

> Intelligent, sensitive, witty films are seldom produced in Hollywood.

> Sensitive, witty, intelligent films are seldom produced in Hollywood.

> Intelligent and sensitive and witty films are seldom produced in Hollywood.

The preceding adjective series meets both tests; therefore, it is a coordinate series and should be separated by commas.

> International peace organizations supported antinuclear demonstrations in the world's capitals.

> Peace international organizations supported antinuclear demonstrations in the world's capitals.

> International and peace organizations supported antinuclear demonstrations in the world's capitals.

The adjective series *international peace* does not meet either test; therefore, it is a cumulative series and should not be separated by commas.

3. The history of the circus goes back to the days of the Roman Empire when chariot races gladiator fights and animal shows were featured activities.

4. Hungry for adventure seeking land to farm and willing to risk life and limb, thousands of Mississippi settlers caught the Oregon fever.

5. Tall and lean brooding and gentle Abraham Lincoln was the imposing figure who led a divided confused country during the Civil War.

6. A third of the country is poorly housed, poorly fed, and poorly educated.

7. Following the Revolutionary War, farsighted courageous leaders like Benjamin Franklin, George Washington, Robert Fulton, and Albert Gallatin planned to build canals to connect towns lakes and rivers across the nation.

8. Most of the town's people were farmers or worked for small local businesses, often bartering food clothing and services.

9. At the peak of the Great Depression, bank closings bankruptcies factory shutdowns and farm and home mortgage foreclosures were at an all-time high.

10. With mustard and relish and onions, the American hot dog has been the favorite of Fourth of July picnics for one hundred years.

37f Use commas to set off parenthetical expressions that function as transitions, express afterthoughts, or offer supplemental information

Parenthetical expressions interrupt the flow of a sentence. Transitional phrases such as *for example, on the other hand,* and *in fact* are parenthetical and are usually set off by commas.

◆ Driving on freeways and turnpikes, for example, is four times more dangerous than flying.

Commas are usually needed to set off conjunctive adverbs such as *accordingly, besides, consequently, furthermore, hence, however, indeed, instead, likewise, meanwhile, moreover, nevertheless, otherwise, therefore,* and *thus.* (See semicolon, 39b.)

◆ Several bystanders who witnessed the crime identified the thief; nevertheless, he was released from custody because of a technicality.

◆ Several bystanders who witnessed the crime identified the thief; he was released from custody, however, because of a technicality.

Always use commas to set off *however* when it is used as a conjunctive adverb; do not use commas to set off *however* when it is an adverb meaning "no matter how."

◆ Sixteen engineers gave similar testimony; however,the Senate
committee was swayed by the attorney general's dissenting
view.

◆ However, the committee votes will have no affect on the
outcome.

Afterthoughts and supplemental information should be set off with
commas.

◆ Mystery writers,some critics maintain,try to make sense of
murder.

37g Use a comma to set off mild interjections, words of direct address, and *yes* and *no*

◆ Oh,I didn't mean to buy so many groceries!

◆ Stop playing those video games,Don.

◆ No,I cannot be there early.

Exercise 37.7: Using Commas with Parenthetical Elements

Insert commas as necessary to set off parenthetical expressions and
words of direct address in the following sentences. If a sentence is
correct, mark it with a C.

1. However much Americans love their Big Macs and chocolate
   shakes, many are sacrificing their affair with junk food for a new
   commitment.

2. Bulging biceps, rippled stomachs, and yes even sinewy necks are
   the new shapes people yearn for.

3. Regardless of the pain and endless hours spent pumping iron
   men and women are dedicating themselves to furious body-
   building.

4. Will chiseled muscles lead to healthier lives? No not if weight lifting is merely an escape from time's relentless craftsmanship.

5. Moreover many bodybuilders express their desire to become a New Age Rambo.

37h Use the comma to set off absolute phrases

An **absolute phrase** modifies an entire sentence rather than a word or phrase, but it is not grammatically related to the rest of the sentence. Absolute phrases are always nonrestrictive—that is, they always supply important but nonessential information to a sentence. (See 69f.)

◆ The Doberman leaped at Rashid's throat, teeth snapping, eyes flashing anger.

◆ Their feet aching from the journey, the four campers climbed into their sleeping bags.

◆ Anuka, her fingers gripping the wheel, accelerated into the curve.

37i Use the comma to set off contrasting expressions and interrogative elements

Love, not hate, is the essence of renewal.

Each person has the responsibility for his or her behavior, right?

37j Use the comma to set off expressions such as *she said* and *he wrote* from direct quotations

The *Tao Te Ching* says, "Not collecting treasures prevents stealing."

"I cannot and will not cut my conscience to fit this year's fashions," wrote Lillian Hellman.

"One writes out of one thing only," says James Baldwin, "one's own experience."

When the expression comes between two or more sentences of quotation, use a period after the expression to indicate the end of the first sentence.

> "The apartment house is nearly finished," she said. "I never thought I would see the day."

(See quotation marks, 40a.)

Omit the comma when a quotation ends with an exclamation point or question mark.

> "Why all this indecision?" she asked.

NOTE: When a comma follows a quotation, always place it within the quotation marks, not after or under them.

> "Of course," she replied.

Exercise 37.8: Using Commas to Set Off Certain Phrases and Quotations

Insert commas as necessary in the following sentences to set off absolute phrases, contrasting expressions, interrogative elements, and explanatory words used with a direct quotation.

1. Many food faddists like to eat natural meat not just the domesticated meat displayed in most supermarkets.

2. Natural meat is game not the kind you play on ball fields and includes a variety of wildlife found in America's forests and mountain ranges.

3. Free for the taking some game is coveted more than others. Venison for instance is the most popular game served at American tables.

4. One chef praises muskrat chili certainly not as common as Texas chili right?

5. Some food faddists see game as a preferred dish in specialty restaurants. "Seldom is the taste so aroused as when a platter of sputtering moose steaks or a brace of mallards is placed on a table" one critic writes. "It's like experiencing the American wilderness in the heart of Manhattan" he claims.

37k Use a comma according to established conventions in numbers, addresses, place names, dates, and friendly letters

Separate long numbers into groups of three beginning from the right.

    5,676   12,345   222,498   231,547,211

Separate each item in an address that is run together on one line. Do not use a comma to set off the zip code.

> 600 Wisconsin Avenue, South Milwaukee, Wisconsin 53172
> 600 Wisconsin Avenue
> South Milwaukee, Wisconsin 53172

Separate each item in a place name.

> I forwarded the package to Harvard University, Cambridge, Massachusetts, where she now teaches.

Separate the month and day from the year in a date.

> The reception will be held at the Hilton on September 21, 2008, in the Twilight Room.

If the day precedes the month, do not use commas.

> 21 September 2008

Conclude the salutation and close of a friendly letter.

> Dear Uncle Joe Bob,   Yours truly,

Exercise 37.9: Using Commas in Letters

Insert commas as necessary in the following letter, including optional commas.

> March 16 2006
> Dear Dat
>
> I have just accepted a sales position with a firm in Newport Beach California about forty-five miles south of Los Angeles. The base salary is $30,000 a year but with commissions I could make another $10,000 to $15,000.
>
> The company will have a training position opening next month. Are you interested? Let me know. My new address is 2701 Fairview Road Costa Mesa CA 92626.
>
> Your friend
> Philip Thi

37I Use a comma to prevent misunderstanding and to show the omission of an understood word

To prevent misunderstanding:

CONFUSING   On Monday morning schedules will be revised.

CLEAR   On Monday, morning schedules will be revised.

CLEAR   On Monday morning, schedules will be revised.

To show an omission:

◆ The French drink wine; the Germans, ~~drink~~ beer.
                                                  ^

◆ For Dr. Sanchez to give one "A" is rare; for him to give two, is
                                                                 ^
unprecedented.

EDITOR'S TOOLBOX

Grammar Checkers and Punctuation

Just as grammar checkers are highly unreliable in flagging and correcting sentence errors, they are also unreliable in flagging punctuation errors.

- Grammar checkers generally fail to flag comma errors except before *which* and *that*.
- They tend to flag all semicolon use, but they generally fail to identify run-on sentences.
- They also tend to flag all colon and dash use, but you still need to determine whether the use is correct.
- They can be effective in identifying missing apostrophes in contractions, and they sometimes flag missing apostrophes in possessives, but not always.
- They are very effective at flagging mistakes in the use of commas and periods with quotation marks.

Whether or not you use a grammar checker, you will have to proofread your work carefully for errors in punctuation.

38 Unnecessary Commas *no* ,

Excessive use of the comma may confuse a reader by separating sentence elements that belong together. The following rules specify when a comma is not necessary.

38a Do not use a comma between a subject and its verb unless a sentence element that comes between them requires commas

◆ Fully grown killer whales, are as long as thirty feet and as heavy as ten tons.

◆ Fully grown killer whales, which travel in pods of ten to twenty, are as long as thirty feet and as heavy as ten tons.

38b Do not use a comma between a verb and its object or its complement

◆ A killer whale will eat, anything it can catch.

38c Do not use a comma between a preposition and its object

◆ Killer whales live in, practically all the tropical oceans of the world.

38d Do not use a comma between an adverb and the word it modifies or between an adjective and the word it modifies

◆ The killer whale has been described as the most socially, intelligent, animal in the world.

38e Do not use a comma between compound words, phrases, or dependent clauses joined by a coordinating conjunction

◆ The engine, and the grill are the most famous features of the Rolls-Royce.

◆ A Rolls-Royce has eighty thousand parts, and takes three months to build.

◆ The Rolls-Royce is proof that fine work is still being done, and that people will pay any price for quality.

38f Do not use commas to separate restrictive elements from the rest of the sentence

◆ The first car, created by Henry Royce and Charles Rolls, was built in 1904.

◆ Fritz Wirth's article, "An Empire on Four Wheels," appeared in January.

38g Do not use a comma after *such as* and *like*

◆ Some writers in Spanish, such as, Gabriel García Márquez and Mario Vargas Llosa, have influenced contemporary American writers.

38h Do not use a comma before the first or after the last item in a series unless a rule requires it

◆ Reading, writing, and arithmetic, should be the spine of education.

◆ Popular college subjects today are, psychology, business, and engineering.

38i Do not use a comma to introduce indirect discourse

◆ The *Tao* teaches that⁄ muddy waters left alone will become clear.

38j Do not use a comma before *than* in a comparison

◆ Hang gliding is more exciting⁄ than skydiving.

38k Do not use a comma with a period, a question mark, an exclamation point, or a dash, all of which stand by themselves

◆ "Return the money at once!"⁄ he pleaded.

Exercise 38.1: Comma Use Review

Correct the following sentences by inserting commas where they are needed and by deleting them where they are not needed. Include all optional commas. If any sentence is correct, mark it with a C.

1. The life of the Chinese heroine Meng Chiang Nu, the Pumpkin Girl, is an example of loyalty dedication and self-sacrifice.

2. The story begins with two families the Meng and the Chiang.

3. During the planting season one year each family planted pumpkins at the foot of a wall that marked the boundary of their properties.

4. Growing rapidly, pumpkin vines soon began to climb the wall and at the top they joined and produced a pumpkin larger than anyone had ever seen before.

5. According to the story the families agreed to divide the pumpkin but when they cut into it they found a tiny baby girl inside.

6. To show she belonged to both the Meng family and the Chiang family they called her Meng Chiang.

7. At about the same time, the Emperor Shih Huang Ti started to build the Great Wall of China.

8. Each time the emperor's men put up a section of the wall however it collapsed before another section could be built.

9. The emperor who felt discouraged sent for the wisest men in the empire to advise him.

10. One wise man told him the only way to stop the collapse, would be to bury a living person in the wall every mile.

11. Since the wall was to extend ten thousand miles the plan would call for the sacrifice of ten thousand people!

12. Another wise man whispered to the emperor "Your Eminence living nearby is a poor man. Since his name Wan means ten thousand bury him in the wall and your great enterprise will be strong along its entire length."

13. Yes, Wan was poor, but he was not stupid.

14. When he heard of the plan he ran, and ran, and ran, until at nightfall he found himself high, in the branches of a tree in a peaceful isolated garden.

15. Beneath him he saw a beautiful girl bathing naked in a pool.

16. Of course it was Meng Chiang grown to womanhood.

17. She sang softly of love, and said aloud "If any man should see me now I would happily be his wife forever."

18. Wan forgot his own safety for a moment and climbed down from the tree and claimed his bride.

19. Unfortunately the emperor's men arrived just after the wedding seized the bridegroom and carried him off to be buried alive in the Great Wall.

20. Having heard of Wan's fate years later Meng Chiang made the hazardous journey to the wall to search for her husband's body.

21. Out of sympathy for her plight, a section of the wall collapsed, and her husband's bones fell out.

22. She was taken to the emperor who was stunned by her great beauty and vowed to marry her.

23. Seeing that the emperor was determined to marry her Meng Chiang asked only that a high altar be built in memory of her husband.

24. On their wedding day Meng Chiang climbed to the top of the altar cursed the emperor for his cruelty and threw herself to her death.

25. The emperor commanded his men to cut her body into little pieces but each piece of her flesh turned into a beautiful silver fish and her soul lives in these fish as a tribute to faithfulness.

---

39 Semicolon ;

Use semicolons in a limited number of situations: as a substitute for a period to indicate a close relation between main clauses and as a substitute for a comma to improve clarity.

39a Use a semicolon between main clauses

When two main clauses are closely related in meaning and are not joined by a coordinating conjunction, you may join them with a semicolon.

◆ In Irish folklore the Sidhe (pronounced "she") spirits

 sometimes appear as men and women;other times they appear
 ^

 as birds and beasts. The Sidhe travel as clouds of dust;they rest
 ^

 as blades of grass.

There must be some basis for deciding whether to use two main clauses with a semicolon between them or two sentences with a period. Generally, the division into separate sentences is better. A semicolon should be used only when the ideas in the two main clauses are so closely related that a period would make too strong a break between them. (See coordinating conjunctions, 67g; comma splices and fused sentences, Chapter 28.)

Stylistically, the semicolon may be used to create a balance between closely related clauses.

◆ Mystics trust spirits;realists trust only facts.
 ^

39b Use a semicolon to separate main clauses joined by conjunctive adverbs

◆ In folklore the Sidhe live under Ireland's rocky soil or beneath
the mutinous seas consequently, some Irish claim the Sidhe are
                ^
never far from them.

NOTE: When a conjunctive adverb immediately follows a semicolon
(as in the preceding example), always put a comma after the conjunctive adverb. When a conjunctive adverb does not immediately
follow the semicolon, put commas before and after the conjunctive
adverb.

◆ The Sidhe live on cold potatoes and milk left on hearths and at
thresholds of Irish homes when feasting, however, they resort
                  ^
to theft and rob Irish cellars of good wines.

39c Use a semicolon to separate main clauses joined by coordinating conjunctions

When the main clauses are long and complex or have internal punctuation, use semicolons to separate them.

◆ The Sidhe sing in glens, dance on boulders, and play
hurling in the fields but they also curse, bicker, and fight
                  ^
each other.

39d Use semicolons to separate long phrases or clauses in a series if they contain commas

◆ Partial to humans, Sidhe spirits will help them in their work
                                   ^
aid them in the search for hidden money, lost jewels, and
buried gold and treat their sick pets, ailing livestock, and ill
        ^
children.

39e Avoid misusing the semicolon

Do not use a semicolon to join dependent clauses or phrases and main clauses.

◆ According to some enthusiasts⁄,only ten thousand Sidhe exist.
     ^

◆ Some believe the Sidhe are headed toward extinction⁄ because fewer and fewer people believe in them.

Do not use a semicolon to introduce a list.

◆ Perhaps the Sidhe will join the ranks of other imaginary creatures⁊ such as unicorns, leprechauns, and magical dwarfs.

Exercise 39.1: Using Semicolons

Delete the unnecessary or incorrect commas and semicolons and in-sert the correct punctuation in the following sentences. If any sentence is correct, mark it with a C.

1. Whereas imaginary creatures may fall from memory; the real mysteries of the world will always arouse our curiosity.

2. One mystery involves strange carvings, many the size of three-story buildings, found on Easter Island, another involves cave drawings at Lascaux, France, painted fifteen to twenty thousand years ago.

3. Easter Island is tiny, volcanic, barren, and isolated; nevertheless, plenty of insects and hordes of rats live there.

4. Mysterious statues dominate the island; their threatening expressions presiding over the landscape.

5. Their faces all share similar features; such as long ears, large eyes, and jutting chins.

6. Some of the statues are toppled over, most, however, still stand, all still have topknots made from red stone.

7. The paintings in the Lascaux caves, are equally mysterious, however the mystery surrounds their purpose, not their origin.

8. Some historians claim the paintings represent hunting magic, others see in them a great symbolic idea that is beyond our

understanding, still others view them as simply the result of creative impulses.

9. Whatever their motivations; the Lascaux cave painters created groups of pictures in sixty-six caves. This achievement required many skills; including the ability to extract minerals from the ground, pound them to powder, and mix them with grease.

10. As children we huddle together in the darkness and scare each other with tales of mysterious monsters, as adults we curl up under a reading lamp with a good book and wonder about the mysterious creations of humankind.

Exercise 39.2: Using Semicolons

Delete the unnecessary and incorrect commas and semicolons, and insert the correct punctuation in the following sentences. If any sentence is correct, mark it with a C.

1. Many Americans are dropping coffee completely from their diets, many others are switching to decaffeinated coffee.

2. Herbal teas and health-food substitutes are reasonable alternatives to coffee drinking, they are drunk hot and offer a reason to pause during the day.

3. "I have measured out my life with coffee spoons," the poet T. S. Eliot once wrote, now, however, he might have to write, "I have measured out my life with teaspoons."

4. Coffee has been nicknamed "mud"; because the grounds look like mud once hot water has been poured through them.

5. Some people drink as much as fifteen to twenty cups of coffee a day; which makes sleeping difficult because of the caffeine.

6. Some people drink coffee to stay alert, then they cannot sleep, finally, they drink coffee the next morning because they are tired from the lack of sleep.

7. Many heavy coffee drinkers who finally quit drinking coffee experience the symptoms of withdrawal; such as headaches, depression, and listlessness.

8. Is there life after coffee consumption has ended? Coffee drinking is such a ritualized part of our experience that giving up coffee would disrupt our schedules, in fact, giving up coffee might change the very fabric of our existence.

9. Imagine having herbal tea with eggs and bacon, sipping caffeine-less cola with the morning paper, taking juice breaks, without coffee all these experiences would be equally dissatisfying.

10. Improved health is not worth the emotional price tag; coffee is the one drink for all occasions.

---

40 Quotation Marks " "

The main use of quotation marks is to assist a reader by indicating the beginning and the end of a direct quotation from speech or writing.

40a Use double quotation marks (" ") to enclose direct quotations from speakers or writers

In a recent lecture on contemporary art, Professor Alvarez said, "Until the general acceptance of Georgia O'Keeffe's work, artists were divided into two groups—artists and female painters. Now we have just one group—artists."

Art historian Sam Hunter sees Georgia O'Keeffe's work as emerging from and going beyond biomorphic abstraction: "O'Keeffe seemed able to invest abstract painting with fresh content and significant new forms."

When quoting a passage that takes up more than four lines in a typewritten paper, do not use quotation marks (unless they appear in the original); instead, set off the quotation from the rest of the paper by putting it in block form. That is, indent the entire passage ten spaces (or one inch) and double-space the lines. The first line of the passage should be indented an additional three spaces (or one-fourth inch) if it marks the beginning of a paragraph.

> All of us are familiar with the superstitious belief that the number 13 is unlucky. But we are not, of course, the only culture that worries about numbers. The famous linguist Charles Berlitz notes,
>
> > In both Chinese and Japanese, the word "four," *shi*, sounds like the word "death." The Japanese often substitute another word for "four"—*yotsu*, taken

> from an alternative system of counting. License
> numbers using 4 in certain combinations are
> shunned by Chinese car owners in Hong Kong,
> Taiwan, and Singapore. They especially avoid the
> number 1414, which in speech resembles the
> words "definite death, definite death."

The indention of the quoted passage indicates that it is all a quotation. Note, too, that the words *four, death,* and *definite death* are placed within quotation marks because those marks appeared in the original.

When directly quoting poetry, work a quotation of one line or less into the text and enclose it within quotation marks.

> Shelley tellingly countered Ozymandias's proclamation of
> omnipotence with the short, ironic comment, "Nothing beside
> remains."

A quotation of two lines of poetry may be worked into the text of your paper or set off from it. To work the lines into the text, separate them with a slash (with one space before and after the slash) and enclose the entire quotation in quotation marks.

> In T. S. Eliot's poem "The Love Song of J. Alfred
> Prufrock," Prufrock's isolation is echoed in the lines "I have
> heard the mermaids singing, each to each. / I do not think
> that they will sing to me."

To set off the lines of poetry from the text, begin each line on a new line, indent it ten spaces (or one inch) unless the poet used varying indentation, and double-space the lines. Omit the quotation marks.

> In T. S. Eliot's poem "The Love Song of J. Alfred
> Prufrock," Prufrock's isolation is echoed in the lines
>> I have heard the mermaids singing, each to each.
>> I do not think that they will sing to me.

A poetry quotation of three or more lines should be set off from the text in block form and presented just as it is printed in the original. Do not use quotation marks or slashes.

When quoting conversation or writing fictional dialogue, put quotation marks around the exact words spoken. Do not enclose descriptive phrases or attributions in quotation marks. Begin a new paragraph for each speaker.

> "Where is he?" Mae asked, coming around the corner of
> the house with a mop and bucket in her hands. "Is he gone?"
>
> "I dunno, Mom," Stacy replied. "He was here a minute ago."
>
> She yawned and scratched the back of her head
> vigorously. "Probably gone huntin' again."

If one speaker or writer is quoted without interruption for more than one paragraph, put quotation marks at the beginning of each paragraph but at the end of only the last paragraph.

NOTE: Do not use quotation marks to enclose indirect quotations—written or spoken information that you have rewritten or summarized in your words.

> His purpose, he said, was to break with the traditions of the
> past and bring new life to the film industry.

40b Use quotation marks to enclose the titles of short works

A *short work* is one included in a larger work or production. Articles, essays, short stories, short poems, songs, chapters and other subdivisions of books and periodicals, as well as episodes of radio and television programs are short works.

> Shirley Jackson's "The Lottery" exposes a small community's
> blind obedience to tradition. [Short story]
>
> "The Microbe Hunters" is this week's episode of *Nova*.
> [Television episode]
>
> Chapter 2, "Entering the Aerobics Program," tells how to take
> the first step toward improving the cardiovascular system.
> [Chapter title]

NOTE: Do not use quotation marks to enclose the titles or section titles of your own papers.

40c Occasionally, quotation marks serve to enclose a word used in a special sense

> I had to take the job. I needed the "prestige" of being employed.

Do not use quotation marks to create an ironic tone, change the meaning of a word, or justify the use of nonstandard English.

INAPPROPRIATE Just being late to class was "traumatic" enough, but when the instructor peered over his glasses and "growled," "Again," I just "totally flipped."

APPROPRIATE Just being late to class was bad enough, but when the instructor peered over his glasses and growled, "Again," I was really embarrassed.

40d Follow standard practice when using other marks of punctuation with quotation marks

1. Always place commas and periods that follow a quotation inside quotation marks.

Although Tom Bender said, "Writers who endure will always write about what they know," he spent years describing the journeys of characters who became lost in exotic lands he never visited.

Scanning the crowd for her son, she said, "It's like looking for a needle in a haystack."

2. Always place colons and semicolons outside quotation marks.

Some of Aunt Maude's favorite expressions are "He runs around like a chicken with its head cut off"; "Where there's smoke there's fire"; and "Don't count your chickens until they've hatched": expressions from the common pot of American clichés.

3. Enclose dashes, question marks, and exclamation points in quotation marks only if they belong to the quotation.

"That's terrible! How can they expect—" she screamed in disbelief.

I am sure you resent him for always asking, "But what does it all mean?"

Long after she had turned the corner, she could still hear him calling, "Eva! Eva!"

When a dash, question mark, or exclamation point is not part of a direct quotation, do not enclose it within quotation marks.

"Something is rotten in the state of Denmark"—and I intend to find out what it is!

Have you ever wanted to tell him, "I don't want to work here anymore"**?**

Please! Stop saying, "Something is rotten in the state of Denmark"**!**

40e Use single quotation marks (' ') to enclose a direct quotation within a quotation

"Let me remind you," the professor said, "of the words of Edward R. Murrow, 'We cannot defend freedom abroad by deserting it at home.'"

WRITER'S TOOLBOX

Using That *in Paraphrasing and Quoting*

Use *that* to introduce a paraphrase, but do not use *that* to introduce a direct quotation.

PARAPHRASE

Director Steven Spielberg's mother said that she never understood her son while he was growing up.

DIRECT QUOTATION

Director Steven Spielberg's mother said, "When he was growing up, I didn't know he was a genius. Frankly, I didn't know what he was."

Exercise 40.1: Using Quotation Marks

Supply quotation marks where they are needed and place punctuation marks correctly in the following sentences. If a quotation should be set off in block form, place a B to indicate at which point the block would begin and an E to indicate where it would end. Make any other changes that would be necessary to handle a block quotation correctly. If no quotation marks are needed in a sentence, mark it with a C.

1. Of all Flannery O'Connor's short stories, A Good Man Is Hard to Find best embodies the full range of her style.

2. O'Connor, Michael Finnegan wrote, mastered the use of caricature in character development.

3. The dictionary defines caricature as follows: The exaggeration of
certain human characteristics in order to create a satiric effect.

4. The portrait of Mrs. Freeman in the short story Good Country
People is an example of caricature: Besides the neutral expression
that she wore when she was alone, Mrs. Freeman had two others,
forward and reverse, that she used in all her human dealings. Her
forward expression was steady and driving like the advance of a
heavy truck. She seldom used the other expression because it was
not often necessary for her to retract a statement. O'Connor even
uses the name Freeman ironically because Mrs. Freeman is no
more free than the speeding truck she is compared to.

5. To reveal the limited natures of her characters, O'Connor often
fills their speech with stock phrases, such as Nothing is perfect;
That is life; and You're the wheel behind the wheel.

6. Sometimes her characters seem too strange to be real, but like all
writers who will endure, she draws her material from life, thus
following Alexander Pope's dictate: Know then thyself, presume
not God to scan; The proper study of Mankind is Man.

7. She studied people, and the absurdity of much of the world delighted her. Sally Fitzgerald writes about O'Connor's letters, She
regaled us with Hadacol advertisements; birth announcements of
infants with names that had to be read to be believed; such news
items as the attendance of Roy Rogers' horse at a church service
in California.

8. Could her intense interest in the absurd behavior of people continue one critic asked and still remain fresh?

9. I've reached the point where I can't do again what I can do well
she wrote in a letter and the larger things I need to do now, I
doubt my capacity for doing.

10. Many prefer distant landscapes such as the magical kingdom in
Coleridge's short poem Kubla Khan, which begins In Xanadu did
Kubla Khan / A stately pleasure-dome decree: / Where Alph, the
sacred river ran Through caverns measureless to man / Down to a
sunless sea.

41 Colon :

A colon has several conventional uses. It introduces sentence elements that explain, illustrate, or amplify portions of a sentence. A colon also introduces formal quotations and separates subtitles and titles, subdivisions of time, parts of biblical citations, and city and publisher in bibliographic entries.

41a Use a colon to introduce a series following a complete sentence

Maya Angelou is best known for four volumes of autobiography: *I Know Why the Caged Bird Sings, Gather Together in My Name, Singin' and Swingin' and Gettin' Merry Like Christmas,* and *The Heart of a Woman.*

They stood on a hilltop and watched the crowd pour across the bridge: families pulling carts piled high with furniture, soldiers in torn uniforms and dragging their rifles by the strap, and children, crying, lost, helpless.

41b Use a colon after *the following* or *as follows* to introduce a statement or series

In the upper-left-hand corner of the first page of your paper write the following: name, course number, assignment number, and date.

The secret to understanding history is as follows: whatever goes around will come around.

41c Use a colon to announce a second main clause that explains the first

She has no doubt about her future: she will first attend medical school and then train as a psychiatrist.

NOTE: Capitalizing the first word of a main clause that follows a colon depends on the style you are following. (See capitals, 48a.)

41d Use a colon to introduce a final appositive

August 6, 1945, is a day we should never forget: the day humanity ignited the earth.

41e Use a colon to introduce a long or formal quotation

In 1962 Rachel Carson's *Silent Spring* sounded the warning:

> The most alarming of all humankind's assaults upon the environment is the contamination of air, earth, rivers, and sea with dangerous and even lethal materials. This pollution is for the most part irrecoverable; the chain of evil it initiates not only in the world that must support life but in living tissues is for the most part irreversible.

41f Use a colon to separate subtitles and titles, subdivisions of time, parts of biblical citations, and city and publisher in bibliographic entries

The Origins of English: A Social and Linguistic History

1:13 a.m.   12:34 p.m.   Matthew 4:6–10
New York: Longman, 2008

NOTE: The MLA and some other styles use a period for biblical citations: Matthew 4.6–10.

41g Use a colon at the end of a formal salutation

Dear Mr. and Mrs. Fritz: To Whom It May Concern:

41h Do not misuse the colon by placing it after a linking verb (separating the verb from its direct object) or a preposition or by placing it in a sentence that lacks a formal introduction for what follows

◆ You will need/ a toothbrush, toothpaste, razor, shaving cream, and change of clothes.

◆ Finchamp, a well-traveled man, has lived in/ Paris, London, Rome, Dublin, and Berlin.

◆ Bluegrass music makes use of several stringed instruments such as; banjo, guitar, mandolin, and fiddle.

Exercise 41.1: Using Colons

Correct the following sentences, inserting colons as needed.

1. After becoming rich I acquired three things I never had before, friends, relatives, and lovers.

2. The assignment for Bible as Literature is as follows, John 21, 17–30.

3. The town meeting broke up following a fiery outburst by one resident, "Either clean up the streets or declare the neighborhood a public-health hazard."

4. He drove nonstop from 530 a.m. to 530 p.m. for one reason to be present for the reading of the will.

5. The secret lesson that comes from studying poetry is simple don't quit your day job.

Exercise 41.2: Using Colons

Use a colon to combine each group of sentences into a single sentence. You will have to revise wording and exclude some words to make the combined sentences read correctly.

1. He drove twelve hours nonstop for one reason. That reason was to arrive before the opening kickoff.

2. The philosopher Sören Kierkegaard contemplated the future with a simply stated attitude. He defined it as fear and trembling.

3. Yahoos were introduced in Jonathan Swift's *Gulliver's Travels*. They are a race of brutish, degraded creatures who have the form and all the vices of human beings.

4. Our forests, our hills, our prairies all have one thing in common. They will soon succumb to land development.

5. Propaganda devices have been given catchy names. Some of the names are "glittering generalities," "bandwagon," "testimonial," "plain folks," and "poisoning the well."

---

42 The Dash —

Use a dash to emphasize a sentence element and to indicate a break in tone or thought. Do not use a dash habitually in place of a comma, a semicolon, parentheses, or a period. Reserve dashes for situations calling for special emphasis or for the infrequent situation when only a dash will make your meaning clear.

In a typed paper make a dash by joining two hyphens (--) without spaces before or after them.

42a Use dashes to emphasize appositives and parenthetical expressions

Judge Sarah Riley sentenced O'Neil—the treasurer of Local 1026 and once the friend of local politicians—to five years.

The craft of surgery—though some would call it an art—demands the steady hand of a miniaturist to work the scalpel through a web of arteries and veins.

42b Use a dash to separate a series that comes at the beginning of a sentence

Aching feet and ankles, throbbing shins, clicking knees, and crumbling hip joints—these physical ailments result from running on asphalt or cement.

42c Use a dash for special emphasis or clarity

Gary March decided to outrage his associates by wearing gray slacks, a brown sport coat, and a pink shirt—but no one noticed.

The meeting was attended by two consultants—a historian and a psychologist.

In the last example a dash must be used rather than a comma to make it clear that the meeting was attended by two consultants, not by four people—two consultants, a historian, and a psychologist.

42d Use dashes to show a break in tone or thought

"I don't—well—I just can't."
"Can't what?"
"Can't seem—OK—I will if you help."

42e Use a dash to precede an author's name after a formal quotation that stands separately from the text, such as an epigraph

Fasten your seat belts—we're going to have a bumpy night.
—Bette Davis

43 Ellipsis Mark ...

An ellipsis mark (...) indicates that one or more words within a quotation have been intentionally omitted, either to avoid including unnecessary or irrelevant portions of a quoted passage or to mark an unfinished statement in dialogue.

43a Use an ellipsis mark to indicate an omission in a quotation that you have edited to fit the purposes of a paper

ORIGINAL PASSAGE

All his books in the Yoknapatawpha cycle are part of the same living pattern. It is the pattern, not the printed volumes in which part of it is recorded, that is Faulkner's real achievement. Its existence helps to explain one feature of his work: that each novel, each long or short story, seems to reveal more than it states explicitly and to have a subject bigger than itself. All the separate works are like blocks of marble from the same quarry: they show the veins and faults of the mother rock. Or else—to use a rather strained figure— they are like wooden planks that were cut, not from a log, but from a still-living tree. The planks are planed and chiseled into their final shapes, but the tree itself heals over the wound and continues to grow.

—Malcolm Cowley

EDITED WITHIN A PAPER

Malcolm Cowley praises the interconnectedness of Faulkner's work:

> All his books in the Yoknapatawpha cycle are part of the same living pattern. It is the pattern . . . that is Faulkner's real achievement. . . . Each novel, each long or short story, seems to reveal more than it states explicitly and to have a subject bigger than itself.

When a complete sentence comes before an omission, as in the sentence above that ends with *achievement,* you should place a period at the end of the sentence before the ellipsis mark. Note also that a complete sentence, even if it is only part of the original sentence, is capitalized. Finally, note that although the quotation is part of a larger paragraph, an ellipsis mark is not used at the end of the quotation.

43b Use a row of evenly spaced periods to indicate that one or more paragraphs of prose or one or more lines of poetry have been omitted from a quotation

And for all this, nature is never spent;
There lives the dearest freshness deep down things;
. . . .
Because the Holy Ghost over the bent
World broods with warm breast and with ah! bright wings.
—Gerard Manley Hopkins, "God's Grandeur"

43c Use an ellipsis mark to indicate an unfinished statement in speech or dialogue

Barry's nervousness got him off to a bad start: "I'm not sure how to begin. It seems as if . . . I don't know how to tell . . . I don't want to appear . . . Miss Jones . . . can I call you Mildred?"

44 Parentheses ( )

Parentheses separate incidental information from the rest of the sentence. They serve approximately the same function as commas and dashes in some situations, though each mark gives a different emphasis to the inserted information.

> Bernard Slye, the famous movie actor, was this year's grand marshal. [Commas imply that the inserted information is equal in importance to Bernard Slye.]

> Bernard Slye—the famous movie actor—was this year's grand marshal. [Dashes give the inserted information more emphasis.]

> Bernard Slye (the famous movie actor) was this year's grand marshal. [Parentheses imply that the inserted information is incidental.]

All three of the preceding sentences are punctuated correctly. Usually, however, commas, dashes, and parentheses are not used interchangeably but are used with different kinds of inserted information. (See comma, Chapter 37; dash, Chapter 42.)

> Billie Jean Stanford, one of our town's leading citizens, donated one thousand dollars to the earthquake relief fund. [Commas used for inserted information that departs from the thought of the rest of the sentence.]

> Billie Jean Stanford—bless her kind heart—donated one thousand dollars to the earthquake relief fund. [Dashes used for a strong break in sentence continuity.]

> Billie Jean Stanford (Bob's mother) donated one thousand dollars to the earthquake relief fund. [Parentheses used for inserted information of only incidental interest.]

44a Use parentheses to enclose parenthetical descriptions or explanations

> Zablonsky Hall (its brick exterior is almost entirely covered with ivy) stands at the top of the hill. [Description]

45

The lecture on phototaxis (the movement of an organism in response to the stimulus of light) gave Nadia the idea for her animated film. [Explanation]

When a parenthetical sentence comes between two sentences, it should begin with a capital letter and end with a period, question mark, or exclamation point.

My uncle was born in 1950. (What a year that was!) Believe it or not, sirloin steak cost only seventy-seven cents a pound, and the average income was around $3,000 a year.

NOTE: Nonessential elements take no special punctuation other than the parentheses. At times punctuation marks may follow the parentheses if those marks are part of the main sentence.

When I feel my stomach churning from fear (usually on the morning of a midterm or final), I do deep-breathing exercises.

44b Use parentheses to enclose letters or figures that label items in a series

To begin playing tennis well, you must remember three fundamental points: (1) tennis is a sideways game, (2) the backhand stroke makes a loop, and (3) the follow-through should end high.

NOTE: When lists are set off from text, the letters and figures labeling them are usually not enclosed in parentheses.

45 Brackets *[ ]*

Always use brackets to enclose your own comments that explain, clarify, or correct the words of a writer you quote.

FOR EXPLANATION

Flora spoke in a soft voice to the other campers: "In all my years [she had been a ranger at Pig Pines for seven summers], I've never seen a more beautiful sunrise."

FOR CLARITY	Ibrahim, the unenthusiastic protagonist, "surveyed the wreckage [of the airplane] and smiled."
FOR COMPLETENESS	The tall, dark-haired man finally spoke: "[I] try to mind my own business. [Why don't] you do the same?"

The word *sic,* a Latin term meaning "thus it is," in brackets marks an error that you have let stand in a quotation and that you did not make when you copied the quotation.

> Roberts set the scene: "And then nite [*sic*] seemed to crush the castle under a heavy blanket of gloom."

Use *sic* only for errors, not for disagreements you may have with a writer you are quoting.

---

46 The Slash /

The slash, or virgule, separates lines of poetry worked into the text of a paper.

> Faustus is astounded at the beauty of Helen, whom Mephistopheles has summoned to his room: "Was this the face that launch'd a thousand ships, / And burnt the topless towers of Ilium? / Sweet Helen, make me immortal with a kiss."

The slash is also used to indicate an option.

> Students may now take eight units of credit/no-credit courses.

NOTE: Do not join pronouns with a slash when referring to non–gender-specific antecedents. Instead, use *or.*

INCORRECT	CORRECT
he/she	he or she
him/her	him or her
his/her(s)	his or her(s)

---

47 End Punctuation . ? !

Period

47a Use a period to end sentences that are statements, mild commands, or indirect questions

The theater department presents a Shakespearean play every year. [Statement]

Be sure to buy your tickets early. [Mild command]

My uncle asked me which play would be performed this year. [Indirect question]

47b Use periods with most abbreviations

Ms.	Dr.	Ave.	i.e.
Mr.	Ph.D.	Blvd.	e.g.

NOTE: Although the title Ms., used before a name in place of Miss or Mrs., is not an abbreviation, it is still followed by a period: Ms. Hansen.

Generally, BCE and CE do not take periods. No periods are needed in certain common abbreviations or in abbreviations of the names of well-known companies, agencies, and organizations.

NBA	CNN	CBS	IBM
TV	USA (or U.S.A.)	NCAA	VW

Do not use periods with U.S. Postal Service (zip code) abbreviations for states.

CA	MA	VT	WY

Do not use two periods at the end of a sentence.

LaToya received her R.N.
The name on the label is William Gordon, Jr.

Question Mark

47c Use a question mark after a direct question

What changes led to this increase in production?

47d Use a question mark within parentheses to indicate doubt about the accuracy of a date or number

The Peloponnesian War ended in 404 BCE (**?**) with a victory for Sparta.

Do not use a question mark within parentheses in an attempt to indicate sarcasm. Instead shape your words to show your intention.

INCORRECT	I never saw such a hardworking (?) supermarket cashier.
REWRITTEN	John is seldom accused of being hardworking.

Exclamation Point

47e Use an exclamation point after interjections, strong commands, and emphatic statements

INTERJECTION	Wow! Look at that little S-car go.
STRONG COMMAND	"Go away!" she shouted at the dog. "Get out of this yard!"
EMPHATIC STATEMENT	I will never give up!

Do not use an exclamation point within parentheses to indicate sarcasm or amazement. Instead shape your words to convey the meaning.

INCORRECT	Gail's winning essay (!) was printed in the *Clarion*.
REWRITTEN	I couldn't believe Gail won the contest and had her essay printed in the *Clarion*.

NOTE: Only one mark of end punctuation is used. Do not combine marks of end punctuation.

INCORRECT	How can you do this to me?/
REWRITTEN	How can you do this to me?

NOTE: A period is not used as end punctuation for the title of a work. A question mark or an exclamation point is used when appropriate.

Watching God
Shopping for a New Car?
Live Now!

PART VII
Mechanics

Turning in an essay with errors is much like giving a speech without knowing you have lettuce in your teeth. No matter how brilliant your insights or how witty your anecdotes, the audience will be distracted by the green bits of lettuce stuck between your incisors.
—Chuck Dawe, *writing teacher*

48 **Capitals** *cap/lc*

In most writing situations, the following guidelines will help you decide when to capitalize. Whenever you are confused about whether to capitalize a particular word, you can check a good dictionary.

48a Capitalize the first word of every sentence

The fog drifted across the field.
Who is responsible for the engine failure?
Do not touch the kettle.

NOTE: Capitalizing the first word of question fragments in a series is optional. Both of the following examples are correct.

What is the best way to become successful? *by* hard work? *through* education? *by* luck?

What is the best way to become successful? *By* hard work? *Through* education? *By* luck?

Capitalizing the first word of a sentence following a colon depends upon the style you are following. The Modern Language Association (MLA) lowercases the first word if the sentence is other than a rule or a principle. The American Psychological Association (APA) always capitalizes the first word.

MLA STYLE   The eye does more than scan the physical world: *it* reveals the soul.

APA STYLE   The eye does more than scan the physical world: *It* reveals the soul.

48b Always capitalize the interjection *O* and the personal pronoun *I* as well as contractions made with *I,* such as *I've* and *I'm*

I beseech Thee, O Father, to help me in my troubles.

Before I write an essay, I outline the main points of my argument.

Although I've been reading French for three years, I'm still uncomfortable speaking it.

48c Capitalize key words in titles

Capitalize the first and last words and every important word in the titles of your papers and the titles of books, plays, short stories, poems, essays, songs, films, and works of art. Do not capitalize coordinating conjunctions, articles, the *to* of infinitives, or prepositions unless they begin or end a title.

> *Guinness Book of World Records*
> "Traveling through the Dark"

NOTE: Capitalize the word immediately following a colon in a title.

> *The Uses of Enchantment: The Meaning and Importance of Fairy Tales*

Capitalize the first word in a hyphenated compound within a title. Capitalize the other parts of the hyphenated compound if they are nouns or adjectives or are as important as the first word.

> "A Clean, Well-Lighted Place"
> "Mysteries of Hide-and-Seek"
> *The Do-It-Yourself Environmental Handbook*

NOTE: The APA capitalizes prepositions of four letters or more.

> *One Flew Over the Cuckoo's Nest*

48d Capitalize the first word in directly quoted sentences or dialogue

> In *Love and Will,* the psychologist Rollo May writes, "The striking thing about love and will in our day is that, whereas in the past they were always held up to us as the *answer* to life's predicaments, they have now become the *problem.*"

> "This is illegal," the detective whispered, taking the crisp twenties. "We're in it together, I guess."

NOTE: Do not capitalize the first word after an interruption between parts of a quoted sentence.

> "Politicians must be courageous," the senator said, "for if they are not, they will never make unpopular decisions."

48e Capitalize the first word in every line of poetry

> To see a world in a grain of sand
> And a heaven in a wild flower,
> Hold infinity in the palm of your hand
> And eternity in an hour.
>
> —WILLIAM BLAKE, "Auguries of Innocence"

If the poet does not follow this convention, use the poet's style.

> anyone lived in a pretty how town
> (with up so floating many bells down)
> spring summer autumn winter
> he sang his didn't he danced his did.
>
> —E. E. CUMMINGS, "anyone lived in a pretty how town"

48f Capitalize proper nouns, proper adjectives, and words used to form essential parts of proper names

PROPER NOUNS	PROPER ADJECTIVES	COMMON NOUNS
Freud	Freudian	psychoanalyst
Texas	Texan	state
France	French	country

The following is a representative list of words that are typically capitalized. Do not capitalize an article that precedes a proper noun unless it is part of the noun.

SPECIFIC PERSONS, PLACES, THINGS

Pat Kubis	the Tower of London
the Atlantic Ocean	*The Old Curiosity Shop*
the Washington Monument	the Grand Canyon
Europe	the *Los Angeles Times*

HISTORIC EVENTS, PERIODS, MOVEMENTS, DOCUMENTS

Desert Storm	the Enlightenment
the Boston Tea Party	the Roaring Twenties
the Middle Ages	the Bill of Rights

NOTE: Do not capitalize centuries, as in eighteenth century, nineteenth century, and so on.

DAYS OF THE WEEK, MONTHS, HOLIDAYS

Friday	September	Fourth of July

ASSOCIATIONS, ORGANIZATIONS, GOVERNMENT DEPARTMENTS, POLITICAL PARTIES

American Bar Association	U.S. Postal Service
League of Women Voters	House of Representatives
Boston Symphony Orchestra	Republican Party
Metropolitan Museum of Art	Democrats

NAMES OF EDUCATIONAL INSTITUTIONS, DEPARTMENTS, COURSES

Westbrook College	Department of English
Chapman University	History 150

RELIGIONS, RELIGIOUS FOLLOWERS, RELIGIOUS TERMS

Christianity	Christians	God
Judaism	Jews	Judgment Day
Buddhism	Buddhists	Holy Ghost
Hinduism	Hindus	the Virgin
Islam	Muslims	Allah

NOTE: Capitalizing pronouns referring to God is optional in general writing but required in most religious writing. Do not capitalize *who, whom,* or *whose* when referring to God.

RACES, TRIBES, NATIONALITIES, AND THEIR LANGUAGES

Native American	European
Iroquois	Gaelic
African American	Asian
Irish	Yugoslav
Latino	Hispanic

NOTE: Capitalizing *black* and *white* when referring to people is optional. Both of the following examples are correct.

In American cities, Blacks and Whites are struggling to revitalize neglected neighborhoods.

In American cities, blacks and whites are struggling to revitalize neglected neighborhoods.

NAMES OF CELESTIAL BODIES

Mars	the North Star	the Big Dipper

TRADE NAMES

Nintendo	Ford	Frisbee	Coke	Xerox

48g Capitalize titles when they come before proper names, and capitalize abbreviations for academic degrees when they come after proper names

Chancellor Carmen Herrera   Carmen Herrera, M.D.
President Cecelia Perdomo   Cecelia Perdomo, Ph.D.

NOTE: Generally, do not capitalize titles that follow a name.

Harold Thomas, treasurer
Adelina Tapparo, professor of history

48h Capitalize abbreviations that indicate time, divisions of government, national and international organizations, businesses, and call letters of radio and television stations

BC	A.M. (or a.m.)	NATO
BCE	P.M. (or p.m.)	IBM
FDIC	YMCA	WQXR

WRITER'S TOOLBOX

Capitalizing Titles

When a word that functions as a title or shows a family relationship comes before a person's name, capitalize it.

> Today Senator Thompson announced that she would seek reelection.

Also capitalize such words when they could be replaced by a name.

> The Mayor announced that she would seek reelection.

Do not capitalize such words in other circumstances.

> A mayor in California announced that she would seek reelection.

48i Avoid common mistakes in capitalization

Do not capitalize common nouns used in place of proper nouns.

INCORRECT   I plan to enroll in College next Fall.

CORRECT	I plan to enroll in college next fall.
CORRECT	I plan to enroll in Bradley College next September.

Do not capitalize the seasons or academic years or terms.

spring	fall	senior year	winter quarter

Do not capitalize words denoting family relations unless they are part of or a substitute for proper nouns.

INCORRECT	My Mother met my Father on an ocean voyage.
CORRECT	My mother met my father on an ocean voyage.
CORRECT	Mother met Father on an ocean voyage.

Do not capitalize general directions unless they refer to specific geographical areas.

south	the South
east	the East
western	East Manhattan

Exercise 48.1: Capitalizing Words

In the following paragraph, capitalize words as necessary. Consult a dictionary if you are in doubt.

in american literature, satire has helped us examine human experience and smile. the humorist kurt vonnegut, jr., author of satiric novels such as *cat's cradle, slaughterhouse-five, breakfast of champions,* and *galapagos,* believes humankind is in trouble. "our brains," vonnegut says, "are too large." according to vonnegut, nature goofed: *homo sapiens's* highly developed cerebral lobes are responsible for the world's troubles. "our brains are terribly oversized," he says, "and must keep creating things to do." he charges that big brains are responsible for the near destruction of native american culture. humankind's big brains caused the civil war in america and world war I. big brains created the third reich in germany that led to world war II and created death camps like dachau and belsen. humankind's oversized brain made the nuclear weapons that were dropped on hiroshima and nagasaki. vonnegut believes our big brains can be used to solve all our problems, but will it happen? he does not know. after all, human beings now think they are the intellectual center of the universe, when in reality they are nothing more than a speck of dust in the milky way.

---

49 Apostrophe ,

The apostrophe indicates possession, the omission of letters in words, and the plurals of letters and words used as words.

49a Use an apostrophe to form the possessive case for nouns and indefinite pronouns

To form the possessive of singular nouns, plural nouns not ending in -s, and indefinite pronouns (such as *no one, someone,* and *everybody*), add 's. (See indefinite pronouns, 67b.)

> Akemi's novel is about an ex-governor's climb to the presidency.
>
> History exists because of humankind's outstanding achievement: the creation of written language.
>
> If only he could be someone's friend—anyone's—but he felt doomed to be everyone's curse.

To form the possessive of singular nouns ending in -s, add 's.

> He rushed into the boss's office.
>
> Little is known about Cheryl Moses's life in Paris during the Depression.
>
> James's reptile collection gives me an eerie feeling.

In the following examples, only the apostrophe is added because adding 's would make pronunciation difficult.

> James' snake collection gives me an eerie feeling.
> The court listened to Socrates' speech.

To form the possessive of plural words ending in -s, add only an apostrophe.

> The girls' basketball team won.
> The victory was the Mustangs' first.

WRITER'S TOOLBOX

Using Apostrophes Correctly to Show Possession

You can check to see if you need to use an apostrophe to indicate possession by rewriting a sentence, using *of.*

A *persons right* to speak freely is protected by law.

REWRITTEN

The *right of a person* to speak freely is protected by law.

CORRECTED

A *person's right* to speak freely is protected by law.

To form the possessive of compound words, add *'s* or an apostrophe (following the rules for forming possessives) to the last word only.

My son-in-law's job is threatened by military cutbacks.

When two or more nouns show joint possession, add *'s* to the last noun in the group.

Raoul, Gus, and Meera's business is facing stiff competition.

When two or more nouns show individual possession, add *'s* to each noun in the group.

Raoul's, Gus's, and Meera's businesses are facing stiff competition.

Exercise 49.1: Using Apostrophes

Insert apostrophes as needed in the following sentences.

1. *Sophies Choice* advanced William Styrons reputation as Americas leading novelist.

2. A kangaroos hop can span forty-two yards.

3. Grooves and Flags fates are intertwined.

4. The Childrens Book Shoppe on 15th Street holds Kids Time, an hour of storytelling, three times each week.

5. Fathers Day and Mothers Day are celebrated yearly, but no special day has been designated for fathers- and mothers-in-law.

49b Do not use an apostrophe with possessive pronouns such as *his, hers, its, ours, yours, theirs,* and *whose*

The manuscript is *theirs;* the income is *ours.*
If you want the truth, it is *yours.*

NOTE: Be careful not to confuse the possessive pronouns *its, whose, your,* and *their* with the contractions *it's* (it is), *who's* (who is), *you're* (you are), and *they're* (they are).

49c Use an apostrophe to mark omissions in contractions

it's (it is)	don't (do not)	o'clock (of the clock)
we're (we are)	you're (you are)	class of '77 (class of 1977)

49d Use *'s* to form the plurals of letters and words used as words

When speaking publicly do not use *well*'s, *huh*'s, and *you know*'s.
I got two *A*'s and three *B*'s.

NOTE: Letters and words used as words are italicized, but the *'s* is not italicized as part of the word. (In handwritten and typed papers, italics are indicated by underlining. See italics, Chapter 51.)

Exercise 49.2: Using Apostrophes

Delete or insert apostrophes in the following sentences. Correct any mistakes in possessive pronouns. If any sentence is correct, mark it with a C.

1. Mississippi is spelled with four *ss* and four *is*.

2. Whos 57 Ford is this? Hers or his?

3. Its the house on the corner.

4. She became rich in the state's lottery.

5. His *what ifs* make the world sound gloomy.

6. It was our mistake, not hers.

7. Who's responsibility is it?

8. The summer of 1992 was as hot as an angry dragon's breath.

9. *Whys* and *how comes* seem to breed on the tongue of every four-year-old.

10. Many writers confuse *their* or *there* with *theyre* and *your* with *youre*.

50 Abbreviations *ab*

In most writing, avoid using abbreviations unless they are commonly accepted.

50a Abbreviate titles before proper names, if you wish

Mr. Douglas Mincr	Ms. Florence Nesbitt
Mrs. Catherine Rojas	Dr. Hanh Tran
Prof. Wilma Steward	Rev. Marion Sylvester
Gen. Doyle Fujimoto	Msgr. Ramon Alvarez

NOTE: Do not abbreviate a title when it is not used with a proper name.

INCORRECT	The Maj. deployed the volunteers in an awkward formation.
CORRECT	The major deployed the volunteers in an awkward formation.
CORRECT	Maj. Olson deployed the volunteers in an awkward formation.

50b Abbreviate titles immediately following proper names

Yung Kee, M.D.	Donald Sporakowski, Ph.D.
Sumi Inoue, LL.D.	Maude Cook, Ed.D.

NOTE: You may use abbreviations for academic degrees without proper names.

She has one goal—to earn an LL.D. by 2012.

50c Use familiar abbreviations for names of corporations, organizations, and countries

HBO   FBI   IRS   USA (or U.S.A.)   AFL-CIO

NOTE: If a name that you plan to use repeatedly is not well known and can be abbreviated, you may write the full name followed by the abbreviation in parentheses the first time you use it; you may then use the abbreviation throughout the paper.

> Parents, teachers, and students formed the Committee for Educational Excellence of Orange County (CEEOC) to improve classroom teaching. CEEOC raises money to support experimental programs that might go unfunded because of limited state resources.

50d Use the commonly accepted abbreviations *a.m., p.m., BCE, CE, no.,* and the symbol *$* with specific dates and numbers only

12:01 a.m. (or A.M.)   1:00 p.m. (or P.M.)
21 BCE   1061 CE
no. 12 $5,501

NOTE: BCE and CE follow a date.

50e Use common English and Latin abbreviations in tables, footnotes, reference lists, and comments placed inside parentheses

> Hudson, Paul D., et al. *A Last Look at the Great West.* 4th ed. 3 vols. New York: Bayside, 2006.

> The four defendants (i.e., Humphreys, Kettler, Rodda, and Gandy) had to be restrained.

50f Do not abbreviate personal names, calendar terms, courses of study, divisions of written works, units of measurement, or geographical names

PERSONAL NAMES

◆ Edw*ard* Walden wrote three unpublished books.

NAMES OF DAYS, MONTHS, AND HOLIDAYS

◆ The ~~Mon.~~ before ~~Xmas~~ is the earliest I begin to shop.
(Monday) *(Christmas)*

◆ Virgos are born during the second half of ~~Aug.~~ and the first
half of ~~Sept.~~
(August) *(September)*

NOTE: MLA style abbreviates the name of the month in the list of works cited; APA style, however, spells out the name of the month in the reference list. (See the examples for periodicals in 60a and 60b.)

EDUCATIONAL COURSES

◆ You must take ~~lit.~~ and ~~bio.~~ to finish the general education
(literature) *(biology)*

requirements.

DIVISIONS OF WRITTEN WORKS

◆ ~~Sec.~~ 4, ~~ch.~~ 3 is due next week.
(Section) *(chapter)*

UNITS OF MEASUREMENT

◆ The car skidded 106 ~~ft.~~ and 7 ~~in.~~
(feet) *(inches)*

NOTE: Long, familiar phrases, such as *miles per hour,* are usually abbreviated (mph).

The Porsche nosed into the turn at 120 mph, fishtailed, and then screeched down the highway.

GEOGRAPHICAL NAMES

◆ The outstanding characteristic of ~~L.A., Calif.,~~ is that it seems to
(Los Angeles, California,)
be able to stretch itself from the ~~Mex.~~ border to San Francisco.
(Mexican)

◆ He grew up in Huntington ~~Pk.~~ on Randolph ~~St.~~ near Miles
~~Ave.~~
(Park) *(Street)* *(Avenue.)*

NOTE: Certain familiar abbreviations for countries are acceptable: USA (or U.S.A.).

51 Italics *ital*

With the almost universal availability of computers for writing academic papers, writers can now use italic (or *slanted*) type, rather than underlining, when distinguishing certain titles, words, and phrases.

51a Italicize the titles of books and other long works

Use italics, not quotation marks, for the titles of books, periodicals, newspapers, plays, films, long poems, long musical compositions, television and radio shows, album titles, and works of visual art. (See quotation marks, 40b.) When italicizing a title, be precise. Do not italicize an initial *a, an,* or *the* unless it is part of the title itself.

BOOK	*The Color Purple*
MAGAZINE	*Vanity Fair*
NEWSPAPER	*The New York Times*
	the *Los Angeles Times*
LONG POEM	*The Waste Land*
PLAY	*Angels in America*
FILM	*The Dark Knight*
TELEVISION PROGRAM	*Project Runway*
RADIO PROGRAM	*Car Talk*
LONG MUSICAL WORK	*The Nutcracker* but: The
	Nutcracker Suite
WORK OF VISUAL ART	*Mona Lisa*
CARTOON OR COMIC STRIP	*Doonesbury*
ALBUM TITLE	*The Wall*
SOFTWARE	*Microsoft Word*

NOTE: Names of legal documents, the Bible, and parts of the Bible are not italicized.

INCORRECT	The *Bill of Rights* contains the first ten amendments to the *Constitution*.
CORRECT	The Bill of Rights contains the first ten amendments to the Constitution.
INCORRECT	The *Bible* is composed of the *Old Testament* and the *New Testament*.
CORRECT	The Bible is composed of the Old Testament and the New Testament.

51b Italicize the names of spacecraft, aircraft, ships, and trains

Discovery   *Titanic*   *Orient Express*   *Spirit of St. Louis*

51c Italicize non-English words and phrases that have not become common expressions

Harrods, Europe's largest department store, tries to live up to its motto—*Omnia, omnibus, ubique*—everyone, everything, everywhere.

Foreign words that have been absorbed into English do not need to be italicized. For example, the words *cliché* and *genre*, both French, are commonly used in English and therefore are not italicized. When in doubt, consult a dictionary to see if a foreign word or phrase should be italicized.

NOTE: Most commonly used foreign abbreviations—i.e., etc., ibid., op. cit., sic—are not italicized.

51d Italicize words, letters, numbers, phrases, and symbols when they are referred to as such

When writing a paper, you should not use *&* for *and*.

Someone had painted an *X* on the oak.

The voters are tired of *maybe* and *perhaps*.

"Mind your *p*'s and *q*'s" was my grandmother's favorite expression.

NOTE: You can use quotation marks instead of italics to set off a word you are defining. Both of the following styles are correct, but you should use one style consistently throughout a paper.

> *Bumbershoot*, which is slang for *umbrella*, is the result of merging *umbr* from umbrella and *shoot* from parachute.

> "Bumbershoot," which is slang for "umbrella," is the result of merging "umbr" from "umbrella" and "shoot" from "parachute."

51e Italics may be used to show emphasis

> I wrote that I wanted the *entire* amount.

Excessive use of italics, however, will only distract the reader and diminish the emphasis.

> I wrote that I wanted the *entire* amount.

51f Do not italicize the titles of your own papers

> Propaganda: Five Ways to Trick a Consumer

Do italicize the title of another work included in your title.

> The Message of *The Autobiography of Malcolm X*

---

52 Hyphen *hyph*

Use the hyphen to divide words, form compounds, and add some prefixes, suffixes, and letters to words.

52a Use a hyphen to indicate that a word is broken at the end of a typed or handwritten line

> Emergency volunteers, medical workers, and federal avia-
> tion experts began sifting through the wreckage.

NOTE: Be sure to divide words between syllables. Whenever you are unsure of the syllabication of a word, check a dictionary. Do not break a one-syllable word.

52b Use a hyphen to form certain compound words

cross-reference	clear-cut
mother-in-law	half-moon
deep-fry	bull's-eye
jack-o-lantern	great-grandfather

NOTE: Since most compound words are not hyphenated, check a dictionary whenever you are uncertain about whether to hyphenate a compound word.

52c Use a hyphen to join two or more words that serve as a single descriptive word before a noun

The one-eyed, one-armed cowboy could hold his own in any two-bit joint he stumbled into.

In Pentagon jargon, two-syllable names indicate jets, and one-syllable names indicate piston-driven aircraft.

Since taking a course in crafts, Beth has produced some well-designed furniture.

The twenty-year-old adventurer will lecture tomorrow.

NOTE: When the descriptive phrase comes after the noun, the words are usually not hyphenated.

Beth's furniture is well designed.

The adventurer, who is twenty years old, will lecture tomorrow.

But when such a phrase is used as a noun, it is hyphenated.

The adventurer, a daring twenty-year-old, will lecture tomorrow.

52d Use a hyphen to spell out the compound numbers twenty-one to ninety-nine and fractions

seventy-five	ninety-nine	one-half	three-fourths

52e Use a hyphen to join certain prefixes, suffixes, and letters to words

Use a hyphen to join a prefix to a word beginning with a capital letter.

> Those who criticize foreign policy are sometimes accused of being anti-American.

Use a hyphen between words and the prefixes *self-*, *all-*, and *ex-* (meaning formerly) as well as the suffix *-elect*.

> self-control   all-encompassing   ex-student   president-elect

Use a hyphen to join single letters to words.

> Z-transfer   U-turn   T-shirt   F-sharp

52f Use suspended hyphens for hyphenated words in a series

> My *mother-*, *father-*, and *brother-in-law* graduated from high school.

52g Use a hyphen to avoid confusion

In creating compound words, use a hyphen rather than doubling vowels and tripling consonants.

- The current college administration has an antiintellectual attitude.

- When the wind blows, the chimes make belllike music.

- The concept of a college without walls is like a wallless room— full of wind.

Use a hyphen to avoid ambiguity.

> re-creation (something created anew)
> recreation (a diverting activity)
> re-sign (to sign again)
> resign (to give up a position)

53 **Numbers** *num*

Follow established conventions when writing numbers.

53a Spell out any number consisting of only one or two words

Eighty-five cyclists started, but only *twenty-one* finished.

The race covered *four hundred* miles of tough Mexican desert over a period of *three* days.

53b Use figures for any number that requires more than two words to spell out

Hurricane Katrina caused 1,300 known deaths and left more than 12,000 families without homes.

NOTE: Be consistent. If there are several numbers, some composed of one or two words and others of more than two words, use numerals for all of them. Also, if numbers are used frequently in a discussion, use numerals for all of them.

53c Use a combination of figures and words for numbers when such a combination will keep your writing clear

The president invited fifty 10-year-olds to the Easter celebration.

53d Use figures for dates; time; addresses; scores and other numerical results; percentages, decimals, and fractions; pages and divisions of written works; and exact amounts of money

DAYS AND YEARS

November 11, 2010   423 BCE   1492 CE   the 1990s

The forms *1st, 2nd,* and so on, as well as *fourth, fifth,* and so on, are sometimes used in dates but only when the year is omitted: *December 5th, December fifth.*

TIME OF DAY

12:15 p.m.   1300 hours   5:43 a.m.

If you are not using a.m. or p.m., write the time in words.

We will meet at twelve-thirty, and we will leave at one o'clock.

ADDRESSES

4345 Sandburg Way   4 Upper Newport Plaza

SCORES, STATISTICS, RESULTS OF SURVEYS

The Hawks beat the Hornets by a score of 133 to 102.

You must score over 600 to qualify.

Out of the 500 surveyed, 498 recognized the name *Tyrone Power,* but only 56 knew he had been an actor, and 16 said they had never "seen one" but had heard they were great to drive.

PERCENTAGES, DECIMALS, FRACTIONS

23 percent (or 23%)   98.6 $12\frac{1}{3}$

PAGES AND DIVISIONS OF WRITTEN WORKS

page 3, pages 110–124   chapter 2   volume 5
act 4   scene 1   lines 5–22

EXACT AMOUNTS OF MONEY

$100,871 $19.76 $123 million

53e Spell out any number that begins a sentence

Two hundred thirteen [not 213] voted for the amendment.

Revising the sentence may be more effective than spelling out the number.

The amendment passed by a vote of 213 to 0.

Exercise 53.1: Writing Numbers

Correct the faulty use of numbers in the following sentences. If any sentence is correct, mark it with a C.

1. In Super Bowl XLII in Phoenix, the New York Giants unexpectedly defeated the previously undefeated New England Patriots seventeen to fourteen with a 13 yard pass in the 4th quarter.

2. 42.5 million people live in Congo, which has a growth rate of three point three percent.

3. Massive mud slides have been known to reach speeds of sixty mph.

4. On October 18th, 1864, 15 Confederate raiders robbed 3 banks in St. Albans, Vermont, and buried $114,522 in gold and currency, $82\frac{1}{2}$ percent of the town's total capital.

5. Nearly 1,000 fans were turned away from the auditorium gates even though they had paid as much as $80.00 for seats.

---

54 Spelling *sp*

Nobody improves poor spelling without working at it. To get started, use a dictionary to check the spelling of words you are uncertain about. If you write on a word processor, use the spell-check program to check the spelling in each paper you write, but be careful—a spell-check program won't distinguish among words that sound the same but are spelled differently, such as *accept, except; their, there, they're; who's, whose; its, it's;* and *won, one.* Also compile a personal list of spelling demons, the words you frequently misspell, such as *occasion, separate, rhythm, negotiator, strategy.* When you use a word on your demon list, double-check its spelling. Finally, remember that basic spelling guidelines and lists of commonly misspelled words will help you eliminate spelling errors.

54a Place *i* before *e* except after *c* or when pronounced like *a* as in *neighbor* or *weigh*

I BEFORE *E*	chief, grief, belief, brief, fierce, frieze, sieve
E BEFORE *I*	ceiling, conceit, receive, freight
EXCEPTIONS	either, neither, foreign, forfeit, height, leisure, weird, seize, sheik

54b Usually drop a silent final *e* before a suffix that begins with a vowel. Usually keep the silent final *e* before a suffix beginning with a consonant

DROP THE *E*	come + ing = coming force + ible = forcible
	fame + ous = famous love + able = lovable
EXCEPTIONS	dying, singeing, mileage, noticeable, courageous

KEEP THE *E*	care + ful = careful
	arrange + ment = arrangement
EXCEPTIONS	awful, ninth, truly, argument, judgment

54c When a final *y* follows a consonant, change *y* to *i* before a suffix except when the suffix begins with *i*

With *y* before a consonant:

> try + ed = tried   messy + er = messier

With *y* before a vowel:

> obey + ed = obeyed   betray + al = betrayal

With a suffix beginning with *i:*

> apply + ing = applying   try + ing = trying

54d Double the final consonant before a suffix beginning with a vowel if the word has only one syllable or is stressed on the last syllable

> drop + ing = dropping   stop + ed = stopped
> forget + ing = forgetting   submit + ed = submitted

54e Form plurals correctly

Add *s* to form the plurals of most words. Add *es* to form the plurals of words ending in *-s, -sh, -ch,* or *-x.* For most words ending in *y,* change the *y* to *i* and add *es.*

| book, books | dress, dresses | bush, bushes |
| fox, foxes | fly, flies | church, churches |

Form the plural of hyphenated words by adding *s* to the main word.

> son-in-law, sons-in-law

Form the plural of family names ending in *y* by adding *s,* such as in *McCurry, McCurrys.* For family names ending in *-s* or *-x* or *-z,* add *es,* as in Rosses, Foxes or Ramirezes.

Form the plural of most nouns ending in *-f* or *-fe* by adding *s.* But the plural of some of these nouns is formed by changing the *f* to *v* and adding *s* or *es.*

| chief, chiefs | dwarf, dwarfs | roof, roofs |
| calf, calves | knife, knives | leaf, leaves |

EDITOR'S TOOLBOX

Spell-Checkers

A spell-checker is a valuable software asset, but it won't solve all your spelling problems. For example, a spell-checker will not flag commonly confused words such as *illusion* and *allusion* or *accept* and *except*. It will not flag words that sound alike but have different meanings and spellings, such as *all together* and *altogether* or *there* and *their*. It will not show you how to spell words not in its dictionary, but it will flag them so you can check the spelling in your dictionary. Nevertheless, a spell-checker is useful because it will flag most typos and most misspellings, allow you to correct the errors on the screen, and integrate the changes throughout the text with one click of the mouse.

Form the plural of words ending in *-o* following a vowel by adding *s*, but form the plural of most words ending in *-o* following a consonant by adding *es*.

    radio, radios   mosquito, mosquitoes

Exception: Form the plural of musical terms ending in *-o* by adding *s*.

    piano, pianos   solo, solos

The plurals of a few nouns are formed by irregular methods.

child, children	goose, geese	mouse, mice
ox, oxen	tooth, teeth	woman, women

Some nouns borrowed from French, Greek, and Latin retain the plural form of the original language.

alumnus, alumni	analysis, analyses
basis, bases	datum, data
medium, media	criterion, criteria

Some nouns are the same in plural and singular forms.

    deer   Chinese   species   trout

Exercise 54.1: Using Spelling Guidelines

Complete the following words by filling in the blanks with *ie* or *ei*, whichever is correct.

1. w __rd
2. p __ce
3. perc __ve
4. n __ce
5. th __f

6. l __sure
7. c __ling
8. ach __ve
9. for __ gn
10. rec __ pt

Add the suffixes to the words below. Be able to explain the rule that applies to each word. Use the dictionary to check your work.

11. unwrap + ed
12. stubborn + ness
13. plant + ing
14. ski + ing
15. commit + ed

16. casual + ly
17. move + ing
18. merry + ly
19. argue + ment
20. write + ing

Write the plural forms of each of the following words. Be able to explain your spelling according to the rules for forming plurals. Refer to a dictionary when in doubt.

21. father-in-law
22. cameo
23. wife
24. loss
25. box

26. crisis
27. loaf
28. alumnus
29. Kelly
30. approach

Commonly Confused Words

Many spelling errors come from confusion over the meaning and correct spelling of commonly used words. Learn the spelling and the meaning of the following commonly confused words.

accept	to receive
except	to exclude
advice	counsel (noun)
advise	to give advice (verb)
affect	to influence (verb)
effect	a result (noun); to accomplish (verb)
all ready	prepared
already	previously
brake	to stop

break	to smash
buy	to purchase
by	near
capital	accumulated wealth; city serving as government seat
capitol	building in which legislative body meets (lowercase for state, uppercase for federal)
choose	to select
chose	past tense of *choose*
cite	to quote
sight	ability to see
site	a place
complement	something that completes
compliment	flattering remark
conscience	moral sense (noun)
conscious	aware (adjective)
coarse	rough (adjective)
course	path, procedure, process (noun)
decent	moral (adjective)
descent	a way down (noun)
dissent	to disagree (verb); difference of opinion (noun)
desert	to abandon (verb); barren land (noun)
dessert	last course of a meal
formally	in a formal manner
formerly	previously
forth	forward
fourth	after third
hear	to perceive by ear (verb)
here	in this place
heard	past tense of *hear*
herd	group of animals
instance	an example
instants	moments
its	possessive of *it*
it's	contraction of *it is*
lead	to show the way (verb); a metal (noun)
led	past tense of *lead*
lessen	to make less
lesson	something learned
loose	to free from restraint (verb); not fastened (adjective)
lose	to misplace; to be deprived of (verb)

passed	past tense of *pass*
past	no longer current (adjective); an earlier time (noun); beyond in time or place (preposition)
peace	absence of strife
piece	a part of something
plain	clear (adjective); level land (noun)
plane	airplane; carpenter's tool
principal	most important (adjective); leader (noun)
principle	basic truth or law (noun)
right	correct (adjective)
rite	ceremony (noun)
write	to record (verb)
road	a driving surface
rode	past tense of *ride*
stationary	unmoving
stationery	writing paper
their	possessive of *they*
there	in that place
they're	contraction of *they are*
to	toward
too	also; excess amount
two	the number following one
weak	not strong
week	Sunday through Saturday
weather	condition of climate
whether	if, either
who's	contraction of *who is*
whose	possessive of *who*
your	possessive of *you*
you're	contraction of *you are*

Exercise 54.2: Using Commonly Confused Words

For each of the following sentences, identify the correct word in parentheses.

1. The ancient temple was the (*cite, sight, site*) of mysterious rituals.

2. The coat does not (*complement, compliment*) the dress.

3. Her job is to (*advice, advise*) the board, not make (*its, it's*) decisions.

4. You must contribute (*weather, whether*) you want to or not.

5. The boys were not (*conscience, conscious*) of the damage they did.

6. I think I know (*who's, whose*) thumbprint that is.

7. He stands as (*stationary, stationery*) as a statue.

8. There is a (*principal, principle*) cause for his joy—money!

9. Can you identify the (*affect, effect*) of the chemical?

10. (*Accept, Except*) for Roberta, no one was in the house last night.

Frequently Misspelled Words

Learn to spell frequently misspelled words. The following is a list of one hundred commonly misspelled "demons."

absence	familiar	personnel
academic	fascinate	precede
accidentally	February	prejudice
accommodate	foreign	prevalent
achieve	forty	privilege
across	friend	probably
all right	fulfill	procedure
already	government	proceed
apparent	grammar	quantity
appearance	harass	quiet
athletic	height	quite
attendance	independent	quizzes
believe	intelligence	receive
benefited	license	reference
Britain	luxury	referred
business	maneuver	referring
calendar	marriage	reminisce
candidate	mathematics	repetition
cemetery	misspelled	rhythm
definite	neither	ridiculous
desperate	ninth	sacrifice
develop	occasion	safety
dilemma	occur	salary
dining	occurrence	satellite
embarrass	optimistic	secretary
emphasize	parallel	seize
existence	pastime	separate

sergeant	succeed	usually
similar	succession	vacuum
sincerely	surprise	vengeance
sophomore	temperament	weird
specimen	tendency	writing
strategy	thorough	
subtly	tragedy	

Exercise 54.3: Frequently Misspelled Words

Test yourself on the list of frequently misspelled words by asking someone to read the words aloud so that you can spell them.

PART VIII

Special College Essays

Writing is about getting something down, not about thinking something up. Whenever I strive to "think something up," writing becomes something I must stretch to achieve. It becomes loftier than I am, perhaps even something so lofty, it is beyond my grasp. When I am trying to think something up, I am straining. When I am focused on just getting something down, I have a sense of attention but not a sense of strain.

—Julia Cameron, *poet and journalist*

55 The Argument Essay *arg*

An argument essay is distinguished from other essays because it has an *argumentative edge*—that is, the writer takes a stand on a controversial issue.

In writing, critical thinking finds its most direct expression in argumentation. By using argumentation, writers attempt to change or reinforce a reader's opinion or to move that reader to take action. Often an argument essay may be emotionally charged, appealing to a reader's feelings with emotional detail or biased language. This is called *persuasive argument.* Or an argument essay may be highly rational, appealing to a reader's intellect with logical discussion. This is called *logical argument.* Political writing relies heavily on persuasive argument, whereas academic writing relies heavily on logical argument. With the exception of highly scientific argument, however, an argument essay seldom appeals only to emotion or only to reason.

The ancient Greeks, who formulated the underlying concepts of logic, identified three factors crucial to the construction of an effective argument:

1. *Logos,* or the quality of arguing soundly, refers to the quality of the evidence—that is, examples, facts, statistics, authority statements, reasonable interpretations.
2. *Pathos,* or the feeling dimension of language, refers to the ability to connect with a reader's emotion—that is, values, attitudes, and psychological needs.
3. *Ethos,* or credibility and honesty, refers to how writers present themselves—that is, knowledgeable, trustworthy, logical, or ignorant, shiftless, erratic.

An effective argument usually blends *logos, pathos,* and *ethos.* The exact mixture varies with the audience and your purpose.

55a Write a purpose statement for an argument essay

Identifying the purpose of an argument essay is similar to identifying the purpose of any college essay (review 4a and 6a); that is, a purpose statement should identify the subject and how you wish to develop it. Consider the following examples.

> I want to argue that the use of animals in scientific research is necessary to protect humankind.

The writer will discuss animals used in scientific research. The method of development is also clear: The writer will argue that research using animals is necessary.

> I want to convince my readers that campus police should be armed.

The subject is arming campus police, and the writer will argue to do so.

> I will argue that films featuring characters who smoke cigarettes should carry the surgeon general's warning that smoking is hazardous to a smoker's health.

Here, too, the subject—films featuring characters who smoke—and the method of development—to argue that the public should be warned about the hazards of smoking—are clear.

55b Develop and evaluate evidence to support your argument

When writing an argument, you are interpreting evidence, not merely presenting facts and opinions. It will usually be the power of your interpretation that wins the day, not the innate truth or falsity of the evidence you marshal in support of your position. Always remember, evidence presented without careful, thoughtful interpretation will not influence most readers (review 2a, 2b, 2c). There are several types of evidence you can use in an argument essay, but some types are more convincing than others.

Facts and Statistics

Often the most convincing argument you can develop is based on facts and statistics. Facts and statistics, when used appropriately, are irrefutable but will not carry an argument in themselves. Instead, they serve as the basis for an inference. For example, research from the Industry Safety Council in Washington, DC, points out the following facts about automobile tires.

- Americans wear nearly 50 million pounds of rubber off their tires every two weeks, enough rubber to make 3.25 million new tires.
- Some 240 to 260 million tires are discarded each year in the United States.

- Billions of tires currently fill up landfill space.
- It takes half a barrel of crude oil to produce the rubber in one truck tire.

In themselves these facts are merely surprising in their magnitude, but if used to argue a case for recycling tires, they could be compelling.

When using facts and statistics, you must be sure the inferences you draw are reasonable. No one, for example, can dispute the fact that four powerful advocates of African American rights—John F. Kennedy, Malcolm X, Martin Luther King, Jr., and Robert Kennedy—were assassinated in the 1960s. But the interpretation of this fact as proof of a powerful anti–civil rights conspiracy is highly debatable.

Informed Authorities

In daily life we rely on a variety of authorities. Dentists evaluate the condition of our teeth. Critics recommend films and books. Weather forecasters tell us to prepare for rain or sunshine. In an argument essay you can rely on authority to support your opinion, but you must be sure your authority is an expert in the field. To argue for special psychological treatment for children who are victims of natural catastrophes, you would rely on developmental psychologists, not law enforcement officers. To argue for government-supported child care, you should rely on educational experts, not political activists.

Avoid using recognized experts in one field as authorities in an unrelated field. For example, a Nobel Prize–winning biologist might have opinions about the economy but is probably not an authority on the economy.

Also avoid using biased authorities. For example, a film executive's opinion about the social effects of violence in popular movies will probably not be an objective opinion.

Avoid using *nameless* authorities. Although "doctors maintain," "three hundred scientists surveyed," and "nationally recognized educators" are often cited by advertisers, to do so in an argument essay would detract from its credibility.

Personal Observations

You can rely on your own observations and the observations of others as evidence to support your opinion. In fact, often the most vivid and dramatic evidence results from personal observations. A traveler's report from a foreign country; a friend's exchange with law enforcement officers; your own encounter with the college bureaucracy; a visit to a polluted river, beach, or industrial site—all can add color and significant information to an argument essay.

When using personal observations as evidence, do all you can to present accurate information. You know how accurate a description of your own experience is because you lived it, but when you present the experience of others, you are in effect vouching for its veracity. It is often wise, therefore, to include more than one account of the same event.

Personal observations become even more compelling when used in conjunction with other forms of evidence. For example, to develop an argument to convince officials to protect an ecologically sensitive salt marsh, you might visit the site and report your observations. If your observations can also be supported by authorities, facts, and statistics, then your observation and the argument's validity will be difficult to challenge.

55c Confront the opposition

During the evidence-gathering process, keep in mind that you must confront the opposing arguments you identified when planning a strategy. If you neglect to confront the opposition, your essay will be ineffective because you will not have dissuaded the reader from those opposing arguments. By confronting objections to your position, you are actively convincing readers that your arguments are sound and that you are a reasonable person, thus making your case even stronger. You can confront opposing arguments by showing that they are unreasonable, unfair, or even weak and emotional. If, however, the opposing position is so compelling that it is not easily dismissed, then concede its strength and go on to make an even stronger case for your position.

One effective strategy to use when planning your essay is to develop a list of arguments that support your position and a list of arguments that oppose your position.

List Supporting Arguments

Begin by developing a list of arguments you might use to support your position. Suppose you want to argue that films featuring characters who smoke cigarettes should carry the surgeon general's warning. You might develop a list of supporting arguments similar to the following:

- Scientific evidence shows that smoking is hazardous to health.
    Smoking causes lung cancer.
    Smoking affects the fetuses of pregnant women.
    Smoking causes emphysema.
- Because of the health hazards of smoking, advertisements for cigarettes have been banned from television and radio. Moreover, cigarette advertisements in magazines carry a warning of the health hazards of smoking.
- Many classic films feature romantic characters who smoke. A famous actor, Humphrey Bogart, died of lung cancer.
- Many current films perpetuate smoking by featuring romantic characters who smoke.
- Several cigarette companies realize the advertising value of having film characters smoke their brands, and they have paid film companies to feature their brands.

List Opposing Arguments

Once you have listed supporting arguments, list opposing arguments. An effective tactic for developing a list of opposing arguments is to discuss the issue with someone who disagrees with your position. The discussion can provide you with valuable information you might have overlooked. Here is a list of arguments opposing the labeling of movies that feature characters who smoke.

- There is no practical way to evaluate the impact on viewer behavior of characters who smoke in films.
- Much information already exists about the hazards of smoking, so film viewers must already be aware of the dangers.
- Films reflect reality. Many people smoke, so why should films be held accountable for reflecting that reality?
- Forcing film companies to label films would be just one more government attempt to interfere with free expression in the arts.

Reconsider Your Position

After developing lists of supporting and opposing arguments, you might reconsider your position. Perhaps the supporting arguments are weak and the opposing arguments are strong. In this situation you would probably be unable to convince readers that you are right, even though you still believe in your original position. Perhaps your position is oversimplified, too extreme, or merely rooted in a preference. In these situations you might rethink your position, attempting to search beyond the obvious in order to modify your extreme thinking or to rephrase your preference so you can support it.

55d Write an argumentative thesis statement and sketch a plan

An argument is predicated on an "assertion," that is, an opinion you want a reader to accept or an action you want a reader to take. When stated in a sentence, the assertion is referred to as a **proposition** or **thesis** (review Chapter 7). Take a stand in your thesis; that is, clearly state your position so readers will have no doubt about your sympathies.

> Television stations should not be allowed to broadcast children's programs that feature violent encounters.
>
> Class attendance should not be a factor in grading.
>
> The high-fashion fur industry should be stopped.

Sometimes you might identify the opposing position in your thesis statement.

> Although censoring magazines that feature nudity would violate freedom of expression, these magazines should not be sold in community vending machines.
>
> Even though some ranchers will lose livestock to wolf packs, for ecological reasons wolves should be reintroduced into the western national parks.
>
> Police maintain that they do not target college-age drivers, but the evidence shows that police consistently abuse their authority near the university.

Notice that in each of these statements the writer takes a clear stand on a debatable point, one with which reasonable people could disagree.

Once you have written a clear thesis statement, you are ready to plan the development of your essay in sentence form. The points you state in your development plan can serve as topic sentences for the finished essay. Your thesis statement and development plan, therefore, will give you a sketch or rough outline for your final paper.

In the following example, the writer wants to argue that movie violence should not be censored. Furthermore, he wants to convince his readers that the skillful use of violence heightens audience interest.

THESIS	Despite charges that movie violence triggers social violence, the evidence shows that no causal relationship exists between imaginary violence and human behavior, and, moreover, violence used skillfully in movies heightens audience interest.
DEVELOPMENT	• Some movies use violence in irresponsible ways.
	• No study has shown a causal connection between movie violence and actual violent behavior.
	• Since violence pervades real life, viewers demand that movies depict violence to reflect reality.
	• Although many movies feature gratuitous violence, others use skillfully crafted violence to engage viewers in positive ways.
	• Even such mild fare as *Bambi* and *The Wizard of Oz* use carefully crafted violence to heighten viewer awareness.
	• The careful crafting of violence to achieve dramatic purposes has its roots in classical literature.

The development pattern of this essay is clear. The author would first write an introduction that presents the thesis statement. He would then concede that many movies feature gratuitous violence, but he would also point out that even if gratuitous violence is a characteristic of many films, it still has no proven effect on audience behavior. Next, the writer would develop the supporting arguments: violence is part of real life; skillfully crafted violence engages viewers in positive ways; even classic children's films use violence; and finally, violence plays a significant role in literature in general.

55e Arranging an argument inductively or deductively

To be convincing, evidence must be arranged so that it all makes sense to a reader. Presenting evidence logically is the most important part of argument writing.

There are two logical approaches to arranging evidence: inductive and deductive. Remember, an *inductive* argument moves from the particular details to generalization. Whenever you begin by first presenting evidence and end by making a logical conclusion from the evidence, you are using inductive reasoning (review 3b). A *deductive* argument is the opposite, and it is similar to college essay arrangement. Whenever you begin with a generalization you assume to be true, consider a specific case of that generalization, and then arrive at a conclusion, you are probably using deductive, or *syllogistic,* reasoning (see 3c). Should you ever include an actual syllogism in an argument? No, but sometimes an argument can be reduced to syllogistic form.

NOTE: Review Chapter 17, Argument Paragraphs, before writing an argument essay.

55f Write an argument essay with a reader in mind

While writing and revising an argument, always keep an eye on your readers. Since you can't be all things to all readers, you might find it helpful to lump them into one of three general categories and then address them appropriately.

Supportive readers already agree with you. There's no need to overload your argument with dry facts and statistics for them. You can emphasize *pathos* over *logos*—that is, rely more on emotion and less on information. Touch the right emotional nerve, and this crowd will carry you away on its shoulders.

Wavering readers are uncommitted or uninformed readers. They are the ones you want to move by using both *logos* and *ethos,* that is, by presenting solid evidence and by establishing your trustworthiness and honesty. Establish the right image, and they will hop on your bandwagon.

Hostile readers are apathetic, skeptical, downright mean. Convincing them of anything is like trying to pull an angry bull's tooth with pliers. Just the facts, please—simple facts, dramatic facts, any facts that will penetrate their intransigence. *Ethos* won't help much, they already see you as a low-down schemer trying to sell them snake oil, and *pathos* will come back at you like a nail-filled mud pie. Just keep writing calmly and rely on *logos*. It's hard to spit in the face of truth.

55g Use the Toulmin model to examine an argument

The philosopher Stephen Toulmin has developed a way to examine the strength of an argument, one that can help you tell if you are covering everything you should. It is a simple system to use in ordinary thinking situations, and it reflects how most people use their minds. The *Toulmin model* consists of three main elements:

> The *claim* is the conclusion you draw from your examination of the information: the thesis.
>
> The *grounds* are the pieces of information related to the issue: the evidence.
>
> The *warrant* is the principle that links the evidence to the thesis: the assumption.

How does the Toulmin model work? Here's a simplified example: Someone makes the suggestion that you and your roommates would have fun camping during the upcoming weekend. You respond by saying, "We can't. We have an examination in freshman composition on Monday."

CLAIM	We can't go camping.
GROUNDS	We have a midterm examination.
WARRANT	Students should stay home and study before a test.

Often a warrant is left unstated because it is usually so obvious that the listener will fill it in. *Students should study the weekend before a test* is a warrant—an assumption behind the claim and the grounds—that most college students would agree with. Sometimes, however, a listener might fill in a different warrant. Suppose that one of your roommates has a warrant that says *Students should relax before a test.* He or she could insist that everyone go camping. You might think this view strange or even unreasonable until you clarified the conflicting assumptions behind each other's thinking.

Notice that a warrant is similar to the generalization used in a syllogism (review 3c) or the conclusion of an inductive chain (review 3b). You could easily argue:

> Students who have a test on Monday shouldn't camp the weekend before.
>
> All of us have a test on Monday.
>
> Therefore, we shouldn't go camping Friday, Saturday, and Sunday.

By using Toulmin's model to identify warrant, claim, and grounds, you can see whether the warrant links the claim and the grounds and whether it should be stated explicitly or left implicit. The model will also help you clarify, or even qualify, your claim and help you determine if you have enough information to convince a reader that your claim is justified.

A Student Argument Essay

Examine the following essay by student-writer Allison Ko in response to this freshman composition assignment:

> Select a controversial subject that is frequently in the newspapers. Write a 500- to 750-word logical argument that takes a position on the subject. Be sure to account for the opposing position within your essay. If the subject you select has undergone extensive public discussion, assume that your reader is familiar with the general elements of the debate and develop specific evidence based on your own observations, reading, and experience.

After your first reading of the essay, turn back and examine the comments in the margin. (Key sentences are italicized.)

War on Drugs: A Losing Battle

Title announces Ko's position.

Are we winning the war against drug use? Last week our local police arrested a narcotics dealer and confiscated over $3 million in cocaine.

Introduction sets up the thesis statement.

The *Register* even published a front-page story under the headline, "Cops Make Record Drug Bust." The "bust" was heralded as a victory in our community's effort to win the war on drugs. But such front-page stories are misleading. Local, state, and federal law enforcement agencies will never win the war on drugs. In fact, we are wasting valuable resources, restricting constitutional freedoms, and overcrowding our prisons in our effort to combat drug use. By making drug use illegal, we have created a "Prohibition" atmosphere with an increase in crime. *The only way to win the*

Thesis has an argumentative edge.

war on drugs is to legalize drug use.

First discussion paragraph opens with an opposing view.

Politicians who support the war on drugs tell us that if we legalize what are now illegal drugs, we are sending our children the wrong message. To do so would be saying, "Yes, drugs can ruin you and your family's lives. They can kill

Transition sentence
shifts to Ko's
position.

sooner or later. We don't advise you to use them,
but if you want to, we'll make them available to
you at the neighborhood drugstore." *Nothing
could be further from the truth.* Ask any of our
school principals. Drugs are already available at
neighborhood "drugstores." Police officers will
tell you the same story. Furthermore, they will
tell you if any mildly enterprising teenagers want
to score drugs, they can do so within ten minutes
of home. Moreover, there is no sound research
that indicates legalizing drugs would create more

Paragraph closes
with a clincher.

users. Common sense may say so, but common
sense, as has been proven time and time again,
is commonly wrong.

Second discussion
paragraph opens
with an opposing
view.

    *Those who actively campaign against drugs
say drug use is our country's biggest social
problem.* One anti-drug champion recently
claimed that over half of all murders were
committed by people under the influence of
drugs. He said that most street crime and home
burglaries were committed by people who needed

Ko agrees with
opposing view but
says her position will
solve the problem.

money for drugs. The high crime rate caused by
drug use is a problem, but if drugs were legalized
and sold at a reasonable price, then addicts
would not have to steal to pay for their addiction.
But as long as drugs are illegal and costly, the
drug-related crime rate will not drop.

Third discussion
paragraph opens by
pointing out a major
flaw in opposition
thinking.

    When anti-drug champions trumpet the high
crime rate caused by drug use, they ignore the
country's biggest drug problem. It is not
marijuana, heroin, amphetamines, or
barbiturates. It is alcohol abuse. The alcohol
manufacturers and marketers want us to believe

Analogy links illegal
drug use with legal
alcohol use.

that alcohol is not a drug, but it is a drug.

Like all illegal drugs, it affects the senses, alters the drinker's psychology, and becomes addictive with prolonged use. According to Mothers Against Drunk Driving, drunken drivers kill someone in America every 32 minutes. Should we therefore prohibit alcohol consumption again? Of course not. We shouldn't because there are many more responsible drinkers than there are abusers.

Transitional paragraph clearly reminds readers of Ko's position.

Instead we now treat alcohol abuse as a medical or psychological problem, and we pass laws that restrict when and where people may drink. I believe all drugs should fall in the same classification as alcohol, and we should end the war on drugs.

Ko extends the legal-drug-use analogy in more detail. She is relying on logos, that is, the development of a reasonable argument, to sway her reader.

Instead of incarcerating drug abusers, we should treat them the same as we do alcohol abusers and help them to lead normal lives in society. There are many responsible people who can and do use drugs recreationally without any harmful effect to themselves or to society. There are religious sects who use peyoto, marijuana, and mushrooms without becoming helpless addicts. And the Netherlands has proved that decriminalization of drug use does not cause a collapse of society or an increase in crime.

Conclusion offers an appeal to ethos. Ko claims to be forthright and honest and calls for action.

I am not an advocate of drug use. In fact, I believe there are many harmful drugs that nobody should become involved with. But I am against laws that make drug use a crime instead of a health problem. Let us start a drug education campaign that uses facts rather than propaganda and grant amnesty to all nonviolent prisoners of the drug war.

Exercise 55.1: Analyze an Argument

Review Allison Ko's essay. Does she effectively use *logos, pathos,* and *ethos?* Find specific examples in her essay.

Exercise 55.2: Applying the Toulmin Model

Apply the Toulmin model to Allison Ko's essay. Identify the claim, the grounds, and the warrant.

WRITER'S TOOLBOX

Conversations and Arguments

A written argument has the same give-and-take as a lively conversation. The main difference is that in a lively conversation you probably feel more confident of what you know, and someone is right there in front of you, asking questions that make you think.

An effective tactic for beginning the writing process is to hold an imaginary conversation. Begin with your fingers on the keyboard or wrapped around a pen. Relax for a moment and imagine someone you know who is informed on the issue you've selected to write about. Then, after a few moments of reflection, begin the conversation.

THE OTHER PERSON	YOU
What's your point?	I claim that . . .
I doubt it, what's your evidence?	One point is . . .
	Another point is . . .
How about this counter argument . . .	That's true, but it doesn't explain . . .
Why are you so sure?	For these reasons, first . . .
What other arguments work against your claim?	I must admit that . . .
How strong is your claim?	I have to limit it to . . .

Once you've fully developed an imaginary conversation, you are ready to fill in the weaknesses of your argument and begin the formal phase of the writing process.

Exercise 55.3: Writing an Argument Essay

Write an argument essay in which you express one of your own deeply felt opinions. If the subject you select has undergone extensive public discussion, assume that your reader is familiar with the general elements of the debate and develop specific evidence based on your own observations, reading, and experience. Use the following list to spark your thinking, but do not feel bound by the subjects. Remember, the suggestions are merely broad subjects; any one of them must be narrowed and focused.

1. Euthanasia

2. Censorship

3. Television violence

4. Film ratings

5. Legalized drugs

6. Animal rights

7. Student codes of conduct

8. Disruptive behavior in public places

9. Subliminal messages in music

10. Civil liberties vs. security

11. Sex education in public schools

12. Video games

13. Smoking in public places

14. The use of torture

15. The power of the beauty myth

56 The Essay about Literature *lit*

Much of your writing in college will be in response to written texts. In American literature you might read a novel, a poem, or a play and write an interpretive essay to explain the work's theme. In history you might read a significant government document and write an analytical essay to explore the assumptions that underlie its intent. In psychology you might read two conflicting views of the mind's structure and write a comparison essay to show how they are similar and different.

Even though the content of written works can be very different, the general strategies for writing about them always apply, no matter what the content. For any such assignment, you can use the basic structure of a college essay. The thesis should embody the purpose; the discussion paragraphs should be organized around topic sentences, each of which develops one subpoint of the thesis; and the conclusion should end the paper in a satisfying way. But within this general structure you should also adhere to several practices common to essays about written works.

To prepare to write about a written work, you must read the assigned work with care. Take notes, reread, identify a subject for your essay, and highlight passages to support your position. Once your preparation is complete, you can begin the writing process.

56a Formulate a thesis statement and develop a plan

No one can examine every aspect of a written work in a brief essay; consequently, you must decide on a topic by selecting a single aspect of your subject. Then you need to develop a limited thesis statement that announces the topic and expresses your attitude toward it. (See thesis statement, 7c.) A thesis developed in response to a written work can take many forms.

AN INTERPRETATION OF CHARACTER IN A SHORT STORY

In "The Chrysanthemums," John Steinbeck portrays a character who senses but cannot understand the need to communicate her deepest feelings.

AN ANALYSIS OF A CENTRAL IMAGE IN A POEM

"Buffalo Bill's defunct" by E. E. Cummings offers an ambiguous image of an American folk hero.

AN EVALUATION OF WRITING TECHNIQUES IN AN ESSAY

Simpson creates this realistic portrait of a hospital emergency room through the effective use of descriptive techniques.

Once you have developed a working thesis statement, you can sift through the evidence you have identified and develop a plan as you would for any essay. (See informal plan, 7b; formal plan, 7d.)

56b Write an introduction that represents the work
and highlights the thesis

Unless you are absolutely certain that your readers are familiar with
the work, use your introduction to acquaint them with it. The most
efficient way to represent the work is to summarize it.

Your summary should be brief, perhaps no longer than eight to
ten sentences. When summarizing, do not get bogged down in extensive detail that will only distract your readers. Instead, create an overview
with just enough detail to make your readers feel comfortable as they
enter the discussion part of your essay.

While writing the summary, follow several common practices.

- In the first sentence state the author, the title, and the author's
  main purpose as you interpret it.
- Follow the opening sentence with a quotation that supports your
  interpretation.
- Throughout the summary section, and whenever appropriate in
  the discussion and conclusion, attribute quotations and ideas to
  the author.
- Use the historical present—the present tense of your main
  verbs—in the summary section and throughout the essay.
- After stating the author's full name in the opening, use only the
  last name in the summary section and throughout the essay.
- End the introduction with the thesis you plan to develop.

In an evaluation of writing techniques, one student wrote the following summary of George Simpson's "The War Room at Bellevue."

Opening sentence names author, title, and the writer's purpose.

George Simpson in "The War Room at
Bellevue" describes a typical Friday night in the
Bellevue Hospital to show why its emergency
team is so highly respected. Simpson writes,

Quote effectively introduced. Note the use of historical present tense.

"Why do injured cops drive by a half-dozen other
hospitals to be treated at Bellevue? They've seen
the Bellevue emergency team in action." In vivid
detail, Simpson describes the nightly events that

Writer uses vivid detail and continues to attribute to Simpson: "Simpson writes," "Simpson describes," "Simpson creates."

unfold in the ER and the victims of accidental
injuries, poisonings, suicide attempts, overdoses,
stabbings, and shootings. From the moment "An
ambulance backs into the receiving bay, its red

and yellow lights flashing . . ." to the end when "blood spatters on the floor" from a knife wound, Simpson captures the grinding pace and traumatic conditions doctors and nurses face. Although few of his readers will ever actually see the inside of the Bellevue Emergency Room, all of them will leave the essay with a powerful sense that they have experienced an ER's nightly

Closes with thesis statement.

reality. *Simpson creates this realistic portrait of an emergency room through the effective use of descriptive techniques.*

If your reader is familiar with the work, an introduction may be composed of snippets of detail. In an introduction to an analysis of setting as it relates to character in Guy de Maupassant's "Moonlight," one student wrote the following.

Opening sentence names author, title, and the writer's central purpose.

Historical present tense is used throughout introduction.

Guy de Maupassant's "Moonlight" deals with a psychological awakening. The principal character, Father Marigan, is a self-satisfied woman-hater who believes he understands "God . . . His plans, His wishes, His intentions." Marigan's awakening comes when he is symbolically seduced by moonlight into realizing, to his dismay, that God's plan includes love between a man and a woman.

Effective use of attribution.

Closes with thesis statement.

Throughout the story de Maupassant uses setting to reinforce the characterization of Father Marigan and to convey the idea that love is natural and good.

56c Write a discussion that develops the thesis

The discussion section of an essay about a written work is like the discussion section of any well-constructed college essay: it should be developed around subpoints expressed in topic sentences. Arrange the discussion according to significant ideas, not necessarily by the structure of the written work you are examining.

Support Observations with an Extended Quotation

One way to develop the topic sentence is to combine your observations with an extended quotation that supports them, as in the following discussion paragraph from an analysis of Flannery O'Connor's "Revelation." (See direct quotations, 40a.)

Topic sentence sets up discussion.

O'Connor creates a conflicting portrait of Mrs. Turpin. We see her from the inside and the outside. Throughout the story she professes Christian love and charity, but in her mind she judges others by superficial standards. For example, at night before sleeping she categorizes and judges people by their economic condition:

Comments set up extended quotation that follows.

Extended quotation in block format (see 40a).

> On the bottom of the heap were most colored people . . . next to them—not above, just away from—were the white trash; then above them were the homeowners, and above them the home-and-land owners, to which she and Claud belonged. Above she and Claud were people with a lot of money and much bigger homes and much more land.

Closing comments tie the quotation to the opening assertion.

This judgmental vision of Mrs. Turpin ends in confusion when rich blacks who own land and "white trash" who've grown rich don't fit into her scheme, but she solves the problem by mentally consigning everyone—white, black, rich, and poor—to boxcars headed for a gas oven, a grim reference to Nazi Germany and the result of categorical thinking when carried to its limits.

Support Observations with Specific Summary

Other paragraphs in the discussion might be developed by accurately summarizing specific aspects of the content of a work as they relate to your point. Consider the following discussion paragraph from an analysis of *Oedipus Rex*.

Topic sentence opens paragraph.

Summarized points support the assertion in the topic sentence.

> *Sophocles uses the imagery of sight and blindness for ironic effect throughout the play.* It is blind Tiresias, the prophet of Apollo, who is the god of foresight and insight, who sees more clearly than those who have eyes. Early in the play, Oedipus promises to bring the dark secret of Laius' death to light for all to see, yet he does so while still blind to his own moral faults. After blinding himself near the play's end, Oedipus sees who he really is and what he has done. Ironically, throughout the play, Oedipus prides himself on his clear-sightedness, but by the end he recognizes that this pride has blinded him.

Support Comments with Brief Quotations

You might also use very brief quotations from a work to support your observations, as does this discussion paragraph from a critical evaluation of *Serpentine*.

Topic sentence sets up the discussion.

Series of brief quotes that support assertion in the topic sentence.

Closes by linking back to topic sentence.

> *A minor flaw in the book comes from Thompson's flagrant use of clichés in place of more thoughtful prose.* He writes, "It was the dead of winter, 1967, and the prison walls were cold as ice." He refers to Sobhraj's courtroom chicanery as a "bag of tricks." His girlfriend clung to him "like moss on an oak." He tries to pass off their tawdry affair as an "epic romance more poignant than Romeo and Juliet." Trite expressions such as these mar every page and blemish an otherwise captivating work.

56d Write a brief conclusion

The conclusion should briefly summarize your thesis and the major subpoints, and it should end with your general view of the work. Here is an effective conclusion from an analysis of Flannery O'Connor's "Revelation."

> Clearly, O'Connor's "Revelation" takes a careful reader into the shadowy mind of a bigot who gains awareness through a personal catastrophe. O'Connor seems to be offering a positive message—that is, there is even hope that a bigot such as Mrs. Turpin can learn not to judge others by the weight of their wallets or the color of their skin.

56e Write a precise title

A title should be brief and should express the idea your essay examines. If the title of the work is included in your essay title, only it should be italicized or put within quotation marks, as appropriate. (See quotation marks, 40b; italics, 51a.)

> E. E. Cummings's "Buffalo Bill's defunct": The Backside of a Folk Hero
>
> Imagery in *Oedipus Rex*
>
> Mrs. Turpin's Revelation

56f Identify your quotations and specific references

In a brief essay about literature, you might be allowed to omit complete citations for primary sources. If so, you should still identify the location of each quotation and specific reference you make. After the quotation or reference, place the page number or numbers from the original work in parentheses and close the sentence with the end punctuation mark after the last parenthesis. (See parenthetical citations, 59c.)

> Hemingway ends the story on an ironic note: "After all, he said to himself, it is probably only insomnia" (72).
>
> Near the end of his life we find that Gimpel has achieved peace. He now understands that soon all illusion will be

swept away. He believes he will truly see without the confusion of ridicule and deception. He will see what is real (85-86).

56g Use the present tense of verbs

The dominant verb tense in an essay about a written work—whether fiction, nonfiction, drama, or poetry—should be the present tense. (See present tense, 33a.)

> In *The Executioner's Song*, Mailer *re-creates* life as it *is lived* in the rural West. He *evokes* people struggling to make a living in gas stations, roadside cafés, movie theaters, small factories, country stores, and on farms. It *is* a world filled with pickup trucks, six-packs, country music, Monday Night Football, deer hunting, motorcycles, and honky-tonk violence. The city slicker *is* suspect, and the easy buck *is* hard to find. The four-wheel-drive Ford truck, not the sleek Mercedes, *is* the status symbol.

56h Avoid common mistakes in essay writing

Do not summarize excessively. Summarize only enough of a work to clarify your thought or a point. A summary should always serve a clear purpose.

Do not refer to authors by their first names, and do not refer to them by title (Dr., Prof., Mr., Mrs., Miss, Ms.). After giving an author's full name in the introduction, refer to him or her by last name throughout the rest of the essay.

Do not miscopy a direct quotation. Always recheck any quotation you use to be sure you have copied it accurately.

Do not set off the title of a work with commas when it follows the word *story, tale, novel, story, book, poem,* or *play.*

INCORRECT	In his poem, "Traveling through the Dark," William Stafford reflects on humankind's relation to nature.

CORRECT	In his poem "Traveling through the Dark," William Stafford reflects on humankind's relation to nature.

A Student Essay about Literature

Examine the following essay by student-writer Kirk Rensfield in response to this reading assignment:

> Select one of the seven literary works read for the unit "On Living and Dying" and write a 500- to 750-word analysis. Explore how effectively the short story, literary essay, or poem you select captures the experience of living or dying. Emphasize "writing techniques" in your essay by linking them to the work's larger implications.

After your first reading, reread Rensfield's essay along with the comments in the margin. To further prepare yourself for this assignment, you should also read George Orwell's "A Hanging," which you will find in most anthologies of essays or in the library in a copy of his collected essays.

The cryptic title is drawn from Orwell's tale.

Introduction sets up thesis statement, follows writing about literature conventions:
1. Names author, title, and purpose.
2. Attributes, using author's last name.
3. Uses quotes.
4. Keeps to the historical present.
5. Closes with thesis.

One World Less

George Orwell in "A Hanging" describes a condemned man's march from a prison cell to his execution by hanging. Orwell begins the march simply: "We set out for the gallows. Two warders marched on either side of the prisoner . . . two others marched close against him, gripping him by the arm and shoulder." Eight minutes later, the prisoner is declared dead by the officer in charge. He "reached out with his stick and poked the brown body; it oscillated slightly. 'He's all right,' said the superintendent." The words of the officer's pronouncement may skirt the reality that a man has just died; Orwell, however, does not blink from that reality. *Although few readers of "A Hanging" will actually see someone hanged, all will leave the essay with a strong sense of what the experience must be like.*

First discussion paragraph opens with topic sentence.

Supports topic sentence with specific detail and quotations from the story.

Orwell creates a vivid reality by generally maintaining an objective perspective, much like a camera photographing the event. For example, like a movie camera moving from a long shot, to a medium shot, to a close-up, Orwell establishes the atmosphere and location of his tale. He begins with an overview, "It was Burma, a sodden morning of the rains." He then moves to the jail yard, "A sickly light, like yellow tinfoil, was slanting over the high walls into the jail yard." He then moves even closer by describing the condemned cells, "a row of sheds fronted with double bars, like small animal cages." Each cell was ten-by-ten feet and held only a plank bed and a pot for drinking water. There, "Brown, silent men were squatting at the inner bars." Finally, his camera concentrates on the prisoner to be hanged, a "Hindu, a puny wisp of a man, with a shaven head and vague liquid eyes."

Second discussion paragraph opens with a transitional phrase and a topic sentence.

Even though the opening perspective seems emotionally detached, Orwell is actually using first person point of view. Throughout the story, the unnamed narrator reports the event much like an objective newspaper reporter, but in one brief passage he does reflect on the experience. Orwell uses the narrator's reflection to create the story's dramatic tension. Orwell writes,

Block quotation used as support for topic sentence.

> I saw the mystery, the unspeakable wrongness, of cutting a life short when it is in full tide. This man was not dying, he was alive just as we are alive. All the organs of his body were working—his bowels digesting food, skin renewing itself, nails growing,

tissues forming—all toiling away in
solemn foolery. His nails would still be
growing when he stood on the drop,
when he was falling through the air
with a tenth-of-a-second to live.

*Follows up
quotation by
relating it to topic
sentence.*

Indeed, the narrator thinks about the significance
of taking a life; he, nevertheless, continues the
relentless march toward the noose. But it is his
reflection on life that elevates the story to a
higher dimension.

*Third discussion
paragraph gives
background, then
states the topic
sentence.*

Experience is composed of two facets: the
outer and inner realities. Orwell captures outer
reality in great detail that is expressed in a
detached, even solemn, tone. *But he also
captures inner reality through the narrator's
thoughts.* They are far from detached. In fact,
they roil with boiling language, and they move
from the particular reality of this hanging to the
universal reality of every person's death.

*Uses block quotation
to support opening
assertion.*

He and we were a party of men
walking together . . . understanding
the same world and in two minutes,
with a sudden snap, one of us would be
gone—one mind less, one world less.

*Closes paragraph
with interpretation
of quote.*

The narrator is beginning to see that all humans
will "be gone." And that with each passing, there
will be "one mind less, one world less."

*The narrator's thoughts round out the
experience of an encounter with death.* The

*Conclusion opens
with rephrasing
of thesis and
restatement of major
point.*

external descriptive detail creates the dramatic
experience of this particular hanging, but the
narrator's internal reflections on death
universalize the experience all humans will
ultimately face.

Exercise 56.1: Writing about a Written Work

Select an anthology of literature that includes fiction, poetry, and drama, such as X. J. Kennedy's *Literature* or Sylvan Barnet, Morton Berman, and William Burto's *An Introduction to Literature*. Browse through the book to find a work that interests you. After reading the work several times, compose a five- to seven-paragraph explication of a brief poem or passage or an analytical examination with character, plot, point of view, setting, symbol, or theme as the subject.

57 The Essay Exam *exam*

In taking an essay exam, you face two important tasks: knowing and understanding the course content, and writing clearly and effectively about it in the time allowed.

The first task means that you will need to study your class notes and review the course textbook in many of the same ways you would for any other kind of exam.

The second task requires that you plan your writing before the exam and then briefly plan again when you read the exam question and prepare to answer it.

Guidelines to Prepare Yourself for the Exam

Begin planning for a timed essay exam as early as possible. Pay attention at the start of the course to the kinds of tests mentioned in the class syllabus or by the instructor. If you know a course will require an essay exam, take notes that focus on relating key concepts and events discussed in lectures and readings.

Also keep any handouts or quizzes given during the course, and pay particular attention to information related to special films, field trips, or presentations by guest speakers.

Since you will need to study the course content as well as prepare for writing about it effectively, give yourself enough time before the exam to prepare adequately for both tasks.

Review Major Course Concepts

Refer to the course syllabus and the table of contents in your textbook to prepare a list of major topics to study.

Be especially sure to include any topics to which a large portion of class time was devoted—such as a series of lectures, special demonstrations, guest speakers, or a class project.

Beneath each topic, list any significant events, examples, persons, dates, or definitions associated with it. As you study for the exam, relate the listed topics and supporting information to your class notes, assigned readings, and any handouts or other course material.

Use Direction Words to Write Practice Questions

An essay exam question usually includes important *direction words* describing how you are to answer. Words like *compare, define, list, show, summarize,* and *evaluate* specify the way your instructor wants you to respond and indicate the scope of the answer he or she expects. As you review major topics covered in the course, you can use such direction words to create and study for potential exam questions.

For example, suppose that in addition to assigned readings about youth gangs, your sociology course also included several lectures on that topic. You would want to use a variety of direction words (shown in bold) to devise potential essay questions about youth gangs:

> **Define** gang membership as viewed by Peters and Walton and **show** how gang activity in central Los Angeles fits that definition.
>
> **Compare** and **contrast** the values of two different types of youth gangs we have studied in this course.
>
> **Explain** the appeal of gang membership beyond the teenage years.

Generating six to ten questions like these will familiarize you with direction words that may appear on the exam, as well as provide you with a means of focusing your preparation.

Prepare a List or Outline

Once you have created a number of potential exam questions, choose one of them and write a brief informal outline of the relevant main points to be discussed. An informal outline for the last question above, for example, might look like this:

> I. The appeal of gang membership beyond the teenage years
>   A. Lack of maturity
>   B. Desire to maintain youth
>   C. Social and financial dependency
>   D. Community prestige

Make an outline such as this for each of the potential questions you devise. You can then use your outlines as a study guide as well as a preliminary plan for writing a practice essay.

Write a Practice Response

Rehearsing a response to likely exam topics will build your confidence and prepare you to handle other questions as well.

Select two or three topics that the instructor emphasized or that you feel are important for other reasons. Devise a potential exam question for each topic, and allow yourself thirty or forty minutes (the usual time allowed for most exam essays) to write a response.

When you have finished, review what you have written for clarity, organization, a clear thesis, and the inclusion of relevant information and examples.

Make corrections to the essay as needed by adding omitted material or deleting anything that did not address the question directly. This practice will reinforce good essay-writing habits and help you to remember the material better.

Make a Spelling List

Your instructor will expect you to be familiar enough with key terms and concepts from the course to be able to spell them correctly.

If you are a weak speller, practice writing words you expect to use in your exam responses, especially those terms that are central to the course. For an exam in a psychology class, for example, you might need to practice writing terms such as *neurosis, Jungian,* and *paranoid;* for an exam in biology, you may want to rehearse words like *synapse, protozoa,* and *cellular.*

Make a list of any such terms that you find difficult, and practice writing them correctly before an exam. Preparing in this way will not only improve your spelling; it will also increase your familiarity with the words and the concepts behind them.

Prepare Yourself for the Exam

After studying and mentally preparing all you can for an essay exam, make sure you are physically ready to do your best. Get a good night's sleep before the exam, and be sure to eat a healthy breakfast or lunch beforehand. You want to be ready to devote all your energy and attention to the exam, not to staying awake or listening to your stomach growl.

57a Writing an essay exam

Be on time for the exam, and bring any necessary items such as a test booklet, pen or pencil, notes (if allowed), a computer disk, or other permitted items. Once you have the exam in hand, take time to read it carefully and to plan your response.

57b Reading and understanding the question

Writing an acceptable response on an essay exam requires that you read and understand the essay question accurately. Do not make the mistake of rushing through the question to formulate a hasty, inaccurate response. Instead, take the time to read the entire exam carefully.

Next, underline the essay question and highlight the direction words in it:

> In a paragraph or two, *discuss* the ways in which evolution may be correctly described as both a theory and fact.

> Briefly *summarize* Jesperson's case against same-sex marriages and *evaluate* his three major arguments.

If you are unsure about what the exam directions say or what is being asked in the exam question, ask your instructor or the exam proctor for clarification.

57c Planning your time

As you read the exam instructions, make a point of circling the time allowed for the test. Consider the steps involved in completing the exam, and decide how long you can take for each. The majority of your time will go to writing the essay response, but you will also need to read and understand the essay question, plan your response, and revise and proofread your finished essay. Allocate enough time for each of these steps, and avoid giving any one of them more time than you can afford.

57d Planning your answer

Briefly plan your essay response by using the exam question's key words (e.g., *define* or *trace*) to direct the form of your answer. Jot down in rough outline form the main points you intend to discuss, and use clustering or other techniques to generate supportive details or examples. Use the outline of your main points as a working plan for writing the essay.

57e Writing your response

An essay exam does not allow you the time to write an introduction and accompanying thesis statement, as you normally would do with other essays. For this reason, you should begin discussing the main points of your response immediately after an opening statement. Begin the essay with a clearly stated sentence that rephrases the exam question itself and serves as the main idea for the rest of the response.

EXAM QUESTION

Explain why Spanish rule in the early nineteenth century did not expand into what later became the northwestern United States.

QUESTION REPHRASED

Spanish rule in the early nineteenth century did not expand into the future northwestern United States because of opposition from the French and economic conditions within Spain itself.

EXAM QUESTION

Compare the wedding rites of the Tair people of West India with one or more traditional American wedding ceremonies.

QUESTION REPHRASED

The wedding rites of the Tair people are far simpler than traditional American ceremonies, but they are also more legally and morally binding.

Use statements such as these to announce your answer and focus your response. Develop the rest of the essay by discussing the main points and supportive information you listed in the working outline you made earlier.

As you complete the essay, write steadily and neatly. Do not expect to recopy your work, as that would sacrifice valuable writing time. Instead, plan to proofread your answer and write in necessary corrections.

Answer the Question

Be sure that you answer the question that is asked and not a different one. Direction words in a question will call for specific kinds of responses—for instance, asking you to *define* a set of terms, *trace* a development, or *identify* and *evaluate* a cause. If you do something other than what is asked—like offering examples instead of defining terms or identifying but not evaluating—your instructor will most likely consider your answer incomplete and give you a low score.

In addition, take care not to wander off the question asked and into one you think you know more about. No matter how well you write on a different topic, your instructor is unlikely to give you credit if you do not answer the exam question. Keep your working outline in front of you, and refer at times to your thesis statement in order to stay on track.

Finally, keep in mind that not all written exams require essay-length answers. Some may ask you to respond to each question in a few sentences, while others may ask for a paragraph or two. When a question explicitly asks you to respond *in a certain length,* make sure your answer stays near the specified range. This is the approximate quantity of writing your instructor has determined is necessary to compose a satisfactory answer.

57f Revising and proofreading

When you have finished your essay, take a few minutes to reread it for completeness and to make minor corrections. If you have left out words or even a sentence or two, add them neatly, using a caret (^) to show where each fits into your writing. Also neatly cross out any irrelevant material and replace it with more pertinent content. Be sure your sentences are complete and that they make sense. Check for punctuation and spelling errors, paying special attention to the spellings of key terms and names of places and individuals. Before you hand in the essay, make sure your name and other necessary information appears on the test booklet cover or at the top of each page.

PART IX
The Research Paper

Despite the telephone, computers, and other information-transmitting technology, the volume of paper work in organizations increases annually. Somebody writes that stuff. It may well be you. Can you predict whether one day you will be publicity chairman of a group? Make public speeches? Design and write brochures, sales materials, procedure manuals? Once you have developed it, writing facility is transferable; you don't need a special course in a specific kind of writing.

—Roger H. Garrison, *writer, professor of English, and educational theorists*

You might think of a research paper as a kind of extended argument essay, an essay more objective in style and based on an investigation of sources and evidence. Like other papers you have written, a research essay presents your opinion about a subject by stating a thesis, or main idea, and supporting it with details and examples. A major difference is that the primary focus of a research paper is on answering an underlying research question such as *Do children's video games increase intelligence? Is ethanol a practical substitute for gasoline in American cars?* Or, as in the sample research paper on pages 390–407, *How widespread is the problem of college plagiarism, and how are campuses responding?* Your own ideas are central to your paper's success, but the evidence you use to support those ideas will come from sources such as books, newspapers, magazines, journals, films, laboratory reports, and even personal interviews. You acknowledge, or document, these sources by citing them in the text of your research essay and then by listing them in a Works Cited or References section at the end of your paper.

As you go about writing a research paper, remember that your own ideas are what the paper is about. If you are writing on the subject of homeless people in the United States, for example, your reader wants to know not only about those people but about what significant information you can provide. Your presentation and interpretation of the facts, your analysis and comparison of other writers' opinions, and your own conclusions constitute the heart of your research essay.

58a Getting started: Find and narrow a suitable research topic

Getting started on a research essay means investigating a broad subject of interest and then moving to a more particular aspect of it, called a *topic*. Your goal in finding a topic—and throughout your research—is continually to refine and narrow the area of investigation. This process will focus your research activities and lead you to an informed conclusion to present in the paper. If you were interested, for example, in the subject of space exploration, one topic for research might be *the benefits of long-range space probes like* Explorer

RESEARCHER'S TOOLBOX

Selecting a Research Topic

The topic you finally select to research and write about will need to meet a number of criteria. As you narrow a general subject to one or two possible topics, check each of your most promising choices against the following guidelines.

- **Be sure the topic meets the requirements** of your research assignment.
- **Focus on a topic that you genuinely want to learn more about.**
- **Use your campus library's resources** to see that sufficient resources about the topic will be available to you.
- **Avoid philosophical topics or those that are based on personal belief,** such as *the value of a family* or *public nudity should be left to personal choice.*
- **Avoid strictly biographical topics**—*Abraham Lincoln as a father*— that have already been discussed fully in book-length studies.
- **Avoid process-focused papers** such as *how cocaine is sold on the street* or *how skin cells turn cancerous.*
- **Avoid topics that are too narrow or too recent** for adequate discussion. A paper on local airport conditions or yesterday's international incident will not allow for adequate use of research materials.
- **Avoid familiar topics** commonly chosen for student research papers. Unless recent developments have added new information or conditions, it will be difficult to impress your instructor with yet another paper on the death penalty or the hazards of smoking.

I *or* Galileo; another topic could be *the physiological effect upon humans of spending prolonged periods of time in outer space.*

Framing a Research Question

Even a closely defined research topic can present too broad an area to research and write about. A topic like *women in the Olympic Games* or a broad question such as *How well do women perform in the Olympic Games?* needs a much more specific focus to promise more than an accumulation of facts. To make your research effective, formulate

questions that focus your discussion and allow you to write an interesting and stimulating paper:

TOPIC	*Television and race*
RESEARCH QUESTIONS	1. Does television promote stereotypes of racial minorities?
	2. Do minority actors have equal employment opportunities in television?
	3. What do popular television shows teach us about race relations?
TOPIC	*Fan violence and sports*
RESEARCH QUESTIONS	1. Are sports promoters doing enough to curb fan violence at games?
	2. What are the causes of fan violence at sports events?

Remember to regard the answer to any preliminary research question as a working hypothesis that your research may or may not confirm and may alter significantly.

Patricia Burton's Research Topic

Education major Patricia Burton, the author of the sample research
paper "College Plagiarism: Easy to Do, But Getting Harder to Get Away
With," on pages 390–407, became interested in her topic after hearing
one of her professors mention the growing problem of student plagiarism on their campus. When the time came in her English class to
select a topic for a research essay, she decided to investigate the issue of
plagiarism but was unsure where to start. She knew plagiarism had a long
history in our society and that its occurrence was not limited to student
papers. She had read of novelists, journalists, song writers, and even
politicians who had been accused of plagiarism. Recognizing that plagiarism itself was too broad a subject for a research topic, Burton settled on college plagiarism as the general subject for her research. But
she knew she still had to focus her paper. Should she investigate the
reasons students plagiarize? Or how professors treat plagiarism when
they discover it in a student's work? As she read, Burton learned that
plagiarism was even more widespread than most people probably recognize. She realized that addressing only the increase in college plagiarism without touching on what colleges are doing about it would leave
her discussion incomplete. Ultimately she decided that her paper
would focus on the question *How big a problem is student plagiarism,
and what are colleges doing to combat it?*

58b Use campus library resources to investigate a topic

Though you will also want to consult print sources in your research, your campus library's electronic resources are probably the best means for investigating a research topic and finding the most current information on it. The library's electronic information system can provide fast, searchable access to its online catalog, reference works, databases, the holdings of other libraries, links to local, state, and federal agencies, sources that are available in both print and electronic forms, and to the millions of sites that compose the Internet. The figure below shows the kinds of options provided by the online catalog at a typical university library. Using such a system, you can download information from an electronic source directly to your own computer or portable drive, or even email it to yourself at home. If you need online material in a printed format, you can send the electronic version directly to the library's copying machines or consult the online catalog to see if your library has the complete work in print form. And if you prefer to work from home or another location, most academic libraries allow you to

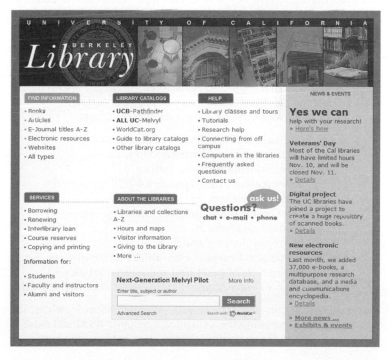

access their online resources, such as the catalog and databases, for free with a required code or student identification number.

Databases Provide Access to a Variety of Sources

A database is a stored, structured collection of information. Most college libraries subscribe to commercial electronic databases to provide students with free access to scholarly material that they would otherwise have to pay for. One of the drawbacks of relying directly on the Internet for research is that nearly all Internet sites charge a fee for accessing or downloading articles from journals, newspapers, and magazines; using your campus library databases allows you access to a wide variety of sources for free.

Companies such as Infotrac, EBSCOhost, and ProQuest offer general and specialized databases containing millions of sources on nearly every subject imaginable. These databases, searchable by topic or keyword, contain complete books; newspaper, journal, and magazine articles; abstracts and dissertations; encyclopedias; and other valuable sources for research. One well-known service, Lexis-Nexis, provides sources on current news, medicine, legal research, and business topics. Another provider, FirstSearch, includes valuable specialized databases such as *WorldCat,* which can locate materials in library collections worldwide.

Special subject databases offered by Infotrac, EBCOhost, and other companies are helpful at first when you are trying to narrow the scope of your research topic and again when you begin researching a topic in depth. Each information service provides different kinds of subject databases; some typical subject databases include:

> *Ask ERIC:* abstracts of articles about education
> *Access Science:* an online science encyclopedia
> *CIA Factbook:* information on countries
> *Contemporary Authors:* biographies and bibliographical
> information on writers
> *Grove Music Online:* music information and scores
> *MEDLINE:* medical research
> *MLA Bibliography:* literary criticism
> *Opposing Viewpoints Resource Center:* articles on controversial issues
> *PsycINFO:* abstracts of periodical and journal articles
> *Health Reference Center Academic:* nursing and allied health articles

Patricia Burton got more than 150 potential sources when she searched for sources using the Expanded Academic ASAP database at her campus library. If your campus library does not have the particular

RESEARCHER'S TOOLBOX

How to Use a Database

- **Use the search function** to list the topic for which you want to find sources.
- **Narrow the search term** (*college plagiarism* instead of *plagiarism*) or use what are called Boolean search terms—*and, or, not,* and others (*dolphins not bottlenose*)—to limit results.
- **Indicate the type of sources you want to find** (peer-reviewed journal, newspaper, magazine, government document, and so on).
- **Use an "Advanced" or "Power" search** to limit your search further (by year, media, country, or abstracts only).
- **When the database includes "Related topics," investigate them** if you need additional sources or perspectives.
- **Read an abstract** to judge whether reading the article would be useful.
- If you work on a computer, **copy and paste relevant parts of the source** as part of your notes or for quoting later in your paper.
- **Write down or copy and paste all the bibliographic information** (author, title, source title, date, volume, pages) you will need to include in your paper's References or Works Cited list.

databases you need for your research, remember that you can also investigate online and on-site resources at other local colleges or even your community library. Public libraries often make databases available for free or for a nominal membership fee.

Databases are not difficult to use, but they can sometimes give you more information than you need or have time to investigate. Narrow the terms of your search all you can, and use other available features to refine your search or to locate more material (see the Researcher's Toolbox above for ways to limit a database search). If you are unfamiliar with searching a database, look to see if the database itself includes instructions or offers a tutorial. You can also ask a librarian for assistance or check to see if your library offers its own tutorial for using a database.

Use Print Indexes to Find Older Periodical Sources

Although the electronic archives of some periodicals contain material published fifty or even a hundred years ago (the *New York Times* online archives go back to 1851), the information in most academic databases may date back only to the early 1970s. If your research requires you to find periodical articles published earlier, you may want to consult a library copy of the printed version of a newspaper catalog such as the *Los Angeles Times Index, New York Times Index,* or the indices to other major national or local newspapers. You can find early articles from magazines and even some journals by consulting the print forms of the *Reader's Guide to Periodical Literature* or *Poole's Index to Periodical Literature.* Many older publications are still available on microfilm at some libraries. If you have difficulty locating older journal, newspaper, or magazine sources, ask a librarian for assistance.

Find Government Sources Online

You can find current information relevant to any research topic by investigating federal and state databases through the Internet. One of the most useful government sites is *gov.com* at *http://www.gov.com.* Here you can link to nearly all federal and state information databases and get help from a "Frequent Questions" area. Use this site to find information about homeland security, natural resources and the environment, food and nutrition, the economy, court decisions, and a host of other research subjects.

Search the Library's Online Catalog for Books

A useful resource when you want to locate books is your library's online catalog, which will allow you to search for books by subject, keyword, author, title, or even ISBN (the International Standard Book Number). Because a catalog may list a hundred or more titles on a topic, you will need to be selective about which ones you track down and spend time examining. Use the online catalog information to preview a book's contents to decide whether or not it will be useful. A catalog entry will tell you how many pages are in a book and whether it includes a bibliography or illustrations; most online catalogs also provide links to such related sources as book reviews, information about and other works written by the author, and non-book materials. Depending on the book you locate and an individual library's preferences, the online catalog may also include a version of the table of contents or an abstract or summary of its major ideas.

If your campus library does not have a book you need, see if its online catalog is linked to a bibliographic database such as *WorldCat* (an electronic catalog of library collections worldwide), which can tell you what libraries near you have the book. You can also find out about the collections at other college and community libraries by accessing their online catalogs through the Internet.

Consult Primary and Secondary Sources

A *primary source* is original material that other sources, called *secondary sources,* are based upon. Secondary sources are materials written *about* a topic. They include books, magazine and newspaper articles, encyclopedia entries, pamphlets, and other works that describe, analyze, or report information. Primary sources are raw materials such as literary works, letters, diaries, government reports, court records, interviews, and laboratory reports. Using a primary source has the advantage of allowing you to make your own assessment of original material; a secondary source gives you someone else's interpretation or analysis. Both can be useful for a fuller understanding of a topic and as a means of evaluating one or the other kinds of sources. For instance, you may want to consult a primary source such as the minutes of a city council meeting to compare its content with an interpretation of the meeting reported in a secondary source.

Use Reference Works for a Broad Understanding of a Subject

Your library's reference section will have print versions of general reference works: dictionaries, encyclopedias, biographical indexes, atlases, yearbooks. Such works can provide basic information about your subject and the sources available, and they can help you to get a broad overview of a research topic.

Dictionaries. Use a dictionary to ensure your own understanding of unfamiliar terms that may be central to your discussion. You may need to provide brief definitions of terms like *ecology* or *Gestalt psychology,* for example, or you may want to describe a word's origin, as Patricia Burton does when she explains in her research paper that *plagiarism* derives from a Latin word meaning "kidnapper." For more extensive treatment of complex terms, you can turn to a specialized dictionary that treats a particular field, such as *Black's Law Dictionary, Encyclopedia of Bioethics, Dictionary of Science,* or *A Dictionary of Philosophy.*

Encyclopedias. An encyclopedia is a good resource to go to early in your research. Works like *Academic American Encyclopedia, The New Encyclopaedia Britannica,* and *The Columbia Encyclopedia* provide general introductory information and usually have bibliographies that can lead you to helpful sources. Electronic versions of general encyclopedias such as *Britannica Online, New World Encyclopedia, McGraw-Hill Concise Encyclopedia of Science & Technology,* and *Encyclopedia Americana* are available, through your college's database subscription as well as in print form. Written and regularly updated by contributors from around the world, the online encyclopedia *Wikipedia* covers traditional and contemporary topics, some of them too current to be found in other encyclopedias. A good resource for background about a topic, *Wikipedia*'s articles include both bibliographies and complete histories of additions made by contributing editors.

In addition, many special-focus works such as the following are available in print form:

> *Encyclopedia of Natural Medicine*
> *Encyclopedia of Psychoactive Plants*
> *Encyclopedia of Women Artists of the American West*
> *New Encyclopedia of Modern Bodybuilding*
> *Rodale's All-New Encyclopedia of Organic Gardening*

Keep in mind that not every work with "Encyclopedia" in its title is written with careful scholarship or by an expert. Moreover, because other authoritative sources are usually more current and specifically relevant, many instructors prefer that you use encyclopedias only to gain a broad understanding of your topic. For this reason, check with your instructor if you feel your paper needs to include information from an encyclopedia.

Bibliographies.   A list of written materials and related works on a particular topic is called a *bibliography*. While all bibliographies provide information about a work's title, author, and publication information, they vary in their emphases and approach. A bibliography may be *selective* and include only a few works on a specific topic; it may be *descriptive* and provide brief annotations or reviews; it may be *evaluative* and discuss the value of the sources it lists; and it might combine any of these approaches. You can use bibliographies to locate sources for research and to get an idea of what other writers have found worthy of writing about a topic.

The most familiar kinds of bibliographies are commonly found at the end of scholarly books or their chapters, at the conclusion of encyclopedia or journal articles, or included with articles in a few popular periodicals like *Scientific American* and *Smithsonian*. The Works Cited list you include at the end of your research paper is a bibliography. Except for the bibliographies listed in the online catalog or a database, the bibliographies available in your library's reference section will be complete works and in print versions.

In addition to print bibliographies, database bibliographies such as *Bibliographic Index Plus* and *The International Bibliography of the Social Sciences* are available at most academic libraries. The online catalog for most libraries also offers *subject guides,* unique bibliographies prepared by the library staff. These guides list sources available on a variety of subjects at that particular library or electronically linked to them via the Internet or a database.

Using the Internet to Find Sources

Use Internet search sites such as *Google, Alta Vista, Lycos*, and others to access content published by government and commercial agencies, libraries, research groups, museums, blogs and newsgroups, and a host of other private and public entities worldwide. The format and quantity of information you get from an Internet search may depend on whether a search site uses *directory* technology, yielding previously selected and stored information sites for a given topic, or a *search engine* that lists all the sites if finds on the Internet that mention the topic. Some search sites, like *Google, Lycos*, and *Yahoo!* allow you to search for information using either a directory or a search engine. To get the best results when searching the Internet, you'll need to understand the advantages of using both options. Patricia Burton used both kinds of searches for her paper on plagiarism. The figure on page 360 shows some of the results she got from using *Google*'s search engine to locate Internet sources on "plagiarism."

The wealth of information available on the Internet is both a blessing and a challenge: It's not difficult to find information, but you have to know how to search effectively to avoid finding more material than you have time to investigate. In addition, the fact that any person or group can publish material on the Internet means you have to evaluate carefully the accuracy, bias, and currency of the information you find.

Directories. The results you get from a directory search begin with a list of general topics and lead step-by-step toward a single more specific topic or resource. Each successive page offers another layer of menu choices on related topics, and you proceed by selecting first one category, then a narrower one, with each selection based on your sense of a category's apparent relevance to your interest. If you were researching "green roofs" (rooftops planted with vegetation to be more environmentally friendly), a series of directory topic choices might look like this:

Arts
Business
Health
News
Science → Environment → Sustainability → Sustainable
    Architecture → Green roofs
Society

In this example, the final directory page would list Internet sites with information about your specific topic, "green roofs."

A multilayered directory search may appear cumbersome, but it can be especially helpful when you first want to explore a potential research subject broadly, examine related issues, or find out what kinds of resources may be available. You cannot always know what related topics may be important to your research, but a directory search engine will find and list likely topics for you.

Because topics and sites are selected by human editors, directories vary in their content, and their results are fewer than those from a search engine; however, they can be more focused and are especially useful when you have a broad topic and want to narrow it or you are having difficulty locating sources on a topic. Some directory sites useful for research purposes are:

Best of the Web	http://botw.org/
DMOZ Open Directory Project	http://www.dmoz.org/

Infomine	http://infomine.ucr.edu
Google Directory	http://www.google.com/dirhp
Librarian's Internet Index	http://lii.org
Yahoo! Directory	http://dir.yahoo.com/ Reference/Libraries

Search Engines. A search engine is a program that finds and lists relevant sources in response to keywords you type into a query, or text box. Unlike a directory program, search engines present no menus of topic choices. They are designed only to find Internet sites containing information related to the search term(s). For this reason, you need to use very specific terms that define accurately what you want to investigate and what sources you want the search engine to find. Always narrow your search terms and use the search limiting features of the search site you are using (see the Researcher's Toolbox below for ways to limit your search).

 RESEARCHER'S TOOLBOX

Narrowing a Database or Internet Search

The results or "hits" you get from a database or Internet search will not be useful if they are inexact or too numerous for you to investigate. To get an accurate list of useful hits, always make the search term(s) as specific as possible. For example, use *college plagiarism* or *college plagiarism causes* instead of merely *plagiarism*. You can also use *operators* to limit the search results, such as the (always capitalized) Boolean operators *AND, OR, BUT NOT,* and other terms or symbols, including quotation marks for an exact phrase match: *reading AND success; atomic OR nuclear power; bears BUT NOT grizzly; "working mothers."*

Not all search systems work alike. Many accept *and* and *or* uncapitalized, and many popular sites, like Google and Yahoo, use different terms and symbols to limit a search:

+ (essential)	*Richard +III*
– (exclude)	*dolphins –bottlenose*
~ (find synonyms)	*~democracy*

Most database and Internet search sites offer guidance for limiting a search and also provide directions for which symbols to use as operators. Go the site's "Advanced Search" or "Search Tips" section for help with limiting your search to sources that match the specifics of your topic.

Since you will get slightly different results with each search site you use, it's a good idea to use more than one search engine for your research (but avoid metasearch engines, which gather only information stored in the databases of other search sites). The most popular site for research is *Google* (www.google.com) and its more academic spin-off, *Google Scholar* (www.google.scholar.com).

To find additional search engine sites, go to *Search Engine Watch* at http://searchenginewatch.com. This site includes a comprehensive list as well as news and reviews of search engine technology.

Evaluate Internet Sources Carefully

A critical mindset is essential when conducting effective research on the Internet because of the vast numbers of people posting information and ideas. You will find that much of the information available on the Internet is commercial in nature, presented to sell a product or at least to emphasize certain characteristics over others. Because it is democratic and essentially unrestricted, Internet content often lacks the usual filtering mechanisms of competition, academic review, financial and legal concerns, and even matter-of-fact judgments about whether something is worth circulating. As a result, you can find on the Internet everyone with an idea, every group with a cause, everything and anything someone thinks is important, necessary, or valuable. Much of it qualifies as all these things and more, and most of us would not want the Internet to lose its democratic, maverick character. That character is a part of the Internet's appeal and a source of its strength as a means of worldwide communication and commerce.

Information found at many Web sites is intended to represent a particular point of view or to promote a cause. Although such sites may support worthwhile causes, they may be highly selective about the information they provide or otherwise biased in the way they present material. For example the Web site sponsored by PETA (People for the Ethical Treatment of Animals) recently criticized the fast-food chain KFC (formerly Kentucky Fried Chicken). The site's authors use carefully crafted language intended to prejudice the audience even before it has read the page contents or viewed the accompanying video. Thus, KFC becomes "Kentucky Fried Cruelty" and the commentary is titled "Cruelty Capitol, USA," implying that something un-American is happening. The video shows scenes of crowded chicken coops and birds being prepared for slaughter; the accompanying text says that KFC suppliers "cram" birds into "waste-filled cages" and "drug them." We are told that "many advisors" for KFC have quit their jobs in frustration over such practices.

The contents of this Web page may well be true, but it is clear that the site uses selective language and content to convey its claims. To use any information from this site in your research would require both that you acknowledge the site's bias and that you investigate and fairly present both sides of the issue. Has KFC responded to the claims made on this site? Have other agencies criticized KFC for its practices? Are the examples shown in the video or described in the commentary typical and recurring? The answers to these and other questions will need to be part of your assessment of the site's reliability if you use its content in your paper.

As Web pages such as this one demonstrate, you need to be especially alert to—and in some instances mistrusting of—Web sources that demonstrate a one-sided approach to an issue, even when that approach supports an admirable cause. Make a point of treating such sources with a critical attitude, one that consciously weighs the evidence and gives equal attention to other sources and opposing points of view.

Assessing the Reliability of Internet Sources. Your judgment of a source's authority and value to your research will develop out of a general understanding of the subject at hand and your own critical thinking skills. Although there are no certain criteria for evaluating Internet sources beyond that, the following checklist can spur your thinking and serve as a guide to determining the reliability of research on the Internet:

PURPOSE

- What is the purpose of the Web site? What audience does it address?

CONTENT

- *Currency:* Does the material appear to be up to date? Is there an indication of how often it is updated?
- *Fairness:* Does the material demonstrate an awareness and consideration of other viewpoints? Is the tone reasonable and temperate? Is there a clear separation of fact and opinion?
- *Evidence:* Does the content provide statistics, examples, or anecdotal evidence to support the author's position? Do the examples and other evidence fairly reflect current data?

Is there evidence of credible research, such as a description of methodology or a bibliography?

- *Credibility:* Would the document's content have credibility outside the Internet world? If so, with whom?

AUTHORITY

- *Identity:* Does the author or the sponsor of the material include an email address, URL, or other means of contact for comments and questions about the site?
- *Qualifications:* Is the author or the sponsor of the content known and accepted as credible? Are other verifiable qualifications such as education, employment, publications, awards, and experience listed?
- *Credibility:* Would the author of this document have credibility outside the Internet world? If so, with whom?

Apply these and similar criteria as you examine sources from the Internet and elsewhere during your research. As you draft your research paper, give extra consideration to how you use Internet information that may appear to your reader to be questionable or unreliable.

58c Keep a working bibliography

A working bibliography is a list of all the sources you consult during your research. You keep a working bibliography in order to have an accurate record of your sources when you cite them in your paper or in case you need to find them again. In most cases, the working bibliography will contain more sources than you will use in writing your paper or include in the paper's Works Cited section.

Record Essential Information

The information you'll need for a working bibliography will depend on the kind of sources and the documentation style you are using for your paper. The Researcher's Toolbox that follows lists the kind of information needed to cite books, periodical articles, database articles, and Internet sources in MLA documentation style. Refer to the relevant sections in this text for the information you'll need for citing other kinds of sources and using MLA, APA, and CSE formats.

RESEARCHER'S TOOLBOX

What to Record in a Working Bibliography

Books

Author, editor, or translator name(s), followed by appropriate abbreviation (*ed., eds., trans.*); title and subtitle; edition; city, publisher, and date (and number of pages for APA papers). For a printed book or a book found on the Web, include the word *Print* or *Web* as appropriate, followed by a period, after the publication date.

Periodical Articles

Author name(s); title and subtitle; magazine, newspaper, or journal title; publication date and page number(s); your date of access (for online sources). For all scholarly journals, include the volume and issue numbers. For print or Web sources, include the word *Print* or *Web* as appropriate, followed by a period, after the page number(s).

Web Sources

Author, editor, compiler, or translator name(s), followed by the appropriate abbreviation (*ed., eds., comp., trans.*); title and subtitle of the source; title of the Web site itself if not the same as the source title; version or edition of the site (if relevant); publisher or sponsor of the site (usually found at the bottom of the Web page; if not found, use *n.p.* for *no publisher*); date of publication (if no date is given, use *n.d.* for *no date*); the medium of publication (*Web*) followed by a period; date of your access. Note: Include the complete URL for the site if a reader would not be able to locate the source without it.

Complete information for MLA Works Cited entries for these and other sources appears on pages 408–419. For APA and CSE References entries, see pages 419–428 and 428–433.

As you locate sources for your working bibliography, you will find many electronic sources in a library's online catalog, in a database, or on the Internet that include a *citation example* for the source. The following "source citation" from Health Reference Center Academic appeared with a database article about tattoos in prisons.

Source Citation: Hellard, Margaret E., C.K. Aitken, and J.S. Hocking. "Tattooing in prisons—Not such a pretty picture. (Author abstract) (Report)." *AJIC: American Journal of Infection Control* 35.7 (Sept 2007): 477(4). *Health Reference Center Academic.* Gale. Orange Coast College Library 14 July 2008 http://find.galegroup.com/itx/start.do?prodld=HRCA.

Look also for links labeled "Cite this source," "Citation Guide," or similar wording. Such citation guides can be helpful because they include the information you will need to cite a particular source; however, the citation forms they demonstrate may not always be accurate or current. Use the information these citation guides provide, but revise the citation form as needed to conform with the documentation style of your paper.

Storing the Working Bibliography

Researchers used to record publication information for each work they consulted on an index card so they could easily rearrange the entries into a particular order, and some researchers still prefer to keep their working bibliography in handwritten form in a notebook. You will find, however, that such methods can be tedious and can lead to inaccuracies, especially when copying a long and complicated URL. Luckily, modern technology has created more efficient methods for entering and storing information.

- Using the library's photocopier, or working from a computer linked to a copier, print a paper copy of the periodical articles, Web pages, or other sources you locate through databases or on the Internet. These printouts will give you the bibliographic information you need and provide ready-made notes to refer to as you write your paper.
- Using your computer's Copy and Paste or Save As function, store bibliographic information about a source in a folder on your own computer or portable ("thumb") drive. You can later copy the information from the folder to your paper as needed.
- Send bibliographic information to a *citation manager* program—reference management software that stores and organizes bibliographic citations. Most academic libraries make such commercial programs as *ProCite, RefWorks,* and *EndNote* available free to their students and faculty. These and similar services can also be obtained through personal subscription.

58d Read and write toward a tentative thesis and working outline

When you have set up a working bibliography (usually about fifteen sources for a college paper), you will be ready to examine your research materials more closely. Your first efforts should be directed toward preliminary reading and establishing a tentative thesis and working outline.

Preliminary reading consists of skimming the most promising materials in your bibliography to give yourself an expanded overview of the topic. You should gain a more detailed sense of the scope and complexity of the topic and a familiarity with the kinds of information you will compare and analyze during the writing process. Work quickly by using tables of contents and indexes to locate information. At this point, take notes only for general information about the topic. Once you have explored enough material, you will start to form an idea (or sharpen an already existing one) of the central point you want to develop in your paper.

1. Develop a Tentative Thesis Statement

Begin by developing a tentative thesis statement, no more than one or two sentences, that presents and limits your topic (see Chapter 7). You may want to revise your tentative thesis during the research or writing stages of the paper, but at this point it will add focus and organization to your research.

Patricia Burton's preliminary reading revealed two major issues related to plagiarism among college students: The increasing degree to which plagiarism was being committed on the nation's campuses, and the attempts colleges were making to prevent and detect plagiarism. Burton decided to include both subjects in her research paper, and she formulated this *tentative* thesis statement:

> College plagiarism has become so increasingly common that campuses are stepping up efforts to combat it and to punish offenders.

2. Develop a Working Outline

Your preliminary reading and your tentative thesis statement should aid you in establishing a working outline for the paper (see Chapter 7). As with everything you have done so far, the working outline need not be in permanent form; it is an early guide, a flexible blueprint to aid you in organizing your research, arranging your ideas logically, and making sure you have not left out an important aspect of your topic. The working outline may simply state the tentative thesis and then list supporting ideas.

Patricia Burton's working outline was roughly organized around ideas in her evolving thesis statement and the research materials she found to support it:

> *Research question:* How large is the problem of student plagiarism, and how are colleges responding?
>
> *Thesis statement:* College plagiarism has become so increasingly common that campuses are stepping up efforts to combat it and punish offenders.
>
> *Definition of plagiarism*
> —*Plagiarius* (Latin) = "kidnapper" of another's words
> —Plagiarism today = using another's words or ideas; submitting a purchased paper.
>
> *Problem of college plagiarism*
> —Surveys show that many students use Internet information inappropriately.
> —Most college students see Internet plagiarism as trivial and not really cheating.
> —Internet homework sites and paper mills make plagiarism easy.
> —Reasons cited for plagiarism: poor planning, pressure for grades, lack of research and writing skills, just because they think they can get away with it.
>
> *Campus responses to plagiarism*
> —Punishments range from failing the assignment or the course to expulsion.
> —Campuses use honor codes to address plagiarism.
> —Instructors increasingly rely on Internet-based services to help detect plagiarism.
> —Some faculty object to policing students or using technology to catch cheaters.
>
> *Conclusion:* Colleges need to protect honest students and the fabric of trust on which society operates.

Notice that the working outline need not be complete. At this stage, it is useful for roughly charting the direction the paper may finally take and in pointing out the research that still needs to be done.

58e Take effective notes

Taking Careful Notes to Avoid Plagiarism

To maintain your academic integrity, you must avoid plagiarism, the worst form of intellectual dishonesty a student can commit. Plagiarism occurs when one writer presents another writer's language or ideas as if they were his or her own.

The consequences for students who plagiarize material by incorporating it in their work—whether deliberately or unintentionally—can be severe. Colleges and universities treat plagiarism as an act of theft that can result in punishment ranging from a failing grade in a course to expulsion from school.

In its most pernicious form, plagiarism occurs when a writer submits an essay written by another student or an essay purchased through a mail-order or online service. Plagiarism may also occur when a writer borrows from a source without properly acknowledging the source or without acknowledging the extent to which the writer relied on the source. A common form of plagiarism occurs when a writer acknowledges direct quotations from a source but does not acknowledge his or her paraphrasing or summarizing that source in other parts of the essay, thus creating the appearance that the material is the writer's original work.

Plagiarism can be accidental. Accidental plagiarism occurs when a writer relies on a source and either forgets or neglects to acknowledge its author in the text of his or her essay and Works Cited list. Such lapses frequently occur in several forms:

- Failure to identify a direct quotation by putting it in quotation marks
- Failure to adequately paraphrase a passage in the writer's own language
- Failure to identify the source of a paraphrased passage
- Failure to credit sources for ideas integrated into the essay

To maintain academic integrity in your writing, adhere to the following guidelines during the research and writing process.

1. *Employ correct note-taking methods.* Learn the differences among summary, paraphrase, and quotation. Know when and how to use each, and employ them correctly.
2. *Store a bibliographic entry for every source.* Consistently include for each note the name of the source's author, the title of the

work, and the page number(s) for any words you copy or adapt and for each piece of information you record.

3. *Use quotation marks.* In your notes and in your essay, put quotation marks around any language you reproduce directly from the source.

4. *Be scrupulous about identifying material downloaded from the Internet.* The Internet is a vast resource for information. It is easy to download material and then cut and paste it into an essay. Just as you must be scrupulous about acknowledging your traditional sources, you must also be scrupulous about acknowledging your Internet sources.

5. *Check and recheck your notes.* During the writing process be sure to integrate your sources into your text accurately. Check and recheck your information and acknowledgments for accuracy.

6. *Cite information accurately.* Cite the source in your text and in the Works Cited section whenever you include material from the notes in your final paper.

For experienced instructors, plagiarism is easy to spot. At the most obvious level, a plagiarized essay might not address the assignment,

WRITER'S TOOLBOX

Avoiding Plagiarism

You can avoid plagiarism by being careful about acknowledging your indebtedness whenever you borrow from another source. You don't need to cite sources of commonly known information such as the number of feet in a mile or the fact that the earth rotates around the sun. But you do need to cite a source any time you incorporate the following kinds of information into your text:

- Quoted words or paraphrased language
- Another writer's particular way of thinking about or describing something
- Facts that are not commonly known
- Numerical or graphical data

Plagiarizing can result from an honest oversight, sloppiness, or outright deliberateness. Take every precaution to avoid plagiarism and its serious academic consequences.

might not read like student work, or might read unevenly, revealing that a writer has not acknowledged a significant source used throughout the essay. Moreover, since there are tens of thousand of plagiarized essays available on the Internet, instructors are determined to fight the problem. As a result, Web sites such as *plagiarism.org* and *turnitin.com* now give instructors the ability to determine if suspect essays have indeed been plagiarized.

The process of researching and writing a research essay is your opportunity to learn what authorities have said about a subject and to develop your own opinion. Don't waste that opportunity by failing to properly acknowledge the work of those who have come before you.

Note-Taking Techniques

Summarizing

Summarizing is a technique for quickly recording information in condensed form and in your own words and style. Summarize whenever you need only a few facts or statistics from a source and you are not concerned about having a larger, more detailed record of its content or an author's perspective. Summarizing is also useful for broadly characterizing the general contents of a source or for registering your own reactions (e.g., "Describes state laws on home schooling. Not as complete as Baker article.").

Convenience and brevity are the keys to effective summarizing. Focus on recording only main points or useful facts, possibly adding a brief note to yourself when doing so seems helpful. Write the notes quickly, without too much concern for your own wording and style. Use synonyms and other wording or symbols to express the information in your own way, but also take care not to distort the meaning of the original. Avoid copying words and sentences from the original, which defeats the purpose of summarizing by taking more time and leads easily to plagiarism. If you must retain exceptional wording from the source, enclose it in quotation marks. Include the work's title, author's name, the source, and the page number for the summarized material on your note card in case you want more information later or need to list the source in your paper's Works Cited section.

The following passage shows how the notes a writer took on Internet health information were used as summary in his research paper. The boxed content quotes the original source material.

SUMMARIZED NOTE

> A better educated population is now emerging. They are capable
> of and require a greater degree of involvement in the decision
> making process. Further, there is a demonstrable shift in "con-
> sumer demand" in favor of "alternative" and more "natural"
> modalities, many of which are utter quackery; and people need
> to be better educated in the scientific method.
>
> Everone, Chadd. *Doctor Internet: How to Use the Internet for
> Health and Medicine: A Procedure Guide and Reference for
> Patients, Facilitators, and Health Professionals* (Berkeley, CA:
> Foundation for Infinite Survival, 1999), 16.

SUMMARY USED IN A RESEARCH PAPER

As one health professional sees the matter, there may be more
informed patients searching the Internet today, but they need to
understand how to examine evidence critically and ask questions
(Everone 16).

Paraphrasing

You **paraphrase** information by clearly restating it in your own
words. Paraphrasing is useful when you need to make a source's language or style more understandable and when it needs revision to
match the style and flow of your own writing when you include the
material in your paper. Unlike a summary, which condenses original
material into its essential meaning, a good paraphrase captures the
sense of each part of the source, whether the source is a single sentence or several pages. For this reason, a paraphrase has no typical
length, although it is seldom much shorter or longer than its source.

Your goal in paraphrasing is to recreate the entire original in different, clearer language that accurately conveys the source's meaning
as well as the attitude of its author. As you interpret the original,
remember that how ideas are stated can change or add to their meaning. Be sure your paraphrase reflects the less evident as well as the obvious aspects of the source's language and style by paying attention to
the author's word choice, emphases, qualifications, and overall tone.
To serve as a later reminder for yourself and to indicate an author's
attitude to your readers, it is often helpful to include brief phrases

that describe the manner in which the source's author relates the original (e.g., "Jenkins argues . . ." or "Henderson concedes that . . .").

Do not make the mistake of simply rewriting the original by rearranging its parts or integrating its words and sentence structures with your own. (Whether or not you cite the source, this practice amounts to plagiarism because the reader will assume the paraphrase is composed of your own wording.) Instead, always rewrite the source in your own style and language, taking care to use synonyms and other words that accurately capture the sense of the original. If you feel you must retain certain exceptional wording from the source, enclose it in quotation marks.

The following examples demonstrate the difference between unsuitable paraphrasing and paraphrasing that achieves its purpose. Notice how the first paraphrase incorrectly repeats words and phrases (shown here in italic type) from the source.

ORIGINAL

Public schools have, apparently willingly, assumed the role of "holding tanks." Social contact limited strictly to "peers" (defined as everyone of the same chronological age) is a fraud. The world for which we have the responsibility of preparing young people is *not* full of their peers. It is full of people both older and younger, from social strata both higher and lower. What are we teaching about this very real world? Not much.
—Bob Pike, "Why I Teach My Children at Home"

POOR PARAPHRASE NOTE

Pike says that *public schools* seem too willing to serve *the role of "holding tanks,"* places where the *social contacts* children have are *limited strictly* to their *chronological peers.* This is simply *fraud. We have the responsibility of preparing* children for a world populated by people *younger* as well as *older,* and from different levels of society. What lessons are they learning about the *real world?* Very few (564).

BETTER PARAPHRASE NOTE

Pike complains that schools seem deliberately to serve as isolated, fraudulent environments in which children socialize only with others their own age. However, the world for which education readies these children is, he insists, populated by people of all ages and from all levels of society. The education we give children about the world beyond the classroom amounts to very little (564).

The second paraphrase effectively rewords the source to avoid unintended plagiarism. In addition, the second paraphrase more accurately conveys the disgruntled attitude of the original author by using the terms *complains* and *insists* to characterize the way he presents his argument. The first version, in contrast, uses only the much less descriptive word *says*, which communicates nothing of the irritation implied in the source.

Once you have written your paraphrase, compare it with the original to make sure you have not omitted key details or distorted the meaning. Remember also to record the source title, author's name, and the page number of the source on your note card so you can properly document the paraphrase when you use it in your paper.

Using Quotation

Take down the precise words of a source when you sense that they will strengthen your research paper's discussion. Quote selectively and accurately, with the expectation of giving your reader only enough quoted material to convey and support your ideas. Blend single words, phrases, and sentences into your own writing as much as possible to keep your discussion flowing and to maintain your style.

> By arguing that people "don't want more taxes, just fewer criminals ruining their neighborhoods," Philips ignores the question of how we pay for more law enforcement.

Keep in mind that a quotation introduces the voice of another writer. Used excessively, it may suggest that you are depending too heavily on others for ideas. When used sparingly and accurately, however, quotation can bring variety and a sense of immediacy to a discussion.

The following are some of the most effective uses for quotation.

1. *Quote from a source to lend authority to what you say.* Use the quotation to reinforce your point, not to make it for you.

   > To do their job right, schools first need more money for teachers, which is why the prestigious 2004 *President's Report on Education* called low teacher salaries "the single greatest roadblock to this nation's quest for educational excellence" (41).

2. *Use quotation when summary or paraphrase would sacrifice the accuracy, precision, or eloquence of the original.*

   > The world's largest single radio telescope has "27 receivers moving on Y-shaped railway tracks, with each arm of the Y stretching 20 km" (18).

   > Americans have historically agreed in principle with Henry David Thoreau, who said, "That government is best which governs least" (Thompson 41).

3. *Use quotation to provide brief examples of language,* as when you discuss a literary work or analyze a political speech.

> Melville describes the whale as "primal," "preadamic," and "as elemental as the substance it swims in" (61, 60).

4. *Use quotation when the original may appear extreme or of questionable veracity.*

> Linguist Mary Hiller states that "half of the world's 6,000 known languages will disappear in the next fifty years because no children living today speak them" (114).

Remember always to put quotation marks around any quotation and to include documentation of the source in both your notes and your paper. Failure to provide either of them each time you quote is plagiarism. Be careful also not to distort the original or to quote out of context. Although you must always use the exact language of the original whenever you quote, there are acceptable methods for altering a quotation to blend with the grammar of your own writing or to suit other needs. For example, use ellipses to show that you have omitted material from a quotation (see ellipses, 43a) and place brackets around your own comments when they interrupt the quotation (see brackets, Chapter 45).

Combining Quotation and Paraphrase

You can sometimes reduce the amount of information you need to quote by combining quotation with paraphrase. The technique is simple: use quotation when the exact wording of the original is important, and paraphrase any part whose meaning, but not whose precise language, is worth recording. You must be careful when using quotation and paraphrase together to distinguish quoted material from paraphrasing by means of clearly placed quotation marks. Use ellipses and brackets to alter quotations as necessary to maintain sense or to omit unnecessary material. The following example demonstrates how to use quotation and paraphrase to record information on a note card.

> Pike argues that when schools serve more like "holding tanks" and limit student contact only to peers, they are "a fraud." The real world "for which we ... [prepare children] is *not* full of their peers." It includes "older and younger" people from various social levels. "What are we teaching [children] about this very real world? Not much" (8).

(See 43a, pages 281–282 for guidance an using ellipses [. . .] in quotations.)

WRITER'S TOOLBOX

Frequently Asked Questions (FAQs) about Student Research

1. **I want to argue against child abuse. Is this a good paper topic?** Who would argue in favor of child abuse? This is a one-sided issue, inappropriate for an argument paper. You might select an unsettled side issue, however, like prevention or laws relating to child abuse.

2. **I can find only three references to my topic in the card catalog. Should I find another topic?** Have you tried your library's online databases or other resources such as *Infotrac* or *Academic ASAP*? Have you tried *Google Scholar*? If you still can't find more, you may need to rethink your topic. Try redefining it based on what you've found in related sources.

3. **My library doesn't have a book I need for my research. Is there some other way I can get a copy?** Ask your librarian about interlibrary loan; you can often get books from other college libraries. Or check *Book Review Digest,* which may have enough information for you to use as a source. The complete texts of many books, especially older ones, are now also available online; try *Google Book Search* or *Books Online*.

4. **Can I interview a friend as a primary source for my paper?** Use personal interviews carefully. Usually people interviewed should be in a position to speak objectively and knowledgeably and should be able to provide insights not available to you through published sources. If your friend fits these criteria, then use that person to support or illustrate information obtained from more widely available sources.

5. **I found over a hundred sources for my topic on the Internet. What do I do now?** Narrow your sources to those that appear most relevant, reliable, current, and authoritative. Look first for sources that are most closely related to your topic, then for clear statements of authorship and sponsorship.

6. **Six of my twelve sources are all from the same magazine. Is that okay?** Probably not. You want a balanced list of works cited—books, journals, magazines—and of sources within each category. The exception might be a range of articles from a scholarly journal that focuses on your topic.

7. **My paper seems like a summary of my sources. How do I bring my own ideas in?** Your thesis statement should offer your own argument and should control the organization of your paper. Be sure your thesis really represents what you want to argue; then support it with ample evidence. Use sources to support or confront your own argument—compare, evaluate, define, make concessions, analyze, and comment just as you would in any discussion.

8. **Are three or four citations enough for a ten-page research paper?** Probably not. You may not be using enough of your research data to support your argument, or you may not be giving appropriate credit to ideas found in your sources. Review your paper to be sure that you are offering enough supportive evidence, and that you have properly cited the sources of that evidence.

9. **I found a lot of information on *Wikipedia.com*. Is this a reliable source?** Collaborative sites like *Wikipedia* can offer up-to-date information on some topics not always included in traditional sources, but you need to tread very carefully, since almost anyone can contribute information to these sites. You can often use *Wikipedia* entries to gain background and basic information and to help locate other, more authoritative sources through the "History," "External Links," and "Bibliography" sections.

10. **I took notes on a lecture in one of my classes. Can I use the lecture as a primary source?** Yes. Just be confident your notes are accurate, and cite the lecturer, date, and place of the lecture in your Works Cited list.

11. **My first draft is much shorter than the required length. What should I do?** Have you supplied ample support for your argument? Have you discussed all the relevant aspects? Is your thesis too narrow to allow expansive discussion? You may need to rethink your argument. If your instructor is willing, maybe she will read your draft and help you see ways to expand it.

12. **I looked at twelve sources but only cited six of them in my paper. Can I include the others in my Works Cited list?** No. If your instructor agrees, you can include a Works Consulted list, but if you have only used a source for general background information, it cannot be included in your list.

59a Revise the thesis and outline

After completing the reading and note taking for your paper, you will probably have rethought your concept of the paper's content and organization. At this point you will want to revise your thesis and then your outline. Begin by sorting the note cards by topic and arranging them in a way that parallels your tentative outline. This process will show whether you have adequate material to support the points in your outline. When the sorting is completed, evaluate your tentative thesis and working outline with an eye for revision. Then rearrange the note cards and rework your tentative thesis to fit the concept you see emerging from the material you have collected.

After reading her notes, Patricia Burton decided her paper should not only address the problem of increasing plagiarism among college students, but that it should also discuss why plagiarism is so easy to commit and what colleges are doing about it. She decided to revise her preliminary thesis statement accordingly:

> *Thesis Statement:* College plagiarism has become so increasingly common that campuses are stepping up efforts to combat it and to punish offenders.

> *Revised Thesis Statement:* College plagiarism has become so easy and pervasive that colleges are stepping up efforts to combat it and to punish those who try to pass off the work of others as their own.

Once Patricia Burton had revised her outline and arranged her notes according to the new headings, she was ready to develop her final outline topic. (See final plan for an essay, 7d.) Burton's formal outline appears on page 391.

59b Write the first draft

You can begin writing the paper at any point in the outline, perhaps writing the middle paragraphs before the introductory and concluding paragraphs. Patricia Burton began her research paper with an example that she considered both highly interesting and significant.

She read a draft of her introduction to a classmate, and she also discussed other sections she had planned for the paper. Burton's classmate urged her to keep the introduction she had planned. It was, he assured her, something student readers would relate to and want to know more about. From that conversation Burton learned an important lesson about writing: Sometimes just talking about your ideas helps to improve them and gives you confidence that you are thinking effectively about your topic.

59c Acknowledge your sources

Acknowledging your sources in your paper lends it authority and credibility and provides readers with the information to locate the sources for themselves. To a large extent, the value of your paper's content and your own integrity as a writer depend on how accurately and fairly you make use of and credit the ideas you borrow from other writers. (See avoiding plagiarism, pp. 369–371.) As you write your paper and integrate information from your sources into it, follow standard documentation practices to ensure the accurate acknowledgment of your sources.

Parenthetical Citations: MLA Documentation Style

Use parenthetical citations to acknowledge quotations (but not common sayings or well-known quotations), summaries, paraphrases, the opinions of others, lines of thinking you adopt, and statistics. In short, use parenthetical citations whenever you borrow information that is not commonly known or believed, especially by people generally acquainted with your subject. Facts or common knowledge— that hydrocyanic acid is a colorless, poisonous liquid or that Abraham Lincoln was the sixteenth president of the United States— do not require parenthetical citations. (See Chapter 60 for additional guidance.)

Because a parenthetical citation must always designate a specific entry listed alphabetically in Works Cited, the information in the citation must clearly direct a reader to that entry. Usually, but not always (see examples below), the author's last name and a page reference are enough to identify the source and the specific location from which you have borrowed material.

> The wings of jetliners built in Europe or Russia are
>
> more difficult to inspect and maintain than those built

in the U.S. because of the way they are manufactured
(Scott 28).

Page references never include *p.* or *pp.* To cite several consecutive pages, join the page numbers with a hyphen. (Seo 78-81). To cite two or more individual pages in one citation, use commas to separate them (Hutton 16, 41, 63).

Keep parenthetical citations as concise as possible so that the interruption in your text is minimal. You are required to give only enough information to guide a reader to the specific source you have fully identified in Works Cited. If you have integrated into your text any information that should be included in a parenthetical citation, such as the author's name, you need not include it in the citation.

> Wilson Bryan Key has taken the mystery from subliminal-
> advertising discussions. He claims to have found subliminal
> messages in vodka ads (99).

Insert parenthetical citations as close to the borrowed material as possible, before a period or comma but after quotation marks.

> In her 1979 essay collection, *The White Album*, Joan Didion
> sounds confused by random violence and personal terror
> (15-20), but by 1982 its meaning has become clear to her:
> "I came to understand, in a way I had not understood before,
> the exact mechanism of terror" (*Salvador* 21).

Set off quotations longer than four typed lines by typing them in an indented block one inch in from the left margin.

> After he was wounded, Walter Ehlers showed the kind of
> courage that eventually earned him the Medal of Honor:
>
> > Ehlers was treated at a field station. The bullet that
> > hit him had actually entered his side, ricocheted
> > off a rib, and exited through his back into his
> > pack—where it pierced a picture of his mother, a
> > bar of soap, and his entrenchment tool. He insisted
> > on returning to action; unable to wear a backpack,
> > he strapped on two bandoliers of ammunition,
> > picked up a rifle, and went to find his men
> > (Collier 76).

Entire Work

If you wish to acknowledge an entire work rather than a specific part of the work, include the author's name in the text rather than in a parenthetical citation. You are not required to cite a page number, although including a work's title in the text may be helpful.

> Peter Brooks's analysis of plot and plotting in *Literary Minds* is established on basic psychoanalytic principles.

Part of an Article or of a Single-Volume Work

When you refer to specific passages or when you quote directly from a work, you must give the relevant page reference in the parenthetical citation.

> Campbell's point is stunningly clear: "Communication is not confined to radios, telephones, and television channels. It occurs in nature, wherever life exists" (67).

> Most people spend more time picking a car than they do a doctor or a hospital (Mathiesen 38), but that is not necessarily bad.

If two authors listed in Works Cited have the same last name, give the first initial as well as the last name: (L. Sanders 34).

For a work with two or three authors, give all the last names. If there are more than three authors, give the first last name listed followed by *et al.*: (Scholes et al. 28-29).

If you list more than one work by the same author in Works Cited, give the title or a shortened version of it after the author's name: (Barthes, *Images* 12-13).

Multivolume Work

In the parenthetical citation for a multivolume work, include the volume number followed by a colon, a space, and then the page reference: (Kroos 1: 210-15). If you refer to an entire volume in general rather than to specific pages, place a comma after the author's name and include *vol.*: (Kroos, vol. 1). If you place the information in your text, write out *volume* and the numeral: Kroos's volume 1 covers the first. . . . Use arabic numerals rather than roman numerals to indicate volume numbers.

> "Feeling-toned complexes" were defined by the early psychiatric community as "failures to react" (Jung 8: 93).

At first the prose is groping, unsure of its footing, but
midway through the work, sharp portraits of avant-garde
artists emerge (Nin, vol. 1).

Work Listed by Title

For a work alphabetized by title in your Works Cited list, use that title
or a shortened version of it in the parenthetical reference. To make
tracing the reference easier for your reader, begin the citation with
the word by which the work is alphabetized. If you are acknowledging a one-page article, omit the page reference.

A debit card, according to MasterCard's president Hogg,
"looks like a credit card but works like a check" ("New Credit
Card").

The *Planning Commission Handbook* clearly states that land
development is not the landowner's god-given right, but is a
privilege granted by a public agency (31-32).

Work by a Corporate Author

Because the names of corporate authors are often long, identify them
in your text and cite the specific page reference in the parenthetical
citation. When necessary, you may offer a shortened version of the
name in the parenthetical citation.

The Commission on Post-Secondary Education in California
states that remedial education in the University of California
and State University systems has dramatically increased (5-10).

Fiction, Poetry, Drama, and the Bible

When citing the Bible as well as literary works available in more than
one edition, include information that will help readers find the relevant passage—chapter, book, scene, line. In general, use arabic numerals rather than roman numerals in citing volumes or divisions of
a work. Roman numerals may be used in citing acts and scenes of a
play if your instructor requires it.

For a novel, give the page number first, a semicolon and space,
and then the divisions, using appropriate abbreviations with periods.

Politics, the undercurrent of the novel, sweeps Julien from
one extreme to another. Nowhere is this more evident than

in the description of the king's visit to Verrières (Stendhal 115-26; pt. 1, ch. 18).

For extended works of poetry, give the division reference first, followed by the line reference. Use a period with no space to separate the two. Do not give a page reference.

> Antenor described Odysseus's ability as a powerful orator: "But when he let the great voice go from his chest, and the words came / drifting down like the winter snows, then no other mortal / man beside could stand up against Odysseus" (Homer 3.221-23).

If the poem is short or not divided into books or cantos, give only the line reference. When acknowledging only line numbers, use *line* or *lines* in the first citation; having established that the numbers designate lines, use only numbers in subsequent citations.

> "For the Anniversary of My Death" begins with the suggestion that after death the soul starts a journey through time "Like the beam of a lightless star" (Merwin, line 5). The poem ends with Merwin's affirmation of concrete experience, behind which lies the mystery of existence.
>
> > As today writing after three days of rain
> > Hearing the wren sing and the falling cease
> > And bowing not knowing to what. (11-13)

For a play give the act, scene, and line references, using periods without spaces to separate the divisions. You may use roman numerals in citing acts and scenes if your instructor requires it.

> The imagery of futile battle is also found in the "To be, or not to be" soliloquy (Shakespeare 3.1.56-89).

For the Bible give the book title, chapter, and verse, using periods to separate the divisions. Within the parenthetical citation (but not in the text itself) you may abbreviate a book title, using a period to end the abbreviation—for example, "Gen." for *Genesis,* "Rev." for *Revelation.*

> In the opening verses of the Book of Job (1.1-5), Job appears to have fulfilled the blessing that God had bestowed on humankind when Adam and Eve were created, "Be fruitful, multiply, fill the earth and conquer it" (Gen. 1.28).

Indirect Sources

Whenever possible, draw your material from an original source, but at times you will need to rely on an indirect source for information. For instance, you may need to use someone's published account of what another person has said. When you do quote or paraphrase from an indirect source, you must indicate in the parenthetical citation that you have done so by putting *qtd. in* ("quoted in") before the acknowledgment of the source, unless, of course, you have clearly indicated in your text that you are relying on an indirect source.

> The poet Michael McClure claims Mailer had a strong belief that he would only be listened to if he were irreverent. When people asked Mailer to moderate his irreverence, he would say, "Hey, I *feel* irreverence, and there's truth in the irreverence" (qtd. in Manso 281).

Two or More Sources in One Parenthetical Citation

To acknowledge more than one source in a single citation, cite each work as you normally would but separate the citations with a semi-colon and a space.

> Whenever we open another novel, we embark on an adventure in which we have a chance to become a new person in the sense both that we can assume the imaginary role the writer thrusts at us and that we can reformulate ourselves by discovering what had previously seemed to elude our consciousness (Gibson 265; Iser 294).

When multiple references in a single citation would be too long, acknowledge them in a note instead. (See the explanatory notes section below.)

Explanatory Notes: MLA Style

Explanatory notes have a limited use in the MLA system of documentation. Notes are used to offer definitions, provide translations, make comparisons between sources, or generally furnish information not strictly pertinent to the immediate discussion in the text.

Identify notes in your text by numbering them consecutively throughout with superscript (raised) arabic numerals. The numerals correspond to notes appearing either at the bottom of the page or on a page titled "Notes" placed at the end of the paper before Works Cited.

TEXT REFERENCE

Although colleges in the United States had historically assumed close supervisory roles over students since the late eighteenth century,[1] the 1960s introduced changes in social attitudes that resulted in fewer restrictions on campuses and new regard for the rights of students to be treated as adults (Kleiner 74).

NOTE

[1]Until the 1960s, colleges and universities continued to act *in loco parentis,* that is, to be legally responsible for minors in the absence of their parents. Changes in social attitudes and the fear of being sued for any involvement in student affairs then pushed schools toward a more "hands-off" approach to supervising students (Kleiner 74).

Works Cited Entries: MLA Style

The documentation formats for citing sources in the Works Cited list for an MLA-style research paper appear on pages 408–419. As you follow those guidelines be aware of the following modifications in MLA style that were made in 2008.

Publication Medium.   The *medium of publication* (the form in which you found the source you are citing) is now required for every work you cite. The publication medium for all printed books and periodicals is *Print.* For any source you access online, the medium is *Web*, even if it originally appeared in another medium. The medium of publication for other kinds of works includes *Film*, *CD*, *Laser disc*, *Performance*, *JPEG file*, and similarly descriptive categories.

In most instances the publication medium, without underlining or italics and followed by a period, appears as the last item in a Works Cited entry:

> Engel, Richard. *War Journal: My Five Years in Iraq*. New York:
>
> Simon, 2008. Print.

Whenever *Web* is the medium of publication, the last item in the Works Cited entry should be the date of access:

> Conrad, Joseph. *Heart of Darkness*. [1902.] *Conrad, Joseph,*
>
> *1857-1924. Heart of Darkness*. Electronic Text Center,
>
> U of Virginia Lib. Web. 3 Mar. 2008.

The documentation examples on pages 408–419 show the medium of publication included in each Works Cited entry. As you proofread your final paper, be sure that the medium of publication appears with every work you cite.

Use of the URL.   Including a URL (Uniform Resource Locator) for an online source is no longer required. Instead, you should give the URL only when your reader may not be able to locate an online source without it. In such cases, give the complete URL (use the computer's copy and paste function to avoid errors), placed between angle brackets and followed by a period. If the URL is long, you may break it into smaller units, but only after a slash:

> *Biology Browser*. 2005. Thompson Reuters. Web. 10 Sept. 2008.
>
> <http://www.biologybrowser.org./cgi-bin/search/
>
> hyperseek.cgi?Terms=mollusca&Range=Any&howmuch=ALL>.

Volume and Issue Numbers.   Where MLA used to omit the issue number for a scholarly journal with continuous pagination (i.e., page numbers continue from issue to issue), MLA now requires that *both* volume and issue numbers be included in Work Cited entries for scholarly journals, regardless of their method of pagination:

> Shamanske, Stephen. "The Monopoly Nonproblem: Taking Price
>
> Discrimination Seriously." *Independent Review* 10.3
>
> (2006): 337-50.

59d Complete the final draft

After you have completed the first draft, put your paper aside for a day or two if possible. This will give you a chance to return to it with a fresh approach. Reread the entire draft carefully several times and at least once aloud to listen for missing transitions or awkward constructions. Watch for careless grammar, spelling, or punctuation mistakes. More important, examine the content to see that you have kept to your thesis, provided ample evidence to support the assertions in your topic sentences, and integrated your own views with those of your sources to create a balanced whole. As a last step, check your citations and list of works cited to be sure they are correct in form, content, and punctuation.

Guidelines for Typing the Research Paper

Although formats for research papers vary, the following guidelines reflect the most common practices for typing the title page, outline (if required), quotations, citations, and Works Cited. Unless otherwise noted, all typing should be double spaced. (See also Chapter 10.)

Title page. Center the title about a third of the way down the page. Do not italicize or underline it or put quotation marks around it unless the words would be treated that way in the paper's text. Ten lines down from the title, center your name. Beneath your name, type the course title, the instructor's name, and the date, each on a separate line.

Your instructor may prefer that you follow MLA guidelines, which recommend not using a title page. In that case, present the identifying information on the first page of the text. Place your name, your instructor's name, the course number and section, and the date on separate double-spaced lines in the upper-left-hand corner of the page, observing the same left-hand margin as the text. Double-space below the date and center your title; then double-space between your title and the first line of the text.

Outline. If your instructor requires you to submit an outline, center the word *Outline* and then type the thesis statement. Use standard outline form, with the topic levels successively indented and numbered with roman or arabic numerals and lowercase or uppercase letters as required. The outline included in Patricia Burton's paper appears on page 391.

Quotations. Indent quotations longer than four typed lines ten spaces from the left margin (or one inch), double-spacing throughout (see 10a). Do not put quotation marks around an indented quotation. When quoting two or more paragraphs, indent the first line of each paragraph three additional spaces (or one-fourth inch). The parenthetical citation appears at the end of the indented quotation, following the period or other end mark. Shorter quotations, not indented, should be enclosed in double quotation marks.

Titles. Use your computer's font selection function to type the titles of all long or independently published works in *italics,* including the titles of books, newspapers, magazines, journals, separately published poems, databases, and entire Internet sites. Enclose the titles of articles and the parts of any long or independent work between double quotation marks ("A Century of Good Deeds").

Punctuation and spacing. Leave only one typed space after a period or other final punctuation mark. Include a comma after each item in a series, up to and including the item before a conjunction (*life, liberty, and the pursuit of happiness*). You may omit the comma before a conjunction when a compound sentence is very short and the relationship of the two clauses is clear without the punctuation (*They objected and Smith apologized.*)

Other punctuation marks. Most computer keyboards have bracket keys. For a dash, use either two unspaced hyphens (--) without space on either side or an em dash, if available.

Notes. Starting on a new page, center the word *Notes* one inch from the top, with the first entry two lines below the title. Indent each note five spaces from the left margin and type the note number followed by a period and a space before the first word of the note. All subsequent lines of the note begin at the left margin. Double-space within each note and between notes.

Works Cited. Type the words *Works Cited* on a new page, centered, one inch from the top. Begin the first alphabetized entry at the left margin two lines below the title. Remember to cite the first author with the last name first; subsequent authors' or editors' names in the same entry are typed in regular order; subsequent lines of an entry are indented five spaces. When you have more than one work by the same author, the name is not repeated; instead, type three hyphens followed by a period. Double-space throughout. Follow periods with only one space.

After you have typed the final version of the paper, carefully read it again for errors in typing. Include, in order, an outline, the text of the paper, the notes, and the list of works cited. Other sections, such as an appendix or glossary, if they are included, precede the notes. When you are satisfied that you have written and typed the paper in a manner that fulfills your own goals and the requirements of your instructor, make a photocopy to keep for yourself and present the original copy to your instructor.

59e A sample research paper

Patricia Burton's research paper, which follows, illustrates the advice given in this chapter. She followed the style for citations and list of works cited given in the *MLA Style Manual* (2008). The comments accompanying the paper identify specific points about the research paper format as well as some of the decisions Burton made while writing.

Include a title page if the paper has an outline and/or your instructor requires it.

Center and double-space title one-third of the way down the page.

College Plagiarism:

Easy to Do, But Getting Harder to Get Away With

Center and double-space your name, course information, and date.

Patricia Burton

English 101

Professor Margo Wills

December 5, 2008

Center Outline *1"* *from top of page.*

Type thesis at beginning of outline.

Outline

Thesis: College plagiarism has become so easy and pervasive that colleges are stepping up efforts to combat it and to punish those who try to pass off the work of others as their own.

Use standard outline form. This outline is organized by topic.

Double-space throughout outline. Leave 1" margins on both sides.

I. Introduction: Use of plagiarism by college students

II. Definition of plagiarism

   A. Origin of the term *plagiarism*

   B. Types of plagiarism

   C. Guidelines against committing plagiarism

III. Widespread frequency of college plagiarism

   A. Results of student surveys

   B. Use of the Internet

      1. Homework sites

      2. Term paper mills

   C. Why college students plagiarize

IV. Campus responses to student plagiarism

   A. Punishments for plagiarism

   B. Use of honor codes

   C. Anti-plagiarism technology

V. Responsibility of colleges to address plagiarism

   A. Protection of honest students

   B. Preservation of social trust

Burton 1

Center paper's
title on first page;
double-space
between lines of
title and text.

College Plagiarism: Easy to Do,

But Getting Harder to Get Away With

Faced with a deadline for giving professors

a working chapter of his dissertation and lacking

the time and inspiration to write it himself,

graduate student Michael Thompson (a pseudonym)

did what instructors fear great numbers of

college students do every day: He went to the

*Burton introduces
topic with an
example illustrating
student plagiarism.*

Internet, copied from a few appropriate

sources, changed or scrambled some wording,

and then prepared the transformed material

as his own work (Thompson). In the end,

Thompson did not submit the plagiarized

material as part of his dissertation. However,

research on college cheating suggests that an

alarming number of college students frequently

do turn in work pirated from books,

newspapers, journals, the Internet, and

other sources for nearly every kind of college

assignment, including research papers, lab

studies, book reports, creative writing

*First paragraph
concludes with
thesis statement.*

assignments, tests, and even personal essays.

College plagiarism, in fact, has become so

easy and pervasive that colleges are stepping

up efforts to combat it and to punish those

who try to pass off the work of others as

their own.

Plagiarism is certainly nothing new to the

world, nor is its practice limited to the halls of

academia. Our modern concepts about plagiarism

and its condemnation go back at least as far as

the first century CE and the Roman poet Martial,

Burton 2

who referred to a writer who had stolen some lines from him as a *plagiarius,* "one who steals the child or slave of another," that is, a kidnapper (Mallon 6). Although Greek, Roman, and other early cultures admired imitations of great works,[1] most instances of plagiarism have been almost universally condemned since the eighteenth century ushered in an increased admiration for originality and respect for copyright laws (Mallon 24). Today revelations about scientists, politicians, journalists, and well-known authors who use unacknowledged content from other sources appear almost regularly in the news.[2] Such acts are almost universally condemned, although public judgment may view them individually as ranging variously from minor ethical lapses to significant acts of immorality or unprofessional behavior.

Formally defined, *plagiarism* is the act of taking someone else's words, ideas, or ways of thinking about or presenting a subject and using that material as if it were one's own. A student who uses another writer's language—whether just a few words, a short phrase or two, or an entire paragraph or page—without putting the material in quotation marks and citing the other writer or source is a plagiarist. Even when the student changes the original wording in some way, the result is still plagiarism. The same is true if the student adopts another writer's way of thinking about or describing a subject, as when explaining a process such as nuclear fusion or someone else's developed concept of loyalty.

Burton 3

Use quotation marks around words used in a special sense.

Rhetorical question varies style and creates emphasis.

And what if the unacknowledged "borrowing" is perhaps unintentional, an inadvertent mistake caused by a careless use of quotation marks or by forgetting what was one's own writing and what was someone else's? The result is the same: plagiarism, pure and simple, intended or not.

Two other forms of plagiarism, both intentional and clearly fraudulent, are also common. In the first, a student turns in a paper he or she has purchased from what is known as a "paper-mill," a commercial company that sells complete essays or research papers by mail or, more usually today, over the Internet. Even though some mills state in their advertising that purchased papers are to be used solely for "research purposes," it is generally known that such papers often end up on an instructor's desk with the student buyer's name as their author (Harris 13).

In another form of plagiarism, the student may commit "self-plagiarism," that is, turning in the same paper in two different courses without an instructor's permission (Whitley and Keith-Spiegel 17; Gibaldi 33). In such an instance, a student may write an essay for an English class about his or her family and then, without notifying either instructor, submit the same or a slightly modified paper to fulfill an assignment in a psychology course.

Separate two or more source citations with a semicolon.

Both in academic settings and throughout the professional world, any form of plagiarism is considered unethical, an unacceptable breach of integrity and trust. Research and publication

guidelines such as those of the American
Psychological Association (APA) and the Modern

Give full name with abbreviation for well-known entities.

Language Association (MLA) are consistently
followed in numerous academic and professional
fields, and they are taught and required of
students on nearly every college campus. These
guidelines discuss the importance of a writer's
integrity in reporting research, and they are
explicit about the inappropriateness of
plagiarism. For example, the *APA Publication
Manual* explicitly warns that "an author does not
present the work of another as if it were his or

Italicize titles of whole works.

her own work" (American 349). The *MLA
Handbook for Writers of Research Papers* goes
even further, condemning plagiarism as a kind of

Use comma or colon as required to introduce block quotations.

double dishonesty:

Indent block quotations ten spaces from the left margin.

> Plagiarism involves two kinds of
> wrongs. Using another person's ideas,
> information, or expressions without
> acknowledging that person's work
> constitutes intellectual theft.
> Passing off another person's ideas,
> information, or expressions as your
> own to get a better grade or gain some
> other advantage constitutes fraud.

Cite source for indented quotation following the final period.

> (Gibaldi 66)

The MLA's guidelines advise that "common sense
as well as ethics should determine" what is
documented and—with the exception of well-
known sayings, quotations, or commonly known

Include changes to original quotation in brackets.

information—student writers should "document
everything that [they] borrow—not only direct

quotations but also information and ideas"
(Gibaldi 73).

What has educators most concerned today is
their sense that despite schools' stressing such

guidelines, great numbers of college students—the
scientists, doctors, politicians, journalists, authors,
and university professors of tomorrow—are
dishonestly submitting and taking credit for
academic work they did not do. Unfortunately,
research suggests that they are right. For
example, two-thirds of high school students—the
college population of tomorrow—cheat on tests,
while an astounding 90 percent cheat on
homework; other studies show that percentages
for college students are almost as high (Carter
and Punyanunt-Carter 336). Given such findings,

it may not be surprising that a University of
Virginia physics professor who used computer
software to analyze his students' papers found
158 suspected cases of plagiarism or that in
a 2003 survey of 18,000 college students,
38 percent said they had plagiarized from the
Internet and 40 percent admitted they had also
plagiarized from books, journals, and other
standard sources (Hansen 6).

These findings agree with results of another
2002-2005 national study of college students in
which 70 percent of respondents admitted to
academic cheating of some kind, while 37 percent
said they had plagiarized material from the
Internet; a surprising 77 percent felt such

cheating was not a serious issue (*Center*). Thus,
it is not hard to understand why TurnItIn.com,

an Internet company whose software services are
used by hundreds of colleges and universities to
detect student plagiarism, reports that about
30 percent of the 100,000 student papers analyzed
each day is not original work (*TurnItIn*).

The Internet provides an undeniably rich
and tempting resource for students, whether they
are merely seeking help with an assignment or
intentionally avoiding doing their own work.
Numerous Internet sites offer study guides,
sample essays and term papers, papers written
to order, book reviews, plot summaries, literary
analyses, and even lecture notes (Harris 169-89).
Many sites also offer free message boards where
students can post questions about classroom
assignments and get help from other users. A
recent posting at *PinkMonkey.com*, for example,
asks readers for help with a literature class
assignment about racism in Joseph Conrad's
novel *Heart of Darkness*. Another student at
SparkNotes.com posts two assigned questions on
distillation from an organic chemistry course.
Like these services, a myriad of other Internet
sites also provide study guides, lecture notes, and
textbook reviews of hundreds of academic
subjects, including art, medicine, biology, history,
literature, mathematics, and astronomy.

While some students may naively rely too
often on Internet resources for research or help
with their homework, many intentionally use the
Internet to plagiarize or to purchase a paper
someone else has written. Thus, in responding to
a study at Rochester Institute of Technology,

*For page number
ranges, give last
two digits of second
number.*

Burton summarizes and integrates quoted material into her own sentences.

16.5 percent of the students said they "sometimes" plagiarized from the Internet, while 8 percent said they did so "often." A different 6 percent admitted that they "sometimes" purchased whole papers from commercial online sources, while 2.3 percent said they did so "often" (Hansen 6).

There can be little doubt that Internet paper mills tempt students with ready-made or written-to-specification papers in any format and on thousands of academic subjects. *CheatHouse.com* advertises itself as "the perfect site for research, late assignments and general reference." A site

Example supports topic sentence and paper's thesis.

named *Academic Term Papers* boasts that it has 30,000 available papers on file, while *ProfEssays.com* promises "custom essays on marketing, management, globalization, medicine, law, philosophy, sociology, literature, history, politics, religion, science, technology, ecology,

Use of sic *in brackets indicates quotation is correct as given.*

psychology, movies and others [sic]." Students can go to *School Sucks* for free essays, term papers, book reports, and even dissertations. *Term Paper Relief* will deliver a paper written to order on any specified topic for $9.95 per page in four days or within 2-24 hours for $24.95 per page. Customers at such sites can specify a paper's subject, length, number and types of sources, and even bibliographic reference styles such a MLA, APA, and Chicago. And while sites like *Academic Term Papers* may remind buyers that term papers are "sold for research and reference purposes only," most emphasize the easy availability of papers on nearly any topic.

Topic sentence states the main idea of the paragraph.

Why students feel compelled to purchase papers or to plagiarize from the Internet and other sources appears to have no definitive answer. Studies show that students plagiarize for a variety of reasons, including stress about grades and academic competition, careless note taking, feelings of intellectual or academic inadequacy, cultural habits, poor planning and procrastination, weak writing skills, and simply the belief that they will not get caught plagiarizing (Harris 2-12). Some experts blame the Internet's huge amounts of readily available information and numerous term paper mills for encouraging the current trend of plagiarism, while others cite the easy copy-cut-paste processes allowed by modern computer software.

Educators generally agree that much college plagiarism is unintentional, the result of poor note-taking or paraphrasing skills as well as a lack of adequate research training in high school (Hansen 4). Studies show that students from non-Western societies may cheat or plagiarize because they come from cultures that deem such activities acceptable (Whitley and Keith-Spiegel 20-21). And although nearly 90 percent of college students say they know plagiarism is wrong (Hansen 3), many still plagiarize because, as the director of a university journalism and mass communication program explains, they think "their professors are too lazy, too busy, or too dumb to catch them" (qtd. in Whitehouse and Nicholls 3). Not surprisingly, students also cheat more often in courses where

Citation refers to a work with two authors.

For material quoted from an indirect source, use qtd. in *before citing the source you used.*

they know the instructor is likely to ignore
cheating (*Center*).

Regardless of why they plagiarize, students
who are caught taking credit for someone else's
words or ideas can face serious and long-lasting
consequences. Depending on the circumstances
and the school, penalties for plagiarizing on a
college writing assignment can range from failing
an assignment or a course to being expelled—or
even having a degree revoked once the
plagiarism has been discovered. At the University
of Virginia in 2001-2002, for example, 48
students were expelled or allowed to leave
because of plagiarism, and three of the students
had their degrees revoked (Hansen 4). In
similar instances, the degrees of two journalism
students at the University of Georgia were held
back because they had plagiarized articles they
wrote for the campus newspaper (Whitehouse
and Nicholls 2), and a University of Ohio
graduate had his Master's degree revoked for
plagiarism he committed in writing his thesis
(Hoag).

As faculty and institutions are also
discovering, penalties for student plagiarism can
extend to those responsible for allowing it to
happen. In 2004 an investigative committee at
one Ohio University campus not only advised that
degrees be held up and possibly denied for
students who had likely plagiarized mechanical
engineering assignments, it also recommended
that two faculty members be fired and another
placed on probation for having allowed "rampant

*Cite a source
without an author
by title.*
and flagrant plagiarism" to occur under their
supervision (qtd. in "Be Tough").

At most campuses, such as the University
of Colorado at Boulder, faculty discuss
plagiarism with their students and include
warnings about it in their course syllabi
(Hansen 16). Although colleges invoke various
degrees of penalties for plagiarism, many
schools also try to set offenders back on the
right track through education and counseling.
At the United States Naval Academy, faculty
mentor students who violate the honor code;
many other campuses require students to
complete a special ethics course on campus or,
to preserve student anonymity, online, such as
in the 8-10 hour program provided free to other
schools by Ball State University (Whitley and
Keith-Spiegel 136).

Nearly all colleges publish honor codes and
academic honesty policies in their catalog, on
their Web site, and in other campus publications.
While some campuses merely list plagiarism
among other non-tolerated offenses, many
address plagiarism specifically and at length. The
online Academic Policies statement of Westmont
College, a liberal arts college in California,
*Quoted material is
integrated with the
writer's own words.* defines "three levels of plagiarism (minimal,
substantial and complete)" and specifies the
consequences for each level, which can range
from rewriting a paper for a reduced grade
to expulsion from the college ("Academic
Dishonesty"). Dartmouth College provides its
students with an online guide that discusses

Burton 11

plagiarism, sources to use for research, and a guide for integrating and acknowledging sources in their writing (*Sources*). Such emphases not only strengthen the legality of an institution's penalty policies, they also raise student and faculty awareness of the importance the institution places on academic integrity. In fact, research shows that published academic honor codes can be highly effective, in many instances lowering cheating overall by as much as a third and reducing cheating on writing assignments by as much as 25-30 percent (Harris 31).

The biggest weapons colleges are using to combat plagiarism today are commercial authentication services with names like TurnItIn, iThenticate, MyDropBox, and Plagiarism Stoppers. As their advertising makes clear, the detection software these companies use is thorough enough to give even the most talented plagiarist cause for concern. The software at MyDropBox can scan some 4.8 billion Web sites (*MyDropBox*), while TurnItIn can compare a student paper to more than 12 billion Internet pages, 10,000 periodicals,

Combine numerals and words to write large numbers.

and some 40 million other student papers (*TurnItIn*). The results tell instructors what percentage of the paper came from other sources and in most cases can identify the source. Some services, like TurnItIn, MyDropBox, and Glatt Plagiarism Services, also provide programs that allow students to check their own work for plagiarism.

The many endorsements and newspaper
headlines about detection services like these
indicate that such services have proven to be
effective in uncovering student plagiarism,
discouraging it, or both. Yet not all faculty agree
that technology is an appropriate way for
colleges to address the problem of plagiarism.
Many instructors resist what they see as
"policing" student writing, and many feel colleges
should place emphasis not on catching plagiarists
but on teaching students the importance of and
the skills to perform ethical research and
writing. Although the use of plagiarism detection
software has been upheld in recent court
decisions (LaRussa), some faculty nonetheless
feel that students' rights to privacy and
copyright protection are jeopardized when their
submitted work becomes part of a service's
database (Hansen 20).

To be fair, Burton discusses opposing points of view.

Those who endorse using technology do not
necessarily disagree, but they also feel that the
extent and seriousness of the plagiarism problem
require new approaches. In the opinion of John
Barrie, founder and president of TurnItIn.com,
"Digital plagiarism is a digital problem and
demands a digital solution." In Barrie's view,
"The status quo doesn't work, and our society's
future leaders are rapidly building a foundation
of shaky ethics while cheating their way to a
degree" (qtd. in Hansen 20).

As Barrie recognizes, students who
plagiarize or commit other unethical acts to
succeed in school are cheating other students out

of the good grades or other academic awards
they deserve. Research shows that those who use
plagiarism or other forms of cheating early in
their college or professional careers often continue
to do so later in life (Whitely and Kieth-Spiegel 5).
Educators consequently have an implicit moral
obligation not only to protect honest students but
to educate early those students who choose
unethical ways to succeed in school. In the view
of Lawrence M. Hinsman, director of the Values
Institute at the University of San Diego,
California, rampant plagiarism in colleges and
the community only lead to a breakdown in social
trust, the very fabric that makes a society's
social, political, and economic entities work
together and endure. "Without trust in public and
business institutions outside the family," he says,
"an economy stops developing after a certain
point" (qtd. in Hansen 7).

*Burton concludes
with summarizing
main ideas,
implications for
society, and
reference to the
thesis statement.*

    As Hinsman suggests, the individual and
social consequences of plagiarism are complex
and far-ranging. The fact that students have to
deal with more information today than ever
before places new and greater responsibilities on
educators, but ultimately it is the students
themselves who must accept their own
responsibility to resist plagiarizing. Clearly, the
ways students ethically access and use that
wealth of information is something they and
those who teach them are still learning together.

Burton 14

Center Notes *at top of page.*

Numerals correspond to those appearing in text.

"See" refers reader to additional sources.

Use notes to clarify or add information that would interrupt the text.

Burton includes titles of alleged plagiarized works in text.

Notes

1. For a discussion of the respect given to imitation and borrowing during classical Greek and Roman times, see Whitely and Keith-Spiegel, page 21 and Hansen, pages 11-12.

2. Major public figures who have been accused of extensive plagiarism and copyright violation include Martin Luther King, Jr., (his doctoral thesis and other works), Alex Haley (*Roots*), Stephen Ambrose (*The Wild Blue, Undaunted Courage,* and other books), Doris Kearns Goodwin (*The Fitzgeralds and the Kennedys*), and Dan Brown (*The Da Vinci Code*). More recent and widely publicized cases involved Jason Blair, the *New York Times* journalist found guilty of extensive plagiarism in his reporting, and Kaavvya Viswanathan, a 19-year-old Harvard sophomore who used unacknowledged material for her novel *How Opal Mehta Got Kissed, Got Wild and Got a Life.* For a discussion of Blair's case, see Hansen.

<table>
<tr><td>*Center* Works Cited
at top of page.</td><td>Works Cited</td></tr>
</table>

"Academic Dishonesty." *Academic Policies.* 2008.

Westmont College. Web. 12 Nov. 2008.

Academic Term Papers. 1998. Academic Term

Papers. Web. 20 Nov. 2008.

Form for a work by a corporate author.

American Psychological Association. *Publication Manual of the American Psychological Association.* 5th ed. Washington: American Psychological Association, 2001. Print.

Form for a work without an author.

"Be Tough on Cheaters: To Discourage Plagiarism, Universities Should Impose Tough Penalties." *Columbus Dispatch* 8 June 2006: 8A.

Publication medium in Web.

Expanded Academic ASAP. InfoTrac. Web. 12 Nov. 2008.

List sources alphabetically by author's surname or title if no author.

Carter, Stacy L., and Narissra Maria Punyanunt-Carter. "Acceptability of Treatments for Plagiarism." *College Student Journal* 41.2 (2007): 336-42, *Expanded Academic ASAP.* InfoTrac. Web. 10 Nov. 2008.

Form for an entire Internet site.

Center for Academic Integrity. 2007. Clemson U. Web. 30 Oct. 2008.

CheatHouse.com. 22 June 2003. Gradua Networks. Web. 10 Nov. 2008.

Form for a book with a later edition.

Gibaldi, Joseph. *MLA Handbook for Writers of Research Papers.* 6th ed. New York: Modern Language Association, 2003. Print.

A work from a library subscription service.

Hansen, Brian. "Is the Internet Causing More Students to Copy?" *CQ Researcher.* InfoTrac. 19 Sept. 2003. Web. 3 Nov. 2006.

Harris, Robert A. *The Plagiarism Handbook.* Los Angeles: Pyrczak, 2001. Print.

Hoag, Rachel. "Ohio University Revokes Master's Degree in Plagiarism Probe." *Associated Press*

Burton 16

State and Local Wire. Academic. Lexis-Nexis.
28 Mar. 2007. Web. 14 Nov. 2008.

Form for a newspaper article.

LaRussa, Tony. "Software to Discourage Cheating."
Pittsburgh Tribune-Review 31 May 2008.
Lexis-Nexis Academic. Lexis-Nexis. Web.
16 Nov. 2008.

Mallon, Thomas. *Stolen Words.* San Diego:
Harvest-Harcourt, 1989. Print.

MyDropBox.com. Sciworth, Inc. Web. 13 Nov.
2008.

PinkMonkey.com. 29 May 2008. PinkMonkey.com.
Web. 20 Nov. 2008.

Internet site names spelled as in source.

ProfEssays.com. ProfEssays.com. Web. 22 Nov.
2008.

School Sucks. School Sucks. Web. 22 Nov. 2008.

Sources: Their Use and Acknowledgement. 5 Nov.
2001. Dartmouth College. Web. 18 Nov. 2008.

SparkNotes.com. 2006. SparkNotes. Web.
20 Nov. 2008.

Term Paper Relief. 2003. Term Paper Relief. Web.
20 Nov. 2008.

Thompson, Michael. "Hidden in Plain Sight." *The
Chronicle of Higher Education* 2 Dec. 2005:
B5. Print.

TurnItIn. 2008. iParadigms. Web. 19 Nov. 2008.

Form for a work by two authors.

Whitehouse, Virginia, and Julia Nicholls. "Inside
These Hallowed Halls: How Journalism
Schools Are Confronting Student Plagiarism."
Quill. Aug. 2004. *Expanded Academic ASAP.*
Infotrac. Web. 14 Nov. 2008.

Italicize database title of source from a library subscription service.

Whitley, Bernard E., and Patricia Keith-Spiegel.
Academic Dishonesty: An Educator's Guide.
London: Erlbaum, 2002. Print.

60   A Documentation Guide *doc*

60a MLA Works Cited and parenthetical note forms

Examples of the MLA Works Cited and parenthetical note forms (if different from the standard style detailed in 59c) follow this list of sample resources. For additional help, visit www.mla.org.

Printed Books

1. A Book with One Author
2. Two or More Books by the Same Author
3. A Book by Two or Three Authors
4. A Book by More Than Three Authors
5. A Book by a Corporate Author
6. A Book in a Later Edition
7. A Book in More Than One Volume
8. A Republished Book
9. A Book in a Series
10. A Book with an Editor
11. A Book with Two Editors
12. A Book with Three or More Editors
13. A Book with an Introduction, Foreword, Afterword, or Preface
14. A Book That Has Been Translated
15. A Book That Includes a Quotation from Another Work
16. A Book with a Title in Its Title
17. A Book with a Publisher's Imprint
18. A Selection in an Anthology or Collection
19. A Religious Work
20. An Article in a Reference Book

Material in a Printed Periodical

21. An Article in a Magazine
22. An Article in a Scholarly Journal
23. A Newspaper Article
24. A Letter to the Editor
25. An Editorial

Sources in Electronic Form

26. A Source on a CD-ROM
27. An Entire Web Site

Printed Books

1. A Book with One Author

Engel, Richard. *War Journal: My Five Years in Iraq.* New York: Simon, 2008. Print.

[Include the medium (in this case *Print*) after the publication date. Use italics, not underlining, for all of the title.]

2. Two or More Books by the Same Author

Bloom, Harold. *Hamlet: Poem Untitled.* New York: Riverhead, 2003. Print.

- - -. *How to Read and Why.* New York: Touchstone, 2001. Print.

- - -. *Jesus and Yahweh: The Names of the Divine.* New York: Riverhead, 2005. Print.

Bloom, Harold, and William Golding. *Wallace Stevens: The*

    Poems of Our Climate. New York: Cornell UP, 1980. Print.

[For multiple works by the same author or authors, list works in alphabetical order by title. After the first entry, use three unspaced hyphens in place of the author's name. If the same author has written a work with other persons, list those works after the single author entries.]

3. A Book by Two or Three Authors

Scalia, Antonin, and Bryan A. Garner. *Making Your Case:*

    The Art of Persuading Judges. St. Paul: Thompson, 2008.

    Print.

Trussel, Mark D., Lynne C. Cosely, and Albert Falman.

    Poverty in the Land of the Free: The Economics of

    Affluence in America. New York: Delacorte, 2008. Print.

4. A Book by More Than Three Authors

Kent, Howard, et al. *Gladiators with Fists: A History of Boxing*.

    New York: Houghton, 2007. Print.

[Avoid long citations in the text and elsewhere by listing only the first author's name (in reverse order), followed by a comma and the abbreviation *et al.*, meaning "and others." When it's necessary to cite all the authors, do it in the order they are listed on the source's title page.]

Kent, Howard, Rosemary Grett, Lyle Davidson, and William

    Nye. *Gladiators with Fists: A History of Boxing*. New

    York: Houghton, 2007. Print.

5. A Book by a Corporate Author

National Center on Addiction and Substance Abuse at Columbia

    University. *Substance Abuse: Its Nature and Consequences*.

    Baltimore: Johns Hopkins UP, 2006. Print.

[Use the abbreviations *U* for *University* and *P* for *Press*.]

6. A Book in a Later Edition

Bergman, Paul, and Sara J. Berman-Barrett. *The Criminal*

    Law Handbook: Know Your Rights, Survive the System.

    7th ed. Berkeley: Nolo, 2005. Print.

[Give the edition as indicated on the title page or elsewhere, using numbers—e.g., *2nd ed.*, *Rev. ed* for "Revised edition," or the year (*2006 ed.*).]

7. A Book in More Than One Volume

L'Amour, Louis. *The Collected Short Stories of Louis L'Amour.* 3 vols. New York: Bantam, 2005. Print.

[If you used more than one volume of a multivolume work, give the total number of volumes before the publication information. Cite a specific volume and page numbers parenthetically in your text (*3:132–35*). If you are using only one volume of a multivolume work, give only that volume number (*Vol.3*) in the Works Cited entry and only page numbers in the text citation (*132–35*).]

8. A Republished Book

Kennedy, John F. *Profiles in Courage.* 1956. New York: Perennial, 2006 Print.

[Include the original publication date of a republished book, if known, after the title.]

9. A Book in a Series

Goldsmith, Jason R. *Atlanta, Again and Again.* Great Cities Series. New York: Albion, 2008. Print.

10. A Book with an Editor

Foster, Frances Smith, ed. *Love and Marriage in Early African American America.* Boston: Northeastern UP, 2008. Print.

11. A Book with Two Editors

Levitsky, Steven, and Maria Victoria Murillo, eds. *Argentine Democracy: The Politics of Institutional Weakness.* Pennsylvania State UP, 2006. Print.

12. A Book with Three or More Editors

Germer, Christopher K., et al., eds. *Mindfulness and Psychotherapy.* New York: Guilford, 2005. Print.

[Avoid long citations in the text and elsewhere by listing only the first editor's name (in reverse order), followed by a comma and the abbreviation *et al.*, meaning "and others." Cite all the editors (in the order they are listed on the source's title page) only when necessary.]

Germer, Christopher K., Ronald D. Siegel, and Paul R. Fulton,
eds. *Mindfulness and Psychotherapy*. New York: Guilford,
2005. Print.

13. A Book with an Introduction, Foreword, Afterword, or Preface

Hanna, Jack. Foreword. *The Rhino with Glue-on Shoes and
Other Surprising Stories of Zoo Vets and Their Patients*.
Eds. Lucy Spelman and Ted Y. Mashima. New York:
Delacorte, 2008. Print.

[Use this form when your focus is on the writer of the supplementary material. Otherwise, cite only the author(s) or editor(s) of the source.]

14. A Book That Has Been Translated

Wiesel, Elie. *Night*. Trans. Marion Wiesel. New York: Hill,
2005. Print.

15. A Book That Includes a Quotation from Another Work

Matte, Richard. *Another Look at Democracy*. Boston: Pitts,
2005. Print.

[The parenthetical citation in your text should read (*qtd. in Matte 121*).]

16. A Book with a Title in Its Title

Shakespeare, William. *Four Great Histories:* Henry IV Part I,
Henry IV Part II, Henry V, and Richard III. New York:
Dover, 2006. Print.

[Do not use italics for the title of a work (Shakespeare's plays, in this example) when it is included within the title of another work. Use italics for the rest of the title.]

17. A Book with a Publisher's Imprint

Applegate, Debby. *The Most Famous Man in America: The
Biography of Henry Ward Beecher*. New York: Three
Leaves-Doubleday, 2006. Print.

[If an imprint, or the name of a special publishing unit, appears on the title page with the name of the publisher, give the imprint name, a hyphen, then the name of the publisher.]

18. **A Selection in an Anthology or Collection**

> Emerson, Ralph Waldo. "Nature." *The Norton Anthology of American Literature: 1820-1865.* Ed. Nina Baym. 7th ed. New York: Norton, 2007. 1110-37. Print.

19. **A Religious Work**

> *The New Oxford Annotated Bible with Apocrypha: New Revised Standard Version.* 3rd ed. Oxford UP, 2001. Print.

20. **An Article in a Reference Book**

> Cochran, Thomas, and Robert S. Norris. "Technology of War." *The New Encyclopedia Britannica: Macropaedia.* 15th ed. 2007. Print.

> Peregrine, D. H. "Rogue Waves." *Encyclopedia of Tidepools and Rocky Shores.* Eds. Mark W. Denny and Steven D. Gaines. Berkeley: U of California P, 2007. 476-77. Print.

> "Robert F. Kennedy." *Who's Who in America.* 62nd ed. 2008. Print.

[Do not cite the editor or publication information for a standard reference work such as a well-known encyclopedia or dictionary. If an article is signed (or bears initials identified elsewhere in the source), cite the article author; if unsigned, cite the article by title. If articles are arranged alphabetically, you may omit volume and page numbers.]

Material in a Printed Periodical

21. **An Article in a Magazine**

> Brown, Steven, and Lawrence M. Parsons. "The Neuroscience of Dance." *Scientific American* July 2008: 78-83. Print.

> "It's Not Easy Being Green." *Newsweek* 16 June 2008: 58. Print.

22. **An Article in a Scholarly Journal**

> Bojowald, Martin. "What Happened Before the Big Bang?" *Nature Physics* 3.8 (2007): 523–25. Print.

[Include the volume number and the issue number, separated by a period.]

23. **A Newspaper Article**

> Gerry, John. "Mothers Told to Pack Leaner Lunches." *New York Times* 16 July 2008, late ed. A10+. Print.

[If the article is signed, give the author's name first. If unsigned, begin with the article title. Omit an introductory *the* from the name of the newspaper. When a newspaper designates an edition, give the edition after the date. If an article appears in a numbered section, add the abbreviation *sec.* and the number, a colon, and the page number (*sec. 4:10.*). When an article appears on nonconsecutive pages, give only the first page number with + after it.]

"NASA Capsule Hurtles Toward Earth," *Tribune* [San Luis Obispo]

15 Jan. 2008: A12 Print.

[If the city of publication is not named in the title of a local newspaper, include that city name in square brackets after the newspaper title. Omit the city name for nationally published newspapers such as the *Wall Street Journal* and the *Chronicle of Higher Education*. Give page numbers as they appear in the source: *A5, D3-4.*]

24. A Letter to the Editor

Gates, Lawrence. Letter. *Chronicle of Higher Education* 26 Sept.

2007: B3. Print.

25. An Editorial

Rennie, John. Editorial. "All Together Now." *Scientific American*

Oct. 2008: 10. Print.

[If you are citing a signed editorial, add the descriptive term *Editorial*, without quotation marks, underling or italic. If the editorial is unsigned, omit the descriptive term.]

"Mr. Bush's War." *Los Angles Times* 4 Feb. 2006: B5. Print.

[If the editorial is signed, begin with the author's name. If unsigned, begin with the editorial's title.]

Sources in Electronic Form

26. A Source on a CD-ROM

Harmon, William, ed. *The Columbia Granger's World of Poetry*

on CD-ROM 3.0: For Windows and Macintosh Operating

Systems. New York: Columbia UP, 1999. CD-ROM.

27. An Entire Web site

Indiana American Association of University Women. 1 July

1999. Indiana State U. Web. 3 Feb. 2007.

<http://www1.indstate.edu/aauw-in>.

The *Rainforest Fund Project*. Ed. Judith Allinson. Web. 16 July
    2008.

United States. Federal Bureau of Investigation. *WI-FI Security:*
    Some Advice from the FBI. 6 May 2008. Web. 20 June 2008.

[List the site title, name of any editor, version number, date of electronic publication or last update, and the name of any sponsoring organization, followed
by the medium (*Web*) and your date of access. If a site does not list all of this
information, include what is available. If a reader may not be able to locate the
source without the URL, list it after the date of your access (see page 386 for
more on including a URL). For an online government publication with no author's name given, cite the government responsible for it, followed by the
agency name, the title of the source, date published or updated, the medium,
and your date of access.]

28. A Part of a Web site

Stull, Richard. "About James Dickey." *Modern American Poetry*.
    2000. Dept. of English, U of Illinois. Web. 2 Nov. 2008.

[Give the author and title of the source, followed by the name of the site, the
date it was published or last updated, the name of the site sponsor, the
medium, and your date of access.]

29. An Online Book

Conrad, Joseph. *Heart of Darkness*. [1902.] *Conrad, Joseph,*
    1857-1924. Heart of Darkness. 1999. Electronic Text
    Center, U of Virginia Lib. Web. 3 Mar. 2008.

[List author, title, and publication information, adding any of the latter in
brackets if relevant and not given in the source; follow this with the Web site
title, date of electronic publication, name of any sponsoring organization, the
medium, and your date of access.]

30. An Online Abstract

Semba, R. D., et al. "Infant Mortality and Maternal Vitamin A
    Deficiency During Human Immunodeficiency Virus
    Infection." *Clinical Infectious Disease* 21 Oct. 1995. 21.4:
    966-72. Abstract. National Center for Biotechnology
    Information. Web. 4 Sept. 2008.

[Cite the original publication information for the source, followed by
Abstract, neither underlined nor in italics, followed by the name of the site
sponsor, the medium, and your date of access.]

31. An Article in an Online Periodical (Not Accessed Through a Library Database)

> Barraclough, Laura R. "Rural Urbanism: Producing Western
> Heritage and the Racial Geography of Postwar Los Angeles."
> *Western Historical Quarterly* 39.2 (2008): 177-202. Web.
> 26 June 2008.

> Posner, Richard A. "Strong Fiber After All." *Atlantic Online.*
> Jan. 2005. Web. 22 Jan. 2006.

[For a periodical article accessed online, indicate the medium (*Web*) after the page number(s). For an article cited only on the Web, give the site name, the date of posting, the medium (*Web*), and the date of your access.]

32. A Periodical Article Accessed Through a Library Database

> Arce, Daniel G., Walter Enders, and Gary A. Hoover.
> "Plagiarism and Its Impact on the Economics Profession."
> *Bulletin of Economic Research* 60.3 (July 2008): 231-44.
> *Expanded Academic ASAP.* InfoTrac. Web. 12 Nov. 2008.

> Daley, Armond. "How to Say No Thanks to Big Oil." *Boston
> Globe* 15 Aug. 2008: A3. *Newspaper Source Plus.* EBSCO.
> Web. 14 Sept. 2008.

> Montooth, Clair, "When Studying Just Isn't Enough."
> *Newsweek* 10 Oct. 2007. *Proquest News and Magazines.*
> ProQuest. Web. 14 Nov. 2008.

[Following publication information about the article, cite the database (in italics), followed by the vendor, medium (*Web*), and date of access. Separate each of these entries by a period.]

33. A Source from a Wiki

> "Adolescence." *Wikipedia.* 17 July 2008. Wikimedia Foundation.
> Web. 2 Jan. 2008.

34. A Source from a Blog

> Donner, Paige. "Greening Hollywood: Solar-Powered ESPYs."
> *Huffington Post.* HuffingtonPost.com. 18 July 2008. Web.
> 8 Sept. 2008.

[Begin with the author's name, followed by the title or subject line. If there is no title, specify *Online posting.* Follow with the name of the forum or site, the posting date, medium (*Web*), and your date of access.]

35. A Source from a Podcast

"The Measure of Race?" *ABC News*. ABC News. 6 Feb. 2008.
Web. 10 Sept. 2008.

36. An Online Audio or Video

Roy, Lesley. "I'm Gone, I'm Going." Dir. Jesse Terrero. 18 July
2008. *MTV Overdrive*. MTV Networks. Web. 17 Oct. 2008.

"FORA.tv." *Joyce Carol Oates—On Writing Characters*. 10 Aug.
2007. *YouTube*. YouTube. Web. 4 May 2008.

37. An E-mail Message

Hatter, Julie. "Membership Requirements." Message to Corrine
Gray. 24 Oct. 2008. E-mail.

38. An Online Radio or Television Program

Paston, Roger. "The Real Costs of a Starbucks." *Fox News
Radio*. Fox News. 20 Oct. 2007. Web. 6 Aug. 2008.

39. A Source from a Digital File

Denning, Trisha J. *Bridge of the Americas*. 2008. Oil on
Canvas. Tuttle Gallery, Newport, California. JPEG file.

Park, Linkin. "Somewhere I Belong." *In the Chamber with
Linkin Park*. 2003. Vitamin. MP3 file.

Porter, Robert. "Native American Tribes of the South Bay
Region." 2007. *Microsoft Word* file.

[For a source stored as a digital file, give the information included when citing
its traditional or original form, followed by a description of the medium. If
you do not have all the information, give what is available.]

Other Sources

40. An Unpublished Dissertation

Piner, Robert Bruce. "Intellectual Ability and Reading Interest in
Pre-School Children." Diss. U of Michigan, 2006. Print.

41. A Sound Recording

Mellencamp, John. "Longest Days." *Life, Death, Love and
Freedom*. Hear Music, 2008. CD.

42. A Film

The Incredible Hulk. Dir. Louis Leterrier. Universal, 2008. Film.

[To focus on the work itself, start with the title, followed by the name of the director, distributor, and year of release. To focus on one person's involvement in a film or play, cite that person first, followed by an abbreviated description of his or her contribution; you may include other writers' or performers' names, as pertinent. For a videocassette or DVD, specify that medium after the release date.]

Leterrier, Louis, dir. *The Incredible Hulk*. Perf. Edward Norton,

Liv Tyler, Tim Roth, and William Hurt. Universal, 2008.

DVD.

43. A Performance of a Play

Othello. By William Shakespeare. Dir. Tony Simotes. Perf.

John Douglas Thompson. Founder's Theater, Lennox, MA.

31 Aug. 2008. Performance.

[Along with the title of the work and the author's name, cite principal contributors or performers and their roles as pertinent to your paper's content. Also include the place and date of the performance.]

44. A Work of Art

Close, Chuck. *Self-Portrait, 1997*. Pace Wildenstein Gallery,

New York. *Art Across Time*. By Laurie Schneider Adams.

Boston: McGraw, 2007. 955. Print.

[Include publication information about the source for a reproduction of an artwork. For an actual work of art, include the medium after the location.]

Rodin, Auguste. *The Thinker*. 1900. Sculpture. Metropolitan

Museum of Art, New York.

45. An Interview

Angelou, Maya. Interview with Dom Swaim. 1987. *Wired for*

Books. Ohio U. Web. 10 Oct. 2008.

Chavez, Hugo. Interview with Barbara Walters. ABC. WABC,

New York. 17 Mar. 2007. Television.

Kimmel, Jimmy. Interview. "Don't They Make a Lovely Couple?"

Newsweek 10 Mar. 2008: 63. Print.

Ramos, Victor. Telephone Interview. 10 May 2008.

[For a published or broadcast interview, begin with the name of the person interviewed and the descriptor *Interview*. For an interview you conduct yourself, list the name of the person interviewed, followed by the type of interview (*personal, telephone, e-mail*).]

46. An Advertisement

Hoag Hospital. Advertisement. *U.S. News and World Report*
    21-28 July 2008: 19. Print.

[Give the name of the product, company, or subject of the advertisement, followed by relevant information about the source.]

47. A Pamphlet

Neighborhood Watch. San Diego: Lighthouse, 2008. Print.

Florida Commission on Education. *Every Child Needs a*
    Computer. Miami: Shores, 2008. Print.

48. A Lecture or Address

Ebadi, Shirin. "Human Rights and Islam and the West." Rice
    U, Houston. 4 Feb. 2006. Lecture.

49. A Cartoon or Comic Strip

Donnelly, Liza. Cartoon. *New Yorker* 30 June 2008: 69. Print.

60b APA documentation style

The American Psychological Association (APA) style of documentation is frequently used in courses in psychology and other social sciences.

Parenthetical Citations: APA Style

The APA parenthetical in-text citation style gives the last name of the author and the date of publication, separated by a comma. For some citations, these two items of information are the only ones necessary, but page references should be added when you present a direct quotation or refer to specific information rather than general concepts. The following examples show the basic forms and placement of APA citations.

AUTHOR AND DATE ONLY

Surveys show a majority of college and university students who say they binge drink are white males (Kalb, 2005).

DATE ONLY

Kalb (2005) points out that surveys show a majority of college and university students who say they binge drink are white males.

AUTHOR, DATE, AND PAGE

Most studies indicate that students are "drinking more, drinking to get drunk, and suffering more severe consequences from excessive drinking" (Keeler, 2003, p. 76).

[For direct quotations, include the page number. Use *p.* for "page" and *pp.* for "pages."]

By their third or fourth year of college, most students seem either to have "brought their drinking under control or dropped out because of personal and academic problems brought on by excessive indulgence" (Myer & Torson, 2005, p. 34).

[Join the names of multiple authors with an ampersand: &.]

Most experts agree that the problem of campus drinking cannot be solved by any single approach, regardless of its apparent success with some students (Myer & Torson, 2005; Hanchett, Krueger, & Davis, 2004).

[For more than one source, list them in alphabetical order by the first authors' names, and separate the citations with a semicolon.]

References: APA Style

In APA style, the sources you cite are listed at the end of your paper in a section titled "References." As you study the following examples of APA reference listings, notice carefully the order in which information is given, the use of punctuation and capitalization, and the spacing between items.

As you prepare entries for your paper's References list, follow the models shown in the "APA Reference Forms" section below and these standard APA practices:

- List references alphabetically by the author's last name or by title when no author is given; indent the second and subsequent lines of an entry five to seven spaces (or one-half inch).
- Follow the author's name with the publication date in parentheses: *Dawes, G. D. (2008).*
- Italicize book titles, but use no italics or quotation marks for the titles of periodical articles. Capitalize only the first word and all proper nouns of a title or subtitle: *Our national security: Are we safe?*
- For publisher's names, write out the names of university presses but omit *Company, Inc., Publishers,* and such; use a shortened version when practical.
- When a DOI (see below) is given for an online periodical source, include the DOI instead of a URL in your entry.
- Include "Retrieved from" information and the URL for each online source lacking a DOI; break long URLs *only* after a slash; add no period or other punctuation at the end of the URL.

DOIs and URLs.   As you research electronic sources on the Web, you will find that the bibliographic information given about many documents includes a DOI (Digital Object Identifier), a permanent identification tag for a document stored in a digital network such as the Internet. Using a URL (Uniform Resource Locator), your computer searches for a Web address; using a DOI, it searches for a particular electronic document. A DOI is more useful to a researcher than a URL because a URL address can change; that is, an electronic document may be removed from one Web site and republished at another. In such a case, the original URL is of no use in locating the document. A DOI, on the other hand, identifies the document no matter where it is located. You can enter a DOI into a search box to locate a particular document anywhere it's located on the Internet or another digital network. When the DOI is given in a source, APA documentation style requires that you include it in your References entry. See model 19 below for citing an article with a DOI.

Only the most frequently encountered sources are illustrated here. For a comprehensive guide to APA documentation style, consult the *Publication Manual of the American Psychological Association*, 6th ed., 2010.

APA References Forms

Printed Books

1. A Book with One Author
2. A Book with More Than One Author
3. A Book in More Than One Volume
4. A Book by an Organization
5. Two or More Works by the Same Author
6. A Book with an Editor
7. A Book in an Edition
8. A Book That Has Been Translated
9. A Work Included in an Anthology or Collection
10. An Article in an Encyclopedia

Printed Periodical Articles

11. A Printed Newspaper Article
12. A Printed Article in a Weekly or Monthly Magazine
13. An Article in a Journal with Continuous Pagination Throughout Each Volume
14. An Article in a Journal with Separate Pagination in Each Issue

Electronic Sources

15. An Online Version of a Book
16. A Periodical Article from an Online Source
17. An Article from a Database
18. An Abstract of an Online Article
19. An Article with a DOI
20. An Article with No DOI
21. An Article in an Online Encyclopedia or Online Dictionary
22. A Dissertation or Thesis from a Database
23. Online Lecture Notes
24. An E-mail
25. A Message Posted to a Newsgroup, Blog, or Other Online Forum
26. Information from a Wiki
27. An Audio Podcast
28. A Consumer Pamphlet

Other Sources

29. A Letter to the Editor
30. A Television Program
31. A Film

Printed Books

1. A Book with One Author

Engel, R. (2008). *War journal: My five years in Iraq.* New York, NY: Simon & Schuster.

2. A Book with More Than One Author

Cline, F. W., & Fay, J. (2006). *Parenting teens with love and logic.* Colorado Springs, CO: Piñon.

[For two or more authors, use an ampersand (&) before the last author's name. For more than six authors, add *et al.* ("and others") after the sixth name.]

3. A Book in More Than One Volume

L' Amour, L. (2005). *The collected short stories of Louis L'Amour* (Vols. 1-3). New York, NY: Random.

[Follow the title with the volume information, with no period after the title.]

4. A Book by an Organization

National Center of Addiction and Substance Abuse at Columbia University (2006). *Substance abuse: Its nature and consequences.* Baltimore, MD: Johns Hopkins University Press.

5. Two or More Works by the Same Author

Bloom, H. (2001). *How to read and why.* New York, NY: Touchstone.

Bloom, H. (2003a) *Genius: A mosaic of one hundred exemplary creative minds.* New York, NY: Warner.

Bloom, H. (2003b). *Hamlet: Poem untitled.* New York, NY: Riverhead.

Bloom, H., & Golding, W. (1980). *Wallace Stevens: The poems of our climate.* New York, NY: Cornell University Press.

[For multiple works by the same author or authors, list works in chronological order. For two or more works written by the same author in the same year, add *a, b,* and so on after the year. If the same author has written works with other persons, list those works after the single author entries.]

6. **A Book with an Editor**

> Foster, F. S. (Ed.) (2008). *Love and marriage in early African American America*. Boston, MA: Northeastern University Press.

[For a work with an editor but no author, list the work by the editor's last name and include the abbreviation *Ed.* or *Eds.* after the editor's name.]

7. **A Book in an Edition**

> Bergman, P., & Berman-Barrett, S. J. (2005). *Criminal law handbook: Know your rights, survive the system* (7th ed.). Berkeley, CA: Nolo.

8. **A Book That Has Been Translated**

> Wiesel, E. (2005). *Night*. (M. Wiesel, Trans.). New York, NY: Hill & Wang.

9. **A Work Included in an Anthology or Collection**

> Cahill, R. D. (2001). Lilacs. In J. Peterson (Ed.), *New literature for now* (pp. 112-118). New York, NY: Norton.

10. **An Article in an Encyclopedia**

> Cochran, T., & Norris, R. S. (1992).Technology of war. In *The new encyclopaedia Britannica: Macropaedia* (Vol. 13, pp. 236-237). Chicago, IL: Encyclopaedia Britannica.

[If no author's name is available, begin the entry with the article title.]

Printed Periodical Articles

11. **A Printed Newspaper Article**

> Tizon, T. A. (2006, February 10). The sky is falling in Alaska. *Los Angeles Times*, p. A1.

[Introduce page numbers for newspaper articles with *p.* or *pp.*]

12. **A Printed Article in a Weekly or Monthly Magazine**

> Brown, S., & Parsons, L. M. (2008, July). The neuroscience of dance. *Scientific American, 299*, 78-83.

Davids, C. (2008, Mar. 12). Up and running for the presi-

dency. *Time, 171,* 32-33.

[Include the month and year for a monthly magazine; give the year, day, and month for weeklies. Include the volume number, italicized, after the magazine name.]

13. An Article in a Journal with Continuous Pagination Throughout Each Volume

Herbst, S. (2008). The rhetorical presidency and the contem-

porary media environment. *Critical Review, 19,* 335-343.

[For a journal with continuous pagination, give only the volume number, italicized.]

14. An Article in a Journal with Separate Pagination in Each Issue

Daughters, G. H., & Heller, R. (2006, May/June). Semantics

and the Web. *IEEE Intelligent Systems 21*(3), 56-63.

[For a journal with separate pagination in each issue, include the volume number in italics, then the issue number (not italicized) in parentheses, with no space after the volume number.]

Electronic Sources

15. An Online Version of a Book

Powelson, J. P. (2007). *A history of wealth and poverty: Why*

some nations are rich and many poor [DX Reader Version].

Retrieved from http://tqe.quaker.org/wealth-and-poverty

[If an online book has a DOI (digital object identifier) include the DOI and delete the url.]

16. A Periodical Article from an Online Source

Carvajal, D. (2008, June 31.) EBay ordered to pay damages

in sale of fake goods. *The New York Times.* Retrieved

from http://www.nytimes.com.

[For a newspaper article accessed directly from a newspaper's Internet site, give the author, publication date, article title, and name of the newspaper, followed by the URL. Omit any other information (page numbers, edition, etc.). If no author's name is given, begin with the article title, followed by the date.]

Johnson, A. (2008, July/August). Guns out of control.

TheAtlantic.com Retrieved June 14, 2008, from

http://www.theatlantic.com/doc/200803u/gun-control

17. An Article from a Database

>Arce, D. G., Enders, W., & Hoover, G. A. (2008). Plagiarism
>and its impact on the economics profession. *Bulletin of
>Economic Research, 60*(3), 231-244. Retrieved from
>Expanded Academic ASAP database (A62373483).

[Do not include database names (e.g. EBSCO) or article identifier numbers for generally available electronic materials.]

18. An Abstract of an Online Article

>Herbert, J., & Estlund, K. (2008) Creating citizen historians.
>*Western Historical Quarterly, 34*(3). Abstract retrieved
>from http://www.usu.edu/whq/current.htm

[Although it is best always to cite the full text of an article, you may cite an abstract as a source if necessary.]

19. An Article with a DOI

>Williams, S. T. (2007, October 30). Safe and legal shipment of
>tissue samples: does it affect DNA quality? *Journal of
>Molluscan Studies, 73*, 416-418. doi:10.1093/mollus/
>eym039

[Include no URL if you give a DOI.]

20. An Article with No DOI

>Williams, B. T. (2007, December). Trust, betrayal, and author-
>ship: Plagiarism and how we perceive students. *Journal
>of Adolescent & Adult Literacy, 51*(4), 350-355. Retrieved
>from http://www.reading.org/publications/journals/jaal/
>current/index.html

[Include a retrieval statement and URL if you find no DOI.]

21. An Article in an Online Encyclopedia or Online Dictionary

>Walser, M. L. (2007). Carbon footprint. In *The encyclopedia of
>earth, content, credibility, community*. Retrieved from
>http://www.eoearth.org

[If an entry has no byline, begin with the title, followed by the date, or by the letters n.d. to indicate no date.]

22. **A Dissertation or Thesis from a Database**

> Loyan, M. F. (2007). *Educated and unemployed: Men and*
>
> > *women who give up on themselves and a career.*
> >
> > Retrieved from ProQuest Digital Dissertations. (AAM
> >
> > 1354678)

[Include the database name, followed by the accession number if one is assigned.]

23. **Online Lecture Notes**

> Kim, H. (2008). *Chapter 18: Inference for a population*
>
> > *mean.* Retrieved from https://eee.uci.edu/classes/
> >
> > ?dept_name=Statistics

24. **An E-mail**

> E-mail communications are not included in APA documenta-
>
> > tion, but information from an e-mail may be cited in the
> >
> > text of your paper in this form: (J. Reynolds, personal
> >
> > communication, Feb. 3, 2008).

25. **A Message Posted to a Newsgroup, Blog, or Other Online Forum**

> Austen. (2008, February 4). Re: One laptop, one child.
>
> > [Electronic mailing list message]. Retrieved from
> >
> > http://en.forum.laptop.org

[List author names as given, including screen names (WhizKid, ROKKO, etc.). For a blog posting, omit "Re:" before the title and use [Web log post] in square brackets as the format description. Include other format descriptions such as "Online forum comment" or "Video file" in brackets as appropriate.]

26. **Information from a Wiki**

> Snowball Earth. (2009, September 11) *Wikipedia.* Retrieved
>
> > September 22, 2009 from http://en.wikipedia.org/wiki/
> >
> > Snowball_Earth

[If the material will change over time, include the retrieval date.]

27. **An Audio Podcast**

> Frederick, R. (2007, December 13). Wild salmon population in peril. *Science Magazine*. Podcast retrieved from http://www.sciencemag.org/rss/podcast.xml

28. **A Consumer Pamphlet**

> State of Illinois. (2007). *Emergency preparedness planning for pets and livestock* [Brochure]. Retrieved from http://www.agr.state.il.us/premiseID/ emergencypreparednessplanningforpets&livestock.pdf

Other Sources

29. **A Letter to the Editor**

> Reiss, K. (2008, August 10). Why can't teachers just teach? [Letter to the editor]. *The Chronicle of Higher Education*, p. B10.

30. **A Television Program**

> Hulme, B. (Announcer). (2008, June 4). *Fox News Channel* [Television broadcast]. New York: Fox News Corporation.

31. **A Film**

> Leterrier, L. (Director). (2008). *The Incredible Hulk* [Motion Picture]. United States: Universal Studios.

60c CSE documentation style

The natural and applied sciences have their own documentation styles that differ from the MLA and APA styles in many ways. Depending on the discipline you are writing for, you may need to refer to scientific style manuals such as:

> American Institute of Physics, *Style Manual: Instructions to Authors and Volume Editors for the Preparation of AIP Book Manuscripts*
> Janet S. Dodd, *The ACS Style Guide: A Manual for Authors and Editors*
> Cheryl Iverson et al., *American Medical Association Manual of Style: A Guide for Authors and Editors*
> Philip Rubens, ed., *Science and Technical Writing: A Manual of Style*

In many of the citation styles described in these and other manuals, each in-text (or parenthetical) citation is a number that corresponds to a full citation in the list of sources at the end of the document. Of the number-sequence documentation styles, the one most commonly used in undergraduate science research is that of the Council of Science Editors (CSE). CSE documentation style is explained throughout the rest of this chapter. (For more information, visit www.councilscienceeditors.org.)

CSE: Three Methods of Citation

CSE documentation style offers writers three different ways to cite sources in-text:

Citation-Sequence.   Sources are numbered as they are cited in the text, then listed in numerical order in the reference list. *Early research by Weber[3] has shown . . .*

Name-Year.   The author's last name and the date of the source are included in parentheses after the material being cited: *Because gravity is less understood than light (Jones 2003) . . .*

Citation-Name.   Sources are first listed in the reference section in alphabetical order according to the authors' last names (or by title when there is no author) and then numbered sequentially. Numbered citations in the text refer to the correspondingly numbered entries in the reference section. Although the numbering methods differ, in-text and References forms are the same for both citation-name and citation-sequence.

These three styles are recommended equally by the CSE. This chapter introduces you to CSE citation-sequence style for crediting sources in the text of your paper and in the section titled References.

CSE Citation-Sequence Style

In CSE citation-sequence style, you assign a sequential number to each source as you cite it in your text; that same number is then assigned to the source as it is listed sequentially in the References:

IN-TEXT CITATION

Clams and other shellfish cannot survive at such
temperatures.[1]

REFERENCES LIST

1. Weber KP. Pacific shellfish diseases. New York (NY):
Oxford University Press; 2006. 157 p.

Alternatively the citation number may be written on the text line, within parentheses:

. . . no traces of iron were found in the sample (4).

Be sure to use only one form—raised numbers or numbers in parentheses—throughout your paper. Check with your instructor to learn his or her preferences for the assignment.

If you need to quote or to document a specific reference, the page number or numbers (using *p.* to indicate one page and *pp.* to indicate more than one page) follow the number assigned to the source.

> In some animals the sense of smell functions as an early
> warning system. "Even in slumbering felines, the nose
> can catch a whiff of danger and rouse the beast to action"
> (5, p. 23). In other animals, however, especially those that
> have been long domesticated, the sense of smell is not so
> acute and may have diminished to the point at which they
> can barely use it to find their dinner bowls (5, pp. 25-27).

When you refer to more than one source in a single in-text citation, separate the numbers with a comma and no space. When you cite a source already cited in your paper, refer to it by its original number.

> The human nose fails miserably from disuse (3,5). Early
> human hunters could smell an animal downwind before the
> eye ever picked it out of the brush, and Native American
> warriors could smell a nearby enemy before they heard a
> war cry (3,6).

CSE References List

Title the reference section *References* or *References Cited.* Center the title at the top of the page. To list your sources in the citation-sequence form, follow the examples given below and these guidelines:

1. Arrange and number the sources in the order in which they are first cited in the text.

2. Begin each entry with the author's last name followed by his or her initials, with no intervening punctuation: *Forest GL.* Separate multiple author names with a comma: *Steadry H, Greene KE.*

3. Do not underline or italicize the title of a source. Capitalize only the first word of the main title and any proper nouns: *Values to keep: rules for living wisely.*

4. For books, give the place of publication, followed by the publisher's name and a semicolon, followed by the publication year and a period. Give the total number of pages, followed by a space and the abbreviation *p.* Do not use "pp."

5. Capitalize the title of a journal as you normally would, but do not underline or italicize the title. You may abbreviate the title unless it is a single word; JNSci instead of *Journal of Natural Science.*

6. For electronic sources, note that CSE style uses *cited* in the same way that MLA and APA use "Retrieved from" or "Accessed."

The following examples are in CSE *citation-sequence* form. Each source in the References list appears in the order in which it is first cited in the paper and is numbered accordingly. When typing your References page, double-space throughout and begin the second and subsequent lines of each entry to align with the first letter of the first line, not with the numeral. If your paper requires citations more complex than these, consult the CSE manual, *Scientific Style and Format,* 7th ed., 2006.

Sample CSE References

1. A Book

Taylor JB. My stroke of insight: a brain scientist's personal journey. New York (NY): Penguin; 2008. 192 p.

2. An Edited Book

Ponder WF, Lindberg DR, editors. Phylogeny and evolution of the mollusca. Berkeley (CA): University of California Press; 2008. 469 p.

3. A Book with Multiple Authors

Trussel MD, Cosely LC, Falman A. Poverty in the land of the free: the economics of affluence in America. New York (NY): Delacorte; 2008. 178 p.

4. **A Journal Article**

> Barraclough LR. Rural urbanism: producing Western heritage
> and the racial geography of postwar Los Angeles. Western
> Historical Quarterly 2008; 39(2):177-202.

[Include the issue number, in parentheses, whenever it appears in the journal.]

5. **A Magazine Article**

> Brown S, Parsons, LM. Neuroscience of dance. Scientific
> American 2008 July; 78-83.

6. **A Newspaper Article**

> Tizon TA. The sky is falling in Alaska. Los Angeles Times
> (National Ed.). 2006 Feb 10;Sect. A:1.

7. **An Electronic Book**

> Hartmann E. Dreams and nightmares: the origin and meaning
> of dreams [Internet]. Cambridge (MA): Massachusetts
> Perseus Books Group; 2001 [cited 2008 Jan 16]. 295 p.
> Available from: http://www.netlibrary.com/
> ?CFID=2695722&CFTOKEN=12140694.

8. **An Article from an Online Newspaper**

> Wald ML. Study details how U.S. could cut 28% of greenhouse
> gases. New York Times [Internet]. 2007 Nov 30 [cited
> 2008 May 16]. [5 paragraphs]. Available from: http://
> www.nytimes.com/2007/11/30/business/30green.html.

9. **An Article from an Online Magazine**

> Martindale D. A dash of nutrition. Scientific American
> [Internet]. 2008 Jan [cited 2007 Sept 3]. [2 pages].
> Available from: http://www.sciamdigital.com/.

10. **An Article from an Online Journal**

> Belling RD. What whales know and we don't. Ocean [Internet].
> 2008 [cited 2008 Feb 9]; 54(3):326–34. Available from:
> http://www.ocean5.even/hdb/vol_54/issue_30343.pdf.

11. An Online Posting

Gura T. Re: anorexia not just a problem for young women.
In:Psych Central [Internet]; 2007 July 24 [cited 2008
May 4]. [1 paragraph]. Available from:
http://psychcentral.com/blog/archives/2007/07/23/
anorexia-not-just-a-problem-for-young-women/.

12. A Home Page

Wildlife Trust [Internet]. New York: Wildlife Trust; 2007 (cited
2008 Oct 12). Available from http://www.wildlifetrust.org/.

PART X

Communicating in the Workplace

Often you will find yourself embarking on an article so apparently lifeless—the history of some institution, or some local issue such as storm sewers—that you quail at the prospect of keeping your readers, or even yourself, awake. Take heart. You will find the solution if you look for the human element. Somewhere in every drab institution are men and women who have a fierce attachment to what they are doing and are rich repositories of lore.

—William K. Zinsser, *journalist*

61 Business Letters

62 Memorandum Form

63 Résumé and Cover Letter

64 Fax and E-mail

65 Creating an Effective Web site

66 Oral Presentations

---

61 Business Letters *bus*

A business letter should be brief, to the point, and representative of your best writing skills. The tone, even if you are writing a letter of complaint, should be courteous. As in all writing, observe the conventions of grammar, usage, and punctuation. Take extra care in proofreading the letter before sending it.

Business Letter Formats

A business letter usually follows one of three basic formats: block style, modified block style, or simplified style.

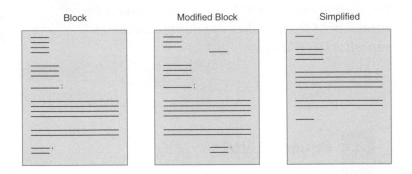

Block   Modified Block   Simplified

Block Style.   Block style is the most formal layout for business letters and is usually written on letterhead stationery. To type a letter in block style, begin all the elements—including date, inside address, salutation, body, and close—flush with the left margin. If there is a second page to a block-style letter, begin the content just below the top margin; don't center it on the depth of the page.

Modified Block Style.   Modified block style appears less formal. Type a modified block letter the same as one in block style, beginning every line at the left margin, with one major exception: The date and the signature lines must begin at the center of the page.

Simplified Style.   The simplified style is usually used for form letters, correspondence with unknown parties, and mass mailings. It is not often used for personal business correspondence. Type a letter in simplified style by lining up all the elements flush with the left margin, as in block style. A major difference, however, is that you include no salutation or complimentary close. The body of the letter begins immediately after the inside address (or after the subject line), with no salutation such as *Dear Ms. Dunlap*. Similarly, include your name and signature right after the last line in the body, with no intervening close such as *Sincerely* or *Yours truly*.

Elements of Business Letters

Return Address Heading. The heading of a business letter includes the sender's return address and the date the letter was written. If you use letterhead stationery, include only the date, typed two line spaces (that is, double spaced) below the letterhead. Don't abbreviate the names of streets, avenues, boulevards, and the like, but do use postal abbreviations for names of states.

> 2701 Fairview Road
> Costa Mesa, CA 92626
> September 21, 2009

The return address should always be flush left on the page, regardless of which letter format you follow. The date should also be flush left if you are using block or simplified style; the date should begin at the center of the page, however, if you are using modified block style.

Inside Address. The inside address includes the recipient's name, title, and mailing address. If the person's title is short, include it following the name and a comma. If the title is long, place it on the line below the name. Write the company name as it usually appears. Again, do not abbreviate the names of streets, avenues, or boulevards. Do use postal abbreviations for states.

> Dr. Robert Sanchez, Chair
> Department of Linguistics
> University of California, Irvine
> 2000 Campus Drive
> Irvine, CA 92612

Begin the inside address two lines below the return address heading and *always* on the left-hand side of the page.

Salutation. Greet the reader with a salutation. You have several options:

1. If you know the person you are writing to, use the name that appears in the inside address: *Dear Dr. Sanchez.*

2. If you are not writing to a particular person and do not know whether the person is male or female, you may use a general salutation: *Dear Sir* or *Dear Madam* (but not *Dear Sir or Madam*).
3. If you are writing to an organization in general, you may greet someone by position: *Dear Dean of Students.* Or you may greet the organization: *Dear Southwest Services.*

When greeting women use *Ms.* unless you know that the recipient prefers *Mrs.* or *Miss.* Always type the salutation two lines below the inside address and end the salutation with a colon.

Subject Line. If you wish to highlight the subject of your letter, type a subject line. A subject line briefly names the subject of the letter. Use the word *subject* or the abbreviation *re* (Latin for "thing"), followed by a colon, to identify your letter's content. Several styles are acceptable.

> Subject: Student Aid
> SUBJECT: Study Abroad
> Re: Part-Time Employment
> RE: Drop Policy

Type the subject line two lines below the letter's salutation.

Body. If possible, keep a business letter to one page in length but never more than two pages. Structure a business letter in three main parts:

1. An *introduction* paragraph that states the purpose of the letter and establishes a courteous tone.
2. One or more *body* paragraphs that develop major points and provide details.
3. A brief *conclusion* paragraph that thanks the reader and suggests possibilities for further action.

Begin each line of the text of a letter at the left margin. Double-space between paragraphs to set them off from each other.

Close. Choose a close that reflects the tone—formal or informal—of the salutation and the rest of the letter: *Sincerely yours, Sincerely, Yours truly, Best regards, Cordially.* Capitalize only the first letter.
Begin the close two lines below the last line of the body. Except for modified block form, align the close with the return address heading, flush left. Follow the close with a comma.

Name and Signature. Type your name four lines below the close. Add any title you hold that may be relevant to the letter's content

(*Student Body Vice President*). If you have addressed a letter's recipient by his or her last name, sign your letter with your full name.

Enclosures.   If you include other material with a letter, add an enclosure notation at the left margin, two lines below your name. You may write out or abbreviate the notation for *enclosure* (*encl.*) or *enclosures* (*encls.*). List important enclosures by name or type. Multiple items should be listed and indented below the notation, or use parenthetic numerals to indicate their quantity.

Enclosure: Transcripts
Encl: Class Schedule
Enclosures: (2)
Encls:
    Photograph
    Copy of Birth Certificate

Copies.   If copies of your letter are being sent to other persons, add a *carbon copy* notation (*cc*) two lines below your typed name or the enclosure notation (if there is one).

cc: Dean William Walsh
CC: Ms. Margaret Johns
Copies to Rodger Faubel
    2715 Orange
    Tustin, CA 92619

When your letter contains sensitive information and you do not want the recipient to know that copies are being sent to others, use a *blind carbon copy* notation on the copy sheets only.

bcc: Internal Revenue Service
BCC: Donald Rayneman, Attorney at Law

Postscripts.   Since a postscript may suggest a last-minute, casual addition, it should rarely be part of a business letter. If you want to include one to emphasize a point not covered in the body of the letter, use the abbreviated form *P.S., PS,* or *PS:* to identify it. Type the abbreviation two lines below the last notation.

P.S. I truly look forward to the four weeks of intense training
    IBM offers.

Paper and Typing or Printing.   Use a good quality paper—20-pound weight, white bond. Write on one side of the paper, single-spacing between lines and double-spacing between paragraphs. Set 1″ margins on the left- and right-hand sides of the paper. Right-hand margins may be left "ragged," that is, "unjustified," if printed. Type or print letters in black or dark blue ink.

Envelope.   Use a business-size (no. 10) envelope. It should be the same width as your letter and about one-third its height. Type your name and address in the upper-left-hand corner. Include any instructions, such as *Attention Accounts Payable,* below that address. Beginning just to the left of the center of the envelope, type the recipient's name, title, and mailing address, as you did for the inside address.

Robin Hanna
12 Antares Avenue
Irvine, CA 92612

                    Dr. Rene Thursten
                    University of California
                    2000 Campus Drive
                    Irvine, CA 92612

---

62   Memorandum Form   *memo*

Unless you are using preprinted company or commercial stationery, begin a memorandum (memo) by typing *MEMORANDUM* at the top of the page. Centering, capitalizing, and underlining are optional.

Two line spaces beneath the heading, type a block of standard information elements: *TO, FROM, DATE, RE* (or *SUBJECT*). Double-space these elements and type them in capitals or with the first letter capitalized. Follow each element with a colon, advance several spaces, and type in the relevant information, keeping each item aligned with the one above it.

Begin the body of the memo two lines below the last element. Single-space the body and begin flush with the left margin (or indent the first line five spaces).

Do not include a closing signature element, but you may add your handwritten initials next to your name or end the memo with your signature, centered at the bottom.

When the memo includes copies or enclosures, note them the way you would in a business letter.

MEMORANDUM

TO: Fine Arts Staff

FROM: Donna Jennings, Chair, Fine Arts

DATE: September 29, 2008

RE: Budget Allotment Meeting

I have several requests to purchase supplies and equipment from department members. Although our supply and equipment budget has been increased by 20% above last year's, we still do not have enough discretionary moneys to accommodate all the requests. As a result, the budget committee will meet to rank the requests by how each one most directly addresses the needs of the entire department. You are invited to attend the meeting and address the committee regarding any proposal before it. The meeting will be held in the Fine Arts Conference Room on October 15, at noon.

Encl: Proposal List

---

63 Résumé and Cover Letter *résumé*

A *résumé* should be an easy-to-read summary of your qualifications for a job. A job résumé usually includes a cover letter that states your interest in a specific position and describes your general abilities.

Creating a Résumé

A résumé follows no standard form, but there are general principles you should observe.

1. Be brief. Keep the length to one or two pages, no more.
2. Stick to the point. Give only the information someone needs to determine whether you are an applicant worth interviewing.
3. Organize résumé information. Arrange the information in categories relevant to the position.
4. Write in brief, active phrases. Summarize information in each category in language that suggests you will be an assertive, proactive employee.
5. Concentrate on the particular position. Tailor a résumé so that the information reflects the experience required for the position.

Personal Data.   List your name, address, and telephone number where you can be reached during business hours. Include a fax number or an e-mail address, if you have either. Do not include your age, marital status, race or ethnicity, religion, height, or weight, all of which the law forbids employers from considering.

Career Objective.   You may include a brief statement of a long-range goal or specific job interests. Keep such a statement brief, no more than a line or two: *Hope to secure a management position in banking. Strong interests in sales and marketing.* Do not use such statements to misrepresent yourself.

Education.   List all schools you have attended from high school on, the most recent first. Include the years you attended, the diplomas and honors you have received, and your area of study. If you did not receive a diploma, list the number of units you completed. Do not mention particular courses you took, but if any of those courses relate to the position, name them in the cover letter.

Employment History.   List your most recent job first. Include each employer's name and address, and identify the position you held. Use short phrases and action verbs to describe your responsibilities: *Taught painting to third graders. Previewed video-game proposals.*

Activities.   You may include a section indicating other activities, memberships, hobbies, skills, or awards that might interest an employer. Do you speak a foreign language? Did you serve as an officer on your campus? Keep in mind that the activities you mention should relate to the position.

References.   Before you provide an employer with a list of references, be sure everyone listed will support your application. Once that is accomplished, you may provide employers with references in one of three ways.

Tom Jenkins
2415 Mann Street
Laguna Beach, CA 92676
(949) 494-0499
tjenkins@aol.com

Career Objective
Employment with a law firm specializing in international contracts and business negotiations.

Education
2006-present   California State University, Long Beach
               Major: History   Minor: English
               Degree: B.A., History
2002-2006   University High School
               Diploma: Graduated with honors

Employment History
2006-present   Forde and Mulrich
               12 MacArthur Avenue
               Newport Beach, CA 92644
                 Duties: Political Research. Responsible
                     for researching statewide and
                     local election initiatives. 15
                     hours weekly.
2005-2006   University Park Library
               221 Sandburg Way
               Irvine, CA 92912
                 Duties: Assistant to the Senior Research
                     Librarian. Maintain research
                     materials. Conduct research on
                     special request. 10 hours weekly.

Activities and Interests
• President of University High chapter of the Green Party, 2005
• Member of the Sierra Club
• Active participant in tennis, camping, and cross-country bicycling

References
Placement Office
California State University, Long Beach
Long Beach, CA 92888
(310) 772-0559

1. Indicate near the bottom of a résumé that *References are available upon request.* If the employer asks for them, you will provide the list.
2. Create a section titled *References.* Type the names, titles, addresses, and phone numbers of several individuals—teachers, former employers, community leaders—who will vouch for your skills and character.
3. File your complete résumé and cover letter with your school's placement center. On your job application, indicate that your résumé, including references, is available through the placement office, and include the phone number. Keep your on-file résumé current; review it each time you apply for a job.

Although there are several acceptable résumé formats, the sample shown on the preceding page is the most commonly used.

Writing a Cover Letter

Keep a cover letter brief. Avoid repeating what is in the résumé. Express your interest in the position, request an interview, and refer the recipient to the enclosed résumé.

Because a company may have several job openings, it is good practice to begin the cover letter by identifying the position you want and by telling specifically when and how you heard about it. Next, briefly refer to an aspect of your résumé that would be particularly relevant to the position. End the cover letter by stating your desire for an interview. Throughout the letter, follow standard business letter guidelines.

64 Fax and E-mail *fax/e-mail*

Treat electronic communications such as faxes and e-mail with the same care as traditional business correspondence.

Sending a Fax

Use the following guidelines when communicating by fax.

1. Since a fax may be received in a mail room or other common area, keep in mind that it may be read by others before being given to the intended recipient. You may prefer to send personal, confidential, or sensitive material by traditional correspondence.

2. Select a letterhead, font sizes, images, and colors that will fax clearly. To ensure readability, use 12-point type for all contents, and remember that colors other than black may not transmit clearly. Avoid sending or retransmitting copies of a fax with fuzzy print or hazy images.

3. Include a cover sheet with your name and your company name, address, and telephone number as well as a fax or e-mail address where you can be reached in case of transmittal problems. Also indicate the total number of pages you are sending (including the cover sheet).

4. Check your fax machine's readout to ensure proper transmission and receipt of your fax, or follow up the transmittal with a telephone call to verify that it was received.

Keep in mind that a fax may not be an acceptable form of communication for all business correspondence. When it is, however, following the above guidelines will help to ensure the effectiveness of your fax and the receipt of a timely response.

Sending E-mail

Although e-mail messages are frequently informal, those written for business purposes need to be easily understood and professional in form and content. Use the following guidelines when transmitting e-mail in a professional environment.

1. If possible, compose offline. This will allow you to compose, revise, and edit any drafts, and it will provide you with a file copy and backup. Once you have finished writing your e-mail, use your computer's Copy function to insert it into the e-mail program.

2. Structure your e-mail so it is easily read. Check for spelling errors and follow standard punctuation and grammar practices. Use indentation, paragraph divisions, capitalization, bullets, and headings as needed to separate content and organize it for a reader.

3. Guide the recipient to the point of your e-mail by including a clear subject line identifying your message's content or purpose.

4. Try to limit an e-mail correspondence to no more than one full screen in length because a lengthy e-mail message is difficult to read on-screen. Use your e-mail program's Attachment function to send additional content as an attached file.

5. Send copies only to those directly concerned with matters treated in your e-mail. Sending unwanted communications takes up other people's time and appears unprofessional.

Like a fax, an e-mail may not be appropriate for all types of business correspondence. Because e-mail programs do not always transmit accurately or reproduce formatting, the original spacing and organization of, say, a résumé that you sent may well be altered. In most instances, you should use e-mail for routine business matters or to communicate with those you have already corresponded with by traditional means.

Finally, keep in mind that e-mail is not a confidential form of communication. Even after you have deleted an e-mail from your message center, it still exists somewhere on your computer system and perhaps on your company's and server's systems as well. Many companies issue guidelines to employees about the appropriate uses of e-mail, warning against using it to discuss personal or potentially litigious topics.

---

65 Creating an Effective Web site *web*

Since its inception, the World Wide Web (WWW) has experienced tremendous growth. Federal and state governments, large and small businesses, and most academic institutions have their own Web sites. Even you, as an individual, may create a Web site for your own personal use or as part of a school or work assignment.

To build an effective Web site you must familiarize yourself with the technical aspects involved in the project. Begin by going to *www. builder.com/Authoring/Basics*. This Web site will give you an overview of the basic computer language, Hypertext Markup Language (HTML), that Web masters use to create documents for the Web. You can also get helpful information on how to go about building your site at *www.builder.com*.

Once you grasp the fundamentals of Web site construction, you must organize and design, that is, you must plan the "vision," or "look," of your Web site.

Organize Your Site

Keep your personal Web site organization and design simple and basic. Construct it for your own Web audience, which more than likely will be made up of people who are surfing for information—which is very different from browsing for information in a library. Web surfers tend to be impatient; they want information—now! If your Web site is haphazardly organized and designed, it will not hold their interest. Remember, with one click of the mouse they can surf away into cyberspace.

Start with a Well-Organized Home Page

Begin by setting up a visually appealing and user-friendly home page. The home page should be clutter-free yet have enough information to entice visitors to the site and clearly explain the site's contents. Use the home page to announce your site's main areas. Visitors can then click on to the main areas to reach the subsections.

To organize your home page effectively, take a few minutes to brainstorm ideas for the page. Consider what your overall vision should be for the site. What is your main message? Is there something you want to showcase? What attention-getting language will work? How can you entice visitors deeper into the site? As you brainstorm, use arrows that move from main sections to subsections to be sure that the material follows a logical sequence.

Use a Visually Appealing Design

Some Web sites are eye-catching and some are duds. To make your site exciting, use interesting graphics. Just as you imagined your site's content, imagine its colors and graphics. Should there be a recurring visual element or a flashing banner? photographs? dramatic color? For a crash course in Web site design, visit *www.builder.com/Graphics/Graphics101/?st.bl.fd.tsl.feat.1284.*

Add Appropriate Links to Other Sites

Effective Web sites offer many layers of information by linking to other sites. Links give Web surfers other resources besides yours. When you link up with other sites, be sure to evaluate them first. Visit them yourself to be sure they are appropriate for your audience.

Also, since Web sites come and go without notification, check your links frequently to make sure that they are still in effect. If any have closed down, remove them from your site.

Carefully Proofread Your Site

There is nothing more embarrassing than having a Web site that is riddled with spelling and grammatical errors. Just as you would proofread a college paper before submitting it, you should proofread your site before launching it.

As you proofread, do not let the graphics distract you. Concentrate on the language, or you risk missing an obvious error. Also have a group of friends or colleagues review the site for spelling, grammatical, and content errors. A final reminder: Always identify the sources of the material you have integrated into your site.

---

66 Oral Presentations *oral pres*

Most people are struck by stage fright when asked to speak in front of others. Even many professional stage actors confess that they frequently experience stage fright before the curtain goes up.

Although the prospect of public speaking is no doubt daunting, there are simple guidelines you can follow in preparing and delivering an oral presentation. By following these guidelines you can tame your initial fear to a manageable edginess, and that in itself can make your presentation a success.

The Speaker-Audience Relationship

Just as you must establish a writer-reader relationship when you write an essay (see section 5a), so too must you establish a speaker-audience relationship when you speak in front of a group. In both instances you are obligated to know a good deal about your subject. And in both instances you are obligated to organize your material carefully so that you clearly communicate it to a reader or to a listening audience.

There is no standard oral presentation. The nature of your assignment will dictate the kind of presentation you will make. But virtually all oral presentations succeed or fail well before the speaker ever stands in front of an audience. So although the kind of presentation you might be required to make will vary, the principles you must employ to make a success of any oral presentation are constant:

- You must carefully organize your material.
- You must repeatedly rehearse your presentation.
- You must use sound speaking techniques when delivering your presentation.

66a Organize your presentation

A solid oral presentation normally has three elements:

Announce Your Subject and Purpose. After a brief, casual, and polite lead-in, such as "Thank you, Professor Bibbit, for the opportunity . . ." or "I appreciate Ms. Chiselwit's invitation to address you today . . .," straightforwardly announce your subject and purpose:

> I chose to read Ken Kesey's *One Flew over the Cuckoo's Nest* for this presentation. I would like to outline for you why I think the novel should be required reading for all college freshmen.

Or:

> Ms. Chiselwit asked me to discuss some effective ways to market and sell our standard copper-plated widgets. I will discuss some of the methods I have used lately that have proved particularly successful, at least to me.

Choose an Effective Method of Presentation. There are several ways to organize an oral presentation, some more effective than others. Select the one that makes you feel comfortable.

Memorizing Your Presentation. Although many inexperienced speakers believe memorization is the path to perfection, it is often the least effective method of oral presentation. It is all too easy for an inexperienced speaker to forget a word or two because of nervousness, then panic and draw a complete blank. Furthermore, a speaker other than a professional actor who attempts a memorized speech often loses effective voice inflection, thus losing the verve and spontaneity of spoken language. Finally, the speaker of a memorized speech seldom makes eye contact with the audience, being so caught up on concentrating on the selected words stored away inside his or her head.

Reading Your Presentation

Reading a presentation has most of the drawbacks of giving a memorized speech, but it has advantages. A good actor, for instance, can make an extremely effective reading. And sometimes it can be effective to read short passages from other people's texts to reinforce your ideas.

Using Notes

Generally, using notes as an aid in giving your oral presentation is considerably more effective than reciting or reading a written speech.

It's easier to have normal voice inflection when you're using notes to jog your memory. It is also easier to make eye contact with your audience, to move away, at least briefly, from your lectern, and to use gestures to emphasize your points and give some visual variety to your audience. All these things make your presentation more dynamic.

If you do employ notes, use note cards—and number them. They're easy to handle. Make sure the notes on each card are brief. You don't want your attention riveted on the cards; that would be almost as ineffective as reading. The only extended writing on a card should be a direct quote from another writer that you use to back up one of your points.

Using an Outline

Your oral presentation, whether you memorize it, read it, or use notes, needs to be tightly organized. The most effective method of tightly organizing your presentation is by outlining it. And using that outline as a memory jog has a few advantages over using note cards. It can be a bit less physically constraining, particularly if you have your outline or the main points of your presentation on display for your audience on a visual aid such as a chalkboard or overhead transparency. Doing so allows you to move away from your lectern more freely and make eye contact with your audience more easily. We discuss these and other visual aids later in this chapter.

Check section 7d in this text for the characteristics of a formal outline. There we point out that formal outlines include a thesis statement—or in oral presentation more often a statement of subject and purpose that serves as a thesis—and the various levels of detail that explain the subject and purpose. The outline for an oral presentation arguing that the jury selection process in this country needs to be changed might look like this:

Oral Presentations

I. Introduction: How juries are selected
II. Problems with the jury selection process
    A. Cross-sectional juries
    B. Homogeneity of jury pools
    C. Preemptory challenges
        1. Example
        2. Example
    D. Bias and nullification
        1. Example
        2. Example

III. Corrective measures
1. Example
2. Example

66b Rehearse your presentation

Making a relatively brief oral presentation requires substantial rehearsal time if the presentation is to succeed. Normally, the more you can rehearse, the better your presentation will be. Like a professional actor, you will have more success if you organize your rehearsals by moving from the simple to the more complex.

Rehearsing Alone

Begin by writing out your entire presentation or by making a very detailed outline. Then read your work or speak from your outline aloud. Reading or speaking aloud is important. Believe it or not, you have to get used to hearing your own voice. You must also determine how long your presentation will take to make sure it will fit into your allotted time.

Then read or speak into an audiocassette. Listening to your voice come out of a machine will give you an entirely different perspective on what you sound like. You will now hear yourself as others hear you. At this point you can more easily make adjustments to your pace, tone, and verbal emphasis.

The final stage of rehearsing alone is speaking in front of a mirror, preferably a full-length mirror. Now you will see yourself as your audience will see you. If you haven't yet added gestures and movement to your presentation, now is the time to do so.

Rehearsing in Front of Others

Ideally, you should rehearse in front of an audience that is similar to your perspective audience. But practically, you will probably rehearse in front of a roommate or two, or a brother or sister, or a parent, or a husband or wife, or any friend willing to listen and, possibly, give advice. This is an important stage in your preparation because speaking in front of a breathing human being is substantially different from speaking to your image in a mirror.

66c Deliver your presentation

Once in front of that audience, though, you will still have to employ the following sound speaking techniques, all of which you will have practiced during your rehearsals.

Using Appropriate Pace

There are two important factors in striking the appropriate pace for your speech. The first is to time your presentation so you start and finish within the time frame you've been given without either rushing or dawdling. A nervous and unpracticed speaker tends to rush, whereas a speaker without much to say stretches thin material even thinner by speaking too slowly.

Just as writers must use clear visual conventions such as paragraphs and punctuation to make their message clear to readers, speakers should also give their audiences visual clarifications (see "Using Visuals" that follows). Speakers, however, rely on voice to make verbal clarifications. That means raising and lowering the voice at appropriate places, speeding and slowing the pace, and pausing to give emphasis.

Using Visuals

When you organize your material, plan to use visuals. Visuals help you to pace yourself and to clarify and emphasize your points. For a short talk, keep your visuals as simple as possible. Handouts, chalkboards, poster boards, flipcharts, and transparencies and slides, for instance, are readily available and can be easily used in classroom and small business presentations, although PowerPoint is often the presentation of choice. But whatever kind of visual aid you choose to employ, use common sense in implementing it. All visuals must be big enough to be seen easily by your entire audience. All visual aids must be simple and uncluttered. When you use a visual, never turn your back to your audience when you use it or waste time writing on a chalkboard or overhead transparency while your audience waits.

WRITER'S TOOLBOX

Using PowerPoint

PowerPoint presentations are used more and more frequently because they provide clear benefits over more traditional visual aids: brighter color, animation and sound, the ability to be transferred easily to handouts. And PowerPoint templates help guide you through the creation of a presentation even if you have never used the program before. But keep in mind that the purpose of any presentation is to convey information—not to show off technology. Like all presentations, PowerPoint presentations should include neatly formatted and easily readable slides that comprise only the information that genuinely needs to be conveyed.

Moving Around the Room

Because just listening to a speaker is pretty much a static activity for a listener, you can make your speech more interesting simply by moving around a little bit. Even minimal movement helps. On occasion, take a step away from your lectern and stand next to it to make a point or two before you move back to your notes. Or walk to the chalkboard you're using to underline or check one of your points. Any kind of movement that appropriately fits into your presentation gives visual variety to your audience and makes your presentation more interesting.

Making Eye Contact

You cannot engage your audience unless you look at them. This means looking them in the eyes, not at the top of their heads. Look around the room as you speak, pausing for moments with individuals. If you don't look your audience in the eyes, you give them the impression that it's really not necessary for them to be there.

Answering Questions

On most occasions when you give an oral presentation you will answer questions at the end. In answering questions there are two important guidelines to follow: (1) Listen to the entire question so you fully understand it, and (2) Never try to answer the question if you don't know the answer.

When you take a question, look the questioner in the eye, nod at appropriate times, do not speak until the questioner is through, and then repeat the question so that you, the questioner, and the rest of the audience all have the same understanding of it. Then answer the question as simply as you can.

Never try to bluff if you don't know the answer to a question. Your audience will always recognize and resent a bluff. There is absolutely nothing wrong with saying "I don't know" or "That's an aspect of the problem I've never considered," or "I'll find out and let you know at our next meeting."

Ending Your Presentation

End your presentation as simply and straightforwardly as you began it: "I've found these sale techniques particularly effective; maybe you will too." "Maybe some of you now agree with me that Ken Kesey's *One Flew over the Cuckoo's Nest* should be required reading for college freshmen." "If there are no more questions, I'd like to thank you for your attention."

If you diligently organize your material, repeatedly rehearse your presentation, and then use sound speaking techniques when you deliver your talk, there is every reason to expect your speech will be a success.

PART XI
Background in the Basics

When you study grammar in school, you are actually studying what you already "know." Note that the verb know *needs those quotation marks because we're not using it in the usual sense. Your grammar knowledge is largely subconscious: You don't consciously know what you "know." When you study grammar you are learning about those grammar rules that you use subconsciously every time you speak—as well as every time you listen and make sense of what you hear.*

—Martha Kolln, *author of textbooks on writing and grammar*

67   Parts of Speech *gr*

There are eight parts of speech in English: nouns, pronouns, verbs, adjectives, adverbs, prepositions, conjunctions, and interjections. The same word can function at different times as more than one part of speech. To identify a word's part of speech, determine how the word is used in a sentence. The word *coach,* for instance, may function as a noun in one sentence and as a verb in another.

NOUN   The *coach* has a gentle way with players.

VERB   I *coach* my daughter's softball team.

67a   Nouns

Nouns name persons, places, things, or ideas. They may be classified as proper, common, abstract, concrete, and collective.

Proper nouns name particular persons, places, things, or events. They should be capitalized: Charles Dickens, London, Christmas.

Common nouns do not name particular persons, places, things, or events. They are not capitalized: writer, city, holiday.

Abstract nouns name intangible qualities, ideas, or characteristics: love, democracy, courage.

Concrete nouns name tangible things that can be perceived through the senses: wind, rain, pencil, nose, knife, needle.

Collective nouns name groups of individuals: audience, family, army, herd, jury, squad. (See agreement of collective nouns and verbs, 29d; of collective nouns and pronouns, 30c.)

NOTE: **Compound nouns** are composed of more than one word: *high school, crosswalk, sister-in-law, Labor Day.* (See hyphen, Chapter 52; forming the possessive case, 49a; forming plurals, 54e.) A dictionary will list a compound noun as a single entry. Referring to a dictionary is especially important for determining the capitalization of compound nouns. (See capitals, Chapter 48.)

67b   Pronouns

Pronouns take the place of nouns. In the following sentences, the pronoun *him* substitutes for *John Franklin,* and the pronoun *them* substitutes for *fans.*

John Franklin ran eighty yards for a touchdown. Six fans ran onto the field to greet him before officials chased them back to the stands.

The word that a pronoun replaces is called the **antecedent** of the pronoun. *John Franklin* is the antecedent of *him,* and *fans* is the antecedent of *them.*

Pronouns are classified as personal, possessive, reflexive, relative, interrogative, demonstrative, and indefinite.

Personal pronouns refer to a person or a thing. They have plural and singular forms.

	SINGULAR	PLURAL
FIRST PERSON	I, me	we, us
SECOND PERSON	you	you
THIRD PERSON	he, she, him, her, it	they, them

Possessive pronouns are forms of personal pronouns that show ownership or relation. (See case, Chapter 32.)

| my, mine | his | its | their, theirs |
| your, yours | her, hers | | our, ours |

Reflexive pronouns are formed by combining personal pronouns with -*self* and -*selves.*

myself	ourselves
yourself	yourselves
himself, herself, itself	themselves

A reflexive pronoun indicates that someone or something named in a sentence acts (or reflects) upon itself.

Margo looked at herself in the mirror.

Reflexive pronouns that are used to emphasize a noun or pronoun are sometimes called **intensive pronouns.**

Margo herself will perform the ceremony.

Relative pronouns introduce adjective clauses. (See subordinate clauses, 70b.)

| who | whom | whose | that | which |

The couple who performed the tango won first prize.

Interrogative pronouns are used in questions.

who   whom   whose   which   what

Whom did you call?

Demonstrative pronouns point to or identify a noun. (See pronoun reference, Chapter 31.)

this   that   these   those

That is your problem.
This is the question: How will we raise the money?

Indefinite pronouns function as nouns in a sentence but do not take the place of a specific person or thing. The following are common indefinite pronouns.

all	any	anyone	each
another	anybody	anything	either
everybody	most	nobody	some
everyone	one	none	somebody
many	neither	several	something

Somebody will reap the benefits.

67c Verbs

A verb may express physical action (*dance, walk, jump*), mental action (*dream, guess, trust*), or state of being (*is, are, were*). A sentence must have a main verb to be complete. (See sentence parts, Chapter 68; sentence fragments, Chapter 27.)

The year 2005 *ended* much like any other year.

Action verbs are classified by whether or not they must be followed by an object, that is, a noun or pronoun that names what is acted upon.

A *transitive verb* takes an object. (See direct object and indirect object, 68e.)

The pitcher tossed the ball.
The voters believed the politician.

An *intransitive verb* expresses action that has no object.

The pitcher smiled.
The stream runs through the canyon.

Although some verbs are transitive only (*destroy, send, forbid*) and others are intransitive only (*tremble, chuckle, happen*), most verbs can function as either transitive or intransitive.

TRANSITIVE	The guide explained the danger.
INTRANSITIVE	The guide never explained.

Linking verbs express a state of being or a condition rather than an action. The most common linking verbs are forms of *be,* such as *am, is, are, was, were.* Words such as *appear, become, feel, grow, look, smell,* and *taste* function as both linking verbs and action verbs. These verbs link the subject of a sentence with a predicate nominative or predicate adjective—a noun, pronoun, or adjective that identifies or modifies the subject. (See subject, 68a; predicate adjectives and predicate nominatives, 68f.)

The butler is the killer.

The predicate nominative *killer* identifies the subject *butler.*

The silence became frightening.

The predicate adjective *frightening* modifies the subject *silence.*

Many linking verbs also function as transitive as well as intransitive verbs.

LINKING	The butler *looked* gloomy.
INTRANSITIVE	The butler *looked* for an escape.
LINKING	Carmen's hair *grew* gray from shock.
TRANSITIVE	Mr. Higgins *grew* plums.

Helping Verbs and Verb Phrases

A verb often includes one or more **helping verbs,** sometimes called **auxiliary verbs.**

COMMON HELPING VERBS

am	has	can (may) have
are	had	could (would, should) be
is	can	could (would, should) have
was	may	will (shall) have been
were	will (shall) be	might have
do	will (shall) have	might have been
did	has (had) been	must
have	can (may) be	must have
		must have been

The verb and its helping verb(s) form a verb phrase.

The comet *has been approaching* earth for two years.

Verbs **459**

In some sentences the verb and its helping verb are separated.

> The day *has* finally *arrived.*
> *Did* they *reach* Georgia?

(See tense, Chapter 33; passive voice, Chapter 35.)

67d Adjectives

Adjectives modify nouns and pronouns. To modify a word means to limit it—that is, to make its meaning more definite. Adjectives limit in three ways.

1. By describing.

> A *tall* woman stepped from the *curious* crowd.
> The *white* and *black* car won the race.

2. By pointing out which one.

> *That* man is my brother.

3. By telling how many.

> *Twelve* children and *several* parents attended.

Adjectives are normally placed directly before the words they modify, but sometimes a writer places descriptive adjectives after the words they modify.

> The stallion, *long* and *lean,* galloped past us.

Predicate adjectives generally follow linking verbs and modify the subject of a sentence. (See predicate adjective, 68f.)

> The runners were *tired* and *thirsty.*

Adjectives or Pronouns?

A word may be used as more than one part of speech. This is especially true of the words listed below, which may serve as adjectives or pronouns depending on the way they function in a sentence.

all	either	one	these
another	few	other	this
any	many	several	those
both	more	some	what
each	neither	that	which

| ADJECTIVE | *This* book is overdue. *Those* books are on reserve. |
| PRONOUN | *This* is the overdue book. *Those* are the books on reserve. |

The definite article *the* and the indefinite articles *a* (used before words beginning with a consonant sound) and *an* (used before words beginning with a vowel sound) may also be classified as adjectives.

67e Adverbs

Adverbs modify verbs, adjectives, other adverbs, and groups of words. Adverbs most commonly modify verbs by telling how, when, where, or to what extent.

HOW	He reads carefully.
WHEN	He reads late.
WHERE	He reads everywhere.
EXTENT	He reads widely.

Adverbs sometimes modify adjectives and other adverbs.

She is *truly* dedicated. [Modifies the adjective *dedicated*]
She studies *terribly* hard. [Modifies the adverb *hard*]

Adverbs sometimes modify groups of words.

Unfortunately, I cannot attend the wedding. [Modifies the whole sentence]

Many adverbs end in *-ly,* but not all words that end in *-ly* are adverbs.

The day was chilly, but the group jogged briskly through the park. [*Chilly* is an adjective; *briskly* is an adverb.]

67f Prepositions

A preposition shows the relation of a noun or pronoun to some other word in a sentence. Prepositions usually introduce a word group called a **prepositional phrase,** which always consists of the preposition and an object of the preposition—a noun or pronoun that relates to another word in the sentence.

The effect of pesticides threatens wildlife in marshes.

Pesticides is related to *effect* because it specifies which effect. *Marshes* is related to *wildlife* because it indicates where wildlife is threatened.

The prepositions *of* and *in* indicate the relations between these words. (See prepositional phrases, 69a.)

Prepositions usually show direction or position. The following words are among the most common prepositions.

above	at	beyond	into	under
across	before	by	of	up
after	behind	down	on	upon
against	below	during	out	with
along	beneath	for	over	within
among	beside	from	through	without
around	between	in	to	

Around the corner and *beyond* the tracks the road turns.

Groups of words, such as *along with, according to,* and *in spite of,* sometimes serve as prepositions. (See idioms, 26c.)

According to the latest report, the company is nearly bankrupt.

67g Conjunctions

Conjunctions join words, phrases, or clauses. They are usually classified into three categories: coordinating conjunctions, correlative conjunctions, and subordinating conjunctions.

There are seven **coordinating conjunctions:** *and, but, or, yet, for, nor,* and *so.* (See subject and predicate, 68a, 68b; main clauses, 70a; compound sentences, Chapter 71.) They connect items of equal weight.

Oranges, lemons, *and* limes are citrus fruits.
The fish bite in the morning *or* after sundown.
The comet hit, *but* no one saw it.

Correlative conjunctions are always used in pairs: *both . . . and; not only . . . but also; either . . . or;* and *neither . . . nor.*

Both the California condor *and* the Maryland darter are struggling to survive.

Neither animal *nor* plant species are safe from human encroachment.

Subordinating conjunctions begin subordinate clauses. Common subordinating conjunctions, several of which also function as prepositions, are *after, although, because, before, if, since, so that, though, unless, until, when, where,* and *while.* (See subordinate clauses, 70b.)

Humans must uncover their fears *before* they can uncover their courage.

When psychology develops a model of human nature, it will not be based solely on neuroses and character disorders.

NOTE: Conjunctive adverbs join main, or independent, clauses. Words such as *consequently, furthermore, hence, however, indeed, moreover, nevertheless, subsequently, therefore,* and *thus* are conjunctive adverbs. (See main clauses, 70a; semicolon, Chapter 39.)

Paralysis was President Franklin Delano Roosevelt's only experience with defeat; *consequently,* he never revealed the extent of his handicap.

Statistics show that advertising generates sales; manufacturers, *therefore,* will continue to support Madison Avenue copywriters.

67h Interjections

Interjections express surprise or strong emotion and have no grammatical relation to sentences. Examples of interjections are *Oh! Wow! Ah! Ouch! Hey! My goodness!*

Ouch! I bit my tongue.

Exercise 67.1: Review

Name the part of speech of each italicized word in the following paragraph, using the abbreviations N for noun, PRO for pronoun, V for verb, ADJ for adjective, ADV for adverb, PREP for preposition, C for conjunction, and I for interjection.

Medical school instructors *believe* that good care *begins* with a record of a patient's medical history; *therefore,* the *skill* of *diagnosis* rests on the simple act of talking with a patient. The doctor must listen, *ask* important questions, and *not only* hear what the patient says *but also* hear what the patient does not say. *This* discussion will enable the doctor to create a diagnosis and a *treatment* plan. *Although* medical interviewing has been part of the *diagnostic* process since medicine began, authorities are *officially* recognizing that *it* is the foundation of any successful treatment. The next time your doctor begins *with* a discussion of your medical history, do not protest with "*Oh no,* not again," but instead appreciate the importance of this process.

68 Parts of Sentences *gr*

Effective writing starts with clear, grammatical sentences. A sentence is a group of words that contains a subject and a predicate and is not dependent on another group of words to complete its meaning. (See subordinating conjunctions, 67g; main clauses and subordinate clauses, Chapter 70.)

NONSENTENCE | Although the celebration ended with a fireworks display.

SENTENCE | The celebration ended with a fireworks display.

SENTENCE | How did the celebration end?

Subject and Predicate

68a Simple subject and complete subject

The **simple subject** is the word or words that act, are acted upon, or are described.

Quail Hill rises at the end of University Drive.
Birds have been nesting among the rocks and shrubs.
Bundled in coats, *students* stroll to the peak each evening.

Sometimes the subject *you* is implied.

Speak to us! [Meaning *You* speak to us.]

The **complete subject** includes the simple subject and the group of words that modify the simple subject.

The student rally began at noon.
The candidate from Benson Hall will speak at two o'clock.

68b Simple predicate and complete predicate

The **simple predicate,** sometimes referred to as the **main verb,** is the word or words that tell what the subject did or how it was acted upon.

Quail Hill *rises* at the end of University Drive.
Birds *have been nesting* among the rocks and shrubs.
Bundled in coats, students *stroll* to the peak each evening.

The **complete predicate** is the group of words that includes the simple predicate and its modifiers.

> The student rally *began at noon.*
> The candidate from Benson Hall *will speak at two o'clock.*

68c Compound subject

A compound subject consists of two or more subjects that are joined by a conjunction and that have the same predicate.

> *Samuel King* and *William Black* took the first aerial photographs.
> Either *he* or *she* will fly the balloon.

68d Compound predicate

A compound predicate consists of two or more main verbs that are joined by a conjunction and that have the same subject.

> The rumble of the train *echoes* through the valley and *rolls* over the hills.
> Space shuttles will *fly* to the moon and *return* with payloads of minerals.

Complements

Some sentences express the writer's thought by means of a subject and a predicate only: *He worked. She arrived.* Most sentences, however, have within the complete predicate one or more words that add to the meaning of the subject and simple predicate.

> They appointed *a new president.*
> He is *an engineer.*

These elements are called **complements,** and they function as direct and indirect objects and as predicate adjectives and predicate nominatives. (See verbs, 67c.)

68e Direct objects and indirect objects

A **direct object** is a word or word group that receives the action of a main transitive verb. A direct object answers the question *What?* or *Whom?*

The Civic League invited *Julio to speak.*
She teaches *fifth grade.*

The **indirect object** of a verb precedes the direct object and usually indicates to whom or for whom the action is done.

The caretaker gave *Kim* the key.

To identify an indirect object, reconstruct the sentence by using the preposition *to* or *for.*

The caretaker gave the key *to Kim.*

Now *Kim* no longer functions as the indirect object but as the object of the preposition *to.*

68f Predicate adjectives and predicate nominatives

A **predicate adjective** is an adjective that follows a linking verb and modifies the subject of the verb.

The animals seem *restless.*

A **predicate nominative** is a noun or pronoun that follows a linking verb and renames or identifies the subject of the verb.

The man with gray hair is *Mr. Sumato.*

Exercise 68.1: Complements

Underline and identify the direct objects (DO), indirect objects (IO), predicate adjectives (PA), and predicate nominatives (PN) in the following sentences.

1. Metaphors create vivid images in people's minds and in their hearts.

2. Highly charged images can become trademarks or handicaps for politicians.

3. Lincoln's "a house divided" won him success, but Hoover's "a chicken in every pot" brought him scorn.

4. In the fear of using vivid language, many politicians give us empty phrases.

5. This vague use of language often sounds dull.

69 Phrases *gr*

Words in sentences function not only individually but also in groups. The most common word group is the phrase, a group of words that may function as a noun, a verb, an adjective, or an adverb.

69a Prepositional phrases

Prepositional phrases begin with a preposition and end with a noun or pronoun. They function as adjectives or adverbs. (See prepositions, 67f.)

> The fibula *of the left leg* is broken.
> As she turned, her mask fell *to the floor.*

69b Appositive phrases

An appositive phrase is a noun or pronoun with modifiers that is placed near another noun or pronoun to explain, describe, or identify it.

> The Wolves' Den, *a hangout for college intellectuals,* caught fire.
> My brother *David, not James,* works nights.

Usually an appositive follows the word it refers to, but it may also precede the word. (See non-restrictive appositives, 37c.)

> *A thrilling love story,* John and Marsha's romance would make a wonderful film.

Exercise 69.1: Prepositional and Appositive Phrases

Combine each group of sentences into one sentence by using prepositional phrases and appositives. You may need to revise wording and delete some words to make the new sentences read correctly. For example:

> The purpose is to enrich a person's life. This is the purpose of a college education. A college education is the best investment anyone can make.

> The purpose of a college education, the best investment anyone can make, is to enrich a person's life.

1. History is the foundation of any liberal arts education. It is a basic subject. History is in most curricula.

2. Sigmund Freud visited the United States. Freud is the father of psychoanalysis. He came to the United States in August and September. The year was 1909.

3. Bodybuilders seem dedicated. They are both male and female. The dedication is self-torture.

4. Personal forgiveness can be granted only by victims, not by observers. Forgiveness is a kind of moral embrace. The embrace is between two people.

5. Upton Sinclair wrote radical novels. Most of his novels are about corruption of the capitalistic system. He was a candidate for governor of California in 1934.

Verbals and Verbal Phrases

A **verbal** is a verb that does not function as the simple predicate of a clause. Instead, verbals (which include infinitives, present participles, and past participles) function as nouns, adjectives, and adverbs.

69c Infinitives and infinitive phrases

Infinitives and infinitive phrases function as nouns, adjectives, and adverbs. An infinitive phrase includes the infinitive—the plain form of a verb preceded by *to*—as well as its complements or modifiers. (See verb forms, Chapter 33.)

> Her favorite pastime is *to dance*. [Noun: names *pastime*]
> I have three choices *to offer* you. [Adjective: modifies *choices*]
> He seems eager *to gain* knowledge. [Adverb: modifies *eager*]

69d Participles and participial phrases

Participles and participial phrases are verb forms that function as adjectives. Present participles end in *-ing* (*running, laughing, flying*). Past participles usually end in *-ed* (*flopped, jumped, dangled*), but a few end in *-en* (*beaten*), and some change entirely (*begun, swum, brought*). (See note on gerunds, 69e; verb forms, Chapter 33.)

> *Tired,* the runner slumped to the ground. [Past participle: modifies *runner*]

The *developing* crisis dominated the news. [Present participle: modifies *crisis*]

Participial phrases consist of a participle and its complements or modifiers.

The cat *howling through the night* belongs to Caesar.

Glutted with inexpensive imports, the automobile market has declined.

Beaten by Lady Luck, the gambler quit the game.

Exercise 69.2: Verbals and Verbal Phrases

Combine each group of sentences by using infinitive and participial phrases. Follow the directions in brackets after each group. You may need to add words, delete words, and/or change tenses. Example:

Time ticks away in relentless beats. It is a major preoccupation of most Americans. [Use a present participial phrase.]

Ticking away in relentless beats, time is a major occupation of most Americans.

1. The Navy keeps accurate world time. This is the Navy's tremendous responsibility. [Use an infinitive phrase as the subject.]

2. Atomic clocks outstrip the performance of the solar system. Every two years atomic clocks must be reset. [Use a present participial phrase.]

3. The Naval Observatory operates about fifty atomic clocks. They are stored in climate-controlled vaults. [Use a past participial phrase.]

4. Navigation satellites are accurate. They are accurate enough to locate an oil well. They are even accurate enough to guide a battleship through fog. [Use two infinitive phrases joined by *or.*]

5. Our lives are conditioned by a steady television diet. Our lives are measured in increments as regular as television commercials. [Use a past participial phrase.]

69e Gerunds and gerund phrases

Gerunds and gerund phrases function as nouns. A gerund is the present participle of a verb, formed by adding *-ing* to the infinitive, and used as a noun.

Dreaming leads to creation.

A gerund phrase consists of a gerund and its complements or modifiers. Like the gerund, the gerund phrase is used as a noun.

I love *dancing until dawn.*
Flying to Rome is costly.

NOTE: Since both gerunds and present participles end in *-ing,* they are sometimes confused. You can avoid confusing them by determining their function in a sentence. Gerunds function as nouns. Present participles, when not serving as part of the predicate, function as adjectives.

GERUND   *Running* keeps me fit for tennis.

PARTICIPLE   The water *running* in the kitchen is a nuisance.

Exercise 69.3: Gerund and Present Participial Phrases

Write two sentences for each of the following words, using the word in a gerund phrase and in a present participial phrase. For example, using the word *diving:*

GERUND   Diving from the ten-meter board is thrilling.

PARTICIPLE   Diving beneath the surface, he saw a world of splendid color.

1. hoping
2. drifting
3. flinging
4. washing
5. speaking

69f Absolute phrases

An absolute phrase consists of a noun and (usually) a participle, plus modifiers, that add to the meaning of a sentence but have no grammatical relation to it.

An absolute phrase differs from other phrases because it does not modify a particular word but instead modifies an entire sentence. An absolute phrase may appear almost anywhere in a sentence.

The palm tree swayed, *its slick leaves shimmering with light.*

A magnifying glass raised to his eye, Sherlock Holmes examined the weapon.

The two of us worked the entire night—*Barbara at the computer and I at the tape recorder*—transcribing our field notes.

Exercise 69.4: Absolute Phrases

Combine each group of sentences using absolute phrases. You may need to add or omit words and change tenses. For example:

> The players were leaning over their cards. They were chatting softly. The poker game continued for hours.
>
> The players leaning over their cards and chatting softly, the poker game continued for hours.

1. Her novel was finished. Renee decided to vacation in Paris.

2. The Mercedes skidded to a stop in the rain. Its brakes were squealing. Its taillights were glowing.

3. The horses rounded the turn. Their nostrils were flaring. Their necks were stretching toward the finish line.

4. The mysteries of the earth have been explored. The 1990s adventurer will turn to the secrets of the mind.

5. The lifeguard sat on the sand. Suntan lotion was glistening on her back, and the wind was gently lifting her hair.

---

70 Clauses *gr*

A **clause** is a group of words that has a subject and a predicate. There are two kinds of clauses: main clauses (sometimes called independent clauses) and subordinate clauses (sometimes called dependent clauses).

70a Main clauses

Main clauses form grammatically complete sentences. They may stand alone or be joined by coordinating conjunctions (see 67g), by conjunctive adverbs (see note, 67g), or by semicolons (see 39a, 39b). (Also see comma, 37a.)

The cobra is a poisonous snake. Its bite is often fatal.
The cobra is a poisonous snake, and its bite is often fatal.
The cobra is a poisonous snake; indeed, its bite is often fatal.
The cobra is a poisonous snake; its bite is often fatal.

70b Subordinate clauses

Subordinate clauses do not form grammatically complete sentences. They are usually introduced by a subordinating conjunction (see 67g) or a relative pronoun (see 67b).

Subordinate clauses function as nouns, adjectives, or adverbs within a sentence. The exact relation in a sentence between the thoughts expressed in a dependent clause and the main clause is indicated by the subordinating conjunction or relative pronoun that joins them.

An **adjective clause** modifies a noun or pronoun. It often begins with a relative pronoun (*who, whom, whose, that, which*) that refers to or is related to a noun or pronoun that precedes it. (See comma, 37c.)

> The trumpet player *who left the stage* fell asleep in the lounge.
>
> Anything *that stands on the seafront* will be leveled by the storm.
>
> Karla is the spy *Smiley seeks.* [The relative pronoun *that* or *whom* is understood.]

An **adverb clause** modifies a verb, an adjective, or an adverb. It begins with a subordinating conjunction such as *when, although, whenever, since, after, while, because, where, if, that,* or *than.*

> *Whenever he is asked,* he plays the banjo.
> I am happy *because it is Saturday.*
> She studies more effectively *than I do.*

A **noun clause** is a subordinate clause that functions as a noun. It may serve as subject, predicate nominative, direct object, indirect object, or object of a preposition. The noun clause is likely to begin with a relative pronoun. (See complements, 68d, 68f.)

SUBJECT	*That life is difficult for some* means little to insensitive bureaucrats.
OBJECT	He described *what he wanted.*

Exercise 70.1: Subordinate Clauses

Combine each group of sentences by using subordinate clauses as indicated in the instructions in brackets. You may need to change some words to avoid repetition. For example:

> Few people have heard of hydrocephalus. Hydrocephalus affects at least a million families. [Use *although* to form an adverb clause.]

> Although few people have heard of the disease, hydrocephalus affects at least a million families.

1. Hydrocephalus is caused by a buildup of fluid in the brain cavity. Hydrocephalus is often called "water on the brain." [Use *which* to form an adjective clause.]

2. As many as eight thousand babies are born with the defect every year. This number does not relieve the mark of shame attached to the disease. [Use *that* to form a noun clause.]

3. Some doctors have attempted to educate the public about the defect. These doctors are prominent in the medical profession. Many people still believe that any child suffering from it will develop a head perhaps twice the normal size. [Use *although* to form an adverb clause and use *who* to form an adjective clause.]

4. Enlarged heads can be avoided. Doctors have developed an operation for hydrocephalics. The operation drains the fluid to avoid retardation in the patient. [Use *because* to form an adverb clause and use *that* to form an adjective clause.]

5. The surgical procedure has brought new hope to the parents of children suffering from the disease. They still worry about the future of their children. [Use *although* to form an adverb clause.]

---

71 Sentence Patterns *gr*

Sentences can be classified according to their structure (simple, compound, complex, or compound-complex) and their purpose (declarative, imperative, interrogative, or exclamatory).

Sentence Structures

Simple sentences have only one main clause and no dependent clauses, although they may have several phrases.

> Years ago the family of a bride would supply the groom with a dowry. [One main clause]

> The bride and the groom were not consulted about the choice of a mate and sometimes met each other for the first time on the day of their wedding. [One main clause with a compound subject and a compound predicate]

Compound sentences have two or more main clauses but no dependent clauses.

> Chauvinism has fueled many political skirmishes, but jingoism has ignited wars. [Two main clauses joined by a comma and the coordinating conjunction *but*]

> Some people are flattered into virtue; other people are bullied out of vice. [Two main clauses joined by a semicolon]

Complex sentences have one main clause and at least one subordinate clause.

> Although he was a cunning investor, Bennett went bankrupt. [One main clause and one dependent clause beginning with the subordinating conjunction *although*]

Compound-complex sentences have at least two main clauses and at least one dependent clause.

> If they wish to live fully, most people need amusement to relax, and many people need intellectual challenges to develop their minds. [Two main clauses joined by a comma and the coordinating conjunction *and* and one dependent clause beginning with the subordinating conjunction *if*]

Sentence Purposes

A **declarative sentence** makes a statement.

> Spelunking requires the skill of a mountain climber and the courage of a coal miner.

An **imperative sentence** gives a command or makes a request.

> Don't walk on the grass.

Please stay off the grass.

(See implied subject, 68a.)

An **interrogative sentence** asks a question.

Which point of view is most valid?

An **exclamatory sentence** expresses strong feeling.

The mountains are glorious!

Exercise 71.1: Sentence Structure and Purpose

Write sentences according to the following directions.

1. Write a simple, declarative sentence that states a fact about your campus.

2. Using the coordinating conjunction *or*, write a compound sentence about a friend.

3. Write an interrogative sentence directed to a politician.

4. Write a declarative compound-complex sentence directed to a parent.

5. Write an imperative sentence that gently directs a child.

6. Write a complex sentence that deals with a foreign country.

7. Using a semicolon, write a compound sentence that deals with a sports event.

8. Using *who*, write a compound-complex sentence describing a friend.

9. Write a series of three simple sentences followed by a complex sentence that deals with a subject you read about in a newspaper.

10. Using a variety of sentence structures, describe a place that is important to you. Identify each sentence as simple, compound, complex, or compound-complex.

PART XII
Background for Multilingual Writers

I am a writer. And by that definition, I am someone who has always loved language. I am fascinated by language in daily life. I spend a great deal of my time thinking about the power of language—the way it can evoke an emotion, a visual image, a complex idea, or a simple truth. Language is the tool of my trade. And I use them all—all the Englishes I grew up with.

—Amy Tan, *novelist*

---

72   Omitted Words   *esl*

Do Not Omit Expletives, Subjects, or Verbs

Are three chapters to read this week has a common second language error. The writer left out a word, the expletive *there*. Corrected, the sentence should read, *There are three chapters to read this week.*

English does not allow you to omit expletives, subjects, or verbs. English does allow you to omit *you* in commands—that is, when *you* is understood: *Read the directions with care.* If your first language allows for these omissions, stay alert! Acceptable omissions in your first language may not be acceptable in English.

◆ *I w*
   ^Worry about my life span because I smoke.

◆ Cultural knowledge *is*^important.

◆ Jorge Lopez, *who*^studied karate, broke a brick with a hand.

An expletive, *there* or *it,* may be required in sentences where the subject follows the verb.

◆ *It is*
   ^Is easy to make mistakes.

◆ Children believe *there*^are scary creatures in the night.

Remember, *is, are, was,* or *were* cannot begin a clause unless the clause is a question, such as *Are you awake?,* or an exclamation, such as *Was I sick!*

Exercise 72.1: Omitted Words

Read the following paragraph. Find the missing subjects and verbs and add them to the text.

> Government loans to college students the lowest in ten years. The president very concerned. Appointed a committee to investigate falling income. Will not meet until next September. The president unhappy about the slow start. Is one

of the problems the president promised to solve during his campaign. Are thousands of needy students in the United States cannot afford a college education. Are unhappy about this problem. Is little hope. Seems to be an unfair policy.

---

73 Noun Markers *esl*

Use Noun Markers

English nouns frequently have markers. Noun markers are words indicating a noun is coming (though the noun might not be the next word). The command *Read stories* is wrong, unless the writer means all stories, which would not make much sense. Corrected, it would read, *Read the stories.*

COMMON NOUN MARKERS

ARTICLES	a car; the car; an automobile
NUMBERS	12 cats; seven dogs
POSSESSIVE NOUNS	Van's stories; China's goal
POSSESSIVE PRONOUNS	my, our, your, his, her, its, their
OTHER PRONOUNS	all, every, any, each, either, neither, few, many, more, most, this, that, these, those, much, several, some, whose

Other words may be placed between the marker and the noun.

The shiny new *motorcycle* belongs to her.
Twelve white *ducks* swim in the lake.
Jon's hopeless *whining* gets nothing done.
Her demanding *schedule* is exhausting.

Of all the noun markers, articles (*a, an, the*) can be troublesome.

Definite Article: *the*

Use *the* before nouns that are specifically identified.

Wear *the* boots you bought in Santa Fe.

Raul had *the* most interesting performance.
The sun rose at six.

A careful reading of the examples above shows that each noun in question is specifically identified by the context.

> I couldn't find the reason for the computer error no matter how hard I tried. After I read the manual the reason became clear.

At first the *reason* is unidentified, so you could use the indefinite article *a*. But *reason* is identified when the writer mentions it the second time; it is the specific *reason* that the writer found that caused the computer error.

Because it is used only with nouns specifically identified, *the* should not be used with plural or noncount nouns when the meaning conveyed is *generally* or *all*.

◆ The cost of printing ~~the~~ magazines is usually paid for by advertising revenue.

◆ Health magazines report studies about drinking ~~the~~ coffee.

Generally, do not use *the* with proper nouns. Proper nouns name people, places, and things: *Leslie Woo, Mexico, Anaheim Stadium.*

There are exceptions. Some plural proper nouns naming places, such as *the Pyrenees, the Sierra Nevadas, the Alps, the Great Lakes,* take the definite article. Furthermore, some countries have an official name that may take *the* and a shorter, more commonly used name that does not take *the.*

FORMAL NAME	COMMON NAME
the Italian Republic	Italy
the Commonwealth of Australia	Australia
the Hashemite Kingdom of Jordan	Jordan
the Principality of Liechtenstein	Liechtenstein

In all these cases the article *the* is used with the descriptive portion of the name, *republic, commonwealth, kingdom, principality, states,* but not with the actual name.

Indefinite Articles: *a, an*

Use the indefinite article *a* or *an* for singular count nouns not specifically identified.

Most nouns refer to things that can be counted, such as *one horse, three cars, five dollars.* Some nouns refer to things that can't be counted, such as *news, fog, sand.*

If a singular count noun is not specifically identified, use *a* or *an.*

> Apple started a revolution in personal computers.
> Deacon has an interesting insect collection.

Which should you use, *a* or *an?* That depends on the sound of the word following the article. Use *a* before consonant sounds and *an* before vowel sounds.

> a rabbit   an awkward rabbit
> an umbrella   a blue umbrella

A word beginning with the letter *h* may have either an initial consonant sound if it is aspirated (*hole*) or an initial vowel sound if it is not aspirated (*heiress*).

> a hand   an hour

Don't use *a* and *an* with plural nouns.

◆ Mariko borrowed money to cover ~~an~~ expenses.

◆ The exhibit consisted of ~~a~~ hastily arranged groupings of native costumes.

Generally, don't use *a* and *an* with noncount nouns.

> Teresa wrote on pollution.
> While you are shopping, please get coffee and soap.

Generally, use an article when you show a particular amount of a noncount noun by placing a count noun first and using *of.*

> a bag of rice   a pile of sand

Exercise 73.1: Noun Markers

In the following paragraph, determine if an article should be used in a space, and if so, which article—*a, an,* or *the.*

> _____ hundred years ago, human beings lived _____ average of forty-five years. Then came _____ flush toilet. Invented by Thomas Crapper in 1860, _____ toilet has been "_____ biggest variable in _____ extending life span,"

according to Professor Gary Ruvkun, _____ geneticist at Harvard University.

In the remainder of the paragraph, determine where articles should be added or deleted.

Human wastes in water can transmit the cholera, diarrhea, and salmonellosis. In developing world, where only 34 percent of population has access to the toilets, life spans can be up to 30 years less than average in the industrialized countries.

---

74 Verb Combinations *esl*

Use Correct Verb Combinations

Van have taken three tests, but only two are difficult, has a common second language error: The writer has not used a correct verb combination. Corrected, the sentence would read, *Van has taken three tests, but only two* were *difficult.*

Helping Verbs. English sentences often require combinations of helping verbs and main verbs. Helping verbs appear before main verbs. Some main verbs will not be complete without helping verbs.

◆ The mail ^*will* ^*arrive* soon.

There are twenty-three helping verbs. Nine are called *modals;* they work only as helping verbs. The others, which are forms of *do, have,* and *be,* can also work as main verbs.

HELPING VERBS
Three forms of *do:* do, does, did
Three forms of *have:* have, has, had
All forms of *be:* be, is, was, were, are, am, been, being
Modals: can, could, may, might, must, shall, should, will, would

After a modal or *do, does, did,* use a plain verb.

may dance	might fly	should bring
do swim	does feel	did hurt

◆ My Web page may expands my clientele.

◆ Your answer does not convinces me.

◆ Did you finished your projects?

After *have, has, had,* use the past participle to form the perfect tense.

have driven   has contributed   had slept

◆ Those hungry guys must have eat the leftovers.
eaten

◆ Julia has accomplish nothing this weekend.
ed

◆ Luis had finish his sculpture just in time.
ed

After the helping verbs *is, was, were, are, am,* use a present participle to form one of the progressive tenses.

is going   was swimming   were eating
are studying   am thinking

◆ Jason was worked on his car.
ing

Be and *been* must be preceded by other helping verbs and followed by a present participle to form one of the progressive tenses.

> *can* or *could* be
> *may, might,* or *must* be
> *shall* or *should* be
> *will* or *would* be
> *has, have,* or *had* been
> *can* or *could have* been
> *may, might,* or *must have* been
> *shall* or *should have* been
> *will* or *would have* been

◆ Rod be leaving soon.
will

◆ Minh been studying late.
has

After the helping verbs *is, was, were, are, am,* use a past participle to form the passive voice.

is repeated   was thrown   were submitted

are appreciated   am assisted

◆ The truth is reveal~ed~ in strange ways.

Be, been, and *being* must be preceded by other helping verbs and followed by a past participle to form the passive voice.

> *is, was, were, are,* or *am* being
> *can* or *could* be
> *may, might,* or *must* be
> *shall* or *should* be
> *will* or *would* be
> *can have* or *could have* been
> *may have, might have,* or *must have* been
> *shall have* or *should have* been
> *will have* or *would have* been

◆ My dog may have been save~d~ by its veterinarian.

◆ The photos were being mount~ed~ in the albums.

Intransitive verbs, those expressing action with no direct object, cannot be used in the passive voice.

◆ The actor was grinn~ing~d broadly.

Exercise 74.1: Correct Verb Forms

Identify the correct verb form for each set of verbs in the following sentences.

1. Scientists (have studied, have study) the effects of exercise on people for years.

2. Information, which (was release, was released) in August, indicates that exercise (is contributing, is contributes) to a longer life expectancy.

3. Further research on exercise suggests that some older people (be coping, may be coping) with mental disorders better because of daily exercise.

4. Unfortunately, many residential communities for the elderly (do not offer, do not offering) enough exercise classes.

5. Now the National Institutes of Health (is encourage, is encouraging) more organized exercise programs across the nation.

Phrasal Verbs   Phrasal verbs combine a verb with a preposition or an adverb. Often phrasal verbs have both idiomatic and literal meaning. For example, *look up* may literally mean *focus on something above you* or it may idiomatically mean *search for information.*

Phrasal verbs are either separable or nonseparable depending on whether an object can be inserted between the verb and the particle. *Clean up,* for example, can be separable phrasal verb, as in *This weekend I will clean the house up.* Generally, phrasal verbs have been common in informal writing, but now they are appearing more frequently in formal writing.

Phrasal verbs must be learned in context. Nevertheless, the following list will help you understand phrasal verbs. Nonseparable phrasal verbs are marked [N].

COMMON PHRASAL VERBS
ask out (ask for a date)
bring up (mention casually; raise a child)
call off (cancel)
call up (call on a telephone)
come across [N] (meet or find unexpectedly)
drop in or drop by [N] (visit unannounced)
drop off (leave someone or something at a place)
fill out (complete a form)
get along with [N] (have a comfortable relationship)
get over [N] (recover from something)
give up (stop trying)
go over [N] (review)
hand in (submit)
help out (assist)
keep on (continue)
leave out (omit)
make up (become friendly again; do past work; invent)
pass away [N] (die)
point out (call attention to)
put away (store; lock up; drink heavily)
put off (postpone, avoid)
run out of [N] (have no more)
take off (leave; remove something)
take over (control; take charge)
turn down (reject)
wrap up (complete)

When the direct object is a pronoun, a phrasal verb must be separated.

◆ I will help out him with biology.
          ^

Exercise 74.2: Correct Phrasal Verbs

Decide which phrasal verb, similar in meaning to the verb in brackets, should be used in the following paragraph.

> Artists must [submit] their entries for the exhibit by Friday, but they are always late. Most artists [postpone] creating their work until the last minute. By starting so late, they cannot [complete] a painting or sculpture on time. Too often judges [reject] late entries. Artists often [invent] dramatic excuses for being late. Last year, one artist actually said, "The dog ate it."

Verbs Followed by Gerunds and Infinitives   Some verbs may be followed by gerunds but not infinitives. Some may be followed by infinitives but not gerunds. Some may be followed by either gerunds or infinitives.

A gerund ends in *-ing* and functions as a noun, such as *cooking, studying, painting.*

An infinitive consists of a verb's plain form usually preceded by *to: to attend, to believe, to convince.*

VERB WITH GERUND	Did he *mention running* in Mason Park?
VERB WITH INFINITIVE	This light *is guaranteed to work* fifteen hours on two batteries.

Verbs Followed by Gerunds But Not Infinitives

admit	discuss	mind	recall
appreciate	enjoy	miss	resent
avoid	escape	postpone	resist
consider	finish	practice	risk
delay	imagine	put off	suggest
deny	mention	quit	tolerate

Authorities *will not tolerate writing* on buildings.

Verbs Followed by Infinitives But Not Gerunds

afford	demand	hope	pretend
agree	deserve	learn	promise

appear	endeavor	manage	refuse
ask	expect	mean (intend)	seem
are	fail	need	threaten
claim	guarantee	offer	wait
choose	happen	plan	want
decide	hesitate	prepare	wish

Some verbs followed by an infinitive must have a noun or pronoun between the verb and the infinitive, such as *advise, allow, cause, caution, challenge, condemn, convince, dare, direct, encourage, forbid, invite, permit, persuade, require, teach, tell, warn.*

> I *urge* you *to enter* the race.
> William *advised* Nona *to avoid* the park after dark.

Some verbs may be followed directly by an infinitive or may have a noun or pronoun between them and an infinitive, such as *ask, expect, need, want.*

> I *want to dance* until midnight.
> I *want* you *to dance* with me until midnight.

Verbs Followed by Gerunds or Infinitives

bear	deserve	love	remember
begin	read	neglect	start
hate	prefer	stop	can't bear
intend	regret	try	can't stand
continue	like		

> The institute *will start researching* the effects of laughter.
> The institute *has started to research* the effects of laughter.

Exercise 74.3: Correct Gerunds and Infinitives

Complete the following sentences with a gerund or an infinitive.

1. Counselors want students [understand] course requirements.
2. They want students [study] the course catalog.
3. They also suggest [examine] and [memorize] college department requirements.
4. Moreover, counselors caution students not [ignore] [read] the detailed requirements for graduation.
5. The Advisory Office would appreciate [know] each student's graduation plans.

75 Faulty Repetitions *esl*

Delete Faulty Repetitions

Childhood it is the leading cause of stress among children has a common second language error. The writer has unnecessarily referred to *childhood* with the pronoun *it*. Corrected, the sentence would read, *Childhood is the leading cause of stress among children.*

Reread your sentences carefully. Delete any words that unnecessarily refer to or repeat other words in a sentence.

◆ Driving ~~this~~ is my favorite method of travel.

◆ The slim woman with short hair ~~she~~ is my doctor.

◆ Professor Park, who lectured on Korea, ~~she~~ used humor to make her points.

◆ That was the year when we graduated ~~then~~.

◆ The party will be held in the restaurant where we held the graduation dinner ~~there~~.

◆ Carl's business trip was made miserable by the clients whom he was visiting with ~~them~~.

Exercise 75.1: Faulty Repetitions

Draw a line through the unnecessary words in the following sentences.

1. The Statue of Liberty, which is located in New York harbor, it was given to the United States by France.

2. A love letter was on the front seat of Tom's Honda where it would be easily found there.

3. The sun it was so hot the sand sizzled.

4. The game occurred on Saturday when thousands of people were at home then.

5. Six people they were honored, and more than fifty they were mentioned.

---

76 Present and Past Participles *esl*

Use Present and Past Participles Correctly

The interesting events interested TV viewers shows how forms of a plain verb can be used as an adjective and main verb. But when you use the present or past participles of a plain verb as an adjective, be sure to do so correctly.

Present participles, such as *moving, running, dancing, flying,* and past participles, such as *moved, ran, danced, flew,* when used as adjectives may precede the noun they modify, or they may follow a linking verb, such as forms of *to be* (*am, are, is, was, were*).

Present Participle Used as an Adjective
> We saw an *interesting* movie.
> The movie we saw was *interesting.*

Past Participle Used as an Adjective
> All *interested* people should attend the debate.
> No one *interested* in buying my car has called.

As you can see from the examples above, the present participle describes the agent causing the feeling or reaction (*movie was interesting*), and the past participle describes the person or thing having the feeling or reaction (*interested people*). In your writing, use the proper participle form for verbs such as these:

amazing, amazed	exciting, excited
amusing, amused	exhausting, exhausted
annoying, annoyed	fascinating, fascinated
boring, bored	frightening, frightened
confusing, confused	interesting, interested
depressing, depressed	shocking, shocked
disturbing, disturbed	surprising, surprised
embarrassing, embarrassed	thrilling, thrilled

Sometimes writers make the mistake of unnecessarily repeating a verb form. They mistakenly use the present participle as an adjective and a past participle of the same verb as the main verb.

◆ The ~~exciting~~ movie excited us.

Exercise 76.1: Using Participles Correctly

Identify the correct participle for each sentence.

1. People across the country were (shocking, shocked) by the news of the explosion in Oklahoma City.

2. The news on television showed how (frightening, frightened) and (confusing, confused) everyone was.

3. The death and destruction left the residents of the Oklahoma City area very (depressing, depressed).

4. However, the rescue of victims who had been trapped for hours was (amazing, amazed), and people were (thrilling, thrilled) to learn that some people survived.

5. Even though the emotional response of people around the nation was strong, nothing could relieve the families of victims, who were (grieving, grieved) over their losses.

Glossaries

Glossary of Usage

Glossary of Grammatical Terms

Glossary of Usage

The entries in this glossary are words and phrases that frequently cause problems for inexperienced writers. Based on recent editions of dictionaries and usage guides, the suggestions for standard written English included in this glossary represent current practice among experienced writers. You should avoid using words and phrases labeled *nonstandard,* and use entries labeled *colloquial* sparingly and with care. They are used primarily in informal speech and writing and, therefore, are usually inappropriate in college and business writing.

a, an   Use *a* before a consonant sound, *an* before a vowel sound.

| a history | a university | a one o'clock meeting | a *C* |
| an hour | an undertow | an orphan | an *F* |

aggravate   *Aggravate* means "make worse." In writing it should not be used in its colloquial meaning of "irritate" or "annoy."

agree to, agree with   *Agree to* means "consent to" a plan or proposal. *Agree with* means "be in accord with" a person or group.

ain't   Nonstandard for *am not* or *aren't.*

all right   *All right* is always two words. *Alright* is a misspelling.

all together, altogether   *All together* means "in a group," "gathered in one place," or "in unison." *Altogether* means "wholly" or "completely." *They made the jungle trek all together rather than in small groups. I did not altogether approve of the plan.*

allusion, illusion   An *allusion* is a reference to something. An *illusion* is a deceptive appearance. *Dr. Conn fills his lectures with classical allusions. Despite the hard facts, she clings to her illusion of true love.*

a lot   *A lot* is always written as two words. *Alot* is a common misspelling.

among, between   *Among* is used to refer to three or more people or things. *Between* is used with two people or things. *Half the treasure was divided between the captain and the ship's owner, the other half among the crew.* Sometimes *between* is used with more than two if the relationship concerns individual members of the group with each other. *The treaty between the five countries guarantees access to deep water ports.*

amount, number   *Amount* refers to a quantity of something that cannot be counted: *Buying a house like that requires a large amount of money. Number* refers to things that can be counted: *The number of students living in dormitories increased by 15% last year.*

an   See *a, an.*

and etc.   *Et cetera* (etc.) means "and so forth"; *and etc.,* therefore, is redundant.

and/or A legalism that many people consider awkward in college and business writing.

anxious, eager *Anxious* means "nervous" or "worried." *Eager* means "enthusiastically anticipating something." *I am eager to start the trip across the desert but anxious about the weather.*

anyone, any one *Anyone* means "any person at all." *Any one* refers to a particular person or thing in a group. Similar definitions apply to *everyone, every one, someone, some one*. *Anyone with the price of membership can join. Any one of the seniors might have started the brawl.*

anyplace Colloquial for *anywhere*.

anyways, anywheres Nonstandard for *anyway* and *anywhere*.

as Avoid using *as* for *because, since, while, whether,* and *who*. *Because* [not *as*] *the firm is almost bankrupt, buying a computer is out of the question. We doubt whether* [not *as*] *they can continue.*

as, like See *like, as, as if, as though*.

awful An overused word for *bad, shocking, ugly*. Colloquially, *awful* substitutes for intensifiers meaning "very" or "extremely."

awhile, a while *Awhile* is an adverb. *A while* is an article and a noun. *Awhile*, therefore, can modify a verb but cannot serve as an object of a preposition. *After six hours on the road, they rested awhile. After six hours on the road, they rested for a while.*

bad, badly *Bad* is an adjective and should be used in formal writing to modify nouns and as a predicate adjective after linking verbs. *Badly* should be used only as an adverb. *The doctor felt bad. The tenor sang badly.*

being as, being that Colloquial for *because*. *Because* [not *Being that*] *the sun has risen each morning of your life, you may expect it to rise tomorrow.*

beside, besides *Beside* means "next to." *Besides* means "except" and "in addition." *The older sister stood beside her father. Besides one stranger, only relatives were on the bus.*

between See *among, between*.

bring, take Use *bring* to carry something from a farther place to a nearer one. Use *take* to carry something from a nearer place to a farther one. *Take these pages to the printer and bring me yesterday's batch.*

bunch *Bunch* should not be used to refer to a crowd or group of people or things. Reserve it to refer to things that grow fastened together, such as grapes and bananas.

burst, bursted, bust, busted The verb *burst* means "fly apart," and its principal parts are *burst, burst, burst*. The past tense *bursted* is nonstandard. *Bust* and *busted* are considered slang, so they are inappropriate in college or business writing.

can, may *Can* indicates ability, and *may* indicates permission. Colloquially, *can* is used in both senses. *If I may use the car, I believe I can reach the store before it closes.*

center around *Center on* is more accurate than *center around.*

climactic, climatic *Climactic* refers to a climax. *Climatic* refers to climate.

compare to, compare with *Compare to* means "regard as similar." *Compare with* means "examine for similarities or differences." *The boy compared his father's bald head to an egg. The investigator compared the facts of the Rineman case with the facts of the Billings incident.*

continual, continuous *Continual* means "often repeated." *Continuous* means "unceasing" or "without a break." *My afternoons are continually interrupted by telephone calls. The waves lap continuously at the shore.*

convince, persuade Careful writers use *convince* when someone changes his or her opinion. They use *persuade* when someone is moved to take action. *The attorney convinced several students that capital punishment is immoral. The attorney persuaded several students to demonstrate against capital punishment.*

could of Nonstandard for *could have.*

credible, creditable, credulous *Credible* means "believable." *Creditable* means "praiseworthy." *Credulous* means "inclined to believe just about anything." *Hitchcock's fantastic stories are hardly credible; nevertheless, as a director he got creditable performances from his actors regardless of whether or not the audience was credulous.*

criteria, data, phenomena *Criteria* is the plural form of *criterion.* Careful writers use *criteria* only in the plural sense. *The criteria were so ill phrased that they were hard to apply. Data* and *phenomena* are plurals of *datum* and *phenomenon,* respectively. They should be treated as plural forms. *New data suggest the drug is harmful. Today's unexplainable phenomena are tomorrow's scientific explanations.*

data See *criteria, data, phenomena.*

deal Colloquial and overused for *bargain, transaction,* or *business transaction.*

differ from, differ with *Differ from* means "be unlike." *Differ with* means "disagree."

different from, different than *Different from* is idiomatic and widely accepted. *Different than* is acceptable when it precedes a clause. *An elephant is different from a mastodon. Paris was different than I had expected.*

disinterested, uninterested *Disinterested* means "impartial." *Uninterested* means "bored" or "indifferent."

don't *Don't* is a contraction of *do not* and should not be used for *does not,* whose contraction is *doesn't. Although the performance doesn't begin for an hour, I still don't think Bernice will be ready.*

due to Many people object to the use of *due to* as a preposition that means "because of" or "owing to." *The class was canceled because of* [not *due to*] *low enrollment. Due to* is acceptable when used as a subject complement. In this position it usually follows a form of *be. His unpredictable behavior is due to alcohol.*

eager See *anxious, eager.*

enthused Colloquial for "showing enthusiasm." The preferred adjective is *enthusiastic.*

etc. See *and etc.*

everyday, every day *Everyday* is an adjective meaning "used daily" or "common" and is always written as a single word. *These are my everyday shoes. Every day* is composed of the noun *day* and the adjective *every* and is always written as two words. *I leave campus every day at 3 p.m.*

everyone, every one See *anyone, any one.*

everywheres Nonstandard for *everywhere.*

every which way Colloquial for *in every direction* or *in disorder.*

expect Colloquial when used to mean "suppose" or "believe." *I suppose* [not *expect*] *the Reynolds clan is still squabbling about the settlement of the will.*

explicit, implicit *Explicit* means "expressed directly or precisely." *Implicit* means "expressed indirectly or suggested." *The threat was explicit—"I'll break your nose!" Although his voice was gentle, his body carried an implicit threat.*

farther, further *Farther* refers to actual distance. *Further* refers to additional time, amount, or other abstract matters. *I cannot walk any farther. Further encouragement is useless.*

fewer, less *Fewer* refers to items that can be counted. *Less* refers to a collective quantity that cannot be counted. *The marsh has fewer ducks living in it, but it also has less water to support them.*

finalize Avoid using *finalize* for the verb *complete.*

former, latter *Former* refers to the first named of two things or people. *Latter* refers to the second of two named. *First* and *last* are used to refer to items in a series of three or more. *Gina and Jose are very successful; the former is a dentist, the latter a poet. Jogging, biking, and swimming require tremendous endurance; the last requires the most.*

further See *farther, further.*

get A common verb used in many colloquial and slang expressions. *Get wise, her prattling gets me,* and the like. Using *get* in such ways is inappropriate in college and business writing.

goes Nonstandard when used instead of *says* or *said* to introduce a quotation. It should not be used to indicate speech. *He said* [not *goes*], *"Leave me alone."*

good, well *Good* is an adjective; *well* is an adverb. *Dr. Hunato is a good golfer. She strokes the ball well. Well* should be used to refer to health. *You look well* [not *good*]. *Are you feeling well* [not *good*]?

had ought, hadn't ought Nonstandard for *ought* and *ought not.*

half *Half a* or *a half* is appropriate, but *a half a* is redundant. *We drank half a* [not *a half a*] *gallon of soda.*

herself, himself See *myself, herself, himself, itself, yourself.*

hisself Nonstandard for *himself.*

hopefully *Hopefully* means "with hope." *They prayed hopefully for the blizzard to stop. Hopefully* is used colloquially to mean "it is hoped" in place of *I hope*; however, *I hope* is preferred in college and business writing. *I hope* [rather than *Hopefully*] *the blizzard will stop.*

illusion See *allusion, illusion.*

implicit See *explicit, implicit.*

imply, infer *Imply* means "suggest." *Infer* means "conclude." *Irving implied that he had studied for the quiz, but I inferred that he was unprepared.*

in, into *In* indicates a location or position. *Into* indicates movement or change. *Beata is in the study with a clairvoyant, who is in a trance. I must go into Murkwood, but I don't want to fall into danger. Into* has also come colloquially to mean "interested in" or "involved in" something, which is an inappropriate use in college and business writing. *My brother is interested in* [not *into*] *restoring Victorian houses.*

individual, party, person *Individual* should be used to refer to a single human being when expressing that person's unique qualities. *Each individual has a right to pursue his or her interests within the law.* When not emphasizing unique qualities, use *person. A romantic person will love the Austrian countryside.* Except in legal documents, use *party* to refer to a group. *Who is the missing person* [not *party*]?

infer See *imply, infer.*

in regards to Nonstandard for *in regard to* or *regarding.*

into See *in, into.*

irregardless Nonstandard for *regardless.*

is because See *reason is because.*

is when, is where A common predication error in sentences that define. *"Bandwagon" is a propaganda device by which* [not *is when* or *is where*] *advertisers urge consumers to become one of the millions buying their products.*

kind, sort, type These are singular words and take singular modifiers and verbs. *This kind of butterfly is rare in North America.* When referring to more than one thing, *kind, sort,* and *type* must be made plural and then take plural modifiers and verbs. *These kinds of butterflies are rare in North America.*

kind of, sort of Colloquial when used to mean *somewhat* or *rather. The picnic was rather* [not *sort of*] *dull.*

lay See *lie, lay.*

learn, teach *Learn* means "acquire knowledge." *Teach* means "dispense knowledge." *I must teach* [not *learn*] *the children better manners.*

leave, let *Leave* means "go away." *Let* means "allow" or "permit." *Let* [not *leave*] *me finish the job. The firm should have let* [not *left*] *her resign.*

less See *fewer, less.*

let See *leave, let.*

liable See *likely, liable.*

lie, lay These verbs are often confused. *Lie* means "recline," and *lay* means "place." In part, they seem to be confusing because the past tense of *lie* is the same as the present tense of *lay.*

lie ("recline")	*lay* ("place")
lie	lay
lay	laid
lain	laid
lying	laying

Lay (meaning "place") is also a transitive verb and as such takes an object. *Don't forget to lay the book on my desk. Today I laid the tile, and tomorrow I'll be laying the carpet. Lie* (meaning "recline") is intransitive and as such never takes an object. *The book lay on my desk for weeks. I can't waste time lying in bed; I've lain there long enough.*

like, as, as if, as though *Like* is a preposition and introduces a prepositional phrase. *As, as if,* and *as though* usually function as subordinating conjunctions and introduce dependent clauses. In college and business writing, do not use *like* as a subordinating conjunction. *The sky looks as if* [not *like*] *the end of the world is near.*

like, such as When introducing a representative series, use *such as.* To make a direct comparison with an example, use *like. The 1980s produced some powerful hitters in tennis, such as Borg, Connors, and McEnroe, but I want to play a game of strategy like Vilas.*

likely, liable *Likely* is used to express probability. *Liable* is used to express responsibility or obligation. *She is likely to finish the project before the weekend. Mr. Wert is liable for his son's destructive behavior.*

lots, lots of Colloquial for *a great deal, much,* or *plenty.*

may See *can, may.*

may be, maybe *May be* is a verb phrase, and *maybe* is an adverb meaning "perhaps."

may of Nonstandard for *may have.*

media, medium *Media* is the plural form of *medium.* Use plural modifiers and plural verbs with *media. These kinds of mass media—television, radio, newspaper—influence our emotional attitudes.*

might of Nonstandard for *might have.*

most Colloquial when used for *almost.*

must of Nonstandard for *must have.*

myself, herself, himself, itself, yourself These and other *-self* pronouns are reflexive or intensive—that is, they refer to or intensify a noun or another pronoun in a sentence. *The family members disagree among themselves, but I myself know how the inheritance should be divided.* Colloquially these pronouns are often used in place of personal pronouns in prepositional phrases. This use is inappropriate in college and business writing. *None of the team except you* [not *yourself*] *has learned to rappel.*

no way Nonstandard for *no.*

nowhere near Colloquial for *not nearly. Brytan's game is not nearly* [not *nowhere near*] *as good as Schrup's.*

nowheres Nonstandard for *nowhere.*

number See *amount, number.*

OK, O.K., okay All are acceptable spellings, but avoid using them in college and business writing.

party See *individual, party, person.*

people, persons *People* refers to a collective mass and emphasizes faceless anonymity. *Persons* refers to individuals who make up the group and emphasizes separate identity. *People surged into the convention hall. Several persons angrily denounced the membership's reluctance to act.*

percent, percentage Both *percent* and *percentage* refer to numbers and should be used only in references to actual statistics. Avoid using them to replace the word *part. The major part* [not *percent*] *of my trouble is caused by mismanagement. Percent* is always preceded by a number (*60 percent; 45 percent*), and *percentage* follows an adjective (*a major percentage*). In formal writing *percent* should always be written out (not %).

person See *individual, party, person.*

persons See *people, persons.*

persuade See *convince, persuade.*

phenomena, phenomenon See *criteria, data, phenomena.*

plus Nonstandard for *moreover. Nguyen Enterprises has a fine economic future; moreover* [not *plus*], *it offers young executives many tax-free perquisites.*

raise, rise Two commonly confused verbs. *Raise (raising, raised, raised),* meaning "force something to move upward," is a transitive verb and takes a direct object. *Rise (rising, rose, risen),* meaning "go up," is an intransitive verb. When the subject of a verb is being forced to move upward, use a form of *raise. Increasing the interest rate will* *raise* *monthly mortgage payments.* When the subject of a verb is itself moving upward, use a form of *rise. Unsteadily the ailing man* *rose* *from the chair.*

real, really *Real* is an adjective; *really* is an adverb. *The linebacker was* *really* [not *real*] *tough to block.*

reason is because Use *that* instead of *because* in the phrase *reason is because,* or rewrite the sentence. *The* *reason* *the MG stalled* *is that* [not *is because*] *the oil had leaked from the crankcase.*

respectfully, respectively *Respectfully* means "with respect" or "showing respect." *Respectively* means "each in the order given." *He* *respectfully* *expressed his opposition to the plan.* The Collector, The Optimist's Daughter, *and* The Human Comedy *were written by John Fowles, Eudora Welty, and William Saroyan,* *respectively*.

rise See *raise, rise.*

says, said See *goes.*

sensual, sensuous *Sensual* refers to pleasures of the body, especially sexual pleasures. *Sensuous* refers to pleasures perceived by the senses. *The poet's* *sensual* *desires led him to create the sensuous images readers find in his work.*

set, sit Two commonly confused verbs. *Set (setting, set, set),* meaning "put or place," is a transitive verb and takes a direct object. *Sit (sitting, sat, sat),* meaning "be seated," is an intransitive verb. When you mean "put something down," use a form of *set. Ralph* *set* *the paint beyond the child's reach.* When you refer to being seated, use a form of *sit. Don't* *sit* *in the wet paint.*

shall, will *Shall,* which was once used to form the simple future tense in the first person, has been replaced by *will. I* *will* *deal with him later.* In first-person questions that request an opinion, *shall* is the correct form to use. *Shall* *I march?* *Shall* *we strike?*

should, would Use *should* when expressing a condition or obligation. Use *would* when expressing a wish or customary action. *If they* *should* *appear, you must be prepared to battle. He* *would* *nap each afternoon when he was on vacation.*

should of Nonstandard for *should have.*

sit See *set, sit.*

someone See *anyone, any one.*

sort See *kind, sort, type.*

sort of See *kind of, sort of.*

such as See *like, such as.*

sure Colloquial when used as an adverb for *surely* or *certainly. Barnett surely* [not *sure*] *was correct in his cost estimate.*

sure and, sure to, try and, try to *Sure to* and *try to* are the preferred forms. *Try to* [not *try and*] *attend.*

than, then *Than* functions as a conjunctive used in comparisons, *then* as an adverb indicating time. *I would rather be in class than* [not *then*] *at work.*

that, which *That* always introduces a restrictive clause. *Which* may introduce a restrictive clause or a nonrestrictive clause. Many writers prefer to use *which* to introduce only nonrestrictive clauses. *This is the class that requires six outside reports. This class, which requires six outside reports, meets once a week.*

theirselves Nonstandard for *themselves.*

then See *than, then.*

try and, try to See *sure and, sure to, try and, try to.*

uninterested See *disinterested, uninterested.*

use to, suppose to Sometimes carelessly written for *used to* and *supposed to.*

wait for, wait on *Wait for* means "await." *Wait on* means "serve."

ways Use *way* when referring to distance. *The trout stream is only a little way* [not *ways*] *from here.*

well See *good, well.*

which See *that, which.*

which, who Never use *which* to refer to people. Use *who* or *that* to refer to people and *which* or *that* to refer to things.

who, whom Use the relative pronoun *who* to refer to subjects and subject complements; use the relative pronoun *whom* to refer to the object of the verb or preposition. *The award was given to the person who deserved it. The award was given to whom?*

will See *shall, will.*

would See *should, would.*

yourself See *myself, herself, himself, itself, yourself.*

Glossary of Grammatical Terms

absolute phrase A phrase that modifies a whole clause or sentence rather than a single word and is not joined to the rest of the sentence by a connector. It consists of a noun and a participle: *Hands trembling, she opened the envelope. Our original plan looks best, all things considered.* See *phrases;* also 69f, 37h.

abstract noun See *noun.*

active voice See *voice.*

adjective A word used to modify a noun or pronoun. It tells what kind, how many, or which one: *Careless drivers must attend seven hours of that class.* A **predicate adjective** follows a linking verb and describes the subject of the sentence: *The speaker was nervous.* See also 68f.

adjective clause A dependent clause that modifies a noun or a pronoun. See *clause.*

adjective phrase Any phrase that modifies a noun or pronoun. See *phrase.*

adverb A word used to modify a verb, an adjective, another adverb, or a whole phrase, clause, or sentence. Adverbs tell how, when, where, or to what extent. *He speaks hurriedly.* [*Hurriedly* modifies *speaks* by telling how.] *She was never ambitious.* [*Never* modifies *ambitious* by telling when.] *Our dog wanders everywhere.* [*Everywhere* modifies *wanders* by telling where.] *He is quite easily confused.* [*Quite* modifies *easily* by telling to what extent.] See also 67e.

adverb clause A dependent clause that modifies a verb, an adjective, another adverb, or a whole clause. See *clause.*

adverbial conjunction See *conjunctive adverb.*

adverb phrase Any phrase used as an adverb. See *phrase.*

agreement The correspondence in person, number, and gender between two words. A verb must agree with its subject in person and number. A pronoun must agree with its antecedent in person, number, and gender. A demonstrative adjective (*this, that, these, those*) must agree with its noun in number. See also *gender, person, number;* also Chapters 29, 30.

antecedent The word or group of words that a pronoun refers to. *When Stacy graduated, she immediately took a job in New York.* [*Stacy* is the antecedent of the pronoun *she.*] See also Chapter 30.

appositive A noun or group of words used as a noun, placed next to a noun or pronoun to explain, describe, or identify it: *The lawyer, a Harvard graduate, easily won her first case.* Most appositives are nonrestrictive and are set off with commas. See also 69b, 38c.

article *The* is a definite article. *A* and *an* are indefinite articles. Articles are classed as adjectives. See also 67d.

auxiliary verb   See *helping verb.*

case   The form of nouns and pronouns classified according to how they function in a sentence. English has three cases: the **subjective** to indicate the subject of a verb or a subject complement; the **objective** to indicate the object of a verb, verbal, or preposition; and the **possessive** to indicate ownership. Nouns and most pronouns change form only in the possessive case (*cathedral's, everyone's*). All other uses require only the plain form (*cathedral, everyone*). The personal pronouns *I, we, he, she,* and *they* and the relative or interrogative pronoun *who* have three case forms. The personal pronouns *you* and *it* have a separate possessive form. See also 49b.

clause   A group of words that has a subject and a predicate. A **main (independent) clause** forms a grammatically complete sentence: *He ran all the way to the station.* Main clauses can be joined to other main clauses with coordinating conjunctions, conjunctive adverbs, or semicolons. (See 67g, Chapter 39.) **Subordinate (dependent) clauses** are not sentences and must be joined to a main clause to form a grammatically complete sentence: *Although he was tired,* he ran all the way to the station. Dependent clauses function as adjectives, adverbs, and nouns. See also Chapter 70.

collective noun   See *noun.*

comma splice   An error occurring when main clauses are joined only by a comma: *Last summer we went camping, everyone laughed at my inability to pitch a tent.* See also Chapter 28, 70a.

common noun   See *noun.*

comparative degree   See *comparison.*

comparison   Adjectives and adverbs have three forms: the **positive degree,** which only describes [*large*]; the **comparative degree,** which compares two things [*larger*]; and the **superlative degree,** which compares three or more things [*largest*]. See also 23a.

complement   A word or group of words that completes the meaning of a subject, an object, or a verb. Complements function as **direct objects, indirect objects, predicate adjectives,** and **predicate nominatives:** *The manager opened the door* [direct object]. *Please send me a letter* [indirect object]. *The sea was calm* [predicate adjective]. *Her father is an accountant* [predicate nominative]. See also Chapter 68.

complete predicate   See *predicate.*

complete sentence   See *sentence.*

complete subject   See *subject.*

compound   Words or groups of words of two or more parts functioning as a unit. **Compound words:** *brother-in-law, lifeguard.* **Compound constructions:** *Betty and Joe* [compound subject] *flew to Chicago. The children giggled and blushed* [compound predicate]. See also 68c, 68d.

compound-complex sentence See *sentence.*

compound predicate See *compound.*

compound sentence See *sentence.*

compound subject See *compound.*

concrete noun See *noun.*

conjunction A word that connects and shows the relation between words, phrases, and clauses. **Coordinating conjunctions** (*and, but, or, nor, yet, for,* and *so*) connect items of equal grammatical rank: *The beauty of the scenery and the friendliness of the people make British Columbia an attractive tourist area.* **Correlative conjunctions** (*either . . . or, not only . . . but also,* and so on) are used in pairs: *You may choose either the vase or the picture.* **Subordinating conjunctions** (*when, while, if, although, because,* and so on) introduce dependent clauses and connect them to main clauses: *The carnival activity began when the sun went down.* See also 67g.

conjunctive adverb An adverb used to connect two main clauses: *Susan practiced faithfully; therefore, she improved rapidly.* See also 67g.

coordinating conjunction See *conjunction.*

correlative conjunction See *conjunction.*

count/noncount noun Count nouns are nouns that may be used in singular or plural form (e.g., *textbook, textbooks; assignment, assignments*). Noncount nouns may be used in singular form only (e.g., *advice, homework*). See Chapter 73.

dangling modifier A modifying phrase or clause that does not sensibly connect to any word in a sentence. See also 21f.

degree See *comparison.*

demonstrative pronoun See *pronoun.*

dependent clause See *clause.*

direct address A noun or pronoun used parenthetically to indicate the person or group spoken to: *I believe, friends, that we will win this election.*

direct discourse The presentation of the exact words, spoken or written, of another: *Steven asked, "Where have you been?"* **Indirect discourse** reports the words of another in paraphrase or summary form: *Steven wanted to know where we had been.* See also 22e.

direct object See *object.*

double negative Two negative words used in the same construction: *I didn't have no reason to stay home.* Double negatives are nonstandard English. The sentence must be revised: *I didn't have any reason to stay home* or *I had no reason to stay home.*

elliptical construction A construction in which one or more words are omitted but understood. *Bob types faster than Margaret* [*types*]. See also 32e.

expletive The word *there, here,* or *it* followed by a form of the verb *be* and used to begin a construction in which the subject follows the verb: *It is easy to spend money foolishly.* [*To spend money foolishly* is the subject of *is.*] See also 29e.

finite verb A verb that makes an assertion about a subject. A finite verb can function as the main (or only) verb in a sentence: *On weekends I work in the garden.* Gerunds, infinitives, and participles are nonfinite verbs and cannot function as main verbs in a sentence. See *verbals and verbal phrases,* 69c and 69d.

fragment See *sentence fragment.*

fused sentence An error occurring when main clauses are joined without a coordinating conjunction or semicolon: *We traveled to Georgia it was a good trip.* See also Chapter 28.

future perfect tense See *tense.*

future tense See *tense.*

gender The classification of nouns and pronouns as masculine (*man, he*), feminine (*woman, she*), or neuter (*house, it*). See also *agreement;* Chapter 29.

genitive case Same as possessive case. See *case.*

gerund A verbal ending in *-ing* that functions as a noun. The form of the gerund is the same as that of the present participle. Gerunds may have objects, complements, or modifiers. *Cigarette smoking is dangerous to your health.* [The gerund *smoking* is the subject of the sentence. *Cigarette* modifies the gerund. *Dangerous* is a predicate adjective complementing the gerund.] See also *verbals and verbal phrases,* 69c and 69d.

gerund phrase See *phrase.*

helping verb A verb used with a main verb to form a verb phrase: *Sarah was living in San Francisco at that time.* See also Chapter 33 and 67c.

imperative See *mood.*

indefinite pronoun See *pronoun.*

independent clause Same as main clause. See *clause.*

indicative See *mood.*

indirect discourse See *direct discourse.*

indirect object See *object.*

infinitive The plain form of a verb, as listed in the dictionary; it usually appears in combination with *to* to form a verbal that functions as a noun, an adjective, or an adverb. Infinitives may have objects, complements, or modifiers. *He promised to mow the lawn.* [The infinitive phrase *to mow the lawn* functions as a noun, the direct object of the verb *promised. Lawn* is the direct object of the infinitive *to mow.*] See also *verbal;* 69c.

infinitive phrase See *phrase.*

intensive pronoun See *pronoun.*

interjection A word expressing surprise or strong emotion: *Oh, here he comes!* See also 67h.

interrogative pronoun See *pronoun.*

intransitive verb See *verb.*

irregular verb A verb that does not form its past and past participle by adding *-d* or *-ed* to the infinitive form: *fly, flew, flown; sink, sank, sunk.* See also Chapter 33.

linking verb See *verb.*

main clause See *clause.*

misplaced modifier A modifier positioned incorrectly in a sentence. See also Chapter 21.

modifier An adjective, an adverb, or a word, phrase, or clause used as an adjective or adverb to limit or qualify another word or group of words.

mood The form of a verb indicating a writer's (or speaker's) intent in a sentence. The **indicative mood** is used for questions and statements of fact or opinion: *John is a good student.* The **imperative mood** indicates a command or direction: *Be a good student.* The **subjunctive mood** expresses doubt, a condition contrary to fact, or a wish: *I wish I were a good student.* See also Chapter 34.

nominative case Same as subjective case. See *case.*

nonrestrictive element A modifier that is not essential to the meaning of a main clause. Nonrestrictive elements are set off by commas: *Mr. Perkins, who retired from the grocery business last summer, is a noted rose grower.* See also 37c.

noun A word that names a person, place, thing, or idea. **Proper nouns** name particular people, places, or things: *James Joyce, Chicago, Fenway Park.* **Common nouns** name general classes: *athlete, singer, hotel.* **Abstract nouns** name intangible qualities: *loyalty, grace, devotion.* **Concrete nouns** name tangible things: *desk, snow, glasses.* **Collective nouns** name groups: *team, squad, committee.* See also 67a.

noun clause A dependent clause that functions as a subject, an object, or a complement. See *clause.*

number The indication of singular or plural in the forms of nouns (*toy, toys*), pronouns (*I, we*), demonstrative adjectives (*this, these*), and verbs (*eats, eat*). See also *agreement;* Chapters 29, 30.

object A word, phrase, or clause that receives the action of or is affected by a transitive verb, a verbal, or a preposition. A **direct object** receives the action of a transitive verb or verbal and answers the question What? or Whom?: *Stan made money tutoring neighborhood children.* [*Money* is the direct object of the transitive verb *make,* answering the question What? *Children* is the direct object of the verbal *tutoring,* answering the question Whom?] An **indirect object** indicates to whom or for whom an action is done: *I gave David five dollars.* [*David* is the indirect object of the verb *gave. Dollars* is the direct object.] An **object of a preposition** is the noun that a preposition relates to the rest of a sentence: *Joan sat by the door of the church.* [*Door* is the object of the preposition *by; church* is the object of the preposition *of.*] See also 67f, 68e.

objective case See *case.*

parenthetical expression A word, phrase, or clause that interrupts the thought of a sentence. See also 37f, 42a, 44a.

participial phrase See *phrase.*

participle A verbal that functions as an adjective, an adverb, or a part of a verb phrase. **Present participles** end in *-ing.* **Past participles** of regular verbs end in *-d* or *-ed: The light from the floating candles created grotesque shapes on the dark walls.* [The present participle *floating* is used as an adjective modifying *candles.*] *He ran screaming down the street.* [The present participle *screaming* is used as an adverb modifying *ran.*] *The thief had taken her favorite bracelet.* [The past participle *taken* is used as part of the verb phrase *had taken.*] See also *verbal;* 69d.

particle Another name for the preposition or adverb portion of a phrasal verb. See *phrasal verb.*

parts of speech The classification of words on the basis of their use in a sentence. The parts of speech are nouns, pronouns, verbs, adjectives, adverbs, prepositions, conjunctions, and interjections. Each part of speech is defined in a separate entry in the glossary. See also Chapter 67.

passive voice See *voice.*

past participle See *participle.*

past perfect tense See *tense.*

past tense See *tense.*

perfect tenses See *tense.*

person The form of pronouns and verbs used to indicate the speaker (first person—*I am*), the one spoken to (second person—*you are*), or the one spoken about (third person—*she is*). See also *agreement;* Chapters 29, 30.

personal pronoun See *pronoun.*

phrasal verb Two-word or three-word verb consisting of a verb form plus a preposition or adverb (e.g., *look over, put up with*).

phrase A group of words lacking a subject or a predicate or both and used as a single part of speech. A **verb phrase** consists of more than one verb: *had been talking, was swimming*. It functions as a predicate for clauses and sentences: *The professor has been lecturing for more than an hour.* A **prepositional phrase** consists of a preposition, its object, and any modifiers: *under the house, after the party*. It functions as an adjective, adverb, or noun: *She wandered to the elm grove beyond the fence.* [*To the elm grove* is used as an adverb modifying *wandered; beyond the fence* is used as an adjective modifying *grove*.] An **infinitive phrase** consists of an infinitive, its object, and any modifiers: *to hear the peaceful music, to learn I had been selected*. It functions as a noun, adjective, or adverb: *To see her again was a pleasure.* [*To see her again* is used as a noun, the subject of the sentence.] A **participial phrase** consists of a participle, its object, and any modifiers: *studying all night, glancing through the album*. It functions as an adjective or adverb: *The man jogging around the track is my brother.* [*Jogging around the track* is used as an adjective modifying *man*.] A **gerund phrase** consists of a gerund, its object, and any modifiers. Like participial phrases, gerund phrases use the *-ing* ending of the verb: *watching the birds, hoping for rain*. Therefore, they can be distinguished from participial phrases only in the context of a sentence. Gerund phrases function as nouns. *Jogging around the track is good exercise.* [*Jogging around the track* is used as a noun, the subject of the sentence.] An **absolute phrase** consists of a noun and usually a participle. It modifies a whole clause or sentence. *The election being over, the loser pledged support to the winner.* See also Chapter 69.

positive degree See *comparison.*

possessive case See *case.*

predicate The part of a sentence that tells what the subject did or how it was acted on. A predicate must have a finite verb. The **simple predicate** is the verb and its helping verb(s). The **complete predicate** is the simple predicate plus any modifiers, objects, and complements. *This play should set an attendance record in New York.* [*Should set* is the simple predicate.] See *finite verb;* also 68b.

predicate adjective See *adjective; complement.*

predicate nominative See *complement.*

preposition A word that shows the relation of a noun or a pronoun (the object of the preposition) to some other word in the sentence. See also *object; phrase;* 67f.

prepositional phrase See *phrase,* 67f.

present participle See *participle.*

present perfect tense See *tense.*

present tense See *tense.*

principal parts The present, present participle, past, and past participle of a verb: *look, looking, looked, looked*. See also Chapter 33.

progressive tense See *tense*.

pronoun A word that takes the place of a noun. Words that function as pronouns are classified as follows. **Personal pronouns:** *I, you, he, she, it, we, they* and their possessive forms, *my, mine, your, yours, his, her, hers, its, our, ours, their, theirs.* **Reflexive pronouns:** *myself, yourself, himself, herself, itself, ourselves, yourselves, themselves,* which are also sometimes used as **intensive pronouns,** as in *I myself saw it.* **Relative pronouns:** *who, whom, that, which, whose.* **Interrogative pronouns:** *who, which, whom, whose, what.* **Demonstrative pronouns:** *this, that, these, those.* **Indefinite pronouns:** *all, both, few, several, nobody,* and so on. See also 67b.

proper adjective An adjective derived from a proper noun: *French perfume, Orwellian nightmare.* See also 48f.

proper noun See *noun*.

quotation See *direct discourse*.

reflexive pronoun See *pronoun*.

regular verb A verb that forms its past and past participle by adding *-d* or *-ed* to the infinitive form: *wander, wandered, wandered; scheme, schemed, schemed.* See also Chapter 33.

relative pronoun See *pronoun*.

restrictive element A modifier that defines or identifies the noun it modifies and is therefore essential to the meaning of the main clause. Restrictive elements are not set off by commas. *All students who have successfully completed sixty units may apply for upper-division standing.* See also 37c and 38f.

run-on sentence See *fused sentence*.

sentence A group of words that contains a subject and a predicate and is not introduced by a subordinating conjunction. Sentences are classified according to their structure. A **simple sentence** has one main clause: *Maria fell asleep.* A **compound sentence** has two or more main clauses: *Maria tried to stay awake, but she fell asleep.* A **complex sentence** has one main clause and at least one dependent clause: *When Maria lay down to rest, she fell asleep.* A **compound-complex sentence** has two or more main clauses and at least one dependent clause: *Maria tried to stay awake because she wanted to study, but she fell asleep.* Sentences may also be classified according to their purpose. A **declarative sentence** makes a statement: *I am going home.* An **imperative sentence** gives a command or makes a request: *Go home now.* An **interrogative sentence** asks a question: *Are you going home?* An **explanatory sentence** expresses strong feeling: *We're going home!* See also Chapter 71.

sentence fragment A portion of a sentence punctuated as though it were a sentence: *Suddenly appearing on the horizon.* See also Chapter 27.

simple predicate See *predicate*.

simple sentence See *sentence*.

simple subject See *subject.*

simple tenses See *tense.*

squinting modifier A modifier placed so it may refer to either a word preceding it or a word following it. See also 21b.

subject The part of a sentence that acts, is acted upon, or is described. The **simple subject** is the essential word or group of words of the **complete subject.** The complete subject is the simple subject plus its modifiers. *A tall, stately gentleman appeared at the door.* [*Gentleman* is the simple subject. *A tall, stately gentleman* is the complete subject.] See also 68a.

subject complement See *complement.*

subjective case See *case.*

subjunctive See *mood.*

subordinate clause Same as dependent clause. See *clause.*

subordinating conjunction See *conjunction.*

superlative degree See *comparison.*

tense The form of a verb and its helping verbs that expresses the verb's relation to time. The **simple tenses** are **present** (*I laugh, you choose*), **past** (*I laughed, you chose*), and **future** (*I will laugh, you will choose*). The **perfect tenses** indicate completed action: **present perfect** (*I have laughed, you have chosen*), **past perfect** (*I had laughed, you had chosen*), and **future perfect** (*I will have laughed, you will have chosen*). The **progressive tense** indicates continuing action (*I am laughing, you are choosing*). See also Chapter 33.

transitive verb See *verb.*

verb A word or group of words expressing action or a state of being. A **transitive verb** expresses action that has an object: *She painted a picture.* An **intransitive verb** expresses action that does not have an **object:** *The artist failed.* A **linking verb** expresses a state of being or a condition. It links the subject of a sentence with a complement that identifies or describes the subject: *Their laughter was maddening.* A verb may be transitive **in one sentence** and intransitive in another: *She paints pictures* [transitive]; *She paints well* [intransitive]. See also 67c; tense, Chapter 33; mood, Chapter 34; voice, Chapter 35.

verbal Also called *nonfinite verb.* A form of a verb used as a noun, an adjective, or an adverb. Gerunds, infinitives, and participles are verbals. Verbals may take objects, complements, and modifiers. A verbal cannot function as the main verb of a sentence. See also *gerund; infinitive; participle; phrase,* 69c, 69d, 69e.

verb phrase See *phrase.*

voice The form of a transitive verb that indicates whether the subject acts (**active voice**) or is acted upon (**passive voice**). Active voice: *Donita wrote a fine research paper.* Passive voice: *A fine research paper was written by Donita.* See also Chapter 35.

Index